The Secret War for the Middle East

The Secret War for the Middle East

The Influence of Axis and Allied Intelligence
Operations during World War II

⫷⫸

Youssef Aboul-Enein
and Basil Aboul-Enein

Naval Institute Press
Annapolis, Maryland

Naval Institute Press
291 Wood Road
Annapolis, MD 21402

Library of Congress Cataloging-in-Publication Data
Aboul-Enein, Youssef H.
   The secret war for the Middle East : the influence of Axis and Allied intelligence operations during World War II / Cdr. Youssef H. Aboul-Enein, USN and Basil H. Aboul-Enein.
      1 online resource.
   Summary: "It can be argued that the Middle East during the World War II has been regarded as that conflict's most overlooked theater of operations. Though the threat of direct Axis invasion never materialized beyond the Egyptian Western Desert with Rommel's Afrika Korps, this did not limit the Axis from probing the Middle East and cultivating potential collaborators and sympathizers. These actions left an indelible mark in the socio-political evolution of the modern states of the Middle East. This book explores the infusion of the political language of anti-Semitism, nationalism, fascism, and Marxism that were among the ideological byproducts of Axis and Allied intervention in the Arab world. The status of British-dominated Middle East was tailor-made for exploitation by Axis intelligence and propaganda. German and Italian intelligence efforts fueled anti-British resentments; their influence shaped the course of Arab nationalist sentiments throughout the Middle East. A relevant parallel to the pan-Arab cause was Hitler's attempt to bring ethnic Germans into the fold of a greater German state. In theory, as the Sudeten German stood on par with the Carpathian German, so too, according to doctrinal theory, did the Yemeni stand in union with the Syrian in the imagination of those espousing pan-Arabism. As historic evidence demonstrates, this very commonality proved to be a major factor in the development of relations between Arab and Fascist leaders. The Arab nationalist movement amounted to nothing more than a shapeless, fragmented, counter position to British imperialism, imported to the Arab East via Berlin for Nazi aspirations"— Provided by publisher.
   Includes bibliographical references and index.
   Description based on print version record and CIP data provided by publisher; resource not viewed.
   ISBN 978-1-61251-336-2 (epub) — ISBN 978-1-61251-336-2 (mobi) — ISBN 978-1-61251-309-6 (hardback) 1. World War, 1939-1945—Middle East. 2. World War, 1939-1945—Secret service—Middle East. 3. World War, 1939-1945—Influence. 4. Middle East—Politics and government—1914-1945. I. Aboul-Enein, Basil H. II. Title.
   D754.N34
   940.54'24—dc23
                              2013030012

21 20 19 18 17 16 15 14 13   9 8 7 6 5 4 3 2 1
First printing

The statements of fact, opinion, or analysis expressed in this book are those of the authors and do not reflect the official policy or position of the Department of Defense or the U.S. government. Review of the material does not imply Department of Defense or U.S. government endorsement of factual accuracy or opinion.

First and foremost, this volume is dedicated to the men and women of Section 60 at Arlington National Cemetery; it is we who are humbled when standing in your presence. We also dedicate our work to military families, who enable us to serve our country. On a personal level, we dedicate this book to our parents, Nagla and Hassan, who worked hard to give us the gift of an education and critical thinking, and introduced us to a wider world. We also thank our late grandparents, Mousa, Youssef, Saadia, and Fawkiah. Before their passing, they bequeathed to us a love for the Arabic language as well as the oral histories of Arabia, the Ottoman Empire, Southwest Asia, Egypt, and the Sudan, that formed our earliest memories of the political and military history of the Near East. Finally, Youssef wishes to remember Maj. Gen. Joe Brown, USAF, my Commandant at the National Defense University's Eisenhower School and his wife (as well as my student), Sue. We lost you both much too soon, as this volume was being delivered to the publisher. I will miss both of you and our conversations.

CONTENTS

List of Maps   ix

Foreword   xi

Preface   xiii

Acknowledgments   xvii

List of Abbreviations   xix

Background   xxi

Chapter 1.   Introduction   1

Chapter 2.   The Palestine Question   4

Chapter 3.   Hashemite Iraq   39

Chapter 4.   Vichy French Syria: Operation Exporter   85

Chapter 5.   Iran: Operation Countenance   100

Chapter 6.   Turkey: Balancing Neutrality   117

Chapter 7.   Axis Efforts in the Arabian Peninsula   126

Chapter 8.   Afghanistan and the Third Reich: Fomenting Rebellions   148

Chapter 9.   Egypt's Internal Struggle: To Declare War or Not?   160

Chapter 10. Conclusion   183

Appendix 1. Excerpts from *The Goebbels Diaries 1942–1943*   193

Appendix 2. Lessons from the 1941 Anglo-Iraqi Revolt   195

Notes   205

Selected Bibliography   237

Index   249

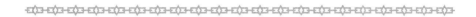

MAPS

Map 1. War of the Radio Waves   37

Map 2. Allies in Disarray in the Near East   99

Map 3. Allies Strike Back   159

FOREWORD

*I have been a conspirator for so long that I mistrust
all around me.*

—Egyptian leader Gamal Abdel-Nasser,
Time magazine interview, July 28, 1958

A comprehensive study of World War II is necessary for serious students of the evolution of America's national security policies. Such students spend hours in a variety of academic institutions—to include our military war colleges—studying Allied coalition building, the rise of Fascism in Europe, Japanese designs on the Pacific, actions in the China-Burma-India theater, and of course the battles, machines, tactics, and personalities who fought on land and sea, and in the air. Few, however, study the covert battlefield where the Allies and Axis fought in the Middle East. Commander Aboul-Enein and his younger brother Basil have written a book that exposes America's military leaders to key aspects of this underground war of diplomacy, intrigue, and propaganda. Their work examines the impact this battleground had on the evolution of Arab Nationalist movements in the twentieth century and militant Islamist groups in the twenty-first century. I have had the great pleasure of attending Commander Aboul-Enein's lectures on Islam, militant Islamist ideology, and modern Middle East politics, and have urged him to put pen to paper and write his findings. Little did I know that what Commander Aboul-Enein does in Washington, DC, for the array of departments and agencies in our security apparatus, and deploying military units, Captain Aboul-Enein did while on active duty in the U.S. Air Force. We are fortunate to have these two brothers who are passionate about educating us on the political history of the modern Middle East. I applaud Naval Institute Press and in particular Mr. Tom Cutler, the director of professional publishing, for giving these two extraordinary officers a forum to write about the region. I look forward to the debate this book will generate, as it educates national security leaders of the United States on the historic and human elements of the terrain that dominates much of our attention today. In practical terms, in the Joint Intelligence Task Force for Combating Terrorism, it is our business to analyze and assess the nuances and psychology of our adversaries, understand the root causes of their grievances, and cultivate empathy for a region and its people. This enhanced understanding, informed by works such as *The Secret War for the Middle East: The Influence of Axis and Allied Intelligence Operations during World War II*, allows us to provide cogent and insightful intelligence on the Middle East and the various forces that shape it today.

Mr. Ed Mornston
Director, Joint Intelligence Task Force for Combating Terrorism
Defense Intelligence Agency
Washington, DC
June 23, 2009

PREFACE

I have never presumed to interfere in British or French affairs. If an Englishman stands up today to say, "We feel responsible for the fate of the peoples of Central and Eastern Europe," then I can only reply to this gentleman: Then we are just as responsible for the fate of the peoples of Palestine, Arabia, Egypt, and, for all I care, of India as well!

—Hitler's November 8, 1939 speech at the Burgerbraukeller on the occasion of the Munich Beer Hall Putsch anniversary

I t could be argued that aspects of the Middle East theater during the Second World War have been overlooked in our current discourse about this conflict, particularly aspects in which the Allied democracies made strategic choices and abrogated democratic values by overthrowing three governments in the Near East, keeping them from being influenced by the Axis. This would leave psychological scars on the region, because it saw democratic values being betrayed by the very Allied powers who claimed to be preserving democracy. Another aspect that is not regularly discussed is the manipulation by the Axis of anticolonial sentiment and the saturation of Fascist slogans as a means of undermining Britain and France in the Middle East. In popular history the threat of direct Axis invasion never materialized in terms of actual ground combat divisions beyond the Egyptian Western Desert with Rommel's Afrika Korps; this direct threat by tactical units or ground combat units did not limit the Axis from aggressively probing the Middle East and cultivating potential collaborators and sympathizers that offered opportunities at the tactical, operational, and strategic levels. These actions left an indelible mark in the sociopolitical evolution of the modern states of the Middle East. The infusion of the political language of anti-Semitism, Nationalism, Fascism, and Marxism were among the ideological by-products of Axis and Allied intervention in the Arab world that would be bestowed on the masses. The status of British and French domination of the Middle East and North Africa was tailor-made for exploitation by Axis intelligence and propaganda. German and Italian intelligence efforts fueled British resentment, and their influence shaped the course of Arab Nationalist sentiments throughout the Middle East. A relevant parallel to the pan-Arab cause was Adolf Hitler's attempt to bring ethnic Germans into the fold of a greater German Reich (state). In theory, as the Sudeten German stood on par with the Carpathian German, so, too, according to doctrinal theory of the time, did the Yemeni stand in union with the Syrian in the imagination of those espousing pan-Arabism through the lens of German National Socialism. As this book demonstrates, this very commonality proved to be a major factor in the development of relations between Arab and Fascist leaders. The Arab Nationalist movement amounted to nothing more than a shapeless, fragmented, counter position to British imperialism, imported to the Arab East via Berlin and Rome for Nazi and Italian Fascist aspirations. Hitler's November 1939 speech quoted at the introduction of this preface, in hindsight, should have provided clues to his views that Germany would compete with Britain and France for the hearts and minds in the region, even though this was an attempt to justify the invasion of Poland in September 1939. Hitler was laying the gauntlet that if Great Britain did not interfere with German possessions, then Germany would not interfere with British possessions.

German and Italian support for the political dogma of Arab Nationalism contributed to the evolution and language of Arab Socialism, Nasserism, Ba'athism, and parts of militant Islamist ideology. While comparisons between militant Islamists and Fascism are not generally useful, we must recognize how the language of Fascism has weaved its way into the diatribe of varying militant Islamist ideologies. Interestingly, on October 28, 2005, President George W. Bush repopularized the term "Islamo-Fascism," much as Prime Minister Winston Churchill described *Mein Kampf* as the "new Quran of faith and war" in *The Gathering Storm*, his first of his famous multi-volume history of the Second World War more than sixty years ago.[1] French writer Maxime Rodinson (d. 2004) coined the term "Islamo-Fascism" to describe the 1979 Iranian Revolution. It is astonishing how phrases and ideas pass through time and space, from individuals that could never be ideologically linked. Rodinson was a former Marxist, a sharp critic of Israel as well as of Jewish settlements in Palestinian lands, and someone that could not conceivably be linked to former President Bush or his administration.

Past military historians have long examined the global and peripheral aspects of the war launched by Nazi Germany. However, Western historians have been more circumspect in the interpretations of Arabic sources with regard to the Middle East theater. This book aims to shed light on the historical parallels and review the forgotten Axis and Allied intelligence as well as propaganda operations conducted in the Near East during a period of political volatility before the conflict and in the midst of World War II, including insights into how this would impact a postwar world in the late twentieth century. It will evaluate Middle Eastern policy conducted by the Axis powers and deliver penetrating accounts gathered from volumes of Arabic, British, American, and German archives, as well as from literature. In particular, the book contains Arabic sources not previously explored in the English language, such as the papers of Egyptian war minister General Saleh Harb during the early part of World War II (1939–1940), which was organized and published in 2009. By studying Arabic sources side by side with Western archives, articles, and books, we synthesize new perspectives on World War II.

The work was first taken up as an interest by the authors in explaining the origins of Arab Nationalist ideologies to men and women of the U.S. Armed Forces. This interest was further enhanced by questions posed to us by fellow military officers and enlisted men and women. Their questions accelerated our exploration into the efforts of Axis penetration and Allied countermeasures in the Near East. Some of our answers appeared in such publications as the *U.S. Army Infantry Journal*, *Armor Journal*, and the *Foreign Area Officer Journal*. This book is an attempt to collect some of these published responses and our notes from seminars, combining them with additional research to expand on these topics. This book was written with the nonspecialist in mind, as our audiences have been officers studying at the National Defense University, as well as personnel deploying to Afghanistan and Iraq. Our goal is to introduce them to a little-discussed aspect of World War II, so they may gain an appreciation for the influence operations, strategic communications, and the use of intelligence in strategic planning. Posing big questions from case studies like Iraq's Rashid Ali Al-Gaylani Revolt in 1941, or Egypt's 1942 Sir Miles Lampson incident is a means by which we intellectually compel classroom and seminar debate about strategy, operations, tactics, and second- and third-order effects of previous policy and current decisions. More importantly, what occurred in the Middle East during World War II will continue to shape perceptions of coalition forces operating in the region.

After World War II the Soviet Union and the United States regularly competed for influence in the Middle East, but the shadow of Allied and Axis intervention in the region was not too far from the thinking of future Nationalist leaders like Iran's Mohammed Mossadeq, Egypt's Gamal Abdel-Nasser, and Algeria's Houari Boumidienne, to name a few. In June 2009 Iran's supreme leader Ali Khamenei delivered a Friday sermon in which he blamed the United States and the United Kingdom for Iranian discontent over the dubious reelection of President Ahmadinejad. Prime Minister Anthony Eden (British premier from 1955 to 1957) wrecked his government in the 1956 Suez adventure, influenced by thoughts of his experiences in World War II, comparing Nasser to Hitler, in his failed quest for forcible regime change. British colleagues have told me in discussions that Eden went to war on a lie that undermined his purpose in forcibly removing Nasser, and that despite being Churchill's protégé, Eden ended as the least successful prime minister in twentieth-century British political history.

The imagery of Western intervention in the affairs of the region continues to be utilized today; the question remains as to whether or not a new generation of youth will see beyond this history. However, we must infuse more nuances into our own political discourse and an understanding of what really happened in the Middle East when it came to clandestine meddling by Western powers. This book attempts to discuss the impact on the Middle East of Allied and Axis covert and overt action during World War II in order to make America's military planners better aware of the human terrain of the region. Readers will also discover that the Allies learned more in their operations fighting Rommel in the Middle East about deception, intelligence, and propaganda. This was needed because in 1940 Mussolini positioned nearly 215,000 men in Libya facing only 50,000 British troops in Egypt. You see Britain's desperate straits in Churchill's volumes on the Second World War, as he deliberates on options to save the Nile Delta and Suez Canal.[2] The seeds of what would become Operation Fortitude, the massive deception operation for D-day, began through trial and error in the sands of Egypt, fighting Rommel.

In 1942 American journalist and commentator Robert L. Baker published *Oil, Blood and Sand*, in which he sounded the alarm on Axis penetration into the Middle East. He opens his book with, "Between the Black and Caspian Seas and the Persian Gulf lies the 'Golden Triangle' of oil that Hitler must win if he is to continue the war with any hope of ultimate victory."[3] It is interesting to read the sense of panic Baker portrays to his readers with the benefit of hindsight, with a chapter entitled, "The Invasion of the Kilocytes," which discusses the radio war for Arab hearts and minds in the Middle East or "New Revolts in the Desert," where Baker refers to Ibn Saud as an Arab Cromwell, and Iraqi prime minister Ali Rashid Al-Gaylani as the Arab Quisling. The problem with this 1942 tome, written in the thick of World War II, is not the hyperbolic scenarios as much as it is the marginalization of Arab grievances and lack of empathy toward Middle Eastern colonialism. This is particularly troubling since the United States had liberated itself from a colonial power. Baker's book sets the stage for the kind of attitude shared by a portion of America's intelligentsia during World War II toward the Middle East, as evidenced by it being reviewed in a 1942 edition of the *New Republic* and a January 1943 edition of *Foreign Affairs*.[4] Rereading Baker's book and the book reviews provides a glimpse into a long-forgotten mind-set among those debating foreign affairs in America.

ACKNOWLEDGMENTS

We would like to express our appreciation to Dr. Christina Lafferty of the National Defense University's Dwight D. Eisenhower School for National Security and Resource Strategy and Dr. Michael W. Ross of the University of Texas Health Science Center for their role as advisers and editors. In order to understand the difficulty of editing this work, they had to reconcile the different writing styles and voices of two authors while making corrections. They both have improved our language and our ability to better articulate our thoughts. In addition, thanks go to Naval War College Seminar student Lt. Cdr. Margaret (Marrie) Read, MSC, USN; Lt. Cdr. Andrew Bertrand, MSC, USN (Ret.); and Lt. Cdr. Jeffrey Pastore, USN, of the Joint Intelligence Task Force for Combating Terrorism; over the years they provided valuable edits and rewrites to several initial drafts of portions of this volume. Lt. Col. Thomas Veale, USA, did more than marshal two drafts of the manuscript through the Defense Department Public Affairs process: he provided helpful improvements to language and structure and worked with another public affairs officer who deserves our thanks, Mr. Dave Thomas of the National Defense University. The Library of Congress Middle East Reading Room in Washington, DC, provided a quiet escape to formulate ideas and handwrite drafts. Ms. Dorothey Corley, a Boston University international relations graduate, helped in editing and discussing the memoirs of Egyptian World War II minister Saleh Harb while acting as my intern at the National Defense University. Commander Aboul-Enein's current intern, Ms. Sara Bannach of George Mason University, provided last-minute research to enable us to make our deadline. In addition, the librarians at the National Defense University's (NDU) Marshall Hall provided rich materials through interlibrary loan and the help of excellent research librarians—specifically, thank you Tim, Mike, Mary, Crafton, Trish, Karen, and Kim, in particular for helping with the last herculean effort of the final revisions and refinement of research. Other libraries that deserve mention are the Pentagon Library, the National Intelligence University's (NIU) John T. Hughes Library, and in particular Gretchen, who in the eleventh hour provided me much-needed page numbers for citations; the Joint Forces Staff College Ike Skelton Library; and Joana at the Marine Corps University Library who aided the NDU librarians with materials. Our thanks also go out to Guy at the U.S. Army Military History Institute in Carlisle, Pennsylvania, who helped through NIU with access to original debriefs of German general Helmuth Felmy; the U.S. Army Center for Military History at Fort McNair, which furnished me with Motter's volume on the Persian Corridor as well as helpful guidance; and finally Salisbury University's Blackwell Library, a place to retreat near Maryland's gorgeous Eastern Shore.

We both would like to express our appreciation for the many members within the Defense Department and U.S. armed services who posed questions to us on the Middle East that led us to explore, debate, and, finally, produce this book. We also would like to extend our appreciation to Mr. Johannes Allert for his editorial input. Faisal, our middle brother, prodded us throughout this project and acted as referee between the two authors on matters of history, politics, and sentences: yes, we do argue and disagree! Appreciation is also merited to Gary Greco for his discussions with Commander Aboul-Enein on the need to educate America's military leaders on the Arab perspectives of war and for forcing me to get a life by prodding me to have the occasional dinner in downtown Washington, DC.

Family support is vital, and this book would be impossible without Cheryl, Maryam, and Omar who had to put up with two brothers, their dad and uncle, repeatedly debating World War II, arguing Middle East politics, and many other topics. Little Sofia keeps us young and her mom, Ana, is part of our support. Youssef thanks his soul-mate Cheryl Anne for listening to him bellow out sentences, waking up with him at three and four in the morning, his most productive time, and keeping him fortified with coffee in the mornings as well as English Breakfast and Earl Grey tea in the afternoons. We would also like to welcome Basil's fiancée, Jackie, the newest member of our family, into the debate on war and policy.

At the Naval Institute Press, Tom Cutler patiently received my letters posted to Annapolis on the progress of the work, and he reciprocated with notes of encouragement and anticipation. Finally, no book is truly complete without a terrific copy editor and map illustrator: Ms. Alison Hope and Mr. Christopher Robinson, respectively, rank among the best.

ABBREVIATIONS

ACIC	Allied Captured Intelligence Center
AOC	air officer commanding
APA	Außenpolitische Amt (NSDAP office of foreign relations separate from German foreign ministry)
APOC	Anglo-Persian Oil Company; later the Anglo-Iranian Oil Company, which became British Petroleum
BapCo	Bahrain Petroleum Company Limited
BBC	British Broadcasting Corporation
BEF	British Expeditionary Forces
Caltex	California-Texas Oil Company
CENTO	Central Eastern Treaty Organization
Chi	Chiffrierableitung (code breaker units of the German armed forces)
CID	Committee of Imperial Defense
CIGS	Chief of the Imperial General Staff
CIU	Central Interpretation Unit
DAL	Deutsch-Arabisches Lehrabteilung (German-Arab training detachment)
DNKK	Dai Nippon Kaikyo Kyokai (greater Japan Islamic league)
FA	Forschungsamt (directorate of scientific research, and internal Nazi Party signals intelligence unit)
GC and CS	Government Communications and Cypher School (Bletchley Park)
Gestapo	Geheime Staatspolizei, "Secret State Police," the official secret police of Nazi Germany and German-occupied Europe
GPU	Gosudarstvennoye Politicheskoye Upravlenie (state political directorate under the Soviet NKVD)
HQ	Headquarters
HMSO	His Majesty's Stationery Office
IDF	Israel Defense Forces
JIC	Joint Information Center (of the general staff)

MEIC	Middle East Intelligence Center
MI	British Intelligence
MI-6	see SIS
MI-14	British Military Intelligence section 14 specializing in German operations
MTC	Mitsubishi Trading Company
MUC	Muslim Ulema Council (post–Operation Iraq Freedom)
NCO	non-commissioned officer
NDRC	National Defense Research Committee
NKVD	Narodnyy Komissariat Vnutrennikh (Soviet People's Commissariat of Internal Affairs)
NSDAP	Nationalsozialistische Deutsche Arbeiterpartei (NSDAP; National Socialist German workers' party)
OKH	Oberkommando des Heeres (supreme high command of the German army)
OKW	Oberkommando der Wehrmacht (supreme command of the German armed forces)
OSS	Office of Strategic Services, the ancestor of today's Central Intelligence Agency
Per Z	The Cryptanalytic and Cryptographic Service of the German Foreign Office
PLO	Palestine Liberation Organization
POW	prisoner of war
RAF	Royal Air Force
Regia Aeronautica	Italian air force
SA	Sturmabteilung (storm troopers)
SAVAK	Iran's national intelligence and security organization
SD	Sicherheitsdienst des Reichsführers-SS (German internal security or intelligence apparatus within the SS)
SIGINT	signals intelligence
SIM	Servizio Informazioni Militari (Italian military intelligence service)
SIS	Secret Intelligence Service also known as MI-6
SOCAL	Standard Oil of California
SOFA	status of forces agreement
SS	schutzstaffel (protection squadron)
UN	United Nations
VEVAK	intelligence and security of Iran

BACKGROUND

Make the lie big, make it simple, keep saying it, and eventually
they will believe it.

—Adolf Hitler

Prior to the German Reich's establishment in 1871 under Kaiser Wilhelm I, neighboring France and Britain had been expanding their overseas colonies. Arriving late to geopolitics of this decade, Berlin, too, established colonies over time in West and East Africa, as well as in a number of archipelagos in the Pacific. German Middle East policy had its origins in the period after the founding of the German Empire.[1] Germany's relationship to the Arab East can be traced to its developed political and economic ties with the Ottoman Empire as far back as the first decade of the twentieth century. During World War I, Germany developed plans to initiate an Islamic Holy War against the Allies. The concerted German-Ottoman campaign involved Germany's attempt to instigate an Arab uprising and represented part of a wider campaign within the broad strategy of the Central Powers that manifested itself in the ongoing construction of the Berlin-Baghdad Railway. The collaborative efforts conducted between Kaiser Wilhelm, Ottoman sultan Abdul Hamid II, and German Orientalist experts such as Baron Max von Oppenheim set the stage for the less-than-successful recruitment of Arab locals, from Libya to Arabia and non-Arab Afghanistan.[2] In 1916 Berlin sent political missions to the Red Sea coast, known as the Hijaz, and to Yemen. These missions were established as intelligence and propaganda bases from which they collected intelligence, conducted military operations against the Allies, and provided assistance to German forces stationed in German East Africa.[3]

The Central Powers failed, however, where the British succeeded in the Arab support against the Ottomans. It may be safe to assert that Germany was to blame, along with the Allies, for the establishment of the modern political culture of the Arab East. Nazism contributed to the German legacy through the support of such figures as the anti-Semitic grand mufti of Jerusalem, the major historical actor of Nazi-Arab collaboration, in World War II.[4] A continuum of

Nazi-Islamist links in the 1930s grew out of the frustrations and aspirations of Orientalist experts like von Oppenheim, Alois Musil, and Curt Prüfer. The relevance of how German foreign policy toward the Arab East evolved in the midst of a global war played a crucial role in what was to come thirty years later with the Axis involvement in the Arab East.[5]

The "Young Turks" became the enthusiastic allies of German imperialism and the advocates of inciting the concept of a global jihad. The grandiose project of a railway extending from Berlin to Baghdad was designed to challenge British command over the Suez and India. This peculiar fusion of ancient and modern, revolutionary and reactionary, resurfaced again in the coming war in the form of Nazi Germany and Arab Nationalism. Historians such as Dr. David Fromkin and Jonathan Schneer have traditionally cited the Balfour Declaration, T. E. Lawrence's Arab Revolt, and the Sykes-Picot Agreement when discussing events that shaped the Arab East. However, evidence has demonstrated the inner workings of German intrigue with individuals like Max von Oppenheim, father of modern German Orientalism and sponsor of holy war.[6] The objective of inciting a Muslim jihad through the Ottoman Empire was a salient part of Germany's design. The first aspect was the systematic provision from Germany to the Ottomans of the sinews of war, from artillery and planes to rail lines and senior military advisers. The second aspect was ideology: as soon as war erupted, General Helmuth von Moltke, chief of the kaiser's general staff, cabled Constantinople asking Enver Pasha to begin inciting Islamic uprisings. Clearly, to dismiss the significance of Germany's pan-Islamist wartime strategy during World War I is to fall victim to hindsight. In the Near East, Germany saw a secret weapon that could decide the war, a secret weapon that the Axis powers reawakened in the upcoming world war as part of a coordinated campaign set against the British.[7]

Origins of the political issues of the Middle East theater during World War II date as far back as before World War I, with the most salient lesson taken by German intelligence planners being the launch of the Great Arab Revolt of 1916. Germany also conducted an Arab Revolt in reverse by establishment of the Office of Jihad at the foreign ministry in Berlin to capitalize on its new ally, the Ottoman Empire. The Germans and Ottomans engaged in inciting anti-British insurgencies in Libya and Afghanistan during World War I. The consequences of World War I set the stage for a beleaguered Arab Nationalist movement in search of a partner to remove the colonial yoke of British and French imperialism. The search for such a partner would come in the radicalism of Europe and the rise of Fascist movements.

Because Arab Nationalists saw themselves as victims of the 1919 Paris Peace Conference, they looked to Nazi Germany as an example. Many others in Europe, Asia, and America were also deluded by the Nazi dictator's ability to economically bring Germany out of depression and restore national pride. Like many who sacrifice complexity for simple answers, they did not dwell on how the Nazis achieved a short-term economic miracle through suppression, autarky, and later needing to sustain this miracle with the search for *liebensraum* (living space) that would be among the focal points of Nazi expansionism. Both Italy and Germany were seen by Arab Nationalists as joining their own confrontation with the post–World War I mandatory powers, which increased the Axis powers' appeal as potential allies for aspirations of Arab Nationalism.[8] Compared to the British and the French, Arabs of that period did not focus on Italy and Germany as colonial powers in the pre–World War II Arab world, which represented an additional advantage of appeal.[9] Yet Italy had a more challenging time propagandizing an anticolonial message when Mussolini was engaged in vicious wars of colonial expansion in Ethiopia and Libya. You will read how Egyptian war minister Saleh Harb would see through this farce, viewing both the British and Italians as imperialists in the region.

The best book on the details of the creation of Middle East mandates from the former Ottoman dominions after World War I is David Fromkin's *A Peace to End All Peace*; for a holistic understanding of the proceedings in Versailles, read Margaret MacMillan's *Paris 1919*.[10]

CHAPTER 1

Introduction

My dear Hitler,
I congratulate you from the bottom of my heart. Even if you
appear to have been defeated, in reality you are the victor.

—Published letter from Sadat to the
vanquished and deceased Hitler[1]

Based on President Obama's historic speech in Cairo in June 2009, the United States has entered a new phase in its relations with the countries of the Middle East. This phase requires a higher level of empathy with the region and an understanding of how radical ideas, conspiracy theories, and even extremist narratives are synthesized. It is imperative that America's military and government officials operating in the region understand the history, perceptions, and grievances of the region that lead to the development of conspiracy theories. In many ways, we must reexamine our military education of World War II from the battles in Europe, Russia, and Japan to those fought both overtly (such as in Operation Torch in 1942) and covertly (such as the anti-British Nazi propaganda in Egypt, Syria, Palestine, and Iraq) to gain a deeper perspective of the region. It is impossible to truly understand Arab Nationalism without comprehending the events from which it arose—namely, British and French colonialism. Moreover, our perspective must derive not just from World War I, but from how this war was exploited by both the Axis and Allies, and in particular, German, Italian, French (Free and Vichy), British, and American intelligence services during World War II. This book will discuss covert operations, political intrigues, diplomacy, and covert propaganda carried out by the Axis and Allies in the Middle East in the years that led up to and during World War II, and trace the emerging Zionist movement during this period. The volume represents a decade of debate between the authors as they sought ways to write, think, and educate their fellow service members in the U.S. armed forces. It stands to reason that Arab Nationalists sought support from the enemies of its enemies, notably the Axis powers of Nazi

1

Germany and Fascist Italy during World War II. But there needs to be a more candid assessment of the ways in which the Axis exploited Arab and Muslim grievances to gain strategic advantages over the Allies. There were contacts between authorities of the Axis governments and notable Arab Nationalists, such as the infamous grand mufti of Jerusalem Hajj Amin Al-Husseini, Egyptian army captain Anwar Sadat, and Iraqi Nationalist prime minister Rashid Ali Al-Gaylani, among others. While the Axis powers before World War II provided some assistance to Arab Nationalists in terms of propaganda and arms shipments, Arab–Axis collaboration was sporadic and gradually took on greater importance with the outbreak of the Second World War.

Of note, in researching this book the authors found that Adolf Hitler was not interested in the Arabs, a group he placed low in his racial pecking order, although his diplomats sought to obfuscate this fact. Not having abandoned hope of reaching an agreement with Britain until the Czech crisis of 1938, Hitler was not particularly eager to stir up trouble in the British-held Near East. However, his inner circle saw things differently and sought to create a climate of anti-British and anti-French hostility to complement the efforts of their Italian Fascist partner, Benito Mussolini. The basic premise of the original 1936 Axis agreement between Hitler and Mussolini was that Rome would be given a free hand in the Mediterranean, while Berlin would dominate Central Europe. Therefore, the Arabs were considered primarily in the Italian sphere of influence. Of course such back room dealing between the Nazis and the Italians was not made with the consent of the Arab Nationalist movements they sought to agitate. Mussolini was eager to play an active role in the Near East. Axis desires to inspire British or French anticolonial movements were not without their challenges: first among these was the reputation of the Italians in the region, who were viewed negatively for their ongoing oppressive colonial policy in Libya.[2] After the expulsion of the British Expeditionary Forces (BEF) from Europe at Dunkirk, Churchill curiously wrote on September 3, 1940, that, apart from the potential invasion of the British Isles, "the only major theater of war which can be foreseen in 1940–41 is the Middle East."[3]

Summing up the position in the Middle East in July 1940, the British chiefs of staff wrote,

> 2. The security of the Middle East hinges on the defence of
>   (a) Egypt and Sudan, where our main forces are based, our Middle East communications are centred, and the Suez Canal is controlled.
>   (b) Iraq, from which we must control the oil of Iraq and Iran and safeguard the Baghdad-Haifa route.
>   (c) Palestine, which is now our most northerly defensive position and contains the western terminus of the Baghdad route.
>   (d) Aden, which is essential to our Red Sea lines of communication.

(e) Kenya, which is our second line of defence in Africa, a valuable base of operations against Italian East Africa and contains a second alternative line of communication to Egypt via Mombasa.[4]

This book will delve into the secret war between the Allies and the Axis in the Middle East that would go on to influence the region for decades after the conclusion of World War II. The Middle East war goes beyond Field Marshal Rommel's and Field Marshal Montgomery's armored divisions clashing in the Western Desert and into the realm of the hearts, minds, ideas, and governments yearning for complete autonomy from colonial rule. It meant the potential for insurgencies in Syria, Iraq, and Palestine that were narrowly averted as well as three successful instances of regime change in Iran, Iraq, and Egypt. In addition, Europe would not be entirely blameless in infusing the language of anti-Semitism among the masses using the medium of radio, which is the language also used by radicals and extremists today. As you read, you will appreciate the impact radio had in providing the Arab masses a new and more destructive vocabulary. It is the hidden war for sentiment, what today in the U.S. military we would call the human terrain. This volume, first and foremost, is a journey of two brothers within America's armed forces. We have been long dedicated to providing an elevated level of dialogue among service members as they deploy to the region. This dialogue was accomplished through seminars, round-table discussions, thesis advising at the National Defense University and National Intelligence University, as well as expanding upon published essays in such journals as *Infantry, Armor,* and the *Foreign Area Officer Association Journal.* Traveling intellectually among and with my fellow officers and non-commissioned officers (NCOs) was the best part of this journey, and this book is an effort to make the reader part of this exploration. Writing about World War II is a complex endeavor for which a person can go off on many tangents. Refer to the notes section throughout the book for occasional amplifications and exchanges between civilian and military leaders or for recommendations for your own exploration into a topic. These notes also provide background on historic events used to amplify the discussion among fellow officers and NCOs attending the authors' seminars, and will hopefully enhance your reading experience.

CHAPTER 2

The Palestine Question

Hitler said that the conquering Arabs, because of their racial inferiority, would in the long run have been unable to contend with the harsher climate and conditions of the country. They could not have kept down the more vigorous natives, so that ultimately not Arabs but Islamized Germans could have stood at the head of this Mohammedan Empire.

—Attributed to Hitler by Albert Speer[1]

Palestine: A British Dilemma

There are three competing elements in dissecting the Palestine question in the lead-up to the creation of Israel in 1948: (1) Zionism, (2) Arab Nationalism, and (3) competition among European powers. The four European powers of World War II—Great Britain, France, Italy, and Germany—intervened directly and indirectly in Palestine in the lead-up to the conflict. In these geostrategic machinations between the Axis and Allies, Palestine occupied a unique role in Nazi Germany's foreign policy thinking. It formed the potential for anti-Allied activities in the Middle East that was exploited by the Abwehr (German military intelligence organization), which was headed by Admiral Wilhelm Franz Canaris. The Germans identified and empathized with the psychological impact of the defeat of the Ottoman Empire during World War I. As an aggrieved nation, German officials understood the power of playing the victim of global events. In particular, Germany's shared outrage with the events and treaties of post–World War I caused a psychological linkage of stoking anti-British and anti-French sentiments among the Arabs. Among the events that shaped the thinking of the region, were these:

- The implementation of the Sykes-Picot Agreement that carved Arab domains of the Ottoman Empire into French and British spheres of influence

4

- The 1919 Revolt in Egypt, stimulated by the British incarceration of Egyptian Nationalist leader Saad Zaghloul (d. 1927), who traveled to Versailles to petition for an independent Egypt
- The 1920 San Remo Conference, in which the British and French agreed that Iraq and Syria were to be British and French mandates, respectively
- Iraq's 1920 Revolt that took less than a year to suppress and was caused by the Iraqi outrage that their country was to be administered as a mandate
- The Balfour Declaration that acknowledged the need for a Jewish homeland in Palestine, but not at the expense of indigenous populations
- The proposed Peel Commission Plan that recommended partition of Palestine into Jewish and Arab sections in 1937

The armed conflict of the First World War, along with diplomatic bargaining, promises, and political agreements connected with them, established the future of the Arab countries and of Arab Nationalism over the next quarter century. With the First World War drawing to a close, British policy became committed to the notion of establishing a Jewish home in Palestine, among the post–World War I efforts to restructure the borders of the evolving modern Middle East from the remnants of the collapsed Ottoman Empire. The British would sideline pledges made to the Arab populations and the ruling Hashemite clan under Meccan ruler Sherief Hussein ibn Ali (ruled 1908–1924) for support against Ottoman forces in the Levant and in Arabia.[2] This commitment to the establishment of a Jewish home in Palestine came in the form of a letter signed by Foreign Secretary Arthur James Balfour to Lord Rothschild and endorsed by the League of Nations. As you read the text of the Balfour Declaration, note promises made to Jewish and non-Jewish communities in a form of diplomatic doublespeak that haunts efforts to resolve the Palestinian-Israeli dispute to this day.

Foreign Office
November 2nd, 1917

Dear Lord Rothschild,

I have much pleasure in conveying to you, on behalf of His Majesty's Government, the following declaration of sympathy with Jewish Zionist aspirations which has been submitted to, and approved by, the Cabinet.

> "His Majesty's Government view with favour the establishment in Palestine of a national home for the Jewish people, and will use their best endeavours to facilitate the achievement of this object, it being clearly understood that nothing shall be done which may prejudice the civil and religious rights of existing non-Jewish communities in Palestine, or the rights and political status enjoyed by Jews in any other country."

I should be grateful if you would bring this declaration to the knowledge of the Zionist Federation.

Yours sincerely,

Arthur James Balfour[3]

A complicating factor was the basis of British engagement with Sherief Hussein of Mecca that was expressed in vague political promises contained in a series of ten letters to and from Sherief Hussein and Sir Henry McMahon, British high commissioner in Egypt, between July 1915 and January 1916. The Hussein-McMahon Correspondence would be a symbol in Arab collective memory of the many empty promises made by the British government in support of Arab autonomy and the recognition of the Arab national identity. The ten letters were riddled with platitudes and ambiguities. Hussein and McMahon would read through the flourishes more into the words, and each preferred to make the sentences fit their idea of what Arab independence meant based on their respective interests. The 1916 Sykes-Picot Agreement and the 1917 Balfour Declaration may be marked in history as giving the impetus for Arab Nationalism in the twentieth century, because they led various Arab subjects of the former Ottoman dominions to unify around grievances, discontent, and the broken promises of self-determination. Of note, President Woodrow Wilson's call for self-determination brought out the likes of Ho Chi Minh, as well as Indian and Chinese Nationalists, calling for independence from colonial rule. For a truly empathetic look at the little-known personalities who shaped the twentieth century from the remnants of colonialism, such as Jamal al-Din al-Afghani in the Middle East, among others, read *From the Ruins of Empire*, by Pankaj Mishra.[4]

The multifaceted policies by the British laid the groundwork for a British-dominated Arab Middle East where both Jewish Zionist and Arab Nationalist goals were to prove irreconcilable over time. Consequently, a system of rule would prevail over Palestine from the time of the country's occupation in 1917–1918 until the British withdrawal of its mandate in 1948. It is important to understand that Arab Nationalism's love affair with Fascism is a result of anticolonial sentiment and a perception of betrayal after the World War I victorious Allied Powers denied Arab self-determination at the 1919 Paris Peace Conference, the 1920 San Remo Conference, and the 1921 Cairo Conference.

When Winston Churchill visited Palestine in March 1921 as secretary of state for the colonies, the debates concerning the future of Palestine and the recriminations over the broken promises were reaching a feverish pitch. In Haifa a delegation of Muslim and Christian Arabs met with Churchill to express their concerns on the intensifying issue of the status of Palestine. Churchill was given a prophetic warning from Arab leaders that has a profound significance in the modern history of the Middle East: "Today the Arabs' belief in England is not what it was. . . . If England does not take up the cause of the Arabs, other powers will. From India, Mesopotamia, the Hedjaz [*sic*] and Palestine the cry goes up to England now. If she [England] does not listen, then perhaps Russia will take up their call some day, or perhaps even Germany."[5]

Arab Enthusiasm and Support for the Nazis: Misplaced Arab Nationalism

Arab public attitudes toward Germany were generally enthusiastic and sympathetic, particularly during the 1930s when the Third Reich was perceived as a possible ally in the fight against Britain, France, and the growing sentiments toward Zionism. This would be cultivated with a deliberate Axis propaganda campaign in the region. Even in the first months of the war, shops in the towns of Syria showed posters with Arabic slogans saying, "No more 'Monsieur,' no more 'Mister'—God in Heaven, on earth Hitler!"[6]

The pro-Axis sentiment in Palestine was analyzed by a Palestinian-Arab newspaper in 1937:

> Palestinian-Arab hostility towards Italy goes back to the period of the Abyssinian War, that is before the Palestinian revolution and not to a period six months ago. The daily manifestations of sympathy with Germany and Italy exist after the relations between these two states and England have become tense. They are not caused by propaganda or by money received nor by enthusiasm for these two countries. They are much more a protest against England. As al-Ahram has justly observed: had the Peel report been favorable to the Arabs, no trace of the so-called Fascist propaganda in Palestine would have been left.[7]

Diverse methods were used in attempts to spread ideas of National-sozialistische Deutsche Arbeiterpartei (NSDAP; National Socialist German workers' party) to the Arab East. These included broadcasts in Arabic from Germany that started around April 1939, of programs of Quran recitals, Arabic music, literary texts, and political commentaries. One of the Arab speakers, the Iraqi journalist Yunus al-Bahri, later wrote his memoirs in 1955 about his time with Radio Berlin under the title *Huna Berlin! Hayyi l-'arab* (This is Berlin! Salutations to the Arabs), which was the customary start of his broadcasts.[8] Radio Berlin-Zeesen also edited an Arab bulletin *Barid al-Sharq* (Orient-Post) that frequently carried excerpts from Hitler's speeches. Of note, Zeesen was a town south of Berlin that had a powerful shortwave broadcasting station that reached the Middle East and beyond. This would be supplemented by Italy's Radio Bari that maintained broadcasting stations in the Dodecanese Islands in the Aegean Sea, as well as the port city of Bari.

However, the immediate requirements of Hitler's foreign policy in Europe during the 1930s necessitated German support for the post–World War I status quo in the Middle East. Hence, support for the idea of a Jewish national home in Palestine, the British mandatory position in Palestine, and British interests in the Middle East were not challenged by the Nazis in the early 1930s. This German noninterference in British colonial affairs also included a refusal by Berlin of any support of Arab Nationalism. The impending war would inevitably change these policies and see an attempt to alter the status quo in the Middle East. An excellent volume that delves into this is Lukasz Hirszowicz's, *The Third Reich and the Arab East*. This book is currently out of print; it was translated from the 1963 Polish edition and published in English in 1966. Hirszowicz demonstrates the cold politics of realism the Nazis were engaging in, and the quick shift in Nazi Middle East policy as a means of destabilizing French and British interests in the region.[9] Hirszowicz is essential reading on Axis policies and decisions pertaining to World War II Middle East.

Owing to the scarcity of economic resources required for Nazi expansionism, the initial success of the German Afrika Korps in North Africa, and the need to undermine Allied control of vital communications links in the Middle East, the Third Reich gradually saw the strategic interest in its involvement in the Middle East. Until Operation Torch in November 1942, the most secure logistical lines of the Allies to the Middle East were from India then around the Cape of Good Hope into the Red Sea, and on to Egypt's major ports. Direct involvement of German forces was stimulated by the poor showing of Italian forces in North Africa under Marshal Rodolfo Graziani, commander in chief of Italian forces in North Africa. This required Hitler to divert German military resources to rescue Mussolini's forces from humiliation. Hitler would also be drawn into military involvement in Greece because of the humiliation Mussolini's legions were enduring in that country. Additionally, developments in Palestine led the Germans to seize the opportunity to adopt a political position on Arab affairs with the objective of agitating Arabs and Muslims against the British. This had less to do with the concepts of self-determination and more to do with a cold calculus that stoking the flames of Arab Nationalism could divert Allied resources into the Middle East. This opened multiple fronts for the British, drawing forces to suppress discontent in Egypt, Iraq, Palestine, Iran, and Transjordan. Even India, at this time, was ripe for a Muslim revolt or Indian Nationalist agitation against the British. Chandra Bose took the opposite position from Mohandas K. Gandhi, organizing an Indian Nationalist army with the aid of the Japanese. As can be seen in a map of the world in 1941, the possibility of the European Axis powers aiding the Japanese who had signed the Tripartite Pact with Hitler and Mussolini in 1940 could not be ignored; this worry manifested itself in vigorous discussions between Churchill and his generals from 1939 to 1942. Of course, Hitler's invasion of the Soviet Union in June 1941 would change these possibilities, and see Rommel complaining of ever-dwindling supplies and troops. Hitler's obsession with Stalin and a Judeo-Bolshevist conspiracy would blind him from seeing the full opportunities the eastern Mediterranean and the Middle East had in crippling the British economically.

After decades of frustration, hostility toward the British mandate in Palestine was always under the surface throughout the 1930s. Arabs in Palestine and in the Middle East greeted the emerging Nazi regime in Germany with enthusiasm. More than a few Arab Nationalist intellectuals viewed the Nazis as liberators coming to rescue the region from decades of British rule. These Arab Nationalist leaders bought the robust Fascist propaganda, or simply saw the Germans as a means of ridding themselves of the British and French, who had occupied various parts of the Middle East for decades. This perception of shared post–World War I victimization of the Germans and Arabs by the British and French would be carefully nurtured by German intelligence operatives in Egypt, Iraq, the Levant, and Palestine. Unlike Britain, Germany capitalized on not being viewed with suspicion and mistrust in the Middle East during the period between the two world wars. Arab Nationalist organizations and societies began to identify with elements of the NSDAP agenda and viewed it as a means of counterbalancing Zionism and European colonial-imperialism. The inequities of the 1919 Versailles Treaty imposed on Germany at the end of the First World War held substantial appeal for Arab leaders, who considered the mandate for Palestine, the Balfour Declaration, and the Sykes-Picot Agreement part of the many injustices that Arabs shared along with the Germans and what was termed the hated "Diktat" of Versailles. This sentiment was fostered and exploited by the Nazis in shaping a favorable atmosphere for Arab uprisings in Palestine and elsewhere in the British and French spheres of the Arab world. The articles and books by Dr. Francis Nicosia of the University of Vermont offer an excellent way to explore these strands of ideological melding between German and Arab victimization narratives.[10] Nicosia's work would be used as a basis for discussion between the authors and America's service members interested in understanding the impact of long-term strategic communications used as a weapon to cultivate hostile areas of operation in the twenty-first century.

Palestinian Arab leaders wasted no time in publicizing their positive assessment of events in Germany in 1933. The German consul general in Palestine, Heinrich Wolff, maintained a consistent dialogue with the grand mufti of Jerusalem, Hajj Amin Al-Husseini. The mufti's views, conveyed to Berlin on March 31, were summarized by Wolff: "The Mufti made detailed statements to me today to the effect that Muslims inside and outside of Palestine salute the new regime in Germany, and hope for the spread of Fascist anti-democratic leadership to other countries."[11] The mufti informed Wolff that Arabs in Palestine were ripe for revolt against the British. The Nazis keenly looked to the future of the spread of Fascism throughout the Near East by capitalizing on pan-Arabism and pan-Islamism. The German consulate in Beirut and the German embassy in Baghdad, headed by Ambassador Fritz Grobba, received letters from Syrian and Iraqi citizens expressing their admiration for Hitler and the NSDAP ideals; these letters also included proposals for closer ties between the Arab world and Germany. Dr. Joseph Goebbels, the infamous Nazi minister of propaganda, obtained favorable reports from sources in the Near East on the extent of pro-German feelings. (See appendix 1 for excerpts of Goebbels' diaries, noting how the Middle East figured into his thinking.) Many Arabs hoped to pursue the aims of Arab Nationalism in Palestine by creating a movement based on the NSDAP model and experiences.[12] In October 1941 Hitler resolved a dispute between German foreign minister Joachim von Ribbentrop and Goebbels by assigning primary responsibility for foreign-language propaganda to the Auswärtige Amt (German foreign ministry). In the foreign ministry's political department, Wilhelm Melchers would direct overall policy concerning the Middle East, and Kurt Munzel would lead the Department of Radio Policy section that focused on Arabic radio broadcasts.[13]

A report outlined Germany's favorable position and the positive propaganda potential throughout the region:

> I have been able to discern with happiness in all the countries of the Near East that, with the exception of the Jews, all the people are following events in the new Germany with much sympathy and enthusiasm. Especially among the youth, national Fascist units are being established against England and France as the oppressors. Everywhere people wish for a man and leader such as Adolf Hitler. German newspapers are read with keen interest, and there is a demand for more propaganda material and newspapers in French and English, as only a few speak German. Such propaganda will serve useful for the Reich.[14]

Scholar Francis Nicosia writes in his book, *The Third Reich and the Palestine Question*, the following, which I have paraphrased: Among German diplomats in the Middle East, there was a consensus that Arab enthusiasm for Nazi Germany lacked any understanding of the substance of NSDAP, the goals of the movement, or the significance of Adolf Hitler. The German consul in Jaffa, Timotheus Wurst, summarized this view in 1935, observing that the Arabs were driven primarily by the anti-Jewish policies of the Hitler regime and to some degree by the disciplined, militaristic, and Nationalistic posture of the Nazi Party.[15]

The German foreign office was hesitant in giving support to Arab efforts to create an Arab national socialist party in Palestine. An unsigned memorandum from the Near East section of the foreign office provided the following explanation:

> The objections that Herr Wolff has raised against the promotion of an Arab National Socialist movement by official German representatives are fully

supported here. Given the notorious political unreliability of the Arabs, one must surely assume that, as a result of Arab indiscretion, such ties would soon become known not only in Palestine and the Near East, but also to London and Paris. Since the end of the war, our efforts in the eastern countries have had the objective of German economic and cultural expansion through meddling in the internal affairs of these countries by our official representatives would likely result not only in economic setbacks, but, because of the preeminent strategic position of Britain and France in the east, would also have adverse consequences for Germany's policy in Europe.[16]

Nicosia further outlines how Wolff was instructed to discourage contact between pro-Nazi Arabs and the various local branches of the Nazi Party in Palestine catering to German expatriates. Moreover, Arab membership in the existing Nazi Party branch in Palestine was further precluded by a decree issued by Ernst Bohle of the Overseas Organization of the Nazi Party in June 1934. According to this decree, party membership abroad was denied to foreigners and reserved exclusively for Germans so that "any appearance of meddling in the internal affairs of foreign countries can be scrupulously avoided."[17] Efforts were made to avoid official contact with politically motivated Arabs in order to retain the goodwill of the British administration toward German consular representatives. This situation would change within a few years to overt agitation of Arabs in the region.

The Abwehr tradecraft capitalized on idealism and on those who despised a foreign government's domination of their homeland. They also made ample use of Germans living in the region, exploiting their homesickness to recruit agents and obtain information. Specific mention was made of Algerians who yearned for independence from France; Algeria had been a French colony since 1832. This tradecraft was implemented by the Abwehr through five hundred North African POWs serving in the French army, who the Abwehr utilized as potential agents and sources. Before reaching judgment, empathize (but do not sympathize) with being a subject people, treated as a second-class citizen within the French colonial system. One's advancement in a colonial system would be based not on merit, but on race or religion. Russian prisoners who spied for Germany did so for various reasons, including a hatred for Communism or a belief that Stalinism had betrayed the original ideals of Communism. David Kahn, in his book *Hitler's Spies*, makes mention of Algerian POWs spying against France, due to over a century of colonial rule of their homeland.[18]

Hitler's views on Palestine can be uncovered by carefully examining a few of his speeches from April 1922 to August 1939. In an address in Nuremburg on September 12, 1938, Hitler conducted a lengthy attack on Bolshevism and democracies before turning his attention to German minorities in Czechoslovakia: "I am in no way willing that there in the heart of Germany through the dexterity of other statesmen, a second Palestine should be permitted to arise. The poor

Arabs are defenseless, and perhaps deserted. The Germans in Czechoslovakia are neither defenseless nor are they deserted, and folk should take notice of that."[19] In this speech he compares the plight of the Palestinians' gradual loss of their land to that of the Sudeten Germans. But only a month later in a speech commemorating the anniversary of the 1923 failed Munich Putsch, Hitler uses the Palestinian question as a means to justify German dominance in Central Europe:

> The gentlemen of the English Parliament can assuredly be quite at home in the British World Empire, but not in Central Europe. Here they lack all the knowledge of conditions, of events, and of relationships. They will not and must not regard this statement of fact as an insult, we for our own part are in the last resort not so well informed on India, or Egypt, not to speak of Palestine. But I could wish that these gentlemen would at this moment concentrate the prodigious knowledge which they possess and the infallible wisdom which is their peculiar property on let us say, precisely, Palestine. What is taking place has a damnable strong smell of violence and precious little democracy. But all that I merely cite as an example, in no way as criticism, for after all I am only the representative of my German people, and not the advocate for the cause of others. And that is where I differ from Mr. Churchill and Mr. Eden who are advocates for the entire world.[20]

The Palestine question had been an issue of contention since World War I, and provided Hitler an opportunity to wage a strategic communication campaign against the British. In a speech in Wilhelmshaven on April 1, 1939, Hitler stated, "Certainly these Englishmen might answer in Palestine the Germans have nothing to seek and what is more, we [Germany] do not want to seek anything in Palestine. But just as little as we Germans have anything to seek in Palestine, precisely so little has England anything to seek in our German living-space (*Lebensraum*)."[21] Arab governments were not the first to exploit the Palestinian question to justify expansionist tendencies or to justify the rationale for war. In a speech to the Reichstag on April 28, 1939, Hitler used the British and French colonization of Arabs and Africans to answer President Franklin Roosevelt's appeal to Germany to cease threatening its neighbors in Europe and Africa. Hitler blurred the lines between European colonialism and the rise of benign American exceptionalism, and lumped or aggregated all democracies in one basket. The Middle East today engages in a similar practice of lumping French, British, and American experiences with secularism and democracy as one, or finding a new colonialist in the United States with such slogans as American imperialism. Addressing the Reichstag, Hitler said, "As for the fact, however, that one nation in Africa is alleged to have lost its freedom—that too is but an error; for it is not questioned if one nation in Africa having lost its freedom—on the contrary practically all the previous inhabitants of this continent have been subject to the sovereignty of other nations by bloody force, thereby losing their freedom. Moroccans, Berbers, Arabs, Negroes, & c., have all fallen victim to foreign might, the swords of which however were not inscribed, Made in Germany but Made by Democracies."[22] This came in response to President Roosevelt declaring that Czechoslovakia, Poland, France, and Ethiopia had seen their independence terminated.

Hitler responded to Roosevelt's request for assurances that the German armed forces abstain from invading several dozen nations, among them Iran, Iraq, Palestine, Syria, and Turkey. Hitler replied in this long Reichstag speech:

> Finally, Mr. Roosevelt asks that assurances be given him that the German Armed Forces will not attack and above all will not invade the territory and possessions of the following independent nations [he lists thirty], in the same way Ireland, the fact has obviously escaped Roosevelt's notice that Palestine is at present occupied not by German troops but by the English, and that the country is having its liberty restricted by the most brutal resort to force, is being robbed of its independence and is suffering the cruelest maltreatment for the benefit of Jewish interlopers. The Arabs living in that country will therefore certainly not have complained to Mr. Roosevelt of German aggression, but they do voice a continuous appeal to the world, deploring the barbarous methods with which England is attempting to suppress a people which loves its freedom and is but defending it.[23]

Toward the end of his speech he mentioned the Arab East again, to attack Roosevelt's logic of a world threatened by Hitler's aggression, and stated, "It is true that I could not cause inquiries to be made of certain of the states and nations mentioned [by Roosevelt in his telegram] because they themselves—as for example—Syria are at present not in possession of their freedom, but are occupied and consequently deprived of their rights by the military agents of democratic states."[24] The propaganda and recruitment value of such a speech was not lost on the Germans, as it was rebroadcast throughout the Arab world to incite anti-British sentiment and to provide opportunities for Axis agents operating in the region. Hitler's speeches demonstrated the failure of the Allies to anticipate a response in which he attempted to portray Fascism as equal to and even less hypocritical than Western democracies in areas of the world where Western democracies maintained the double standard of a colonial administration and a military presence. It is worthy to debate the utility of President Roosevelt's mention of subject states like India, Palestine, and Syria in which he argued with Churchill in the 1943 Casablanca Conference. The president argued with the prime minister that maintaining the British colonial status quo was becoming untenable when fighting for democratic ideals against the Axis powers. The anti-American sentiment would grow in the Arab East after the Roosevelt administration; that sentiment stemmed from the ambiguous expression by U.S. public officials, culminating with President Truman's overt sympathy with Zionism in Palestine, the creation of the state of Israel, and what was seen in the Middle East as a selective alliance with Britain against Arab independence. This led the Arabs to believe that the

United States supported Britain's policies in the Arab world as evidence of the hypocritical attitude of the United States in advocating independence and self-determination for minorities on the one hand, while supporting British imperialism on the other. President Truman's secretary of state, General George C. Marshall, would attempt to repair this misperception during the Cold War.

Italian Engagements in Palestine

It is impossible to discuss the events of World War II without understanding the ending of World War I, and events in the Middle East are no exception. Italy's disappointment with the Paris Peace settlement of 1919 strengthened French and British dominion in the Mediterranean and fueled the sentiments of Fascist Italy after 1922. Mussolini's aim was for the Mediterranean Sea to be mare nostrum (Latin for "our sea"). The Italian dictator's goal was to replace Britain and France as the dominant power in the Mediterranean and Red Seas. With the exception of a desire to share in the control and operation of the strategic Suez Canal, Italy posited no specific claims against the British in the Near East. Though anxious to protect and promote its own influence in Palestine, Italy did not seek to replace the British as the mandatory power.[25]

Before the Second World War, Italy's policy, with the exception of its policy toward Libya, was one of peaceful penetration that consisted of developing ties with Arab leaders, tapping into their demand for arms, and presenting Fascism in a favorable light via various Italian-sponsored propaganda outlets. Italy adopted an assuring policy with respect to the Islamic religion; that policy served as a tool for both colonial and foreign policy purposes. Italian propaganda efforts included the construction of mosques in Libya and East Africa, the encouragement of Islamic academics in Italy's colonies, and the assistance for pilgrims from Italian domains to perform the hajj (pilgrimage to Mecca). These were all conducted to improve Italy's image in the Arab East, and explore the potential of empowering the Muslim minority against the Christian majority in Ethiopia. Italy's financial subsidies to Ethiopian Muslim pilgrims wanting to travel to Mecca were welcomed by the Saudi government. The ruling al-Sauds, whose finances were adversely affected by both the loss of revenue caused by the world depression and the decrease in Muslim pilgrims visiting Islamic holy cities of Mecca and Medina, needed revenue from where they could get it. In 1937 the Italian authorities in Ethiopia and representatives in Jeddah made efforts to accommodate the pilgrims and to ensure their transportation from the port of Jeddah to Mecca. Italy helped some 1,900 Muslim Ethiopians reach the holy places, where they publicly praised the generosity of Mussolini and spent much-needed Italian cash in the holy sites controlled by the al-Saud family.[26]

Mussolini accepted London's need for a link with British India through Palestine and Transjordan and did not dispute British control of these territories;

however, Italy expressed interest in succeeding France as the mandatory power overseeing the Levant and other territories. Albania, Corsica, Nice, Syria, and Tunis were the major aims of Italian revisionism in the Mediterranean during the interwar period—that is, the recreation of Roman glory. Mussolini was supportive of the aims of the Zionist movement and the idea of a Jewish national home in Palestine during the 1920s and 1930s. He was once of the opinion that European power and influence in Palestine and the Near East were best promoted through the support of Zionism, but was torn. Both Italy and Britain came to the realization in the late 1930s as the clouds of war began to descend over Europe that support for the Arabs would prove fruitful. The Italo-Ethiopian War from 1935 to 1936, followed by the Spanish Civil War that began in 1936, forced Mussolini to conclude that his aims could only be achieved by confronting Anglo-French opposition to his expansionist policies and by striving to make Italy a respected power among nations.

Toward this end, Rome began an anti-British campaign in the Near East and a program of financial support for Arab insurgents in Palestine. In 1934 Mussolini initiated a program to improve the Italian image in the Arab world in preparation for his Ethiopian campaign. Repressive policies, particularly in Libya, were scrapped, and a new public works program, to include the building of schools and hospitals, was implemented in the Libyan colony, described by the Italians as the three sections of Fezzan, Tripoli, and Cyrenaica, a remnant of how the Ottomans had divided Libya before Italian colonization. Previous to the Ottomans, it was a designation of the region made by the Romans—for instance, Fezzan is a Latin-derivative of Phasania, meaning land of the pheasants.

Mussolini was interested in winning Arab sympathy for Italy at the expense of Britain and France; the Palestinian turmoil provided him with the opportunity to do so. On May 24, 1934, Italy pioneered the first Arabic language radio broadcasts on its Radio Bari station. Radio Bari began broadcasting daily Arabic language programs with anti-British propaganda, which was intensified during the Palestinian Revolt. At times Italian propaganda in Arabic also criticized the Jews in Palestine. Radio Bari broadcast to its Arab listeners popular anti-British propaganda. One of the drawbacks to Radio Bari was that it broadcast in a formalized literal Arabic instead of in regional dialects; however the novelty of the radio station and being the first to broadcast in Arabic made up for this deficiency.[27] British foreign secretary Anthony Eden would face two occasions in Parliament when questions by lawmakers were posed about Radio Bari and the anti-British influence they were having in the Near East.[28]

In the course of researching this book, the authors stumbled upon a newspaper article first published in London on January 9, 1938, and reprinted the next day in the *Sydney Morning Herald*, with the headline, "Arabs Prefer Bari." The article discusses the challenges British officials have in countering Italian propaganda.[29] In addition, Italian propaganda was not limited to radio broadcasts:

Italian aircraft scattered leaflets in Arabic boasting of Italian conquests of British Somaliland and claiming air superiority over Gibraltar and Malta.[30] This became one of the major points of friction in Anglo-Italian relations during the late 1930s. In response to Radio Bari's anti-British propaganda, the British established the Palestine Broadcasting Service in 1936; and BBC Arabic Service broadcasting through the entire Middle East would air in 1938.[31] Not to be outdone, Radio Berlin began its virulent anti-British Arabic broadcast in 1938, with the Iraqi journalist Yunus al-Bahri, opening the broadcast, "This is Berlin! Salutations to the Arabs."[32] This war of the radio waves was another aspect of the World War II Middle East, with Radio Berlin-Zeesen even broadcasting readings from the Quran to attract listeners and alternating broadcasts with the opening, "This is the Voice of Free Arabism."[33] When the Germans occupied Greece, they established a transmitter in Athens to increase their reach into the region. The British Royal Air Force (RAF) and Special Operations Executive (SOE) began to set up radio transmitters in Jaffa starting in 1941 to compete with the aggressive Axis propaganda radio inciting the region.[34] Ironically, the British set up Egypt's radio in 1926, but handed it over to Egyptian programmers and directors, and did not utilize it for propaganda purposes. In 1936 King Ghazi of Iraq set up his personal radio station inside his al-Zuhoor Palace; the king delivered anti-British speeches to Baghdad listeners. That same year Radio Baghdad came on line. In March 1936 the Palestine Broadcasting Service aired from British-mandated Palestine delivering programs in Arabic, Hebrew, and English; the transmitter was in Ramallah. In April 1940 Radio Tehran delivered Farsi programs, music, and shows to the Iranian masses. Reading about the various radio stations and the competition for hearts and minds made me recollect the controversy surrounding Donald Rumsfeld's short-lived idea of creating an Office of Strategic Communication in 2003. It was viewed as a propaganda arm instead of understanding the secretary's view of how media, perception, and disinformation were killing American combat troops in Iraq. He was searching for ways to address the toxic atmosphere created by anti-American media outlets in the region.

Italy established relations with Amir Shakib Arslan (hereafter Arslan) of Syria.[35] A fierce Arab Nationalist born into a Druze family and residing in the Swiss city of Geneva, Arslan served as the unofficial representative of Syria and Palestine at the League of Nations. He was also the editor of the newspaper *La Nation Arabe* (the Arab Nation).[36] Of note, Arslan oversaw the translation of Hitler's *Mein Kampf* into Arabic before the project was cancelled due to cost overruns. What is unique in the Arslan translation is his attempt to mimic Arabic literary style versus the editions that were published in Arabic by the German foreign ministry. Jeffrey Herf discusses this in his 2009 book, *Nazi Propaganda and the Arab World*.[37] The next translation of Hitler's manifesto would be completed in 1963 by Luis Heiden (aka Luis al-Hajj), an escaped Nazi war criminal who was hiding in Egypt.[38]

Arslan was influenced by both the teachings of the Persian Islamist Nationalist, Jamal al-Din al-Afghani (d. 1897), and by al-Afghani's disciple the Egyptian grand mufti and Islamic reformer, Muhammad Abduh (d. 1905). Arslan was particularly hostile toward France and sought to exploit Franco-German and Franco-Italian friction in order to win both Germany and Italy for the Arab cause. He was a strong supporter of the Ottoman Empire and carried negative sentiments toward the Hashemites for their support of the Arab Revolt during the First World War. Arslan, unlike other leading Arab figures of practical politics, realized the futility of seeking an alliance with the Axis. Instead, despite his early flirtation with the Italians, Arslan eventually advocated Arab neutrality in the upcoming conflict.

There is also evidence the grand mufti of Jerusalem received money from Italy throughout the 1930s and that Arslan acted as the intermediary between Rome and the grand mufti.[39] In September of 1940 Count Galeazzo Ciano, Italian foreign minister, told the German ambassador to Rome, Hans Georg von Mackensen, that he maintained relations with the mufti for years and provided him substantial financial aid.[40] In April of 1939 Ciano stated to chief of the Luftwaffe (German air force) Hermann Goering that Italian money helped pay for smuggled arms into Palestine.[41] Italy's efforts to sway Arab opinion were designed to put pressure on Britain to accept the annexation of Ethiopia and to attain some measure of national equality among European colonial powers in East Africa and the Red Sea, rather than to undermine the Allied position in the Levant. The result of Italian involvement in Palestine and the Arab East as a whole was an unlikely partnership between an aspiring colonial power (Italy) and an anticolonial movement (Arab Nationalism). Incompatibility between Fascist colonial aspirations, Nazi domination, and Arab Nationalist yearnings were bound to come to the surface. "Ideological and strategic incompatibility" is a description aptly used in Francis Nicosia's title of his article, "Arab Nationalism and National Socialist Germany: Ideological and Strategic Incompatibility," and can also be fixed on Fascist Italy's efforts to manipulate the emotions of the Middle East.

Origins of the Arab Revolt of 1936

It is important to understand the origins of the Palestinian revolt that occurred in 1936. It is usually viewed as being caused by the following four major events:

1. The incitement made by Izz Ad-Din Al-Qassam
2. The establishment of the Arab Higher Committee chaired by Hajj Amin Al-Husseini
3. The Peel Commission interlude
4. The recommencement of the revolt

On April 19, 1936, riots began in Jaffa initiated by the followers of Sheikh Izz Ad-Din Al-Qassam, the spiritual leader and founder of Al Kaff Al Aswad (the Black Hand), an anti-Zionist and anti-British underground Islamist militant organization. Al-Qassam, born in 1882 on the coastal city of Jableh in northern Syria, was educated in the prestigious Al-Azhar University in Cairo. Upon graduating he spent a short time in Turkey as a religious teacher. After the Italian-Turkish War concluded on October 18, 1912, he began collecting funds and enlisting 250 volunteers for Omar Mukhtar, the famous Libyan resistance leader who fought Italy from 1911 to 1931.[42] As you will read in chapter 9, the Egyptian war minister during the outbreak of World War II, Saleh Harb Pasha, would be impacted by the Italo-Libyan War, leading the Libyans fighting Italian forces alongside another famous leader, Mustafa Kemal Atatürk, who would also provide leadership in battle against the Italians in the deserts of Libya.

Al-Qassam later enlisted in the Ottoman army during World War I; there he received military training and acted as a Muslim chaplain at an Ottoman army base near Damascus. Following the implementation of the 1916 Sykes-Picot Agreement, he conducted guerrilla warfare against French forces in the Levant. With the establishment of the Black Hand organization, classified as a terrorist group by the British mandatory authorities, he arranged cells and enlisted men to conduct a widespread campaign of attacks against Jewish communities, British installations, and rail lines.[43]

Al-Qassam often cooperated with and received financial assistance from Al-Husseini. However, the two men went their separate ways, presumably due to Al-Qassam's independent activities committed without the consent of the mufti. Al-Qassam found financial relief from Hizb al-Istiqlal (Arab Nationalist Independence Party) founded by Awni Abd al-Hadi. His continued attempts to forge a coalition with the mufti failed since the mufti was engaged in diplomatic negotiations with the British at that time. In November of 1935 Al-Qassam, fearing British reprisals, moved his base to the hills between Jenin and Nablus. The British police launched a manhunt and surrounded his safe house in the West Bank town of Ya'bad, thirty-two miles from Jenin. In the consequent gun battle, Al-Qassam was killed. His death became an inspiration for militant organizations in subsequent years. The militant wing of Hamas was dubbed Izz Ad-Din Al-Qassam brigades, and they used artillery called "Qassam" rockets.[44]

With the death of Al-Qassam, the Qassamiyun (devout followers of Al-Qassam) staged a general strike in Jaffa and in Nablus and launched attacks on Jewish and British quarters. These strikes were prompted by the Arab Higher Committee, the political foci of the Arab community in Palestine, chaired by Al-Husseini. Substantial funding arrived from Italy, among other sources.[45]

The mufti explained to Italy's consul general in Jerusalem, Mariano de Angelis, that his involvement in the conflict with the British arose from the trust he reposed in Mussolini's backing.[46] In Massimiliano Fiore's book, *Anglo-Italian*

Relations in the Middle East, 1922–1940, readers gain an idea of the sums of money provided to the grand mufti; several payments of £20,000 were not uncommon. With this money as well as cash collected from donors in the region, the mufti formed a paramilitary youth organization, al-Futuwwah (the Youth Vanguard) that was based on the Hitler Youth. The Arab Higher Committee stated that the strike would continue until the British administration agreed to halt Jewish immigration. Palestinian guerrillas targeted a major oil pipeline from Kirkuk to Haifa to put pressure on the British colonial administration in Palestine.[47]

Dr. Fritz Grobba can be described as Nazi Germany's most effective agent and foremost German envoy of Middle Eastern affairs. Among his duties was German ambassador to Iraq in 1932 and to Saudi Arabia in 1938. Grobba was born in Gartz, Germany, on July 18, 1886. He obtained his degree in law and oriental languages from the University of Berlin, was well versed in Arab culture and Near East history, and was fluent in Arabic and Turkish. We often pay much attention to British Arabists and neglect the Arabists that the losing side of World War II produced. Grobba harbored much faith in the potential of the pan-Arab movement, and in late 1937 believed that the friendship of the Arabs for Germany was, in his own words, "almost instinctive." He wrote those words when two Axis-sympathetic governments were installed in Iraq.[48] In 1938 the grand mufti met with Nazi intelligence chief Admiral Wilhelm Canaris with plans to smuggle weapons into Palestine for anti-British Arab cells through Saudi Arabia. The operation was aborted, however, because of concerns the British would link the weapons to Berlin.[49]

Reeva Simon's book on the militarist origins of tyranny in Iraq, *Iraq between the Two World Wars*, contains an excellent collection of writings and quotes by Grobba, including these: "[T]he friendship of the Arabs for Germany [was] still active in the leading class in Iraq, Syria, and Palestine" and, "[E]ven if Arab friendship towards Germany is determined above all by the Arab's own interest, it is an important factor for Germany, which we can make both political and economic use of."[50]

Grobba would receive requests from Arab sources for weapons and other supplies for Arab insurgents in Palestine. One such request came from Fawzi El-Qawukji, a former officer in the Iraqi army who commanded Arab units in Palestine during the revolt. El-Qawukji requested large amounts of German weapons, to be paid for by the mufti's Higher Committee. In January 1937 Grobba was visited by members of the Arab Higher Committee who hoped to secure German arms and money for future efforts in Palestine.[51] Francis Nicosia's book, *The Third Reich and the Palestine Question*, republished in 2000, is an essential volume in attempting to begin to trace the Axis money trail to Middle East insurgencies in World War II.

Although the Peel Commission did not finish its deliberations in Palestine until six months later, there was anticipation in the Middle East and in Europe that the Commission would recommend the creation of an independent Jewish state in part of mandatory Palestine.

The source of weapons used by the Arab insurgency remains unclear to this day; it was difficult for Britain to trace the origin of the weapons during the first phases of the revolt leading up to the subsequent unrest and violence. Nicosia discusses how British foreign office and German foreign ministry records indicate that both London and Berlin suspected financial and arms assistance for the Palestinian Arabs from diverse sources, such as the Soviet Union and Italy. The statistics of the Handelspolitische Abteilung (Section for trade policy) in the German foreign ministry revealed a relatively modest export of German war materiel to the Arab states of the Middle East between 1936 and 1939. The most likely and immediate sources of weapons and financial assistance were neighboring Arab states. According to the deputy inspector general in Palestine in 1936, large sums of money had been collected in Egypt and the Levant by the mufti's Central Relief Committee for the Arab cause in Palestine. In August of 1936 German consul general in Jerusalem Hans Dohle reported to Berlin that weapons and ammunition were coming into Palestine from Transjordan, in spite of King Abdullah I's (ruled 1921–1951) efforts to mediate between the rebels and British authorities. In October Grobba reported from Baghdad that the Palestinian rebels had procured weapons through an Anglo-Belgian consortium for the Ethiopian government in its war against Italy, but that one ship with weapons was transferred by the Saudi government to Palestine via Transjordan.[52]

In early 1937 Grobba again reported to Berlin on his suspicions about Russian (Bolshevik) assistance to the Arabs.[53] This report was not unreasonable; during the attempts to create the French and British mandates in Syria and Iraq, Bolshevist operatives circulated propaganda to undermine their efforts in an attempt to spread Communist ideals. A report made by Hans Dohle to the mufti and published in Nicosia's *Third Reich and the Palestinian Question* stated, "The elite units of the Arab terror organization are moving more and more under Russian influence. With Russian help, Arab guerrillas have to possess good, modern weapons. After a recent visit of a Soviet Russian trade representative in Jaffa, the possibilities of Russian weapons deliveries for the Arabs via the southern Palestine coast have been discussed. In view of the intense supervision of Greek ships, which played a role in weapons smuggling during the recent unrest, agreements were concluded for the use of Egyptian sailboats."[54]

The Peel Commission Committee would meet on November 11, 1936, led by Lord William Wellesley Peel. It investigated the reasons behind the uprising and proposed a solution, issuing its report on July 7, 1937. In that report the Committee proposed ending the mandate and dividing Palestine into two parts.[55] While an ongoing contentious issue, the partition was not equal portions of Palestine given to the Palestinians and the Israelis, and the plan would prove impossible for the Palestinians to accept due to the inequity and quality of the land designated to its people. Yet understanding the history is just the beginning as we attempt to find an acceptable solution to the Palestinian-Israeli dispute.

The Peel Report recommended the transfer of Arab Palestinians from territories allocated for the Jewish state. Arab leadership consequently rejected the plan, and the revolt resumed in the autumn of 1937. With the assassination of British district commissioner Lewis Yelland Andrews, Britain declared martial law and outlawed the Arab Higher Committee.[56] An arrest warrant for Al-Husseini was issued. Although the 1936 Revolt was futile, it signified the birth of the national Arab Palestinian identity and features prominently in the narratives of Palestinians, whether Nationalist or Islamist.

The Grand Mufti: Hajj Amin Al-Husseini

Perhaps the most prominent figure and symbol of Arab Nationalist and Nazi collaboration in World War II was Al-Husseini. His influence extended beyond Palestine and saw no boundary between religion and politics, and played a major role in integrating Palestinian and Arab Nationalism with Islamic schemes. Born in 1895 to the prominent Al-Husseini clan in Jerusalem, he belonged to the Hanafi jurisprudence of the Sunni sect of Islam, one of four Sunni schools of Islam. His father, Tahir Al-Husseini, was chief justice of the Sharia (Islamic) courts of Jerusalem. After learning to speak Turkish fluently at an Ottoman government school in Palestine, he attended Al-Azhar University in Cairo in 1912, where he studied Islamic theology, Arabic studies, and Islamic jurisprudence.

While in Cairo, Al-Husseini attended an educational institution known as Dar al-Dawa wal-Ershad (the Institute for Propagation and Guidance) created by the Syrian Islamist Salafi intellectual Mohammed Rashid Rida (1865–1935).[57] Rida politically promoted a rejuvenation of the Caliphate for pan-Islamism. Rida witnessed the forcible French eviction of King Feisal ibn Hussein from Syria in 1920 in the Battle of Maysaloon. King Feisal would later be installed by the British as king of Iraq (ruled 1921–1933) in a British-orchestrated plebiscite designed to bring calm to Iraq's 1920 Revolt, which was objecting to the British mandate over Iraq. These colonial events shaped Rida, who, while living in Egypt, stoked Islamist political sentiments and directly influenced such young students as Hassan al-Banna, founder of the Egyptian Muslim Brotherhood.[58]

At Dar-al-Dawa wal-Ershad, Al-Husseini was also exposed to the teachings of Jamal al-Din al-Afghani, which taught him the tactics of Islamist incitement and radicalism. In this view, the Middle East was colonized because of the Muslim's lack of faith and the need to reestablish the ethic of jihad. Al-Afghani and his disciples also believed that Muslim rulers who enabled colonization were apostates who should be killed. It was Al-Afghani who would inspire two strands of Salafism: the radical strand of Rashid Rida, and the progressive strand of Muhammad Abdu, who wanted to reform society and make it compatible with the challenges of the industrial age. Al-Husseini continued his studies at Cairo University College of Literature and received formal training in leadership and administration at the secular Ottoman School for Administration in Istanbul. After attending the military academy in Istanbul, and following the outbreak of World War I, he received his commission as an artillery officer in the Ottoman army, entering the College for Reserve Officers.[59]

Al-Husseini joined the 46th Infantry Regiment stationed at Izmir in southwest Turkey and had a follow-on assignment to the 47th Infantry Regiment stationed in the Turkish city of Smyrna. His allegiance to Ottoman Islamic unity was gradually eroded by the harsh Ottoman Turkification of the Arab provinces and the suppression of Arab Nationalist organizations. In November 1916 he left the Ottoman Army on disability leave and returned to Jerusalem, where he began aiding the Arab Revolt led by Feisal bin Al Hussein Bin Ali El-Hashemi, who later became King Feisal I of Iraq. After the Treaty of Versailles, Al-Husseini was embittered by the sidelining of the Arab Revolt prompted by the Sykes-Picot Agreement and by the influx of Jewish immigrants into British-mandated Palestine. Rioting broke out among Palestinian Muslims during the procession of the Nabi Musa (the prophet Moses) festival, which was used as an occasion to protest the implementation of the Balfour Declaration of a Jewish homeland. Al-Husseini, then an Islamic tutor at the Rashidiya School in East Jerusalem, was charged with incitement and sentenced by military court to ten years' imprisonment, but was among those agitators pardoned by British authorities in an attempt to not further inflame Arab civil discord.[60]

With Arab protests at their peak after the First World War, the Palin Commission (formally the Palin Court of Inquiry) was set up in May of 1920 by Major General P. C. Palin to examine the rioting in Jerusalem during April 4–7, 1920, in the wake of violent Arab protests against the growing presence and political demands of the Jewish community. The report was completed on July 1, 1920, at Port Said, and was submitted in August 1920, though it was never published. Palestinians attacked Jewish inhabitants in Jaffa and five Jewish colonies on May 1, 1921. The British high commissioner for Palestine, Sir Herbert Samuel, appointed the chief justice of Palestine, Sir Thomas Haycraft, to determine the causes of the Arab violence; hence, another commission was set up to investigate the Jaffa riots of 1921.[61]

The Haycraft Report highlighted Arab fears that extensive Jewish immigration would lead to Palestine becoming a Jewish dominion. With the ineffective conclusions of the Palin Report and the Haycraft Commission of Inquiry in the early 1920s, Al-Husseini directed his efforts to thoughts of pan-Arabism and the idea of a Greater Syria, to consist of Palestine, Lebanon, Transjordan, and Syria, with Damascus as its political heart. However, this plan collapsed in the face of British and French determination in implementing the 1916 Sykes-Picot Agreement through several post–World War I conferences, beginning with Versailles in 1919 and ending with the Cairo Conference in 1921. Al-Husseini turned from Damascus-centered pan-Arabism to a Palestinian ideology centered on Jerusalem, which sought to block Jewish immigration to Palestine. From the time of his election as mufti, Al-Husseini exercised control over the anti-British and anti-Zionist underground groups, Al-Fida'iyya (the Self-Sacrificers), and Al-Ikha Wal-Afaf (Brotherhood and Purity).[62]

British High Commissioner of Palestine Sir Herbert Samuel, in an attempt to appease Arab Nationalists, granted Al-Husseini amnesty in April 1921 following the death of his half-brother, the mufti Kamil Al-Husseini. This allowed him to return to Jerusalem, where he took the position of grand mufti of Jerusalem. The following year the British established the Supreme Muslim Council and appointed Al-Husseini to lead the organization, designed to transition Arabs toward self-governance and give them a representative voice. Al-Husseini, making use of his new position, took an active role organizing anti-Jewish riots in 1929. The British hope of giving him responsibility, as a means of incorporating him in the British mandatory system, backfired, as he resorted to incitement and violence as a means of garnering influence through populism. The appeasement of Al-Husseini only elevated his hatred of both the British and Jews. He was among the leaders that formed the Arab Higher Committee that incited discord and managed the uprising in 1936. In 1937 the British outlawed his committee and he escaped to Damascus once again, where he continued his rebellion against British authorities.[63]

The rise of Nazism increased pressure on Britain from Zionist groups to allow larger numbers of immigrants into Palestine. Al-Husseini, in an attempt to find a European patron, expressed solidarity with Nazi Germany as early as 1937. His earliest contacts were with the German consul in Damascus declaring his support for the Third Reich. In 1937 the mufti met with Nazi officials Hauptschanführer Adolf Eichmann and SS (Schutzstaffel, or protection squadron) Oberscharführer Herbert Hagen in Syria. Following this meeting Al-Husseini became an agent of the Third Reich. His close association with the Nazis became a subject of discussion in the testimony of SS officer and Eichmann subordinate Dieter Wisliceny, who supplied an affidavit on the grand mufti's close association with the SS during the Nuremberg tribunals.[64] However, the British failed to charge the grand mufti and found Wisliceny's testimony to be suspect.[65]

After years of violence against the British and the Jews and following an assassination attempt on the British inspector general of the Palestine police, the British authorities officially declared the Arab Higher Committee illegal and the mufti fled the Palestine mandate for good in 1937. Al-Husseini stopped in Beirut, Baghdad, and Tehran before arriving and settling in Berlin in 1941. One of the most essential of these stops was Baghdad where, in April 1941, a group of army officers led by an Iraqi lawyer and politician, Rashid Ali Al-Gaylani, seized power and established a pro-Axis regime in Iraq. One of the officers supporting the Gaylani coup was a young officer, Khairallah Tulfah, who became better known as the uncle, paternal mentor, and later father-in-law of the late Iraqi dictator Saddam Hussein. Tulfah, impacted partly by Fascist propaganda, would write a perverse pseudo-intellectual ten-page pamphlet in the 1940s, "Three Whom God Should Not Have Created: Persians, Jews, and Flies," that would be made into Ba'athist propaganda in 1981 and distributed as part of the ideological indoctrination to children.[66]

After the 1929 Riots at the Western Wall that were instigated by Arab mobs in Jerusalem, armed Zionist formations such as Haganah began to gain popularity in British-mandated Palestine.[67] Though such groups had existed before 1929, the riots prompted a more efficient military organization and mobilization.[68] Irgun was an offshoot of Haganah, founded in 1937 and based around more-radical ideals pioneered by Ze'ev Jabotinsky.[69] As a right-wing revisionist, Jabotinsky rejected Communist and Fascist ideologies and advocated a form of government where liberty, individuality, and equality were valued.[70] Within Irgun, leadership was divided between David Raziel, who was in charge of the military wing, and Abraham Stern, who was Irgun's political leader.[71] Stern's personal ideology differed greatly from Jabotinsky's. Stern believed the British were inherently a barrier to the development of a Jewish state, and suggested an anti-British rebellion with help from states such as Fascist Italy.[72] The divide between the two men grew wider after the publication of the White Paper of 1939, which limited Jewish immigration to Palestine and placed restrictions on land purchases between Arabs and Jews.[73] This enraged Stern, who argued for intensified anti-British raids in retaliation.[74] Stern finally left Irgun to form his own organization, Lohamei Herut Yisrael (Lehi; fighters for the freedom of Israel), in 1940.[75] Subsequent to their split from Irgun, Lehi, or the "Stern Gang" as it came to be known, began to appeal to Nazi planners who saw it as a means of agitation in the Middle East as well as an effort to expel the British from the region, albeit in hindsight unsuccessfully.[76] Additionally, Lehi carried out small-scale assassination attempts against British soldiers between 1941 and 1943.[77] While the British used Irgun to target the grand mufti, Lehi would undertake an assassination in Egypt that would delay the establishment of a Jewish homeland in Palestine.

The chairperson of the Jewish National Council in Palestine proposed to the British foreign office that an assassination attempt should be conducted on Al-Husseini while he was still residing in Baghdad in 1941. With Churchill's approval, the plan was to be conducted by members of the Jewish ultra-Nationalist group, Irgun, led by David Raziel. They were to be flown to Iraq in order to capture or kill Al-Husseini. However, a lone German messerschmitt (fighter plane) strafed a convoy in May 1941, killing Raziel and others on board. Following this incident, the operation was abandoned.[78] While not the subject of this book, readers may wish to explore operations conducted by Irgun during World War II, and its more violent splinter group, Lehi, which conducted outreach to the Fascists in return for help evicting the British and setting up a Jewish state in Palestine. Lehi would be involved in the assassination of Resident Minister of the Middle East Lord Moyne in Cairo in 1944. Moyne's murder would anger Churchill, and would require the intervention of Chaim Weizman to manage the British prime minister and distance the Zionist project from the militant methodology of Lehi. In order to keep British support, other Jewish organizations, namely the Jewish Agency for Israel, rushed to cooperate with all the demands of British officials. However, it was too late, as Churchill had already ordered postponement of debate on the Palestine Committee Report, which would have given the Jews an independent state.[79]

Despite some aid to the Iraqis from Syria, which was still controlled by the pro-Axis French Vichy government, the Germans were unable to maintain the Gaylani coup, and it was crushed by British forces. In Syria a committee was created to mobilize support for the pro-Axis regime; this formed the core of what later became the Ba'ath Party today. Rashid Ali Al-Gaylani later joined up with Al-Husseini in Berlin, where both sought political protection from the Nazis. Gaylani also established contacts with the other Axis powers and was granted legation asylum in Japan and Italy. After the occupation of Iran in the aftermath of Operation Countenance, Al-Husseini fled to Italy with the aid of Italian diplomats who provided him secured passage. Al-Husseini arrived in Rome October 11, 1941, and contacted the Italian Servizio Informazioni Militari (SIM; Italian military intelligence). On October 27 Al-Husseini met with Mussolini and was granted 1 million (lira; approximately $40,000) in support of Axis-friendly cells in Palestine.[80] Admiral Canaris also met the mufti earlier in the summer of 1938 while traveling incognito to Lebanon, quite possibly to supply financial assistance to him. On at least one occasion, Ambassador Grobba met with Musa el-Alami, the mufti's secretary, in Damascus and gave him £800 (sterling; approximately $3,500) that Grobba stated "was entrusted to me in Berlin for this purpose," that is, to agitate anti-French sentiments in Syria on the eve of war.[81]

Al-Husseini developed the official draft declaration of German-Arab collaboration that was submitted earlier in 1940 by another private secretary, Uthman Haddad, stating the following eight points:

(1.) Recognition of the complete independence of the already [nominally] independent Arab countries: Iraq, Egypt, the Sudan, Saudi Arabia and the Yemen;
(2.) Recognition of the independence of the Arab countries under British mandate (Palestine and Transjordan) or protectorates by Great Britain (Kuwait, Dubai, Oman, Hadhramaut);
(3.) A statement to the effect that Germany and Italy would have no objections to Syria and Lebanon attaining full independence;

(4.) Abrogation of the reservations to the full independence of Egypt and the Sudan contained in the treaties with Great Britain, with Italy reserving only the right to safeguard her imperial communications line through the Sudan by agreement with Egypt;

(5.) A statement that Germany and Italy would not make use of such means as the mandate system which abridges the full independence of the Arab countries;

(6.) Recognition of the right of the Arab countries to unite and a commitment to create no obstacle for the Arab national programme in this respect;

(7.) Condemnation of the Jewish national home in Palestine as an illegal entity and recognition of the right of the Arabs to solve the Jewish question in accordance with the Arab nationalist aspirations and in the same manner as in the Axis countries; prohibition of all Jewish emigration to Arab countries;

(8.) Italy and Germany only desire that the whole Arab nation enjoy full prosperity and assume their historical and natural place in their properly due living space within the framework of the new world order and in economic cooperation with the Axis powers on the basis of mutual benefit. From the Arab countries, it is desired that they recognize the status quo in everything concerning the property of churches and Christian missions, the right to worship of the various religious Christian sects, and to philanthropic activity.[82]

It was signed and approved by Mussolini, and the draft was forwarded to the German consulate in Rome.

Upon his arrival in Berlin on November 6, 1941, the mufti met with Nazi foreign minister Joachim Von Ribbentrop and German ambassador to Iraq and Arab envoy Grobba, and was officially received by the führer on November 28, 1941. Hitler stated to Al-Husseini that after the defeat of the Soviet Union as German armed forces struck through the Caucasus into the Middle East, "Germany would have no further imperial goals of its own and would support Arab liberation." He further stated, "Germany's objective would then be solely the destruction of the Jewish element residing in the Arab sphere under the protection of British power."[83] According to transcripts of the meeting, Al-Husseini conveyed "to the Fuhrer of the Greater German Reich, admired by the entire Arab world, his thanks of the sympathy which he had always shown for the Arab and especially the Palestinian cause, and to which he had given clear expression in his public speeches."[84] This demonstrates Hitler's wider genocidal aspirations in the destruction of not only Europe's Jews, but of Jews beyond Europe and Russia.

The meeting between Hitler and Al-Husseini took place a few months before the notorious Wannsee Conference that met on January 20, 1942, and bureaucratized the "Final Solution" of the Jewish question (the methodical and industrialized genocide of 6 million Jews). The mufti discussed a draft agreement with German secretary of state to the foreign office Ernst Von Weizsäcker and approved of Nazi support in the elimination of any future Jewish national home in Palestine. Von Weizsäcker and the mufti's secretary Haddad would spend much time together negotiating a basis of understanding between the Nazis and the mufti. The mufti also conducted meetings with SS Reichsführer Heinrich Himmler. In addition, the mufti's years in Nazi Germany were spent in a confiscated Jewish mansion in Berlin as head of the Nazi-Arab Cooperation Section; there he continued his anti-Jewish propaganda campaign. With his introduction to Himmler, he became actively involved in the grotesque campaign against European and Slavic Jews in the Final Solution. The Nazis recruited two SS divisions from Yugoslavia's Muslim population and one from Albania's Muslim population: these were the Bosnian 13th Waffen-SS Handschar (Dagger) Mountain Division, the Bosnian 23rd Waffen-SS Kama Division, and the Albanian Skanderbeg 21st Waffen-SS Division. Al-Husseini used his prior military training coupled with his religious credentials (serving as a military chaplain on occasion) to involve himself in the training of these divisions. Each division grew to about 22,000 and carried out orders of the mufti that included genocide against Bosnian Serbs, Gypsies, and Jews. These Balkan divisions swore an oath to the Third Reich specifically written by Heinrich Himmler. Himmler wrote on the importance of integrating Muslim units, when training of select Muslims by the SS experienced tensions over race:

> All Muslim members of the Waffen SS and police are to be afforded the inalienable right of their religious demands never to touch pork, pork sausages nor to drink alcohol. . . . In all cases a diet of equal value will be assured to them. I hold all commanders, company commanders, and other officers, especially those officers and NCOs involved with economic administration (SS logistics), to be responsible for the most scrupulous and loyal respect for this privilege especially to be granted to the Muslims. They have answered the call of the Muslim chiefs and have come to us out of hatred for the common Jewish-Anglo-Bolshevik enemy and through respect and fidelity for the man they respect above all, the Fuhrer, Adolf Hitler. I do not wish that through folly or narrowness of mind of an isolated person, a single one of tens of thousands of these brave volunteers and their families should suffer from ill humor. . . . I forbid jokes and facetious remarks about Muslim volunteers.[85]

Such was the depth of Himmler's plan to exploit Muslims for Nazi purposes. "I have nothing against Islam because it educates the men in this division for me and promises them heaven if they fight and are killed in action. A very practical and attractive religion for soldiers."[86] This cooperation was not so much a matter of ideological affinities or similarities between NSDAP and Islam as it was part of SS opportunism to expand support, motivate, and exploit Muslim volunteers via religious and cultural sensitivities as well as communal aspirations into a new and modernist ideological mixture.[87]

No doubt Himmler's attitudes were shared by the Nazi elite and expressed an intimate understanding regarding fragments of Islam that could be manipulated and exploited by the Nazis. Himmler had a very utilitarian view of religion in the advancement of shaping the global will toward his perceived view of the German master race. In a speech to the 13th SS (Handschar) Mountain Division in January 1944, as the Allies were gaining in North Africa and threatening Italy, Himmler said to the Muslim SS division he created,

> We have the same aims. There can be no more solid basis for living together [than] common aims and common ideals. For 200 years Germany has not had the slightest cause of friction with Islam. . . . Now we Germans and you in this division, you Muslims, share a common feeling of gratitude that God—you call him Allah, but it's the same—has sent our tormented European nations the Fuhrer, the Fuhrer who will rid first Europe and then the whole world of the Jews, these enemies of our Reich, who robbed us of victory in 1918 so that the sacrifice of two million dead was in vain. They are also your enemies, for the Jew has been you enemy from time immemorial.[88]

The Handschar SS Division fought against the Yugoslav Partisans led by General Josip Broz Tito, and carried out police and security runs in Hungary. SS conscription in Yugoslavia during the war produced 42,000 Waffen-SS and police troops. Al-Husseini had flown from Berlin to Sarajevo in order to inspect arms, observe training exercises, and bestow blessings on the Islamo-Fascist arm. In a speech to a Bosnian Muslim Waffen-SS Division as well as a radio broadcast in January 1944, Al-Husseini stated,

> This division of Bosnian Muslims, established with the help of Greater Germany, is an example for Muslims in all countries. There is no other deliverance for them from imperialist oppression than hard fighting to preserve their homes and faith. Many common interests exist between the Islamic world and Greater Germany, and those make cooperation a matter of course. The Reich is fighting against the same enemies who robbed Muslims of their countries and suppressed their faith in Asia, Africa, and Europe. . . . Further, National Socialist Germany is fighting against world Jewry. The Koran says: "You will find that the Jews are the worst enemies of the Muslims." There are also considerable similarities between Islamic principles and those of National Socialism, namely in the affirmation of struggle and fellowship, in stressing leadership, in the ideas of order, in the high valuation of work. All this brings our ideologies close together and facilitates cooperation. I am happy to see in this division a visible and practical expression of both ideologies.[89]

In the Balkans, between 115,000 and 128,000 Muslim soldiers served at some stage in various Waffen-SS or Wehrmacht units or associated local militias.[90]

Prior to the Allied meetings in Cairo, a telegram submitted from Himmler to Al-Husseini, dated November 2, 1943, stated,

> [T]he National Socialist movement of Greater Germany has, since its inception, inscribed upon its flag the fight against the world Jewry. It has therefore followed with particular sympathy the struggle of freedom-loving Arabs, especially in Palestine, against Jewish interlopers. In the recognition of this enemy and of the common struggle against it lie the firm foundation of the natural alliance that exists between the National Socialist Greater Germany and the freedom-loving Muslims of the whole world. In this spirit I am sending you on the anniversary of the infamous Balfour declaration my hearty greetings and wishes for the successful pursuit of your struggle until the final victory.[91]

According to German minister of armaments and war production Albert Speer, Hitler had stated, "[W]hen the Mohammedans attempted to penetrate beyond France and into Central Europe during the eighth century, they were driven back at the battle of Tours. Had the Arabs won this battle, the European world would be Mohammedan today. For theirs was a religion that believed in spreading the faith by sword and subjugating all nations to that faith. The Germanic people would have become heirs to that religion. Such a creed was perfectly suited to the Germanic temperament."[92]

Throughout the war, Al-Husseini implemented teams of Arab saboteurs in the Levant to attack Allied infrastructure such as telephone lines, pipelines, bridges, and railways. One such sabotage team was armed with a substantial quantity of poison with instructions to dump it into the Tel Aviv water system. In 1942 Al-Husseini helped in conscripting Arab students, refugees from Syria and Iraq, and POWs in Germany into the Arabisches Freiheitkorps (Arab Freedom Corps, Arab units in the German Army who fought on the Russian front). Gaylani and Al-Husseini preferred Arab units within the Axis armies to be under their own national colors. Proposals of a full-scale Arab Legion were suggested by the mufti in conversations with Mussolini and Ciano during his first visit to Rome in October of 1941. The ideas were passed on to Von Ribbentrop, Weizsäcker, and Hitler. After consideration by the German foreign ministry, an announcement was made from Hitler's headquarters that Hitler wished the immediate formation of such a legion to operate in Cape Sounion, forty-three miles southeast of Athens. The Deutsch-Arabisches Lehrabteilung (DAL; German-Arab Training Detachment) was formed in early 1942 and in Arabic was referred to as *al-mafraza al-'arabiya al-hurra* (the Free Arab Corps).[93]

By May of 1942 the detachment comprised only 130 men. The reason for its low conscription was due to the rejection by the Axis for recruitment of Arabs from Italian and French colonies; this disappointed Al-Husseini, who had proposed to enlist captured Arabs from Algeria, Tunisia, and Morocco; and North

African émigrés. Director of the political department of the German foreign ministry, Ernst Woermann, wrote in a memorandum, "In our Arab policy, we always distinguish between Near East and North African Arabs. Our Arab policy does not apply to the area west of Egypt. We are not interested in cultivating nationalism in North Africa because of our policy toward Italy, France and Spain."[94] During this same period, Indian Nationalist Subhas Chandra Bose proposed plans to form an Indian legion that would later incorporate upwards of 40,000 Indian POWs into an anti-British army of invasion from Burma.

After World War II, Al-Husseini fled to Switzerland, then Paris, before settling in Cairo. He escaped house arrest in Paris where he had been sentenced by the Yugoslav Supreme Military Court to three years' imprisonment and two years of deprivation of civil rights after his conviction as a war criminal.

The mufti established the Islamishe Zentralinstitut (Islamic Central Institute) in Dresden to serve as grooming center for future Muslim leaders supportive of Nazi objectives. It is noteworthy how the European Nationalist movements of the late nineteenth century, the rise of Fascism in the aftermath of World War I, and the covert intervention of the Axis powers in the Middle East shaped the evolution of Arab Nationalist and Islamist movements. It is important to understand how Fascism was synthesized into the politics of the region, and to face the reality that this was a regrettable import from Europe. In his memoirs Al-Husseini professed, "[O]ur fundamental condition for cooperating with Germany was a free hand to eradicate Jews from Palestine and the Arab world. I expressed to Herr Hitler for an explicit undertaking to allow us to solve the Jewish problem in a manner befitting our national and racial aspirations and according to the scientific methods innovated by Germany in the handling of its Jews. The answer I received was: The Jews are yours."[95] Al-Husseini also provided German intelligence chief Admiral Canaris and Colonel Franz Seubert with a highly detailed report of a possible Allied invasion of French Northwest Africa said to have been leaked to him by Muhammad V, sultan of Morocco. The invasion, including the date, unfolded exactly as the sultan of Morocco had disclosed to the mufti.[96]

In 1946 Al-Husseini was appointed a leader of the Muslim Brotherhood, then sponsored by Egypt's King Farouk (ruled 1936–1952) as a counter to antimonarchist groups and British control over his country, and was invited to settle in Cairo that same year. When Gamal Abdel-Nasser gained control of Egypt in 1952, Al-Husseini remained in exile at Heliopolis in Cairo until 1959, before departing for Beirut, where he died in 1974. The mufti had a falling out with Nasser over the creation of the Palestine Liberation Organization (PLO), an organization the mufti refused to endorse until his death.

The Nation Associates, a block within the United Nations campaigning for the creation of a Jewish state in Palestine, documented the alliance of Al-Husseini and the Axis powers in a memorandum submitted to the UN in May 1947, which was traced from the files of the German High Command in Flansberg:

No. 792-PS
17 September 1945
Source of Original OKW Files, Flensburg

[Excerpt]
LEADS: CANARIS, IBN SAUD, GRAND MUFTI.
SUMMARY OF RELEVANT POINTS (with page references):

1. Only through the funds made available by Germany to the Grand Mufti of Jerusalem was it possible to carry out the revolt in Palestine.
2. Germany will keep up the connection with the Grand Mufti. Weapons will be stored for the Mufti with Ibn Saud in Arabia.
3. Ibn Saud himself has close connections with the Grand Mufti and the revolting circles in Transjordan.[97]

The Allies, preoccupied with German and Japanese war criminals, made no effort to bring Al-Husseini to justice. The Yugoslavian courts unsuccessfully sought his extradition. The Allies were likely deterred by Al-Husseini's prestige in the Arab world and the emerging Cold War competition. From Egypt, Al-Husseini aided in the recruitment efforts and propaganda for the 1948 Arab–Israeli War. When the Jordanian monarch Abdullah I gave the position of grand mufti of Jerusalem to another, Al-Husseini was implicated in the conspiracy that led to the assassination of the king in 1951. Al-Husseini was denied entry into Jordanian-controlled Jerusalem by Abdullah's son King Talal (ruled 1951–1952) and later his grandson the late King Hussein (ruled 1952–1999).[98]

Al-Husseini retired from public life in 1962 after serving as president of the World Islamic Congress, an organization he helped found in 1931; he eventually died in exile in Lebanon on July 4, 1974. He never returned to Jerusalem after leaving in the 1930s. The Al-Husseini family continued to play an active part in Arab–Israeli affairs. Abdel Kader Al-Husseini, a nephew of the grand mufti, founded the militant group Munazzamat al-Jihad al-Muqaddas (the Organization for Holy Struggle), which he commanded as the Jaysh al-Jihad al-Muqaddas (Army of the Holy Warriors). He underwent a degree of military training with the Germans during World War II and took part in the pro-Axis coup in Iraq. In January 1948 Abdel Kader Al-Husseini and a force of one thousand attacked Kfar Etzion, approximately fourteen miles south of Tel Aviv. The Arab attack on Kfar Etzion was thwarted by Jewish settlers, who held their positions until they were reinforced by the Palmach force. In early April 1948, Abdel Kader was involved in the retaking of the village of Qastel, taken by the Haganah in Operation Nachshon. He was in Damascus gathering financial support and additional weapons, and had returned to Jerusalem to lead the attack on Qastel. Abdel Kader Al-Husseini was killed while approaching a position not yet taken by Arab forces in the battle for Qastel. Demoralized at the death of Abdel Kader Husseini, the Arab forces fell back.[99]

Among the many that supported and sympathized with Nazi Germany were some familiar faces. Nasser expressed his disheartenment at the Third Reich's demise in 1945. Anwar Sadat was a voluntary cooperator in espionage on behalf of Germany against British forces in Egypt. In Sadat's autobiography referring to the Beer Hall Putsch, he stated, "When Hitler marched from Munich to Berlin, to wipe out the consequences of Germany's defeat in World War I and rebuild his country, I gathered my friends and told them we ought to follow Hitler's example."[100] During the war, Nasser and Sadat established contact with agents of the Axis powers, particularly several Italians, and planned a coup to coincide with Axis offensives. Abdul-Aziz Ibn Saud of Saudi Arabia, Nuri Al-Sa'id of Iraq, as well as Nahas Pasha of Egypt all tried on several occasions to make contact with Berlin. It was said that Nasser described the author of *Mein Kampf* in 1939 as the "strongest man in Europe."[101]

Nazi Fifth Column in Palestine

The historian and scholar Francis Nicosia traces the cells of the NSDAP as being first established in Palestine in 1932 with six members.[102] By mid-1937 membership had increased to approximately three hundred, consisting of local branches at Sarona and Jaffa with 108 members, Haifa with 90 members, Jerusalem with 66 members, and Bethlehem with 19 members. The active process of *Gleichschaltung* (synchronization) was pursued by the NSDAP headquarters in Berlin and the NSDAP cell in Palestine. This strengthened ties between Germany and the Nazi Party organization in Palestine. An information campaign, undertaken by the Nazi Party in Palestine, included courses, literature, and organized excursions to Germany for conferences. Radio and German news services were prominently displayed. Some communal German language libraries were purged of inappropriate German authors and replaced with Nazi literature. The NSDAP in Palestine took advantage of feelings of isolation, weakness, and vulnerability in its efforts to enlist the German communities in Palestine for the New Germany. The Party provided a sense of psychological comfort with the ability to identify with a dynamic movement and a strong fatherland. The cultural and social isolation of the German communities in Palestine made many yearn for German culture. Germans living in the Middle East sought to address this homesickness through the Nazi Party, which set up functions for German expatriates in the region.[103]

Attempts were made to establish Arab offshoots of the NSDAP in Arab countries. In April 1933 Palestine correspondent for the Egyptian newspaper *al-Ahram*, Joseph Francis, approached Heinrich Wolff with the idea of creating an Arab offshoot of the Nazi party. Dr. Grobba was approached by Abdul Ghaffur el-Bedri, an anti-Sherifan ex-officer and editor of the Baghdad newspaper *al-Istiqlal*, with a similar request for German assistance in establishing such a party. In both cases the response from the German foreign office was negative and no efforts were made to create Arab cells of national socialist parties. Consul General in Palestine, Heinrich Wolf, said, "[A] direct connection between Mr. Francis and members of the Ortsgruppen of the NSDAP in Palestine would be regrettable, as German citizens then would be suspected of interfering in the domestic affairs of Palestine."[104] The overriding motive was to avoid any perceived encroachment on British positions in the Near East.

Radical Change of German Policy in Palestine

Hitler capitalized on the unrest in Palestine in an attempt to embarrass the British and to press his notion of mutually agreed upon spheres of interest. In his speech at the Reichstag on February 20, 1938, he attacked the British parliament and pressed for their persistent criticism of political and radical persecution in Germany. He referred to the harsh sentences given to Arab rebels by British military courts in Palestine and argued, "I advise the members of the English house of Commons to concern themselves with the judgments of British military courts in Jerusalem, and not with the judgments of German courts of justice." On September 12, 1938, at the closing session of the Nuremberg Party congress, Hitler compared the Sudeten Germans with the Arabs of Palestine, stating, "My task, and the task of us all, my fellow Germans, is to ensure that in no way will we allow a second Palestine to emerge here in the heart of Germany through the cleverness of other statesmen. The poor Arabs are defenseless and perhaps forgotten. The Germans in Czechoslovakia are neither defenseless nor are they forgotten."[105]

With the news of the 1937 Peel Commission Plan for the partitioning of Palestine and creation of a Jewish state, Germans in control of foreign policy reexamined their position toward the Palestine question. The German foreign ministry sent a letter on June 22, 1937, to all German outposts and embassies overseas. The document dealt specifically with the Palestine question and declared that Germany's interests revolved around undermining the British in the Arab world. It stated, "It was the primary goal of Germany's Jewish policy to promote the emigration of Jews from Germany as much as possible. The formation of a Jewish state or a Jewish-led political structure under British mandate is not in Germany's interest, since a Palestinian state would not absorb world Jewry, but would create an additional position of powers under international law for international Jewry, somewhat like the Vatican state for political Catholicism or Moscow for the Comintern."[106] After reaffirming Germany's opposition to the creation of a Jewish state in Palestine, German foreign minister Konstantin von Neurath observed, "There exists a German interest in the strengthening of the Arabs as a counterweight against such a simultaneous growth in the power of the Jews."[107] He concluded, however, that direct German involvement in the Palestine conflict was not in Germany's best interest.

With the political ascendancy of Hitler in 1932, the German foreign ministry began the process of Nazifying its policies. Dr. Grobba, German envoy to Baghdad, received a directive from Berlin to the effect that the "German understanding of Arab national aspirations should be expressed more clearly than before, but without making definite promises."[108]

German Nationalist Ideology and the Development of Arab Nationalist Theory

Some of the major political parties of the Arab Nationalist movement had acquired, to a degree, certain elements of NSDAP and Fascism. These were namely the Ba'ath Party, the Syrian Socialist Nationalist Party, the Kata'ib (Phalange), Misr al-Fatat (Young Egypt), and the Futuwwa (Youth Movement).[109]

Michel Aflaq, one of the founders of the Ba'ath Party, came into contact with NSDAP ideas during his academics at the Sorbonne between 1928 and 1932. Hitler's political program combining Nationalism and Socialism had fascinated Aflaq as he read Alfred Rosenberg's *Mythus des Zwanzigsten Jahrhunderts* (The myth of the twentieth century), the most influential Nazi text after Hitler's *Mein Kampf*.[110] Sami al-Jundi, a cofounder of the Ba'ath Party, described in his memoirs how Aflaq and Zaki Arsuzi spent long discussions regarding democracy, Communism, and Nazism. He wrote, "[W]hoever has lived during this period in Damascus will appreciate the inclination of the Arab people to Nazism, for Nazism was the power which could serve as its champion, and he who is defeated will by nature love the victor."[111]

Another party directly influenced by NSDAP was the Syrian Socialist Nationalist Party founded by Antun Sa'adah. The party's ideology was secular, Nationalist, and totalitarian with a life-long leader—Sa'adah himself—at its head. Other components of this ideology were the social Darwinism doctrine of survival of the fittest, the superiority of certain races, and an emphasis on military power. An admiration of NSDAP ideals was seen when Sa'id Aql, a lawyer, poet, and party member, wrote a party hymn to the tune of *Deutschland Über Alles*. French authorities accused the party of being subservient to the Nazi regime and arrested party members, including Sa'adah, who they accused of having connections to Italy and Germany; the charges were dropped due to the lack of substantive corroboration between Sa'adah and German officials.[112]

At the 1936 Summer Olympic Games in Berlin, two Lebanese represented the Soccer Federation of Lebanon. One of them, whose name was Pierre Jumayyil, stated, "We Orientals are by nature an unruly and individualistic people. In Germany, I witnessed the perfect conduct of a whole, unified nation."[113] Jumayyil, founder of the traditional right-wing Lebanese party, the Phalanges, modeled the party after Fascist parties he had observed as an Olympic athlete during the Berlin Olympic Games. In an interview with British journalist Robert Fisk, Jumayyil stated,

> I was the captain of the Lebanese football team and the president of the Lebanese Football federation. We went to the Olympic Games of 1936 in Berlin. And I saw then this discipline and order. And I said to myself: "Why can't we do the same thing in Lebanon?" So when we came back to Lebanon, we created this youth movement. When I was in Berlin then, Nazism did not have the reputation which it has now. Nazism? In every system in the world, you can find something good. But Nazism was not Nazism at all. The word came afterwards. In their system, I saw discipline. And we in the Middle East, we need discipline more than anything else.[114]

From its beginnings in the early 1930s, the Young Egypt Party emulated European Fascism—a green shirt uniform, a Nazi-style salute, a paramilitary organization with obedience to a leader, and ultra-Nationalist slogans based on the tune of *Deutschland Über Alles*. In 1934 Young Egypt leader Ahmed Hussayn paid a visit to the German envoy in Cairo, Eberhard von Stohrer, to express his sympathy for the new Germany. In 1938 Hussayn visited Europe and Germany, and in an open letter to Hitler, called the Reichsarbeitsdienst (Reich labor service) "a return to true Islamic society, when there was no employer and no employee but when all were brothers cooperating together."[115]

In a second open letter to Hitler written in Arabic on July 24, 1938, Hussayn expressed the following that summarized the reasons why many Arab Nationalists admired Hitler and the Third Reich:

> In Egypt, we suffered in our foreign policy and our international standing exactly what Germany was suffering in her first years after the War. Egypt belonged to those peoples which greeted the news of your success with a sense of great relief: it increased her confidence in herself and strengthened her belief in her approaching success in the realization of the national goals, to which she aspires. You have improved the situation of the members of this people by ending the terrible unemployment, by guaranteeing work, and by the fact that you ended the class struggle by making the people feel itself one people, first in the army, then in the compulsory work where the rich work next to the poor, the doctor next to the engineer and the baker and the farmer, where all work on the same basis of equality with their hands and their bodies on German land to serve all Germans. You have abolished factionalism [*ta'ifiyya*] between workers and employers . . . all this has rendered Germany good service . . . and created the physical, mental and social culture for the Youth of your country to make them strong members of a social body.[116]

Unlike the previously mentioned political parties, the Futuwwa movement in Iraq was a youth organization composed of highly educated students of military age, who received paramilitary training led by Dr. Sami Shaukat, director general of the Iraqi ministry of education. Shaukat was ordered by Prime Minister Nuri Sa'id of Iraq to educate the Iraqi youth on the military spirit based on the German model. In 1933 Shaukat addressed the students of the Central Secondary School in Baghdad:

> The nation which does not excel in the Profession of Death with iron and fire will be forced to die under the hooves of the horses and under the boots of a foreign soldiery. If to live is just, killing in self-defense is also just. Had Mustafa Kemal not had for his revolution in Anatolia forty thousand officers trained in the Profession of Death, we would not have seen Turkey restoring in the twentieth century the glories of Yavouz Sultan Selim. Had not Pahlavi had thousands of officers well versed in the sacred profession we would not have seen him restoring the glory of Darius. And had Mussolini not had tens of thousands of Black Shirts well versed in the Profession of Death he would not have been able to put on the temples of Victor Emanuel the crown of the first Caesars of Roma. . . . Sixty years ago, Prussia used to dream of uniting the German people. What is there to prevent Iraq, who fulfilled her desire for independence ten years ago, from dreaming to unite all the Arab countries?[117]

Reichsjugendführer (Reich youth leader) Baldur Von Schirach visited Iraq, Persia, Syria, and Turkey in December 1937 and suggested an acceleration of military training. A delegation of the Futuwwa participated in the march of the Hitler Youth at the *Parteitag* (party convention) in Nuremberg in September 1938. Impressed by the Olympic Games in Berlin, an Iraqi Olympic Committee was established. Shaukat also developed anti-Jewish ideas that were indebted to German anti-Semitism and called for the annihilation of the Jews in Iraq as a prerequisite for Iraqi national revival.[118]

Interestingly, Hassan al-Banna, founder of the Egyptian Muslim Brotherhood in 1928 (the first Islamist political party), commented in 1938 on the concept of the "strong nation":

> In the contemporary world there are many ideologies [*da 'awdt*], most of which are based on a sentiment of nationalist fanaticism [*'asabiyya qaumi-yya*] which seduces at present the hearts of the peoples. In Germany Hitler preaches Aryan nationalism, in Italy Mussolini calls for Latin nationalism, thereby coloring Italian fascism, Ataturk extols Turanian Nationalism and propagates it in Turkey, and the English, pretending their country to be the oldest democracy in the world, think that Anglo-Saxon blood is so perfect that no other race can compare with it. This is the reason for the slogans "Germany above all . . . " or "Italy above all" and "Rule Britannia . . . " and other slogans calling the peoples of this age.[119]

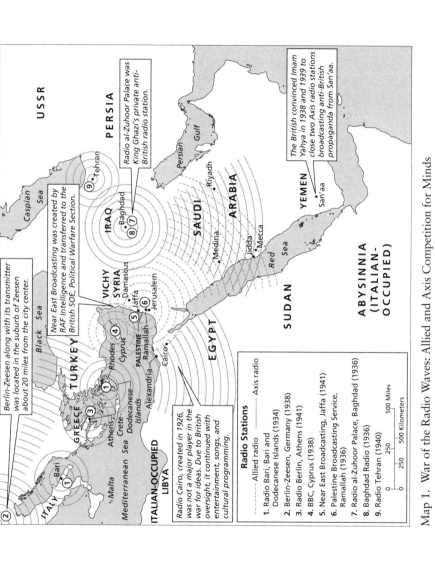

Map 1. War of the Radio Waves: Allied and Axis Competition for Minds

Text labels within the map:

USSR

PERSIA

Caspian Sea

Black Sea

Tehran (9)

Baghdad (8)(7)
IRAQ

Radio al-Zuhoor Palace was King Ghazi's private anti-British radio station.

Berlin-Zeesen along with its transmitter was located in the suburb of Zeesen about 20 miles from the city center.

Near East Broadcasting was created by RAF Intelligence and transferred to the British SOE, Political Warfare Section.

Persian Gulf

Riyadh

SAUDI ARABIA

The British convinced Imam Yahya in 1938 and 1939 to close two Axis radio stations broadcasting anti-British propaganda from San'aa.

YEMEN
San'aa

Medina
Jidda
Mecca

Red Sea

TURKEY

GREECE

Athens
Crete
Rhodes (4)
Cyprus
Dodecanese Islands

(1)

(3)

Mediterranean Sea

Malta

ITALY
Bari (1)

ITALIAN-OCCUPIED LIBYA

Alexandria

Cairo

EGYPT

SUDAN

VICHY SYRIA
Damascus
Jaffa
Jerusalem
PALESTINE
Ramallah (5)(6)

ABYSSINIA (ITALIAN-OCCUPIED)

(2)

Radio Cairo, created in 1926, was not a major player in the war for ideas. Due to British oversight, it continued with entertainment, songs, and cultural programming.

Radio Stations

------ Allied radio   ——— Axis radio

1. Radio Bari, Bari and Dodecanese Islands (1934)
2. Berlin-Zeesen, Germany (1938)
3. Radio Berlin, Athens (1941)
4. BBC, Cyprus (1938)
5. Near East Broadcasting, Jaffa (1941)
6. Palestine Broadcasting Service, Ramallah (1936)
7. Radio al-Zuhoor Palace, Baghdad (1936)
8. Baghdad Radio (1936)
9. Radio Tehran (1940)

0   250   500 Miles
0   250   500 Kilometers

Resonant Lessons on Islamist Militant Ideology and Fascism

It is vital to examine the past to discover that Islamist militants, violent Arab Nationalists, and European Fascists have collaborated when their interests merge. Reading about Al-Husseini one also gains an appreciation that the initial British tactic of appeasing Islamic radicals with titles and positions was not effective; he merely used his legitimacy to pursue the tactic he knew best, choosing violence over negotiation. Al-Husseini offered a template for organized incitement and violence, a technique advocated by some Palestinians in dealing with the Israelis. It was a tactic that predates the PLO or the current intifada (uprising). Finally, note Al-Husseini's obsession with the Nazi Final Solution; this obsession with Hitler and the Final Solution was found in Islamist militant Web sites and literature. Until 2004 Egypt's anticorruption tsar was Hitler Tantawi, who was given his first name at a time when thousands of Egyptians felt the Nazis were an acceptable way to get the British out of the Middle East.

Al-Husseini was a perfect manifestation of a collision of jihadists, violent Arab Nationalists, and Fascists. He was also another tragic example of an Arab leader who chose a negative path in the quest for Palestinian independence. There were leaders who worked toward positive change, such as Palestinian academics Hanan Ashrawi and Saeb Erekat, and others who did not, such as the late Sheikh Ahmed Yassin and Abdel Aziz al-Rantissi, the Hamas founder and former leader, respectively. Arab masses and intellectuals must recognize those who had a negative impact on their modern historical development and cease their praising of such figures as Al-Husseini who represents the kind of Arab leaders that negatively influenced events. Two considerations of Nazi anti-Semitism were observed: one was the tendency to drive the Jews out of Germany, and the other was the movement to capitalize on the Jewish question in political scheming within the Third Reich. These considerations and their limitations formed the seed of what materialized among Hitler's inner circle as the Final Solution of the Jewish question. Moreover, the resolution to the Palestine question remained unresolved and would worsen under the slogans and propaganda wafting onto the shores of the region from Italy and Germany.

CHAPTER 3

Hashemite Iraq

My Grandfather Invented Iraq.

—*Wall Street Journal* op-ed column, Winston S. Churchill
(grandson of Prime Minister Winston Churchill),
March 16, 2003

Ottoman Military Administration of Iraq

This chapter will rely primarily on the work of Iraqi military historian Akeel Naseeri, whose book *Al-Jaysh wal Sultah fee Iraq al-Malaki* (The army and authority in Iraq under the monarchy, 1921–1958) is among the best Arabic works on Iraq's turbulent civil-military relations; it was published in Syria in 2000. In 2006 the authors of this book introduced America's military readers to Naseeri's book in an effort to train U.S. combat units deploying to Iraq by using primary Arabic works of significance. Naseeri's book was first highlighted by the authors in a March 2006 edition of the U.S. Army journal, *Infantry*.[1] Portions of this chapter have been taken from the two authors' article in *Infantry*; where appropriate, this chapter has been enhanced with both Arabic and English sources.

Before the creation of modern Iraq in the aftermath of World War I, the Ottoman Turks administered the region as three distinct quasi-autonomous entities. These three regions were centered on Mosul, Baghdad, and Basra. Each of these separate *vilayet* (provinces) had a duly appointed Ottoman *pasha* (an honorific Ottoman title equivalent to a British lord). From 1534 to around 1870 these pashas governed these provinces on behalf of the Ottoman sultan. One of their main functions was collecting taxes for Constantinople. Ottoman governor of Baghdad Midhat Pasha (governor 1869–1872) restructured the three provinces of Mesopotamia, with Baghdad retaining central control over Mosul and Basra. Iraq, although not in existence at the time, was slowly taking shape, with Baghdad becoming the central capital of the Ottoman-governed Mesopotamian province. Thus the British did not so much create modern Iraq as they inherited three Ottoman provinces that were driven toward central management and control from Baghdad.

The Ottomans used a divide-and-rule system to maintain dominance over Mesopotamia, capitalizing on divisions such as urban mercantile aristocratic families versus agrarian tribes that farmed along the Euphrates River; one tribe against another in Iraq's desert and semi-nomadic regions; Shiite versus Sunni; and various Shiite *hawzas* against each other.[2]

The latter half of the nineteenth century witnessed significant reform of the Ottoman army. Chiefly, these reforms included opening Prussian-style military academies and the creation of a modern general staff on the German model. For Arab subjects of the Ottoman Empire, the pivotal reform was the establishment of officer ranks, military schools, and officer academies.[3]

Arabs experienced Ottoman military service as a full-time profession in the late nineteenth century. Arab officers trained in the 1870s onward would rise to command in Syria, Iraq, and Egypt. For Mesopotamia the hub of military activity was the 16th Ottoman Army, which was charged with providing security in the three provinces along the Tigris and Euphrates Rivers.[4]

The origins of a modern army in Iraq can be traced to 1870. Ottoman governor Midhat Pasha established an intermediate military school in Baghdad.[5] This institution was tailored to take children who completed elementary school and provide them with three years of instruction in technical military fields (drill, artillery, engineering, and tactics). By the outbreak of World War I in 1914, three intermediate schools had opened: two in Baghdad and one in Suleimaniyah. If students passed this phase of their military education, they matriculated to the only military high school in Mesopotamia, which was located in Baghdad and served as an academy preparatory school.[6] Those who excelled in their studies in preparatory school entered the Ottoman Military Academy in Constantinople. Mesopotamia (the three provinces of Baghdad, Mosul, and Basra) was allocated sixty to seventy slots yearly, the largest share of any of the Ottoman Arab dominions. After four years at the Ottoman Military Academy, students received an officer's commission as a second lieutenant; a few went on to further specialized training in cavalry, infantry, engineering, and medicine. On the eve of World War I about a thousand Iraqi officers were in the service of the Ottoman sultan.[7]

The first group of about 250 joined the Arab Revolt and served under the banner of Sherief Hussein of Mecca and his three sons, Princes Abdullah, Feisal, and Ali. They were motivated by British promises of creating an Arab homeland that stretched from Arabia to the Levant and Iraq. After World War I and subsequent to the revelations of both the Balfour Declaration and the Sykes-Picot Agreement, they felt betrayed. Members of this group evolved into Arab Nationalist leaders and played an important role in the development of modern Iraq as well as the development of what today is the fighting force known as the Arab Legion with the oversight of General (Sir) John Glubb Pasha.[8]

This group included Jafar Al-Askary and Mouloud Mukhlis, as well as Nuri As-Sa'id and Jawdat Farouki. Their efforts, alongside British intelligence officers like T. E. Lawrence, were able to divert the Ottomans from their attacks on the Suez Canal and Tsarist Russia by causing them to devote forces to suppressing the Arab Revolt (1916–1918) in Arabia. This scheme tied down several divisions that might have been used in an Ottoman thrust toward the occupation of the vital Suez Canal in Egypt, or even used as a threat to General Edmund Allenby's forces marching from Egypt into Palestine. It is this group of Arab officers, inspired by Arab Nationalism and self-determination from the Ottomans, who fought with the Arab Revolt and would keep the Ottoman garrison in Medina encircled. This Arab army occupied the Red Sea Port of Yanbu and finally marched with Allenby's British forces to Palestine and Damascus. They went on after World War I to form the core of loyal military officers for both King Abdullah bin Hussein of Jordan and King Feisal bin Hussein of Iraq, and held ministerial positions in Iraq, including prime minister in the case of Nuri As-Sa'id.[9]

The second group of about three hundred Iraqi Ottoman graduates remained in Ottoman service and considered defiance of the sultan a sacrilege. They fought and commanded Ottoman troops in the Balkans, Mesopotamia, Palestine, Russia, and Greece, as well as in the Sinai. This group returned and was repatriated into the new Iraqi army under King Feisal; it played a role on the fringes of the new Iraqi mandate. To what degree they experienced bitterness regarding the dismantling of the Ottoman Empire remains uncertain. One can assume that their loyalty to King Feisal was tainted by their certain resentment over the fate of the Ottoman Empire.[10]

Jafar Al-Askary became the first of King Feisal's military leaders to arrive in what would become Iraq; he served as war minister in several Iraqi provisional governments that existed until 1932, the year Iraq transitioned from the British mandate to quasi-independence. (The term "quasi-independence" is used because, although granted independence in 1932, Iraq in reality was given greater autonomy that was heavily influenced by British interests. The king's governments were labeled "provisional" until Iraq's formal independence in 1932.) In 1920 Jafar Al-Askary implemented the process of repatriating Iraqi military personnel who were dispersed throughout the Middle East and in Ottoman theaters of battle, and absorbing them into the new Iraqi army. Among the challenges he faced during the first provisional government (January 1920–September 1921) was retaining Arab officers and troops who fought French forces in Syria, who were defeated in the 1920 Battle of Maysalun, into the nucleus of a new Iraqi army. The Battle of Maysalun is a defining event in twentieth-century Syria, akin to the Alamo, and represents the last stand of Arab forces in defense of an Arab kingdom that had declared independence in 1918. French forces would evict King Feisal of Syria, who two years later would become King Feisal of Iraq in a

British-engineered plebiscite, designed to quell unrest in Iraq.[11] As of the writing of this book, the casualty rate inflicted by Syrian military units largely loyal to dictator Bashar al-Assad has topped 90,000, with no end in sight. Understanding this history from the Syrian viewpoint is important when considering any type of intervention in the region. For instance, if an intervention force included the French, it is prudent to expect aspects of this history to be used to incite and create a hostile atmosphere.

The French, working with Al-Askary, eagerly released 240 military personnel of the Arab Revolt to Jafar Al-Askary. During the second provisional government (September 1921–August 1922), War Minister Al-Askary focused on freeing Iraqi troops who had served the Ottomans and were now held as prisoners in such places as ship hulks in Greek harbors and throughout Arabia and Yemen.[12]

Aside from bringing in former trained Arab combatants who served in the Arab Revolt or under Ottoman colors, Askary and a dozen Hashemite officers from the Arab Revolt debated other aspects of creating a modern Iraqi army during the first provisional government. That discussion included deciding to field an all-volunteer force; determining who would be eligible to serve in the army; and creating zones of training whereby those joining in the north of Iraq would train at Hilla, sixty miles south of Baghdad, and those joining in the southern or central regions would train in Baghdad.[13]

Arab Views on the British Mandate of Iraq

Two political attitudes existed among this cadre of repatriated Arab officers and troops brought together from Ottoman service. Some argued for an alliance with Britain and for allowing the British mandate to take its course to create a modern and regionally powerful Iraq. Another significant faction of officers, known as the radicalists, desired immediate independence for Iraq and union with French-mandated Syria. This group rejected King Feisal and the British mandate and included senior officers like Sabbagh, Sidqi, Shabeeb, and Jawad, all of whom provided a host of officers to serve in Iraq's military. It was in this climate that King Feisal and his advisers began promoting and assigning Sunni-Sherifan (Arab Revolt) officers to senior ranks in Iraq's new army. Out of 304 officers who returned to Iraq after World War I, 191 were Sunni and primarily non-Iraqi, and eight were above the rank of colonel in the Ottoman system. Of those eight senior officers, only three were originally the three Ottoman provinces that made up Iraq. An officer corps, dominated by twenty to thirty primarily Sunni families, evolved under the monarchy. The lion's share of Iraq's military leadership came from these twelve families: Askary, Said, Saddoun, Suweidi, Sahrurdi, Shabandar, Bajaje, Gaylani, Daftari, Jaderjee, Hashimi, and Ayubi.[14]

These military families intermarried and promoted each other's interests within the Iraqi armed forces, and dominated the Iraqi officer corps of the monarchic period (1922 to 1958). Their descendants exist in today's Iraq and no doubt continue to protect their interests beyond the post-Ba'athist period. Some of these officers were eliminated by Saddam Hussein, who saw them as elitists or felt they posed a threat from a military coup; others perished in the wars against Iran, Kuwait, and the United States.

King Feisal I

When French forces evicted King Feisal from Syria in 1920, the British installed him as king of Iraq through negotiations at the 1921 Cairo Conference and decided to transition the country to independence in ten years (1922–1932) under his rule. King Feisal, of the Hashemite clan of Mecca, was descended from Prophet Muhammad. He knew that as a Sunni outsider from Arabia, asked to rule over predominately Shia Iraqis, he was in a difficult situation. However, he was attuned to the ways that the Ottomans governed Iraq and quickly assessed that the Shiite *hawzas* (clerical clusters) stood against the British mandate; the mercantile urban families stood against Hashemite (sometimes called Sherifan) rule in Iraq; and the Sherifan officers of the Arab Revolt who fought for Arab self-determination on the British side now stood against the British experiment in Iraq but were divided on the course the new country should take. Should Iraq follow Iraqi Nationalist or Arab Nationalist agendas? Should Iraq attempt to regain the unity of Arabs as it was under the Ottomans? Or should Islam be the unifying force of the country?[15]

Initially, the urban elite of Iraq's major cities refused to build a middle- and upper-middle-class cadre around King Feisal or serve in the newly created Iraqi army. A few Iraqis did join the army as officers but were against a monarchy they deemed as alien, and they sought to undermine it from within. Clerics, both Sunni and Shiite, primarily directed their anger at the British and excluded demonstrating against King Feisal. They had stimulated the 1920 uprising that opposed the enforcement of the Sykes-Picot Agreement and the mandate systems.[16]

The rebellion lasted well into 1921 and led to a commitment of thousands of British troops. Sheikh Al-Dhari, a key leader of the 1920 revolt, was a Sunni clerical leader who incited an urban riot against British forces in Iraq. His descendants today head the Muslim Ulema Council in Iraq, a Sunni Islamist- and Salafi-inspired organization that some argue is the more reasoned face of what was the Sunni insurgency in Iraq that would turn against the foreign fighter elements of al-Qaida in Iraq.

Iraqi officers of the 1920s could be classified as one of the following:

- Collaborators of the British and the Hashemite monarch in the name of stability and order

- Urbanites who strived toward a gradual shift in political power to the urban mercantile class
- Sons of tribal chiefs who were sent to look after regional interests and report on policies from Baghdad that appeared unfavorable to their tribe or region
- Ottoman officers who joined the Iraqi army as mercenaries
- Arab intelligentsia (the effendi class) who strived toward a unified national agenda with Syria, Jordan, and Lebanon
- Iraqi intelligentsia who strived to create an Iraqi national identity and regional hegemony
- Those who safeguarded Shiite or Sunni interests through the use of their commission[17]

British Views on the Creation of Modern Iraq

The future of Iraq was the subject of much debate among British colonial officials. The Cairo clique represented by Sir Percy Cox believed that immediate independence for Iraq coupled with indirect British rule was the best course for the newly emerging nation. In that manner King Feisal could establish himself without overt British support that undermined his tenuous legitimacy as king of Iraq.[18]

The Delhi clique, represented by A. T. Wilson, wanted direct British rule over Iraq as the only means of guaranteeing short-term stability until such time that Iraq's mandatory status ended and they could establish institutions of governance, thereby creating a sense of national unity. The British politicians discussed Iraq's divisions and proposed establishment of an Iraqi army as a means to foster national identity. The key determining issue in London was how to manage the Iraqi mandate with little investment in security and commitment of British forces. This debate was clearly demonstrated in the memoirs of Winston Churchill. A concise case for getting Iraqis to assume more responsibility in securing British interests in Mesopotamia was made in three letters written by T. E. Lawrence to three different British newspapers between July and August 1920.[19] Central concepts of these three letters are the following:

- Criticizing British policy makers essentially setting up in Mesopotamia a government that is English in fashion and conducted in the English language. He advocated raising two divisions of local volunteer troops, making Arabic the official language of government, and looking to the dominions of Canada and South Africa as a model on how Iraqi governance should evolve under the British mandatory system.
- Advocating the tapping of British officials with significant experience in India, Sudan, Egypt, and other colonies to act as advisers to King Feisal behind the scenes.

- Warning London against being compared to the Ottomans, citing that the Ottomans killed two hundred Arabs yearly to maintain the peace. He argued that the 1920 Revolt had cost more than 10,000 Arab lives and that the British were losing their legitimacy as a benign hegemony.[20]

The British crafted the 1922 Anglo-Iraqi Treaty that defined the terms of the ten-year mandate and imposed the following security terms that would be a source of constant tension between Askary, Nuri As-Sa'id, and King Feisal on the one hand, and British authorities on the other. Issues of contention that relate to security included these:

- Cooperating with British forces to quell internal riots and civil disobedience
- Defining a percentage of Iraq's total revenue that would go to the military
- Assigning a British flag officer as inspector general of the Iraqi army
- Providing the British high commissioner in Iraq unimpeded access to Iraq's military installations and oversight of all Iraqi military operations carried out by the army
- Recruiting 7,500 Iraqis as levy forces (locally recruited constabulary)
- Basing six RAF squadrons in Iraq
- Agreeing to undertake the training of the Iraqi officer corps and furnish advisers and trainers in Iraq[21]

Problems with this treaty included the Levy Force that evolved into a better-equipped and elite Iraqi force that the regular Iraqi army resented. Arab historians single this out as an example of how the Ba'athists modeled their Republican Guard forces on the British Levy Force. The Iraqi provisional government ruling on behalf of King Feisal sought to reduce the initial four battalions used to secure British installations and officials from four in 1922 to two after 1927. The terms of the treaty further undermined King Feisal's legitimacy and bolstered the radicals within the Iraqi military establishment. Oversight over the Iraqi army and its internal security operations was the main point of contention through a period of four provisional governments; it was an all-consuming issue of the third provisional government of Prime Minister Saddoun (January 1928–April 1929). Initial Iraqi plans for an all-volunteer force were debated repeatedly, with Iraqi generals favoring a general draft as a means of wresting control from the British.[22]

However, those generals were vested in the preservation of the Hashemite monarchy who thought a general draft provided training to Shiites, Kurds, and undesirable Sunni tribes. These tribes formed a force, prepared at the expense of the central government, and served under a tribal sheikh. Kurds and a minority sect known as Yazidis voiced objections to the idea of a draft. Among those who stood against conscription and expansion of the army initially was Prime Minister Nuri As-Sa'id. His opposition changed when he realized the expansion of the army was a defining issue in ending British oversight of Iraq by 1932. In the end, the Iraqis adopted a three-layered defense of regular volunteers, four-year conscripts, and three-year conscripts. The Iraqi provisional government forced Yazidis and other minorities to submit to conscription, which further undermined the armed forces.[23]

Solutions to King Feisal's Problems

To address the challenges of ruling Iraq, Feisal brought in loyal officers and troops who had fought with him during the Arab Revolt, an event made famous with the notoriety of T. E. Lawrence. His first order of business was to create a security force that maintained internal order and suppressed any vocal objections to his rule. King Feisal I and one of his trusted military advisers, Tewfik Suweidi, worked to create a cadre of loyal Sunni officers from remnants of the Arab Revolt, his fight against the French in Syria after World War I, and the disintegrating Ottoman army. This cadre evolved in time to sixty-one army officers, fifty-one of whom were former Sherifan officers who had fought in the Arab Revolt, and maintained security for King Feisal until 1941. Despite British efforts to create a parliamentary monarchy in Iraq, King Feisal used the army to control a parliament rife with dissent and revolutionary ideas aimed at undermining his authority.[24]

The new Iraqi army was the only defense against Wahhabi encroachment from Arabia, a matter that preoccupied Iraqi Shiites in the 1922 Karbala Conference. The Iraqi army, supported by the British RAF, was used to subdue Saudi-incited tribes and to keep Iraqi Sunni tribes from entering the Al-Saud tribal confederacy. The urban intelligentsia saw in the Iraqi army a chance for Arab self-determination denied them by the European victors of World War I, a chance for unity, and a return to the past glories of the Arab Empire. A carryover from Ottoman times, military training slots were allocated to sons of tribal chieftains as a means of guaranteeing loyalty. It made political sense because it allowed King Feisal to undermine the hold that the twenty to thirty martial families had in the Iraqi military.[25]

Uprisings and Revolts

It is a testament to coalition forces and the recently trained Iraqi security forces that rioting and violent protest has not been as prevalent and undertaken at a national level as they had been during the British mandate. Modern Iraqi history is replete with serious riots, insurrections, and violent incitements, such as the Hilla and Najaf Uprising of 1918, the 1920 Revolt that engulfed Baghdad and Basra, and the Filahiya Insurrection in Baghdad and southward that lasted until the mid-1930s.[26]

Iraqi forces supported by the British RAF put down 130 uprisings and revolts from 1921 to 1932. After the British mandate ended in 1932, there were ten major uprisings in five years centering in the Kurdish regions of Nasiriyah and Diwaniyah as well as the Shiite area of Basra.[27]

Worse was to come after Iraq became independent in 1932. Starting with the Kurdish Bakr Sidqi Revolt that began on October 29, 1936, during the reign of King Feisal's ineffectual son King Ghazi I (ruled 1933–1939), six major military coups took place in the course of five years. Two officers were motivated by the example of Mustafa Kemal Atatürk (presided 1920–1938) in Turkey and Shah Reza Pahlavi (ruled 1925–1941) in Iran, who were ridding themselves of foreign influences and dictating modernity, order, and independence. Atatürk and Pahlavi were former military officers. The coup staged by Bakr Sidqi, chief of the Iraqi general staff, under the short-lived prime ministership of Hikmat Sulayman, had a goal to lessen Iraq's political and military dependence on Britain and sought closer ties with Germany. At the end of 1936 a German general staff officer, Colonel R. Heins, came to Baghdad to assess the needs of Iraqi armament.[28]

Some Iraqi officers were a product of the same Ottoman schools that produced the founder of modern Turkey, Mustafa Kemal Atatürk, and events in Iraq were made worse when Prime Minister Nuri As-Sa'id made use of the army to eliminate political enemies. This is what Prime Minister Nuri al-Maliki is doing to Kurdish and Sunni political adversaries today. The pro-British Nuri As-Sa'id's rise to prime minister was sanctioned by a pro-German Iraqi military largely due to the mutual dislike of Jamil al-Midfai (prime minister 1937–1938). Midfai was forced into exile in Transjordan following his short pro-Axis hold on power, mainly because he was threatening the hold of seven military officers on the monarchy. Midfai was not a constitutional monarchist, but he wanted to use his office to extend patronage to his supporters.[29] However, these pro-Axis Iraqi officers' infighting would bring about the third military coup d'état in Iraq, which should have been a warning to British officials of what was to come in the form of Prime Minister Rashid Ali Al-Gaylani in 1941.

The Iraqi army was not immune to the political turmoil in the country and the various Nationalist, monarchist, Marxist, reformist, and Fascist currents. The first Communist cells within the army were uncovered in 1935. In 1937 more than sixty-five soldiers were imprisoned for supporting the Iraqi Communist Party. In 1938 Military Regulation 51 was imposed for any person or group that imported subversive doctrines into the armed forces.[30] The discovery of huge oil fields near Kirkuk and the installation of King Feisal I placed Iraq firmly into British control. Yet the rise of anti-British sentiments gave birth to several anticolonialist and Arab Nationalist movements as well as secret societies; the British resorted to military force when their interests were threatened, as in the case of addressing the pro-Fascist Gaylani coup of 1941.[31] This would be one of three instances of regime change undertaken by the British during World War II (Iran, Iraq, and Egypt) that secured the region from Axis influence but left a scar on the political psychology of the region.

Rashid Ali Al-Gaylani and the Nazi Connection in Iraq

To understand Britain's 1941 intervention in Iraq, it is important to appreciate the history outlined in previous chapters of interactions between Britain and Iraq. It is a history lived and carried in the minds of Iraq's leaders of World War II. While some of these Iraqi leaders benefited from British involvement, many did not, and this added to the resentment of a country. The underlying animus carried by every Iraqi is being subjected to the status of a mandatory state and that British oversight was imposed, which maintained control of Iraq's defense and foreign policies. Rashid Ali Al-Gaylani was born in 1892 to a prominent aristocratic Sunni family in Baghdad. His father would be the first prime minister of Iraq, Abd-al Rahman Al-Gaylani. The first Al-Gaylani provisional government of Rashid Ali's father lasted from 1920 to 1922. Ironically, Rashid Ali's father negotiated the 1922 Anglo-Iraqi Treaty that established the veiled British mandate over Iraq. How much the son wanted to redeem the shame of his father can only be a matter for speculation.

Rashid Ali Al-Gaylani studied law in Baghdad and began his career in Iraqi politics in 1924, in the government led by Yasin al-Hashimi, who appointed Gaylani as minister of justice and then minister of the interior. Both men opposed any British involvement in Iraq's internal politics. They rejected the Anglo-Iraqi Treaty signed by the pro-British government of Nuri As-Sa'id in 1930 that altered the terms of the 1922 treaty, and formed their own party in 1931, dubbed Hizb al-Ikhwa al-Watani (Party of National Brotherhood) to promote a Nationalist agenda and oppose the 1930 Treaty of Alliance with Britain. Gaylani became prime minister in 1933 and, by King Ghazi's approval, became head of the royal *diwan* (council).[32] The Anglo-Iraqi Treaty of 1930 granted use of air bases to the RAF in Basra and Habbaniya, the right of troop transit at all times, and, in times of war, access to all Iraqi facilities. Iraq's independence in 1932 found Iraqi leaders wanting to redefine the relationship with Britain. During the outbreak of World War II, Iraq broke off diplomatic relations with Germany, but did not declare war; after 1940, Iraq kept its relations with Italy. The Italian legation in Baghdad became a center for anti-British propaganda, and intelligence collection against the Allies. As you will read in chapter 9, Egyptian political leaders would also seek to redefine its relationship and duel over the language of the 1936 Anglo-Egyptian Treaty.[33]

During the 1930s Gaylani was influenced by Al-Husseini, an ex-Ottoman artillery officer, who had become a schoolteacher and then rose to infamy as the grand mufti of Jerusalem. The mufti was exiled from the British mandate of Palestine for his anti-British activities and was active traveling the Middle East fomenting anti-British sentiment and courting Fascist leaders, chiefly Hitler. Al-Husseini established a record of organizing anti-Jewish and anti-British riots in the late 1920s and found support from Hitler's Germany.[34] An advocate of capitalizing on anti-British sentiment in the Middle East was

SS-Obengruppenführer Reinhard Heydrich, who fomented an unsuccessful revolt in Romania and wanted to try again in the more fertile revolutionary soil of Iraq. Heydrich was among those who chaired the infamous Wannsee Conference that operationalized the Final Solution. Before his assassination in 1942, Heydrich was the Third Reich's top policeman, and head of Reich main security that included the SD (Sicherheitsdienst des Reichsführers-SS, the intelligence agency of the SS), the Gestapo (Geheime Staatspolizei, "Secret State Police," the official secret police of Nazi Germany and German-occupied Europe), and Kriminalpolizei (the criminal investigative unit). Heydrich planned large-scale subversions in Iraq using the SD, and argued with Ribbentrop to insert police attachés around the globe in German embassies to coordinate revolutionary activities within Allied domains.[35] Heydrich saw an opportunity to utilize Arab Nationalism as a means of undermining Britain's influence in the Middle East.

By 1940 Gaylani founded his own association of fierce Arab Nationalists. One influential group of officers was a cabal of four colonels known as Al Marba Al-Dzahabi (the Golden Square). These four influential, militant pan-Arabists included Salah Eddin Al-Sabbagh, Kamil Shabib, Fahmi Sa'id, and Mahmud Salman. The virulently anti-British clique looked to Germany for support, enthusiastically encouraged since the 1930s by German ambassador Grobba. By this time the majority view amongst Iraqi political circles was that Britain's demise at the hands of the Axis powers was only a matter of time.[36]

It was at that time that the ideological foundations of what in later years became the Ba'ath Party were laid. Ba'athism, a fusion of Arab Nationalism with Fascist ideas, was created by two Syrian students, Salah al-Din al-Bittar and Michel Aflaq, who previously studied in the Sorbonne. But, in accordance with the requirements of the Anglo-Iraq treaty, Iraq broke off relations with Nazi Germany in September 1939, and the Ba'ath party was not organized until 1947.[37]

As a prelude to independence, the Anglo-Iraqi Treaty of 1930 preserved for Britain important stakes in Iraq, specifically (1) commercial interests in Mosul and Kirkuk oil fields, (2) air bases next to Baghdad and Basra, (3) vital strategic land and air link with India, and (4) the right to transport troops through Iraq. The treaty that was revised in 1936 had granted Britain air bases at Habbaniya near Baghdad and Shaibah.[38] Robert Lyman and Howard Gerrard describe the history of British bases in Iraq and their defense in their book, *Iraq 1941: The Battles for Basra, Habbaniya, Fallujah and Baghdad*. The book is an excellent campaign study and was recommended by the authors to U.S. troops deploying in support of Operation Iraqi Freedom as a means of discussing the terrain. We have paraphrased some passages from that book of relevance to understanding the region from an operational perspective: A large RAF base was established at Lake Habbaniya on the Euphrates, fifty-five miles west of Baghdad, to replace the RAF cantonment at Hinaidi, on the outskirts of Baghdad. RAF

Habbaniya, formally named RAF Dhibban, became operational in October 19, 1936. Habbaniya became an important staging post on the aerial route to India and the Far East and a potential route whereby Cairo could be reinforced in time of emergency. Adjacent to the airfield were the aircraft hangars for the flight training school and the Iraq communications flight.[39]

The long-established base at Shaibah, sixteen miles southwest of Basra, was occupied in 1920 and retained after the Ottoman defeat in World War I during the Mesopotamian campaign, together with base and port facilities at Basra. In its fourth article of the 1930 Anglo-Iraq Treaty, it dictated,

> [S]hould . . . either of the High Contracting parties become engaged in war, the other High Contacting party will . . . immediately come to his aid in the capacity of an ally. In the event of an imminent menace of War, the High Contracting Parties will immediately concert together the necessary measures of defense. The aid of His Majesty the King of Iraq in the event of war or the imminent menace of war will consist in furnishing to His Britannic Majesty on Iraq territory all facilities and assistance in his power including the use of railways, rivers, ports, aerodromes and means of communication.[40]

The Iraqi rail link connecting the Persian Gulf via Baghdad to Tripoli in Lebanon and the Bosporus in Istanbul was British owned. British investments in an oil pipeline connecting Kirkuk to Tripoli and Haifa made British defenses a necessity. The fifth article, appendix 1 of the 1930 Anglo-Iraqi treaty declared, "[I]t is understood between the High Contracting Parties that responsibility for the maintenance of internal order in Iraq . . . for the defense of Iraq from external aggression rests with His Majesty the King of Iraq. Nevertheless His Majesty the King of Iraq recognizes that the permanent maintenance and protection in all circumstances of the essential communications of His Britannic Majesty is in the common interest of the High Contracting Parties."[41]

Upon the resignation of Nuri As-Sa'id on March 28, 1940, the mufti was asked to facilitate the transition of government to Rashid Ali Al-Gaylani. A cordial understanding had developed between the two since the reception that Gaylani afforded the mufti in October of 1939. On March 31, 1940, Gaylani replaced Nuri As-Sa'id as prime minister. The new cabinet was formed, headed by Gaylani. Nuri As-Sa'id took the foreign affairs section, with Taha El-Hashimi as defense minister, Naji Shawkat as justice minister, Naji al-Swaydi as finance minister, Omar Nazmi as head of communications and public works, Sadeq Bassam as minister of education, Amin Zaki as minister of trade, and Rauf El-Bahrani as minister of social affairs. Moreover, Al-Husseini was an important political factor in Iraq. The U.S envoy in Baghdad wrote, with reference to the mufti, "[M]y investigations convince me that he is the most highly respected and influential individual in Iraq today, both in religious and political circles. . . . He has gained a large following in Palestine and Syria and he is now developing a similar influence in Iraq. He is thus becoming a power to be reckoned with in the Arab world."[42]

Consequently, when Italy entered the war in June 1940 Iraq did not sever relations with Rome. Hence, the Italian envoy, Luigi Gabrielli, remained in Baghdad and the Iraqi government thus preserved the possibility of contact with the Axis. Following the death of King Feisal I in 1933, his son Ghazi took the throne until Ghazi's untimely death on April 4, 1939, in a car accident. His death would be followed by the ascendancy of a weak regency of the new four-year-old King Feisal II. The power was in the hands of his uncle, Prince Abdal-Illah until 1953, when Feisal II came of age. However, Abdal-Illah remained a chief adviser and companion of the young king, and a strong advocate of a pro-Western foreign policy. Because of his friendship with Britain, the regent was the subject of political intrigue by extreme Nationalists determined to undermine his position.[43] King Feisal II would rule from 1953 to 1958, and would be brutally overthrown by an Iraqi military coup led by General Abdal-Karim Qassim. In a scene reminiscent of the murder of the Russian tsar and his family, King Feisal, his family, and servants were machine-gunned in the palace courtyard in Baghdad.

Though Abdal-Illah supported Britain in the war, he was unable to assert control over Gaylani, who used the start of World War II to further Iraqi Nationalist objectives. Gaylani refused to allow troops from India and Australia to cross through Iraq to the North African front. He also rejected calls that Iraq break ties with Italy and sent his justice minister, Naji Shawkat, on a secret mission to Ankara. Born in 1893, Muhammad Naji Shawkat was a graduate of the Ottoman Law School in Istanbul. He was the assistant general prosecutor in the Iraqi city of al-Hila during World War I. Shawkat joined the Ottoman army as a reserve office. After two years of involvement in the Ottoman defense of Iraq, he was captured by the advancing British in March 1917. Afterwards, Shawkat joined the Arab Revolt and was appointed as a legal adviser to Yasin al-Hashimi's infant military command of the Damascus Arab government. He was appointed as representative of Iraq in Ankara. This mission's intent was to make contact with the German ambassador to Turkey, Franz von Papen, and to win German support for his government.

The German foreign ministry archives contain detailed records, which are excerpted here: Shawkat carried a letter of introduction from the grand mufti describing him as "the person in whom you can place complete confidence in discussing the general questions concerning the Arab countries."[44] He asked Von Papen "to convey to His Excellency, Adolf Hitler, my sincerest felicitations on the occasion of the great political and military triumphs which he has just achieved through his foresight and great genius." The mufti observed that "Palestine, which has for the past years been fighting the democracies and international Jewry, is ready at any time to assume an active role and redouble her efforts both at home and in the other Arab countries. The Arab people, slandered, maltreated, and deceived by our common enemies, confidently expect that the result of your final victory will be their independence and complete liberation, as well as the creation of their unity, when they will be linked to your country by a treaty of friendship and collaboration." Von Papen met with Shawkat on July 5, 1940, and emphasized that "the future development of the political situation in the Near East was a matter of interest primarily to Italy and that, therefore, I could be regarded only as an intermediary for proposals and wishes addressed to Italy via the Reich government." Shawkat replied that "as the Arab movement had fought Anglo-French imperialism, so it would have to oppose Italian colonialism. It was therefore to the interest of the Axis Powers for Germany to use her influence with Rome, in order to support a solution that would be compatible with the interests of the Arab movement."[45]

With the diplomatic aid of an Iraqi passport provided by Gaylani, the mufti dispatched his private secretary, Uthman Kamal Haddad, a Lebanese Arab activist from Tripoli, to Berlin and Rome. When he reached the Axis capitals, Haddad claimed to represent an inter-Arab committee. Haddad, who stayed in Berlin from August until October of 1940, presented himself to Dr. Grobba and other senior officials of the German foreign office. He reported to his German interlocutors the formation of an Arab coordination committee chaired by Al-Husseini. Members included, for Iraq, Rashid Ali Al-Gaylani, Naji Shawkat, Naji al-Swaydi, the Golden Square colonels (Salah Eddin Al-Sabbagh, Kamil Shabib, Fahmi Sa'id, and Mahmud Salman), and Yunis al-Sab'awi; for Syria, Shukri al-Quwwatli and Zaki al-Khatib; and for Saudi Arabia, Yusuf Yasin and Khalid Al-Hud Al-Qarqani. Haddad proposed that the Axis governments support the preliminary draft declaration of German-Arab collaboration outlining the declaration on Arab affairs developed by Al-Husseini. Haddad elaborated that the term "Arab countries" covered the North African countries as well as countries of the Arab East. This declaration was accompanied by a letter in which both Italy and Germany expressed their agreement with the Iraqi government's wish to restore diplomatic relations with Germany. Iraq's willingness to accord Germany and Italy a favorable position with respect to the exploitation of Iraqi mineral resources, particularly oil and petroleum, was a significant concession to the Germans. Finally, the resumption of anti-British uprisings in Palestine and Transjordan would be an added tactical bonus for Berlin in their struggle to undermine the British globally. In this context, Haddad proposed to the Germans that

A general uprising would tie down the 30–40,000 troops which Britain maintained in Palestine and together with the prevention of Indian troop movement across Iraq, would substantially relieve Italy's military positions in the eastern Mediterranean. If the British regarded the prevention of troop movements as a provocation and responded militarily, Iraq would be ready to defend her neutrality with all means and to admit all German agents or experts necessary for this purpose.[46]

Geoffrey Warner's 1974 book, *Iraq and Syria, 1941* contains Haddad's discussions with the Italians. Among his proposals that were thoroughly studied by one of Ciano's Middle Eastern experts, Giovanni Guarnaschelli, concluded, "[A] public declaration recognizing the unlimited independence of the Arab states does not correspond to our interests." Guarnaschelli further stated, "Apart from other and more direct reasons, it is felt that free access to the Indian Ocean will never be assured if the Suez Canal Zone, Sinai, the Sudan and Aden are not controlled by us."[47] Arab Nationalists were perfectly justified in suspecting that Rome entertained extensive imperial ambitions in the Arab world. Commenting on the meeting between Von Papen and Shawkat, Ernst Woermann, the director of the political department of the German foreign ministry, wrote on July 21, "There can be no doubt that we must give Italy absolute precedence in organizing the Arabian Area. This consequently rules out any German claim to leadership in the Arabian area, or a division of that claim with Italy. All views about the Near East received indicate a unanimous anti-Italian attitude among the Arabs. We ought not to allow ourselves to become involved in this Arabian game and ought not to arouse their hope that they could get from us support against Rome."[48]

The Baghdad government under Gaylani, by agreement with the mufti and the four Iraqi colonels of the Golden Square, requested of the Italian envoy to Baghdad, Luigi Gabrielli, that the Italian government should issue a declaration ensuring their sympathy and support for the Arab national aspiration. Gabrielli made the following note verbale (an unsigned diplomatic communication expressed in third person), which circulated among interested parties: "His Excellency Count Ciano, the Italian Minister of Foreign Affairs, has instructed me to inform Your Excellency that coherently with the policy so far followed Italy aims at ensuring the complete independence and territorial integrity of the Levant as well as of Iraq and the countries under British Mandate. In consequence, Italy will oppose any eventual British or Turkish pretensions for territorial occupation whether in Syria, Lebanon, Iraq."[49]

German diplomacy in Iraq also concerned itself with the question of Italy's attitude. The Italians were by no means thrilled about German meddling in eastern Mediterranean affairs. However, they took no initiative in conducting joint covert or overt activities and neglected to propose any common financing of Arab figures close to the Axis. After Mussolini's failures in North Africa and the Balkans, Germany no longer had any inclinations to cease from political activity on their own accord in the Arab territories. Assertions appeared in unofficial documents stating that Rome should not be given much attention regarding Axis efforts in Iraq and that certain matters should be settled without Rome's involvement. This lack of coordination among the Axis would in hindsight be one of the major flaws that led to their defeat by the Allies who even set up combined military staffs. The German military demanded that the decision to give Italy freedom of action in the Arab countries be reexamined and that all political activities in the Near East be directed from Germany and that Berlin would assume the initiative in Iraq.[50]

Final opportunities to amend relations with Britain came in July of 1940, with the arrival in Baghdad of Lieutenant Colonel Stewart Francis Newcombe, a colleague of T. E. Lawrence; Newcombe had been sent on a semi-official mission to find out what could be done to appease the Arab Nationalists. Those who took part in the discussions were Nuri As-Sa'id, Gaylani, representatives of the grand mufti Husseini, and British ambassador Sir Basil Newton. Topics of discussion included Arab grievances about Palestine, Syria, and Arab unity. The British government was not prepared to make any concessions to the Arabs on any of the issues raised during Newcombe's mission. A circular sent from London to the Dominion governments was sent on August 22 on Arab policy stating

> As regards Syria, we are discouraging any Arab policy likely to disturb the situation which has so far remained calm. In Palestine, the situation remains such that we cannot accede to the Arab requests for general amnesty, nor proceed to the first step in constitutional development laid down in the White Paper. In general since in the present circumstances, it is not practicable politics to make a major concession and since the value of immediate minor concessions appears doubtful we are impressing upon the Arabs that our policy is fixed by the White Paper of 1939 and the most we can do is to uphold it. The idea of an Arab Federation remains as yet vague. We do not believe a practical scheme can be evolved. We would only be likely to intervene in order to secure our essential interests or fulfill announced obligations.[51]

It is doubtful whether Gaylani and Grand Mufti Amin Al-Husseini ever entertained much hope of winning concessions from the British. The failure of the Newcombe mission, therefore, reinforced their prejudices and enabled Husseini and Gaylani to concentrate on their negotiations with the Axis.[52]

The Allies, and in particular Britain, grew concerned with Iraqi negotiations to renew ties between the Nazi regime and Iraq. The discussion between Nazi and Iraqi officials included promises to provide military support to Germany when its armies reached Iraq. At a later meeting, Al-Husseini's private secretary acted as the representative for the Iraqi government, and Gaylani guaranteed Germany that Iraq's natural resources would be made available to the Axis war effort in return for German recognition of the Arab state's right to independence and political unity.[53]

By December 1940 the British demanded the removal of Gaylani, and in January he was replaced with General Taha Pasha El-Hashimi, another pan-Arabist but rather more acceptable in temperament to Britain. This only aggravated Iraqi mistrust of Britain, and Iraqi nationalist supporters in the Baghdad government agitated for action. Together with some of his pro-Axis colleagues, Gaylani made plans to assassinate Abdal-Illah and depose Taha El-Hashimi. Needless to say, the change in ruling parties and Iraqi political intrigues did not bode well for Great Britain. As relations stood in the summer of 1940, Gaylani neither allowed the concentration of British troops in Iraq nor severed diplomatic ties with Italy. Making matters worse, the Iraqi government was in the process of renewing diplomatic relations with Berlin. Members of Iraq's intelligentsia seeing Nazi victories in France and believing in the likelihood of an Axis victory in the Western Desert began to challenge the Hashimi government. Hashimi realized that in order to begin a pro-British foreign policy he had to dismantle the Axis sympathetic cluster of Iraqi officers—the Golden Square—by gradually removing its members from important positions in the Iraqi army and to do so without provoking a serious backlash. Hashimi attempted to transfer Kamil Shabib from his command of the 1st Army Division near the Iraqi capital to a less influential position as commander of the 4th Army Division in Basra. Hashimi then transferred Salah Eddin Al-Sabbagh, commanding the Baghdad 3rd Army Division, to command the 2nd Army Division in Mosul. The army officers easily discerned his plan as transferring Axis sympathetic commanders away from centers of the power in Baghdad and dispatching them to commands in the north and south of Iraq. In addition, the leaders of a mechanized force and air force were reassigned in a shuffle of colonels.[54]

Robert Lyman's two books on the 1941 Gaylani Revolt offer a detailed study on Iraqi political intrigues of the time. Lyman's volumes reveal a February 28, 1941, meeting consisting of Mufti Husseini, Gaylani, and members of the Golden Square. During that meeting the movements of the Hashimi government were reviewed. Those in attendance came to two decisions: (1) that breaking off relations with Italy was inconsistent with Arab interests; and (2) if Hashimi were to insist on carrying out policies deemed unacceptable to Iraqis, he should then be compelled to resign in favor of Gaylani. As increasing elements of the Iraqi military began siding with Gaylani, the Golden Square moved to depose Taha El-Hashimi, and Iraq's royal family fled to Habbaniya and then by air to Basra on April 2, 1941. Iraq's monarch was assisted by the American consul to Baghdad, Paul Knabenshue. The American diplomat allowed 150 British citizens to take refuge in what would be nicknamed "The White House on the Tigris."[55]

The Lyman book describes how, at Basra, the regent Abdal-Illah was smuggled on board the protective hull of the British river gunboat HMS *Cockchafer*. Abdal-Illah spent the next two months as a guest of the British in Jerusalem. On April 3 Gaylani regained power, declaring a National Defense government. The coup leaders immediately planned to deny any further concessions to Britain as well as to retain diplomatic links with Italy and expel prominent Iraqi pro-British politicians from the country. A military clash with Britain became inevitable. On April 9 a joint German and Italian statement of support was cabled to Gaylani, promising his government both military and financial assistance. Axis statements led Iraqi Nationalists to believe that assistance was forthcoming in the event of a conflict with Britain. It was time for London and Delhi (British India) to dust off contingency plans for a campaign drafted around August 1939 to send forces to the Persian Gulf in the event of threats to the British-controlled Iranian oil fields. The primary threat in British war games at the time was the Soviet Union, not Iraq. The plan called for three infantry divisions to be built up in Iraq, in Basra; the plan was given the code name Operation Sabine.[56]

Initial Axis Armaments in Iraq

Francis Nicosia's work paints an excellent picture of the buildup of Iraqi generals who wanted to reduce their reliance on British aid and materiel. He describes how the coup of October 1936 brought to power a new government in Iraq that sought to reduce British political and military dependency, and to establish closer ties with Germany. In March 1937 Ambassador Grobba notified Berlin that the new Iraqi government received permission from London to look elsewhere to satisfy some of its arms requirements. The Iraqi government was interested in more-advanced weaponry, mainly artillery, anti-aircraft guns, and fighter aircraft from Germany. In April the German war ministry notified the foreign ministry that most of the weapons could not be delivered due to cost and production problems, as well as Germany's own rearmament needs. German firms negotiated with Baghdad the first German–Iraqi arms agreement in December 9, 1937. Germany concluded two further arms transactions with Iraq before the outbreak of the war. Both these agreements were known and even approved by London.[57]

During the war Hitler ordered planes and arms sent to Baghdad in support of Gaylani. Luftwaffe colonel Werner Junck met with Reichsmarschall Goering, who named Junck commander of aviation for Iraq. At the direction of General Hans Jeschonnek, Goering's chief of staff, the Luftwaffe sent Werner Junck to Iraq. Junck's unit flew two squadrons amounting to fifteen Heinkel-111s and fourteen Messerschmitt-110s into Mosul through Vichy French air bases in Syria. In addition, to assist in transporting German airborne troops to Iraq, Junck was lent thirteen Junkers-52 and Junkers-90 transport aircraft. All but three of these transports were returned for the preparation for the invasion of Crete. The Luftwaffe task force under Iraqi colors called Fliegerführer Irak (flyer command Iraq) was to operate out of Mosul. The Luftwaffe units arrived in Mosul on May 12, 1941. Junck visited Baghdad on May 16 and held a meeting with Dr. Grobba, Gaylani, General Amin Zaki, Colonel Nur Eddin Mahmud, and Colonel Mahmud Salman. They agreed to the following priorities: (1) prevent British forces from arriving to reinforce Habbaniya; and (2) capture Habbaniya, assuming that the Iraqi army would make the actual ground assault while the Germans provided air cover and a few German airborne formations. Junck decided to launch a surprise attack that very day on Habbaniya, deploying six Bf-110 fighters and three He-111 bombers. A train arrived in Mosul via Turkey on May 13 carrying 15,500 rifles with 6 million rounds of ammunition, 200 machine guns with 900 ammunition belts, and four 75-mm field guns together with 10,000 shells. Hitler's Directive No. 30 on the Middle East, dated May 23, 1941 stated the following:

> The Arab Freedom Movement in the Middle East is our natural ally against England. In this context the uprising in Iraq is of special importance. This strengthens the forces hostile to England in the Middle East beyond the Iraqi frontier, disrupts English communications, and ties up English troops and shipping at the expense of other theaters. I have therefore decided to hasten developments in the Middle East by supporting Iraq. Whether and how it may be possible, in conjunction with an offensive against the Suez Canal, finally to break the British position between the Mediterranean and the Persian Gulf is a question that will be answered only after BARBAROSSA [the German invasion of the Soviet Union].
>
> In connection with my decision I order the following for the support of Iraq: (a) Support by the air force, (b) Dispatch of a military mission, (c) Arms deliveries.
>
> The military mission (cover name—Sonderstab F [Special staff F]) will be under the command of General [Helmuth] Felmy. Its tasks are: (a) To advise and support the Iraqi armed forces, (b) Where possible, to establish military contacts with forces hostile to England outside of Iraq, (c) To obtain experience and intelligence in this area for the German armed forces. The composition of this organization will be regulated, in accordance with these duties, by the Chief of the High Command in the Armed Forces. Chain of command will be as follows: (a) All armed forces personnel sent to Iraq, including liaison staff in Syria, will be under the command of the head of the military mission with the proviso that orders and guidelines for the aviation units will come exclusively from the High Command of the Air Force, (b) The head of the military mission will be subordinate to the Chief of the High Command in the Armed Forces, with the proviso that orders and guidelines for the aviation units will come exclusively from the High Command of the Air Force, (c) The members of the military mission are, for the time being, to be regarded as volunteers (in the manner of the Condor Legion). They will wear tropical uniforms with Iraqi badges. Also, Iraqi markings will be worn by German aircraft.
>
> The employment of the air force in limited numbers is intended, apart from direct effects, to increase the self-confidence and fighting spirit of the Iraqi people and armed forces.
>
> The Chief of the High Command in the Armed Forces will issue the necessary orders in this respect. (Deliveries to be made from Syria, in accordance with the agreement reached with the French in this matter, and from Germany.)

The direction of propaganda in the Middle East is the responsibility of the Foreign Office, which will cooperate with the High Command in the Armed Forces, Operations Staff—Propaganda Section. The basic idea of our propaganda is: The victory of the Axis will free the countries of the Middle East from the English yoke, and will give them the right to self-determination. All who love freedom will therefore join the fight against England. No propaganda is to be carried out against the French in Syria.

Should members of the Italian Armed Forces be employed on duties in Iraq, German personnel will cooperate on the lines laid down in this directive. Efforts will be made to ensure that they come under the command of the Head of the German Military Mission.

Signed,
The Supreme Commander of the Armed Forces,
Adolf Hitler.[58]

During an interview conducted by the British foreign office, the captured Nazi leader Rudolf Hess, who served as Hitler's secretary and deputy, pointed out that "in any peace settlement Germany would have to support Rashid Ali (Al-Gaylani) and secure eviction of British presence from Iraq."[59]

French admiral Jean-François Darlan signed an agreement with German ambassador to Vichy France Otto Abetz in May of 1941; this agreement was known as the Paris Protocols. The Paris Protocols granted the Germans military facilities in Syria, Tunisia, and French West Africa. In return, Vichy France asked for the re-commissioning of seven torpedo boats, the reduction of the occupation costs, and the easing of communications through France's demarcation line. Specifically, the following written guarantees were submitted to the Reich government:

- Restoration of France's state sovereignty over the entire country with the line of demarcation constituting only the limits for the stationing of German troops on French territory
- A special status for the disputed Alsace-Lorraine territory until the conclusion of a peace treaty
- The gradual release of war prisoners
- The reduction of occupation costs
- A public statement renouncing German claims on the territories of Syria, North Africa, and West Africa
- The abolition of the control commissions in Africa or the weakening of their prerogatives

The Paris Protocol relating to Syria and Iraq was formulated on the evening of May 23. The Vichy government was obligated to (1) turn over to Iraq about three-quarters of the war materiel stored in Syria; (2) agree to the landing of German and Italian planes, and provide them with fuel and make available to the Luftwaffe a special base at Aleppo; (3) permit the use of ports, roads, and railways for transport to Iraq; (4) train in Syria Iraqi soldiers equipped with French arms; (5) make available to the German High Command all information on British strength and plans in the Middle East in the possession of French intelligence; and (6) defend Syria and Lebanon with all available forces. In return, the German High Command of the armed forces agreed to the strengthening of French forces in Syria beyond the limits fixed by the Armistice Convention. Ultimately, however, only the part of the Paris Protocols relating to the Levant was carried out. Sections devoted to cooperation in Tunisia, regarding the important military base at Bizerte, as well as at Dakar in French West Africa and at Brazzaville in Equatorial Africa, were not.[60] Michael Bloch's 1992 biography of Nazi foreign minister Ribbentrop may explain the tense relationship between the Vichy French and the Germans. Bloch reveals that Ribbentrop may have seen events in Iraq as a means of deflecting Hitler from Operation Barbarossa, the disastrous invasion of the Soviet Union. He also argues that the Vichy French allowed the Nazis access to weapons' stores and overflight to rescue Gaylani in return for permission to rearm the Vichy French navy, to release French prisoners held by the Germans, to relax the occupation costs, and to renegotiate lines of demarcation between Vichy- and German-occupied northern France. Another revealing aspect of Bloch's book is the inability of the Iraqis to utilize German arms, since they mainly had been trained on British weapons.[61] Resenting the Royal Navy's July 1940 attack on the French fleet anchored at Mers-el-Kébir in Algeria, Darlan negotiated a preliminary agreement that released Vichy war stocks in Syria, including aircraft, and permitted passage of German war materiel across Syria, providing a Syrian overflight for the Germans.[62]

Following the fall of pro-Axis forces in Iraq, Darlan told the German ambassador in France that he was concerned lest the British attack Syria: "I would therefore urgently request you to intervene with the German high command with a view to ordering the evacuation of personnel and of German and Italian air force materiel sent to the Levant."[63] Darlan's views in hindsight would be proven correct as Churchill compelled General Wavell to create a force that would deprive the Vichy French of Syria. It would be among the many strains in the relationship between the prime minister and his commander in chief of the Middle East. German agents, with ample funds, proceeded to stimulate anti-British and anti-Zionist feeling among the Arab peoples of the Levant and Iraq during the British intervention in the Gaylani Revolt. The Luftwaffe conducted attacks on the Suez Canal from bases in the Dodecanese Islands. With Syria under German influence, Egypt and the oil refineries at Abadan were vulnerable to heavy air attacks and airborne troop landings; in addition, the communication lines between Palestine and Iraq risked being severed, thereby weakening the British diplomatic position in Turkey.[64] The Germans had conducted successful airborne operations in Belgium, as part of the invasion of France, in Norway, and in a mass airborne operation against Crete. In the German airborne assault on Crete, seven thousand British Commonwealth troops were evacuated to Egypt in a mini-Dunkirk on the eastern Mediterranean. In discussions about intervening in Iraq, the use of airborne troops figured prominently in Axis staff planning.

Unfortunately for Berlin, by the time Hitler was moved to declare in his Directive No. 30 that "the Arab liberation movement as our natural ally," Churchill had anticipated and preempted Axis intervention in Iraq.[65] The Iraqis made things worse for themselves when on May 17 they mistakenly shot down the plane of Major Axel Von Blomberg, Germany's negotiator sent to coordinate military support for the Gaylani coup and to make arrangements for a council of war with the Iraqi government. Von Blomberg was to raise the German-led Arabische Brigade (Arab Brigade) in Iraq utilizing volunteers from Iraq, Syria, Palestine, and Saudi Arabia. Blomberg, son of Field Marshal Werner Von Blomberg, possessed extensive experience in the Near East, gained during World War I on the Sinai front. He was Grobba's brother-in-law and had served under the kaiser as an ensign in the 61st Infantry Regiment at Toru, Poland, as well as in the Luftwaffe since 1912. During World War I Blomberg operated in the Sinai Peninsula. With the death of Blomberg, the military mission to Iraq would be headed by Luftwaffe general Hellmuth Felmy. Felmy was no T. E. Lawrence, however, and his Arab Revolt in Iraq did not materialize into an effective unit, and instead operated from Athens under the name of Sonderstab F (Special Staff F), a unit that concerned itself with Arab affairs, with Felmy acting as military attaché. Ambassador Grobba represented the German foreign office in Iraq for Sonderstab F. As such, he would be responsible for the direction of mission-related propaganda in addition to his diplomatic duties in Baghdad.[66] Despite energetic efforts by Dr. Rudolf Rahn, the German representative on the Italian armistice commission in Syria, to run shipment of arms, munitions, and spare parts to the insurgents through Turkey and Syria, and the intervention of approximately thirty German planes bolstered by a dozen Italian planes, Iraq's five divisions proved no match against the British forces that were supported by about two hundred aircraft.[67]

Efforts to ship arms to Iraq were not limited to the European Axis powers; with the assistance of Canaris and German intelligence, they attempted to receive shipments from Japan. German officials raised this question with the Japanese ambassador to Berlin, Hiroshi Oshima, and the Japanese foreign minister, Yosuke Matsuoka, during the latter's visit to Berlin. Rashid Ali Al-Gaylani made requests for war materiel on a commercial basis to the Japanese chargé d'affaires in Baghdad and the Japanese military attaché in Tehran. Canaris promised aid, but the transport of arms from far-off Japan would take months, and Basra, Iraq's lone port, was firmly in British hands. Japanese–Iraqi negotiations on the matter of arms supply lasted from October 1940 to January 1941, but did not amount to anything tangible.[68] A series of discussions between Mussolini and Hitler at the Brenner Pass can be considered one of the great "what ifs" of the Middle East campaign. Hitler offered Mussolini assistance in bombing the Suez Canal in their discussions of July 7, 1940, but instead the Italian dictator decided to dwell on restructuring the Middle East after the British defeat and completing his East African empire. During the October 4, 1940, Brenner Pass meeting, Hitler discussed the planned invasion of Crete to establish more bases from which to attack the Suez Canal. Actual German bombing began on January 17, 1940, and German warplanes began mining approaches to the canal on November 4, 1940. What if Mussolini had focused on combined arms tactics and not on flights of fancy with the German dictator?[69]

Fascist and Iraqi Nationalist Showdown with British Forces in Iraq

The two senior British commanders in the region in May of 1941 were General Archibald Wavell and General Claude Auchinleck. Wavell was appointed Middle East commander in chief on July 4, 1939. His successes in the war against the Italians in North Africa and East Africa drew him to the attention of British war planners. By February 7, 1941, his Western Desert Force commanded under his subordinate General Richard O'Conner had defeated the Italian Tenth Army in Libya at Beda Fomm, taking 130,000 Axis prisoners, and was driving the Italian forces from Libya. His troops in East Africa outmaneuvered the Italians; at the end of March his forces, under the leadership of William Platt, won the decisive battle at Keren, in Eritrea, resulting in occupation of the Italian colonies in Ethiopia and Somaliland.[70]

In February Wavell was ordered to halt his advance into Libya and to begin Operation Lustre, a futile attempt to provide military aid to Greece, an operation pushed by Churchill. Wavell dispatched 50,000 Commonwealth troops and a great deal of equipment to Greece, dangerously depleting North Africa of necessary resources to prevent Libya and Egypt from being overrun by Rommel's Afrika Korps. The Afrika Korps arrived in Libya February 10 to March 12, 1941, and rapidly advanced across the Egyptian border. Wavell was now forced to fight in the Western Desert, East Africa, and Iraq. On June 22, 1941, he was ordered to swap commands with Auchinleck, who at the time was in charge of British forces in India.[71]

The Iraqi coup could not have arrived at a more inconvenient time for Britain, specifically for Wavell and Churchill. The Afrika Korp's blitz in North Africa with the siege of Tobruk, the German drive into the Balkans and Greece, the pyrrhic German victory in Crete during Operation Mercury, and the Baghdad Putsch were all taking place with uncanny synchronicity. Auchinleck became increasingly concerned that the lack of robust action could lead not only to the loss of British positions in Iraq, but also to disastrous consequences for British India. Churchill's first move was to secure the Iraqi port city of Basra. In an effort to do so, Churchill, on April 8, 1941, sent the following dispatch to the secretary of state for India, L. S. Amery:

> Some time ago you suggested that you might be able to spare another division taken from the frontier troops for the Middle East. The situation in Iraq has turned sour. We must make sure of Basra, as the Americans are increasingly keen on a great air assembling base being formed there to which they [the Americans] could deliver [supplies] direct [to Iraq]. This plan seems of high importance in view of the undoubted Eastern trend of the war. I am telling the Chiefs of Staff that you will look into these possibilities. Gen[eral] Auchinleck also had ideas that an additional force could be spared.[72]

Upon receiving the Churchill communiqué, General Claude Auchinleck promptly offered to divert an infantry brigade and regiment of artillery originally intended for Malaya to Basra. The major component of what the British would call "Iraqforce," was the 10th Indian Division commanded by Major General William Fraser. Fraser's convoy set off from Karachi on April 12th with the following orders: "(1) To occupy the Basra-Shaibah area in order to ensure the safe disembarkation of further reinforcements and to enable a base to be established in that area. (2) In view of the uncertain attitude of the Iraqi Army and local authorities, to face the possibility that attempts might be made to oppose the disembarkation of his force. (3) Should the embarkation be opposed, to overcome the enemy by force and occupy suitable defensive positions ashore as quickly as possible. (4) To take the greatest care not to infringe the neutrality of Iran."[73] The king's own Royal Regiment landed in Shaibah following a four-day journey from Karachi that had taken them via Sharjah Fort in Trucial Oman and Bahrain in what was the first-ever strategic airlift by British forces in war.[74]

The king's Royal Regiment traveled in five Armstrong Whitworth Atlanta aircraft lent to the RAF for the operation by Imperial Airways, as well as in twelve Vickers Valentia biplane transports. The seaborne convoy contained Brigadier General Donald Powell's 20th Indian Infantry Brigade. Powell considered three options: (1) To land at Kuwait and move north to Basra by land, thus reducing the difficulties associated with an opposed landing but involving a 112-mile march with little water en route, providing the Iraqi forces at Basra advance warning of British intentions. The subsequent line of communication would also be vulnerable to guerrilla action. (2) To land at the entrance of the Shatt-Al-Arab at Al-Fao. The route from Al-Fao to Basra, however, was hindered by water channels that would impede the advance. (3) To execute a coup de main directly up the Shatt-Al-Arab to the dock area, carrying the deception that the landing was merely in support of Britain's treaty rights. Powell opted for the third option.[75]

India was determined to follow up this landing with another convoy to bring the 10th Indian Division up to strength. London decided on April 23 that the

20th Indian Brigade landing would be reinforced to divisional size, and the Port of Basra needed to be expanded in order to adequately accommodate the full complement of three divisions planned for Operation Sabine. The Iraqis decided not to oppose the landings at Basra but rather to carry out troop dispositions designed to isolate and threaten RAF Habbaniya instead. With the onset of hostilities at Habbaniya, Powell sought to consolidate his position around the town of Maqil near Basra while a Gurkha detachment was dispatched to guard the RAF airfield at Shaibah. The Iraqi army made no attempts to oppose the British positions at either Maqil or Shaibah. On May 6 the 21st Indian Brigade landed at the Maqil docks in support of Powell's efforts to secure the township of Ashar. The aim was to occupy the Iraqi naval and military headquarters, the police barracks, government quarters, the post office, and the telephone as well as telegraph exchanges.

That same day, British chiefs of staff telegrammed Wavell:

[S]ettlement by negotiation cannot be entertained except on the basis of a climb down by Iraqis, with safeguard against future Axis designs on Iraq. Realities of the situation are that Rashid Ali [Al-Gaylani] has all along been hand-in-glove with Axis Powers, and was merely waiting until they could support him before exposing his hand. Our arrival into Basra forces him to go off at half-cock before the Axis was ready. Thus there is an excellent chance of restoring the situation by bold action, if it is not delayed. . . . Defense Committee direct that Air Vice-Marshal Smart should be informed that he will be given assistance, and that in the meanwhile it is his duty to defend Habbaniya. Subject to the security of Egypt being maintained, maximum air support possible should be given to operations in Iraq.[76]

On May 7 Churchill telegrammed Smart: "[Y]our vigourous and splendid action has largely restored the situation. We are all watching the grand fight you are making. All possible aid will be sent."[77] The efforts to establish a foothold in the Basra area, expand a base for future operations in Iraq, and protect the Iranian oil refinery at Abadan proved in hindsight to be a considerable military achievement for British arms. The Iraqis worked to deny the transport routes northwest toward Baghdad: they removed locomotives and river crafts, and uprooted and destroyed rail and telegraph lines. Both the 20th and 21st Indian Brigades and the HQ of the 10th Indian Division gradually established a firm base in Basra and, through offensive action across the region, removed any threat of Iraqi interference in operations to the north. This was not part of Auchinleck's original plan, but it played a useful role in subduing local dissent and sponsored the creation of a regional government favorable to the rule of the regent.[78]

Auchinleck also saw fit to secure the transfer of four hundred infantrymen from India to Shaibah. However, on April 10 Gaylani stated that his coup was a matter of internal politics. He stated that nothing should preclude Great Britain from exercising its rites of passage under the Treaty of Alliance. Ambassador

Cornwallis found the Gaylani government's pacifying stance encouraging, and expressed to the British government that a landing at Basra may be viewed by Baghdad as a deliberate act of provocation. Lord Linlithgow, viceroy of India, spoke in defense of the landings by rightly stating, "[W]e are moving into a position that affects our general standing in the Middle East, that has the most important potential repercussions on India and Iran, that affects our oil supplies (so vital to the admiralty) in Iran and Bahrain and (to a lesser extent) Kuwait; and I have no doubt that we must be prepared to take a strong line now."[79] One of Gaylani's first acts was to send an Iraqi artillery force to confront the British air base at Habbaniya while other British forces landed at Basra. Constructed in 1934, it was situated on low ground by the River Euphrates and was overlooked by a plateau one thousand yards to the south that rose to around 150 feet at its highest point. The base had a force of ninety-six mostly obsolete planes, most of them Gloster Gladiator biplanes and a few Bristol Blenheim planes.[80]

On April 29 Iraqi dispositions streamed out of Baghdad westward along the roads toward the Euphrates at Fallujah. At the same time, the Euphrates embankments were severed, and flooded the low-lying area around Habbaniya, thereby effectively cutting it off from the east. The British embassy reported these troop movements early morning on April 30. During that day an estimated two brigades of Iraqi troops advanced toward Habbaniya and further brigades occupied the town of Ramadi, fourteen miles west of Habbaniya on the Euphrates. The troops involved were instructed to deploy on a training exercise to the high ground between Lake Habbaniya and the cantonment. The only thing to arouse suspicion was the fact they were given live ammunition.[81]

The Iraqis placed the British embassy under siege, and the road from Baghdad to Fallujah was blocked. Simultaneously, Iraqi troops seized the oil fields at Kirkuk, shutting down the flow of oil to Haifa and opening up pipelines to Tripoli in Lebanon. This was the same flow that Britain originally closed down with the collapse of France a year prior to this event. A lone Audax biplane sent up to report, returned with the information that at least one thousand troops supported by artillery and armored vehicles were dispersed across the plateau. It was estimated that the Iraqi disposition had deployed on the escarpment the following:

- Three infantry battalions
- An artillery brigade
- Twelve Crossley six-wheeled armored cars
- A mechanized machine gun company
- A number of flat light tanks
- In addition, it was estimated that an infantry company based at Fallujah was advancing to Baghdad supported by a horsed infantry brigade.[82]

The British had 2,200 troops composed of the Iraq levies to defend the base, and twenty armored cars. The base housed the 4th Service Flying Training School. At the start of the campaign, base personnel were as follows: seventeen British officers, five NCOs, three surgeons, forty Assyrian officers, and 1,134 local Iraqi troops composed mainly of minority groups. It also consisted of a machine gun section, a 3-inch mortar section, and an anti-tank rifle. Together with civilian workers, the population of the cantonment in the spring of 1941 was some nine thousand. Its defenses consisted of a seven-mile-long iron fence and a local constabulary of 1,200 Iraqi and Assyrian levies.[83]

Encouraged by hints of German assistance and German triumphs in Greece and Crete, Gaylani advanced against the British. The Iraqi leader violated the 1930 Anglo-Iraqi Treaty by besieging the air base at Habbaniya on April 30, 1941. By the second day of fighting, a few more Blenheim fighter bombers had arrived. British infantry were shuttled by air from Shaibah to reinforce Habbaniya. The Vichy French government in Syria aided the new pro-Axis Iraqi government and provided a conduit for German assistance to keep the Iraqi National Defense government alive. Gaylani collaborated with Nazi German intelligence units and eventually accepted military assistance from Nazi Germany.[84] In a desperate gambit, Gaylani appealed to Hitler for aid, and the Germans demanded that Vichy French air bases in Syria and Lebanon be made available as staging areas. In addition, the Germans requested that Vichy French arms depots in Syria be used to arm the Iraqi coup leaders.

Lyman and Gerrard's volume *Iraq, 1941* provides an excellent blow-by-blow description of the details of the battle between Iraqi and British forces. It is a volume the authors recommended when orienting U.S. military personnel deploying to Iraq as a tactical case study on culture, terrain, and ground operations. By May 2 the Iraqi force on the escarpment had expanded to nine thousand troops with twenty-eight field guns and two dozen armored vehicles. Appointed in November 1939 was Air Vice Marshall H. G. Smart, who was air officer commanding (AOC) Iraq at RAF Habbaniya. An Iraqi officer arrived at the main gate with the following message to Smart: "For the purpose of training we have occupied the Habbaniya hills. Please make no flying attempts or personnel leaving the cantonment. If any aircraft or armored car attempts to leave, it will be shelled by our batteries, and we will not be held responsible."[85] Smart cabled his concerns to British ambassador in Baghdad, Sir Kinahan Cornwallis. Meanwhile, Iraqi forces had simultaneously occupied vital bridges over the Tigris and Euphrates Rivers and reinforced their garrison at Ramadi, effectively cutting off RAF Base Habbaniya from any supply except from the air.[86]

To secure Iraq, Prime Minister Churchill ordered General Archibald Wavell to protect the Habbaniya Royal Air Base. In Cairo, AOC Middle East, Air Chief Marshal Sir Arthur Murray Longmore, ordered eighteen Vickers Wellington bombers from Egypt to Shaibah. Air Vice Marshal Smart launched preemptive air strikes against the plateau without issuing an ultimatum. The attack came entirely as a surprise to the Iraqi forces on the escarpment. Many Iraqi soldiers thought that they were participating in a training exercise or drill. The fact that the British were prepared to fight rather than negotiate a peaceful surrender came as a surprise to Gaylani and the Iraqi colonels of the Golden Square. When news of the attacks reaching Baghdad, the grand mufti immediately declared a jihad against the British and the flow of oil through the remaining pipeline to Haifa was stopped through the seizing of the Iraq Petroleum Company oil plants.[87]

On May 4 attacks continued from both Habbaniya and Shaibah. The attack was devastating for the Iraqi air force, costing twenty-nine aircraft. After five days of incessant bombing the Iraqi army was dealt a demoralizing blow: leaflets dropped over Baghdad assured the local population that Britain's argument was with the Rashid Ali Al-Gaylani government. On May 11 five more Gladiator fighters arrived from Ismailia on the Suez Canal.[88] This force saved Iraq for the Allies but overstretched scarce forces needed to confront Rommel's Afrika Korps that would reach to within sixty miles of Alexandria. The events in Iraq also demonstrated how the years of anti-British propaganda would bear fruit in the Gaylani Revolt.

Wavell's Apprehension

General Wavell was overcommitted and short of resources needed to reinforce Iraq, particularly with the presence of Italian divisions in North Africa; he believed that Iraq was a minor aggravation. Wavell was in Cyrenaica addressing Rommel's assault on Tobruk. The general's response to the London dispatch read as follows: "I have consistently warned you that no assistance could be given to Iraq from Palestine in present circumstances and have always advised that a commitment in Iraq should be avoided. My forces are stretched to the limit everywhere and I simply cannot afford to risk part of forces on what cannot produce any effect. I can only advise negotiation with Iraqis on basis of liquidation of regrettable incident by mutual agreement with alternative of war with British Empire, complete blockade and ruthless air action."[89]

Furthermore, the general believed that the expedition deprived him of his only response force to Vichy-controlled Syria. London replied:

> We much deplore the extra burden thrown upon you at this critical time by events in Iraq. A commitment in Iraq was however inevitable. We had to establish a base at Basra, and control that port to safeguard Persian oil in case of need. The line of communication to Turkey through Iraq has also assumed greater importance owing to German air superiority in the Aegean Sea. . . . Had we sent no forces to Basra the present situation at Habbaniya might still have arisen under Axis direction, and we should have also have had to face an opposed landing at Basra later on instead of being able to

secure a bridgehead there without opposition. There can be no question of accepting Turkish offer of mediation. We can make no concessions. The security of Egypt remains paramount. But it is essential to do all in our power to save Habbaniya and to control the pipeline to the Mediterranean.[90]

Wavell left Iraq's RAF base at Habbaniyah lightly guarded by a Levy Force backed by armored cars. Despite overstretched British forces in Egypt and North Africa, Churchill insisted on overthrowing the Gaylani regime in order to preserve British strategic interests in the Gulf. Prime Minister Churchill correctly understood this was a war of mechanization in the air, on the sea, and on land; therefore the military required petroleum. An Indian division sailed for Basra, along with a hybrid force of a British brigade composed of (Transjordanian) Arab Legion assembled in Jordan under Lieutenant General John Bagot Glubb (Glubb Pasha). General Sir Edward Quinan would be assigned to the improvised task force assigned the name "Iraqforce."[91]

The German and Italian threats to Crete, Libya, and Iraq exacerbated Britain's ability to defend the Suez Canal. An Axis-occupied Iraq jeopardized the safety of the eastern Egyptian frontier and proved to be an ideal base for German and Italian air missions into northern Egypt. Egypt's front was under intense pressure from Rommel, who was in the process of besieging Tobruk. A significant thorn in the British side was the guerrilla leader Fawzi El-Qawukji. He had served in the French-Syrian Army during the 1920s and received formal military training at the French military academy at Saint-Cyr. He deserted in order to join the Druze rebellion in 1925–1927 and remained an outlaw thereafter. He was pardoned by Vichy France in 1941 and agreed to fight against the British. He was wounded in battle on June 24, 1941, and evacuated to Athens. After the war he led the Palestinian Liberation Army in the war of 1947, in which Glubb Pasha, former British officer and Transjordanian military adviser and creator of the Arab Legion, fought. Colonel Humphrey Wyndham of the Household Cavalry Regiment described El-Qawukji as "a very fine guerrilla leader and a very formidable opponent."[92]

German envelopment was of great concern to British commanders. It was expressed by Major General Sir John Kennedy, deputy director of military operations, who stated in spring 1941, "[W]hether we can hold onto the Middle East depends on one thing and one thing alone—whether the Germans concentrate seriously against us there. If they do, they will be able to develop attacks in considerable strength from the west through Libya, from the north through Turkey, and possibly from the northeast through the Caucasus and Persia."[93]

Opposing Forces during Operation Sabine

Lyman describes the British forces as comprising the following: (1) RAF Habbaniya 4th Service Flying Training Squadron and Iraq levies; (2) RAF

Shaibah, Force Sabine (Iraqforce) and H4 Transjordan Blenheim Detachment; (3) Habforce–Kingcol, Arab Legion; and (4) a navy presence of seven ships in the northern Persian Gulf. The Iraqi forces comprised four infantry divisions with some 60,000 troops, two mechanized battalions, one mechanized artillery brigade (equipped with twelve 3.7-mm howitzers), one field artillery brigade (equipped with twelve 18 pounders and four 4.5-mm howitzers), twelve armored cars, one mechanized machine gun company, one mechanized signal company, and one anti-air/anti-tank battery.[94]

The Iraqi armed forces challenging the British position were led by the following: the 1st and 2nd Infantry Divisions, headquartered in Baghdad, led by Colonel Kamal Shahib; the 3rd Infantry Division, headquartered in Kirkuk, led by Colonel Salah Eddin Al-Sabbagh; the Independent Mechanized Brigade, headquartered in Baghdad, and led by Colonel Fahmi Sa'id; a navy flotilla consisting of four Thorneycroft gunboats, one pilot vessel, the *King Feisal I,* and one *Algerine*-class minesweeper, the *Alarm,* based in the Shatt-Al-Arab waterway; and an air force of sixty plus operational aircraft that included Italian Savoia Marchetti (SM)-79 bombers and Breda Ba-65 fighters based at Rashid airfield commanded by Air Force chief colonel Mahmud Salman.[95]

In view of the situation, London decided to organize a relief force to go to the aid of Habbaniya. This force was named Habforce, and was commanded by Major General George Clark; it consisted of the 1st Cavalry Regiment supported by one royal field artillery regiment. One mobile infantry battalion and three mechanized squadrons from the Transjordan Frontier Force were assembled. This force was short of equipment and would have to travel a total of 535 miles to reach Habbaniya.[96]

Major General John Glubb was then a major in command of the small task force of the Arab Legion that reached Habbaniya on May 18 after crossing five hundred miles of desert. As the British forces advanced toward Iraq from Jordan, RAF bombers virtually annihilated the Iraqi air force and extended their attacks to Syrian air bases that serviced German He-111 bombers and Me-110 fighters. The Iraqi army established itself on the high ground to the south of the Habbaniya Air Base. An Iraqi envoy was sent to demand that no movements of either ground or air were to take place from the base. The British refused this demand and opened fire on the Iraqis, knowing the relief force was only hours away.[97]

The British forces surrounded at Habbaniya consisted of two thousand troops, twenty armored cars, and a few Bristol Blenheim fighter bombers. With help from the ground forces at the base and the Iraqi levies comprising mostly Assyrians and Kurds, the Iraqi troops were pushed back to Fallujah, using a combined air, ground, and artillery assault from within the British air base upon the Iraqi forces surrounding them. The air battle was taken to the remaining Iraqi air bases. Habbaniya essentially lifted the siege with its own resources. A secondary mission of Habforce was to establish a line of communication across the desert, and to provide a flying column for operations.[98]

This roving column was known as the Kingcol after its commander Brigadier General J. J. Kingstone. The Kingcol (derived from the first four letters of Kingstone's name and "col" for roving column) was made up of the headquarters of the 4th Cavalry Brigade and Signals, Household Cavalry Regiment; one battery of the 60th Field Regiment; 1st Anti-Tank Troop Regiment, a detachment of the 2nd Field Squadron; two companies of the 1st Essex Regiment; a detachment of the 166th Light Field Ambulance; a desert mechanized regiment; and an improvised Arab Legion detachment from Jordan under General John Glubb Pasha, supported by eight attack armored cars.[99] On May 12, 1941, the column was attacked by high-flying aircraft showering the trucks of the 1st Essex. The offending aircraft was a Heinkel-111 of the newly arrived Fliegerführer Irak flying out of Mosul.[100]

The arrival of German aircraft over Iraqi skies in mid-May was the direct result of fevered consultations between Baghdad and Berlin in the days following Smart's preemptive strikes on the forces occupying the high grounds over Habbaniya. However, the Luftwaffe found conditions in Iraq intolerable. Supplies of fuel and equipment were sparse and each passing day resulted in a reduction of force due to the unrelenting attacks carried out by the RAF. The eventual withdrawal of the Luftwaffe in these circumstances was inevitable and ultimately led to all Luftwaffe personnel evacuating on the last remaining Heinkel He-111.

Once the Allied reinforcements arrived in two columns (Kingcol, headed by Brigadier J. J. Kingstone, and Habforce, headed by Major General John George Walters Clark) across the desert from Palestine and Transjordan, the Iraqi army was cleared from Fallujah and pursued along the river valley to Baghdad, which fell within a week. The nominal restoration of the regent Abdal-Illah (caretaker for the child monarch Feisal II) on June 1 and the pro-British government ensured that access to its strategic oil resources was maintained. When the government of Gaylani collapsed, the Germans withdrew their military, ceasing all major intervention in Iraq. However, the Axis powers did not completely absent themselves from military activity or from subversive political maneuvering in the Middle East.[101]

Unsettled by Vichy France's invitation to the Germans to use Syrian air bases, Churchill ordered the invasion of Syria and Lebanon, which fell on July 14, 1941, after a six-week campaign. Nuri As-Sa'id was reinstalled as prime minister of a pro-British government on October 10, 1941; Iraq broke diplomatic relations with Vichy France a month later. Using Iraq as a staging area, British forces invaded Iran with Soviet intervention from the north on August 25, 1941, installing pro-British Mohammad Reza Pahlavi. Allied (British) occupation of Iraq continued until October 26, 1947. The last British soldier left Iraq on May 30, 1959, with the closure of the strategic Habbaniya Air Base in Iraq. The process eventually yielded a British victory, one that reflected unanimity. The strategic and tactical control of the Iraqi operation fell under the influence of three primary command centers: London, Cairo, and New Delhi. From the outset of the crisis, it was evident that each camp was going to advocate the policy that most accommodated its own regional interests. Churchill and Sir Claude Auchinleck favored armed intervention, while Wavell and the British ambassador to Iraq Sir Kinahan Cornwallis, both well accustomed to the potentialities of Arab Nationalism, believed in diplomacy.[102]

Gaylani fled to Iran, Istanbul, and Rome, and finally ended up in Berlin, where Hitler provided him protection as head of an Iraqi government-in-exile. After World War II he was exiled to Saudi Arabia and later Egypt, returning to Iraq only in 1958 following the revolution that overthrew Iraq's Hashemite monarchy. Once again Gaylani attempted to seize power, plotting a revolt against Brigadier General Abdul Karim Kassim's government. The revolt failed and Gaylani was sentenced to death but was later pardoned. In 1961 Gaylani was granted amnesty and released from prison, eventually settling in Beirut, where he died four years later. Gaylani's reputation was revived by the late Saddam Hussein, who portrayed him as a national hero.

It is worth mentioning that it was also during this time after the fall of the pro-Axis regime in Iraq that one of the most dramatic and violent anti-Jewish pogroms erupted in Baghdad. Following the defeat of Gaylani and the colonels of the Golden Square by British forces, Iraqi soldiers and tribesmen vented their frustration by attacking the Jewish community in June 1941. Al-Farhud (a Kurdish term indicating a murderous breakdown of law and order) was carried out against the Jewish population of Baghdad during the Jewish holiday of Shavuot; this was a turning point in the history of Iraqi Jews. The Arab Nationalist–inspired attack on the Jewish community, after years of anti-Jewish and Nazi propaganda promulgated in the schools and in the media, resulted in the death of about 137 Iraqi Jews and the destruction and plundering of Jewish shops and houses. The Farhud is referred to as the forgotten pogrom of the Holocaust and marks the beginning of the end of the Jewish community of Iraq, a community that had existed for 2,600 years.[103] Finally, in discussions with America's military men and women today, the authors remind their colleagues that the airfield H-4 near the Jordanian border that was used by the British in 1941 was both targeted and later used by U.S. forces in Operation Desert Storm and Operation Iraqi Freedom.

Quarrels within the Arab Leadership

A fundamental issue that involved the struggle for leadership of the Arab independence movement arose in Rome and Berlin. The two main protagonists in this struggle were the grand mufti Al-Husseini and Prime Minister Gaylani. Since their escape from Iraq, both leaders had initiated political maneuvers within the Axis camp to assert their control and influence over the future direction of the Arab movement. After the mufti's arrival in Berlin, he discovered that Gaylani obtained a letter from Berlin that recognized him as the premier of a liberated Iraq. Al-Husseini requested a similar letter recognizing his own leadership position within the Arab community of the rest of the Middle East.[104]

Other incidents revealed the depth of mutual discontent and jealousy that characterized the relations between Gaylani and Husseini. One such incident occurred when both leaders visited Rome in the winter of 1942 and the Italians gave "pride of place" to Gaylani. This action provoked Al-Husseini, prompting him to vent his dissatisfaction at having been allocated a secondary position. But the conflict between the two men was deeper than the complexities of official recognition and matters of diplomatic protocol. The heart of their dispute was a struggle for political leadership between two rival claimants whose personal ambitions and goals, though similar, were in effect mutually exclusive.[105]

The issue revolved around the question concerning who was the legitimate spokesperson for the Arabs in the Middle East. Al-Husseini's claim of leadership was of the entire Arab independence movement, whereas Gaylani's claim was only in relation to his position as former Iraqi prime minister. The dispute between the two men led to a struggle of personalities within the German foreign office culminating in an administrative struggle between SS Obergruppenführer Erwin Ettel, the Nazi Party official in charge of Arab affairs, and his foreign office counterpart, Ambassador Grobba. To Ettel, the mufti ranked as an *Alte Kampfer* (old fighter) who won the respect and admiration of the Arab population majority in the Near East. Al-Husseini was a fanatical idealist who differed from conventional leaders like Gaylani, whom Ettel characterized as tainted by his exposure to the liberal democratic system.[106]

Grobba, on the other hand, feared that the unity of the Arab independence movement was jeopardized and the intra-Arab political struggle had migrated to Berlin. To Grobba, Al-Husseini was the spiritual leader of the movement, while the government constituted under the leadership of Gaylani demonstrated its concrete political usefulness through its revolt in Iraq. In Grobba's views neither of them could claim sole leadership of the Arab movement. Instead, Grobba offered to refrain from taking any initiatives in resolving the leadership dispute and to treat both leaders equally, while carefully weighing their specific contribution potential toward the Axis military effort.[107]

In addition to the demands of recognition and leadership issues, military concerns also aggravated the conflict. One such specific issue was the utilization of the Deutsch-Arabisches Lehrabteilung based out of Cape Sounion, Greece, under the command of Felmy. The Wehrmacht wanted to deploy this unit to service on the eastern front but faced stiff resistance from Al-Husseini, who was adamantly against Arab units being sent to fight against the Russians in the Caucasus. He dispatched a letter to Field Marshal Wilhelm Keitel, head of the supreme command of the German armed forces, expressing his obligation as spokesman for the Arab cause not to have this unit sent to the eastern front; instead, he insisted that the unit be under Arab command and under an Arab banner to fight only on Egyptian, Palestinian, or Syrian soil. Gaylani, however, was more accommodating than the mufti and agreed that the German military could decide the best use of the Arab volunteer units.[108]

Al-Husseini, aided by Ettel, set out to undermine Grobba's position in the foreign office by accusing him of political intrigue and deception, and to eliminate Grobba's influence in Arab affairs. However, the foreign office was reluctant to get involved and refused to assume any responsibility in regulating the leadership dispute. Although Ettel continued to recommend that Berlin work with both Arab leaders, they did admit that if circumstances forced them to choose between Gaylani and Al-Husseini, they would choose the latter because of his prestige and influence over the Arab world. To Al-Husseini, NSDAP and Islam shared a common weltanschauung (worldview) as he compared the notion of a *Führerprinzip* (absolute leader) to the office of the caliphate, which provided spiritual, political, social, and military leadership in the Islamic world. The foundations of the NSDAP aspired to a similar centralization of power and authority in the hands of the führer, and linked this to the concept of the caliphate.[109] It demonstrates either a complete misunderstanding of the evolution of the institution of the caliphate after the death of Prophet Muhammad in 632 AD, or the typical Nazi method of manipulating history to suit their megalomaniacal agenda. In many ways, militant Islamist groups of the twenty-first century also synthesize a fantasy of what the caliphate was based on their own perverse and modernist worldview. The Nazis used fragments of history, and the militant Islamist fragments of Islamic history and theology to weave a new narrative.

Arab Volunteers in the German Armed Forces

Despite the limited cooperation conducted between the Axis powers and the Arab Nationalist movement, the contingent of Arab soldiers that served with the Axis forces during World War II was considerably smaller than the number of Arabs who fought for the Allies. As mentioned earlier, preliminary steps were made to develop an Arab Legion under the command of the German army. Hitler designated Sonderstab F in the Wehrmacht Southeast as "the central office in the field to participate in all planning and measures in the Arab area."[110] The Sonderstab F was a hastily improvised German-Arab unit founded in 1941 as a military mission to Iraq for deployment in the Arab East. The Sonderstab F and its subunits had a total strength of 5,931 officers, NCOs, and enlisted men. The Sonderstab F lacked any firm Arab policy regarding the course of German political, military, and propaganda efforts in the Near East. Eventually the Sonderstab F was used as a supply of substitutes for unavailable German combat personnel. The mission of the Sonderstab F changed gradually as the political and military climate of Germany and the Arab East deteriorated to the point where the Sonderstab F transformed into a regular corps committed in combat.[111]

Segments of the Arab volunteers with the German army were student recruits in Germany. Some came from Syria after the capitulation of the Vichy French army, and a few Iraqi men were sent by Gaylani. A very small number were recruited from Arab civilians, notably Egyptians, who had been arrested in Germany as enemy aliens following the outbreak of the war. They remained in internment camps until June 1941, when they were released by the German foreign office under the direct recommendation of Ribbentrop, who stated that their release should be "exploited politically" or used for radio and language services.[112]

The Arab volunteers of the German Arab Training Battalion were issued a specially designated brassard (armband) with the colors red, green, white, and black, and the words *Freies Arabien* (free Arabian) with its Arabic translation. By May 1942 only 130 Arab soldiers and NCOs were trained by German officers. In late 1942 there were eight hundred Arab combatants compared to approximately half a million Arab soldiers fighting along the Allied side. For the recruits, volunteering for the German army offered a hope to improve their situation and return to the Middle East as a fighting unit deployed against French and British forces. Instead, the unit was sent to the eastern front where it participated in the fighting at Stalino in September 1942 in anticipation of a breakthrough across the Caucasus into the Middle East. In January 1943 it was transferred to Tunis by way of Sicily. The Vichy French government also organized Arabs, Berbers, and French citizens living in North Africa into a volunteer force dubbed La Phalange Africaine (the African phalanx). This unit managed to recruit 406 men, of which 132 were local Arabs and Berbers in Tunisia.[113]

The Arabs who joined German units were largely recruited among POWs serving with the British and French armies in North Africa between February 1941 and May 1943. Recruitment ended with Rommel's defeat at El-Alamein and the capitulation of the Afrika Korps. After the defeat of the Afrika Korps in Tunisia on May 13, 1943, a number of Arab soldiers were taken prisoner while the rest were evacuated, supplemented with a newly recruited German-Arab 845th Infantry Battalion and again stationed in Greece, where they were charged mostly with guard duties. Remnants of a small Arab paratrooper company rallied to their old German officers and fought in the Battle of Berlin in the final weeks of the war. Captain I. G. Schacht led the Arab Parachute Company in Tunisia; he describes his experiences with the Arab company in a 1945 personal letter: "During the fighting in March and April 1945 in Pomerania and on the Oder marches, the Arab company fully proved its effectiveness. In at least two instances I owed my life to the Arabs. Their losses were in proportion to their courage."[114]

According to estimates found in Antonio Munoz's research published in a 1994 book, *Lions of the Desert*, between 1941 and 1945, of some 2 million men who served in various labor brigades, transport, and guard units or ethnic and national division units set up by the Third Reich for volunteers in the occupied territories, about 372,000 to 445,000 were of Muslim background and tradition. Ethnicities stemmed from Soviet Eurasians, people from the Balkans and India, Arabs, and North African Berbers; 1.4 percent of the total Muslims in the German armed forces were of Arab or Berber origin. The near-totality of Muslims who were involved in military collaboration with Germany were not Arabs but rather were Eurasian and Balkan. An estimated 500 Syrians, 150–200 Palestinians, 450 Iraqis, and approximately 12,000 Moroccans, Tunisians, Algerians, Libyans, and Egyptians joined the Axis between 1941 and 1945. Most served in the *Freies Arabien*, the Sonderverbande 287 and 288, the Phalange Africaine, and the Sonderstab F.[115]

Arab Inmates in Nazi Concentration Camps: The Forgotten Victims

Gaylani wrote the following to the Aufklärungsamt für Bevölkerungspolitik und Rassenpflege (Dr. Walter Gross' Office for Enlightenment on Population Policy and Racial Welfare) in October 1942:

> The Axis enemies in their propaganda state that the Germans consider the Arabs among the lower castes. In my capacity as the Premier of Iraq, I can give an assurance that the Arabs do not give this claim any importance after what they have seen and felt Germany's treatment and help to them. But as the enemy propaganda goes on repeating these lies, I should like to receive an answer from an official source regarding the German consideration of the Arab race. I should be very grateful to get from you a reply on the opinion of Germany on the subject.
>
> Signed,
> Rashid Ali Al-Gaylani

Dr. Gross' reply was as follows:

> In answer to your Excellency's letter of 17th October, 1942, I have the honor to give you the racial theory regarding the Arab caste. The racial policy has been adopted by Germany to safeguard the German people against the Jews who, biologically, are different from the Middle East races. Accordingly, Europe has been opposing Jews for decades. The Germans do not fight the Jews because they are Semitic or because they come from the East, but for their character, egoism and their hostility to society . . . while Germany forbids the entrance of the Jews into her territory, she welcomes all Arabs of Semitic origin and cares for them. The attitude of the Germans for the Arabs is that of respect. Not a single official German source ever stated that the

Arabs originated from a lower caste. On the contrary, the racial theory of National Socialism considers the Arabs of a very high caste. The oppression of the Arabs of Palestine is being followed in Germany with great interest and Germany confirms the demands of the Arabs.[116]

In contrast to the exhaustive research conducted in over six decades with regard to the collaboration of Arab politicians with the Axis powers, Arab victims of Nazi Germany have received little attention. New preliminary research into Arab inmates of Nazi concentration camps between 1939 and 1945 reveals a forgotten aspect of the Holocaust. Although not incarcerated for racist or religious reasons, their fate was no less than that of millions of other non-Jewish inmates considered undesirable or troublesome for the Third Reich. Arabs did not belong to the class of "privileged" inmates but rather were the forgotten victims of Nazi Germany's policies.[117]

Most Arab inmates were arrested in France starting in 1943 and were taken by the Sicherheitspolizei (German security police) to the concentration camps, while a smaller number were arrested in different cities of the Reich and Austria. There were also records of transports of Arabs from Brussels and Tunis. The dates and places of arrest and imprisonment and categorizations of inmates helped define a few possible reasons for their incarceration and deportation. Identification of some Arabs as so-called NN (*Nacht und Nebel,* and designated political prisoners or resistance helpers) inmates and their committal to Hinsert, Mauthausen, and Gross-Rosen camps indicated that they fought for or collaborated with the French Resistance. A number of Arabs sent to the concentration camps presumably breached their contract as slave workers or POWs bound for work in occupied Europe and were sentenced by courts on grounds of absence from work, crimes against wartime economy, and other offenses.[118]

Databases and archives of the concentration camp memorial sites revealed people who, by their names and birth places, might have been Arabs. According to some studies, possibly 350 to 1,500 Arab inmates were sent to Nazi concentration camps. While not close to the scale of Jewish incarceration and systematic deliberate liquidation, evidence for Arab presence is found in Auschwitz (25 inmates), Bergen-Belsen (21), Buchenwald (152), Dachau (78), Flossenbürg (39), Sachsenhausen (38), and Mauthausen (57), to name a few. Two Arab inmates were at Sachsenhausen at the time of Al-Husseini's and Gaylani's collaborators' visit to the Sachsenhausen camp in July 1942. Most of the inmates came from French North Africa or Vichy French Algeria (205), Morocco (23), Tunisia (19), Egypt (5), Iraq (4), Vichy French Lebanon (1), Palestine (4), and Vichy French Syria (1). Some Arab Jews came mostly from Libya and Yemen. Ninety-five percent of Arab inmates fell under the SS category of *politische* (political) or *schutzhaftling* (protective custody), which was marked with a red triangle on prison clothes. Most Arab inmates were registered as French and in addition had the letter "F" inside a red triangle.[119]

German Misinterpretation of Iraq: A Strategic Error?

The Iraqi campaign represented a stance of resolution and action in the eyes of the British. Although some leading Nazi officials advocated the exploitation of the fragile British position in Iraq, Churchill expressed after the war that "Hitler cast away the opportunity of taking a great prize for little cost in the Middle East."[120] Grobba was to say after the war in his memoirs, "The rejection of every unilateral German initiative in the Arab region was due to the fact that Hitler's enemies in the Foreign Office worked against any expanding the war to the Middle East. In part, they did not recognize the opportunity there and in part obstructed it."[121] This is Grobba's assessment of "wasted opportunities" in regards to Nazi Germany's Middle East policy during the 1930s. According to his memoirs, Germany did not take advantage of the Arab hostility toward both Britain and France. General Franz Halder, chief of the general staff between 1938 and 1942, concurred with Grobba's assessment in his foreword to a study on German involvement with Arab national movements, prepared for the U.S. Army by two former German officers involved in the Arab East during the war. Halder observed,

> German efforts to exploit the Arab nationalist movements against Britain lacked a solid foundation. Occupied by other problems more closely akin to his nature, Hitler expended too little interest on the political and psychological currents prevalent in the Arab world. . . . In the diplomatic, propaganda and military fields, Germany had neglected to prepare the ground for a serious threat to Britain in the area of that country's important land communication route between the Mediterranean Sea and the Indian Ocean. . . . No uniformly thought out plan was developed for the exploitation of the Arab nationalist movements.[122]

Although Hitler did approve the shipment of arms to Iraq, he was reserved about the news concerning British troops disembarking at Basra with provisions on the way. Replying to the foreign office, Hitler said, "In view of the English landings in Iraq, it was too late."[123] On May 3, a day after the start of hostilities at Habbaniya, Ribbentrop pushed for German action in the region. Ribbentrop appealed, "If the available reports are correct regarding the relatively small forces the English have landed in Iraq so far, there would seem to be a great opportunity for establishing a base for warfare against England through an armed Iraq. A constantly expanding insurrection of the Arab world would be of the greatest help in our decisive advance toward Egypt." Ribbentrop, in his brief to Hitler, added the following statement: "The figures regarding the British in Iraq show again how weak England still is at the Suez Canal."[124]

Ribbentrop was not alone in lobbying the exploits of initial German-Iraqi action in support of the Gaylani Revolt. In fact, Ernst Woermann, chief of the German foreign ministry's political department, and Ernst Freiherr Von

Weizsäcker, secretary of state under the foreign ministry, were two diplomats that were staunchly opposed to Operation Barbarossa. Along with Grobba, they were essential in bringing to Ribbentrop's attention the possibility of German achievements in the Arab East. In his memoirs Ribbentrop stressed Germany's need to identify itself with Arab Nationalism and its drive for independence, stating, "In the last war, we did not take advantage of the opportunities that we had as a result of the friendly attitude of the Arabs towards us, because we did not promise the Arabs the independence that would have been a precondition for their active rebellion."[125]

Earlier, State Secretary of the German Foreign Ministry Weizsäcker gave the mufti's secretary, Haddad, the following declaration, which was broadcasted by German and Italian Arabic radio services on October 23, 1940: "Germany, which has always been animated by sentiments of friendship for the Arabs and cherishes the wish that they may prosper and assume a place among the peoples of the earth in accordance with their historic and natural importance, has always watched with interest the struggle of the Arab countries to achieve their independence. In their efforts to attain this goal, Arab countries can count upon Germany's full sympathy also in the future. In making this statement, Germany finds herself in full accord with her Italian ally."[126]

Italy forced officials in Berlin to refrain from taking any lead in Arab affairs. At the same time, Germany refused to launch any initiative that would serve to encourage the outbreak of liberation movements in the Levant and as a consequence jeopardize the working relationship with Vichy France. Instead, German officials reaffirmed their support for Italy's interpretation of the October 23 declaration. As Weizsäcker stated, "As long as we are still in the war, we should tell the Arabs only what we are fighting against, namely England, and only speak of the 'liberation of the Arab world' without any detailed reference to any goals for the future."[127] However, the question of rendering aid to the Arab independence movement ultimately came to the test following the March 1941 coup in Iraq that returned Rashid Ali Al-Gaylani to the post of prime minister. It is important to note that Hitler's decision to send aid to the pro-Axis faction in Iraq occurred only after hostilities had begun.[128] This may be fine in hindsight, but when Weizsäcker was an active diplomat, the Germans really saw the potential of exploiting anti-British discontent in the Near East, and coupled this with extensive studies to derive not only military operational benefits, but access to lines of communication, and natural resources that are the sinews of war.

To understand the level of detail with which the Germans examined Iraq, the Marienbad Research Institute provided detailed maps and sketches of railroad points in which 12,000 tons of chrome were transported through Iraq, and highlighted a bridge over the Euphrates River that could disrupt supplies of chrome. German strategic planners used the private sector to derive targeting information, in this instance focusing on Iraq.[129]

Though contact between the German armed forces and the foreign office over the Iraqi situation was absent, there were a number of officers who were aware of the region's great potential, and were at least partial to the Arab East as a substitute front to Barbarossa and the Russian front. Principal advocates were commander in chief of the Kriegsmarine (German navy), Grand Admiral Erich Raeder, and Hermann Goering. Raeder believed that a campaign against the Soviet Union should be postponed, stating, " The C-in-C, Navy, recommends postponing this until after victory over Britain, since demands of German forces would be too great, and an end to hostilities could not be foreseen. . . . Russia, on her part, will not attempt to attack in the next few years."[130]

The German naval staff further asserted that operations in the eastern Mediterranean could prove "decisive for the outcome of the war."[131] Raeder, endorsed by Mussolini, went on to state, "Duce (Italy) urgently demanded a decisive offensive of Egypt's Suez for fall of 1941; requiring 12 divisions. This stroke would be more deadly to the British Empire than the capture of London."[132] Raeder pushed for a German seizure of Gibraltar (with Spanish assistance) and the Suez Canal, followed by a move on Palestine and Syria.[133] On February 13, 1941, Raeder pointed out to Hitler and senior military commanders that the British position in the central Mediterranean was weak, and that Axis air and sea forces currently had the upper hand; he urged that "The Suez and Basra positions are the western pillars of the British position in the Indian Ocean. Should these positions collapse under the weight of concentrated Axis pressure the consequences for the British Empire would be disastrous."[134] By concentrated Axis pressure, Raeder meant coordination with the Japanese and a combined naval plan of attack on Alexandria and Suez in conjunction with Rommel's Afrika Korps, who would be pushing east from Libya. Hitler was too obsessed with planning for the June 1941 invasion of Russia and blinded by his pathological hatred of what he termed Judeo-Bolshevism to see the unique strategic opportunity presented to him by Raeder and Rommel.

Mussolini's intelligence apparatus assessed that the United States would intervene in Egypt on the side of the British; this assertion was shared by the Italian and German dictators alike. This assessment was deduced from the massive American Lend-Lease aid flowing into Egypt for British forces fighting Rommel, combined with intercepts of Brigadier General Russell Maxwell establishing a military mission in Cairo.[135] The Italians could not understand that Lend-Lease meant equipment only, and could not fathom that American combat forces would not eventually follow into Egypt; it was a classic case of mirror imaging in intelligence analysis.

An additional memo outlining an alternative to Barbarossa was written by the head of the German naval historical office, Rear Admiral Kurt Assmann, and was discussed in a briefing with Hitler:

The British power position in the eastern Mediterranean is under the severest pressure as a result of the Balkan campaign and the occupation of Crete, but it is . . . not yet broken. All the signs indicate, moreover, that the British are in no way inclined to give up their position in the eastern Mediterranean. On the contrary, England appears determined to maintain her position in this area by every means. This is based, as in all areas of decisive importance for the British Empire, upon the exercise of control of the sea by the British battle fleet. . . . It alone is in the position to protect the maritime lines of communication which are essential for the control of the eastern Mediterranean position and to secure the power political influence in Egypt, Palestine, Iraq and to a considerable extent in Turkey, with its ramifications in the African, Indian and even the Far Eastern regions. Upon its shoulders, too, rests the prestige of the British Empire in the eastern Mediterranean. As always, therefore, it remains the aim of German-Italian strategy to destroy the British fleet as the controlling factor, to drive it out of the eastern Mediterranean and to eliminate its bases and operational possibilities in the Mediterranean.[136]

On June 30, 1940, a memorandum drafted by General Alfred Jodl, chief of the operations staff of the High Command of the German armed forces, stated two distinct possibilities regarding Britain's defeat: "(1) A direct assault on the British Isles (Operation Sealion), and (2) Enlarging the war on British periphery."[137] He submitted a memorandum to Hitler that first included the Mediterranean area as a potential theater of operations.[138] The most essential strategy was the seizure of Gibraltar and capture of the Suez Canal, thereby sealing off the Mediterranean. By mid-September the Luftwaffe was unable to achieve the necessary air superiority over the channel and southwest England. This forced Hitler to alter his views about Sealion. A peripheral strategy now appeared more relevant. Grand Admiral Erich Raeder told Hitler on September 26 that the "British have always regarded the Mediterranean as the pivot of their world empire."[139] Raeder went on to state,

[A]n advance from Suez through Palestine and Syria as far as Turkey is necessary. If we reach that point, Turkey will be in our power. The Russian problem will then appear in a different light. Fundamentally, Russia is afraid of Germany. It is doubtful whether an advance against Russia from the north will, by then, by necessary. There is also the question of the Dardanelles. It will be easier to supply Italy and Spain if we control the Mediterranean. Protection of Italian East Africa is assured. The Italians can wage naval warfare in the Indian Ocean. An operation against British India could be feigned.[140]

Jodl suggested utilizing the Abwehr to provide assistance to the Arab countries as part of the peripheral strategy. German official statements constantly spoke of liberation of the Arab world, without detailed reference to any goals for the future. The German attitude to Arab Nationalism was largely one of indifference. Even the prospects of gaining access to Middle East oil did not have the lure one might have expected, for Hitler and his military advisers were convinced that the war would be a short one, and the oil supplies provided by Romania were sufficient for Germany's needs. Interestingly, this indifference was enough to sustain the hopes of Gaylani, Naji Shawkat, and Al-Husseini.[141]

Admiral Assmann further stated, "[I]n spite of other considerable demands upon German armed forces (BARBAROSSA), all current problems in the area must be tackled and all operational possibilities at present available unconditionally utilized in order to be able to exploit the full considerable successes recently obtained in the Mediterranean at a time when the help of the United States to England has yet to reach decisive proportions."[142]

During his testimony at the Nuremberg Trials, the former chief of the Luftwaffe Herman Goering stated that Germany should have "attacked England at Gibraltar and Suez." Goering stressed, "The exclusion of the Mediterranean and Near East as a theater of war, the key point Gibraltar-North Africa down to Dakar-Suez, and possibly extended further south, would have required only a few forces, a number of divisions on the one side and a number of divisions on the other, to eliminate the entire insecurity of the long Italian coast line against the possibility of attack." Goering concluded his views on a Mediterranean campaign by stating that he "urged Hitler to put these decisive considerations in the foreground and only after the conclusion of such an undertaking to examine further the military and political situation with regard to Russia."[143]

One of the rare contacts between the foreign office and the German High Command provided evidence to the German military's interest in a Near Eastern campaign. Speaking in response to a memo from Woermann "regarding arms deliveries to Iraq and the associated Arab questions," the German High Command presented a summary of "its wishes regarding a strengthening of German activity in the Arab countries."[144] The German High Command called for a reexamination of Italy's freedom of action in the region and making a move to redirect "political activity in the Middle East from Germany and to take quick and vigorous action in this matter."[145] It goes on to stress the importance of German "recognition of the independence of Arabia as a war aim of the Axis. We are in a favorable position in so far as we need not promise the Arabs a merely 'tolerable' solution of the Jewish question in Palestine but can with a good conscience make the Arabs any concession in this field."[146]

While meeting with Benito Mussolini to discuss the Iraq situation, Ribbentrop voiced the following idea: "[I]f a sizable arms shipment reached Iraq, airborne troops could then be brought into the area, which could then with the material on hand advance against the English and from Iraq, in certain circumstances, they could attack Egypt from the east."[147] Mussolini found Ribbentrop's proposal commendable, stating, "Iraq had to be helped in any case . . . for in this way a new front would be opened up against the English and a revolt not only of the Arabs, but also of a great number of Mohammedans would be started." Mussolini was convinced that "the possessions of this center of the British Empire with its oil wells might have an even more profound impact upon the British world position than a landing in the British Isles themselves."[148]

One can conclude that had Hitler succeeded in defeating Russia in 1941, the amount of time required to conquer territory in the Middle East could have been measured in months. German military planning at the strategic level planned for options of moving the German army in Russia to the Caucasus, then Turkey, and then to Syria. In addition, the military forces needed might have amounted to twenty to thirty armored and infantry divisions for such a task, a mere fraction compared to the four million men assembled for Barbarossa. Knowing that a concentration in the Middle East might have resulted in an Axis victory, it is easy to understand why German policy in the eastern Mediterranean in the spring of 1941 is worthy of criticism. Assuming that Hitler was discouraged by the failure of Barbarossa and selected a drive into the Arab East, the Axis gain would have been the enormous reserve of oil of both Iraq and Persia. Germany would have been in an excellent position to flank and threaten Soviet oil fields in the Caucasus. Italy's ability to participate in Axis operations was severely shortened after its navy's oil stocks ran out in June of 1941 and the Italians were requesting some 500,000 tons of oil in "supplementary requirement for the first half of the year."[149]

One can conclude that the mineral resources lifted from the Arab East would have given Hitler the vast versatility needed for Barbarossa. Furthermore, in view of the Suez Canal's significance, one can infer that an effective German pincer action would have stalled the Allied flow of communications and supplies. The closure of the Suez Canal would have severely handicapped the British ability to transport materiel from the Mediterranean theater to the Pacific theater. An exploitation of the pro-Axis coup in Iraq would have most likely changed the face of the war and would have afforded the Axis its stocks of oil, which would have revitalized the needed firepower of the Italian Navy. Thus, an Axis victory in the Near East would have cut off British possessions in India and British-held Africa.[150] Fritz Grobba explained,

> The Iraq conflict offered Germany a unique opportunity to gain a foot-hold behind the British frontline in the Middle East from which to launch a very effective pincer operation against Egypt and the Caucasus. Successful German operations in Iraq and Egypt would have opened the way to India and, by posing a serious threat to India, would have created favorable conditions for an agreement with England. . . . This opportunity was not recognized in time by influential policy makers at the Foreign Office and the Army High Command, and was, due in part to their opposition to Hitler, consciously not seized upon. The lack of understanding of the Middle East on the part of high-level German military leaders and the opportunities

arising from exploiting the indigenous movements for the German war strategy had already come to the fore in the First World War.[151]

Churchill was to later state, "Hitler certainly rejected a brilliant opportunity to gain a great prize in the Middle East with a minimum of investment."[152]

Conclusion

There are many lessons that American forces and military planners can learn from the Axis and Allied experiences in Iraq, as well as from the construct of the Iraqi military during the Ottoman and monarchic periods. But first, the writings concerning Iraq's development as a nation-state require reexamination with an eye to Operation Iraqi Freedom that has taken Iraq into a new phase as a nation-state. British memoirs, British intelligence reports, and German sources, as well as several key Arabic books, allow a fuller view of the evolution of Iraq's political and military history. These sources also provide us with an explanation of how the Iraqi military had interjected itself in the country's political life. British influence in Iraq was limited to only a small segment of the population, the Sunni Arabs. In the end, the focus of the British presence in Iraq was to maintain access to strategic bases and air routes to India as well as energy resources. Therefore Iraq's constitution and electoral politics during the monarchy were geared toward maintaining Britain's position in Iraq. The United States and coalition partners more than eight decades later have striven to include and empower the various segments of Iraqi society. Even when the Sunnis boycotted the January 2005 elections, other population groups within the Iraqi provisional government showed great statesmanship and included Sunnis in the drafting of the constitution and in the government in general. Recently, Prime Minister Nuri al-Maliki has begun moving against his Sunni and Kurdish political rivals, which can only increase fears of sectarianism. The experiment is ongoing and is not immune from the violence across the border in Syria. Integrating Iraqis in quelling violence was also a key improvement in the management of Operation Iraqi Freedom with the bringing in of the Sunni tribesmen under the label "Sons of Iraq."

The British handling of the 1920 Revolt lasted four months and led to more than 2,000 British (including Indian auxiliaries) and 8,450 Iraqi casualties.[153] It is unclear if World War II military planners attempting to quell the 1941 Gaylani Revolt thought of the 1920 Revolt. On the positive side, the British mandate in Iraq did plant the seeds of modern industrial capabilities for Iraq in the political, military, and economic, as well as petroleum, sectors. Much of the British infrastructure in the petroleum industry was still found operational by U.S. forces in Operation Iraqi Freedom several decades later. However, on the negative side, the British focus during the mandatory period was not to get Iraq on its feet and give the Iraqi people the liberty to choose their form of government, but rather to maintain British dominion in the region. It is vital to distance Operation Iraqi Freedom from any references to the old British mandate system. This includes rebutting such news channels as Al-Jazeera, wherein the terms "imperialism," "colonialism," "occupier," and "the United States" are used interchangeably in programming. This conjures up memories of the past for many Iraqis, which is an unfair and out-of-context characterization of U.S. intentions in Iraq.

Other lessons learned from the Iraqi monarchy were the call for constant vigilance against anti-government cells within the Iraqi military and the need to enshrine in culture and in the constitution an apolitical officer corps, emphasizing the peaceful and constructive methods officers can bring forth grievances to seniors. As to the Kurds, while the clouds of war gathered over Europe in 1939, General Maxime Weygand obtained promises from Kurdish Nationalist leaders to refrain from any action that might antagonize Turkey.[154] Weygand hoped for Turkey to join an alliance against the Germans; eventually he would become a Vichy collaborator after the 1940 fall of France, working with the Nazis and against de Gaulle's Free French forces. Aside from the Kurds being used as Iraqi levies supporting the British in World War II, in 1942 the Society for the Revival of Kurdistan was organized in Mahrabad, Iran.[155] The party mainly comprised academics whose primary goal was to develop an independent Kurdish state.[156] The Soviets would carve out a small section of northwestern Persia in 1945, declaring it the Republic of Mahrabad on January 22, 1946. This republic would last until December 15, 1946, when upon the evacuation of Soviet forces from Iran, the shah's army would reclaim the territory in what was the first Cold War showdown between the United States and the Soviet Union over Iranian sovereignty. It was not lost to the Axis and Allies that Kurdish Nationalist resistance had been an internal problem in Turkey, Syria, Iraq, and Iran. This was made worse by famine in Kurdish regions of Iraq in 1943 and in Turkey by the government in Ankara imposing legislation forcibly assimilating the Kurds in 1938.[157]

Further examination concerning the greater narrative of the Middle East is required at all levels of our advanced military education in the twenty-first century. Arabic books spanning the Ottoman, Hashemite, and Ba'athist periods require not only translation, but also analysis and discussion amongst America's civil-military professionals. Included in appendix 2 of this book is an exposé of this conflict written by Iraqi army officer and military historian Mahmood al-Durrah, who fought against the British in the 1941 Gaylani Revolt. The abridged and synthesized translation of al-Durrah's Arabic book *Al-Harb Al-Iraqiyah Al-Britaniah* (the Iraqi-British war, 1941) was published in 1969 and was introduced to U.S. military readers by Commander Aboul-Enein in the November/December 2008 edition of the U.S Army *Armor Journal*.[158] This was at a time when U.S. forces were still actively engaged in Operation Iraqi Freedom, and was part of the authors' personal effort to provide Arabic work of military significance and to incorporate these perspectives in the training and discussion of units and personnel deploying to Iraq. A question I would pose as a case study in discussion is, Did Rashid Ali Al-Gaylani espouse Nazi ideology, or was he a pragmatist wanting to secure Iraq's autonomy from the British? Another question is to force comparisons between Gaylani's relationship with the Nazi regime and that of the grand mufti of Jerusalem. I leave the readers to ponder these questions and reach their own conclusions.

An excellent piece of literature that extrapolates Iraq's military-political past into current events takes the form of a booklet published in 2003 entitled *U.S. Policy in Post-Saddam Iraq: Lessons from the British Experience*, edited by Michael Eisenstadt and Eric Mathewson.[159] Perhaps the biggest lesson for America's military planners is the ability of an adversary to gradually create a hostile environment against forces present in the region; the Axis investment in years of anti-British propaganda bore fruit with revolts in the region. It led the British to choose between securing Egypt against Rommel, peacekeeping in Palestine, or seeing Iraq implode and fall under Axis influence. The Axis upset the balance of British power whereby British Palestine provided strategic depth to defend Egypt and the Suez Canal. In addition, Palestine provided air routes to India and overland routes to Iraq. The Baghdad-to-Haifa road was a means by which British planners intended to flow British Indian army units to reinforce Egypt. Haifa was the terminus for an oil pipeline that provided vital petroleum supplies from Iraq and an alternative light naval base to ease the traffic at the massive port in Alexandria.[160] The stakes could not have been higher. We will see in the next chapter another operation that would divert Axis and Allied resources in Syria.

CHAPTER 4

Vichy French Syria
Operation Exporter

Choose the neighbor before the house.

—Syrian saying

Political Prelude

The defeat of pro-Axis Iraqi regiments led by Prime Minister Rashid Ali Al-Gaylani and the British effort to end the siege of the Habbaniya Royal Air Base led to the reevaluation of asymmetric agitation in the Middle East by Axis powers. Although the European, Russian, and North African fronts in World War II garner much attention when students learn about World War II, it is vital that students also reexamine obscure campaigns such as the one in Syria. These campaigns offer potential lessons in the current war on terrorism that now occupies three major ongoing crises of strategic interest to the United States today in Iraq, Afghanistan, and Syria/Lebanon.

British military planners designed Operation Exporter, which was to put an end to German influence and agitation in the Middle East theater of operations. British military and political leaders were concerned that Vichy (pro-Nazi) French occupation of Syria was a strategic threat to surrounding Allied oil supplies in Iraq, Iran, and the Persian Gulf region. Operation Exporter combined British and Free French forces in a plan to invade Syria in June 1941. The Luftwaffe was attacking the Suez Canal from the Dodecanese Islands and could possibly operate against Syria, specifically with airborne troops. The aims of the Allies were to occupy Syria and Lebanon, thereby preventing the establishment of an Axis presence that could threaten British bases in Palestine and oil refineries at Abadan and, consequently, enhance Britain's broader strategic position in the eastern Mediterranean.[1]

Syria and Lebanon had been French protectorates since 1919. From 1920 British colonial policy makers worked diligently to create in Iraq a centralized government ruling over a population that was disparate and heterogeneous in the extreme. It had no ties of loyalty to the nation-state of Iraq nor did it have affection for its ruler King Feisal I; the only constants were tribal allegiances. Syria, on the other hand, was governed under France's colonial policy and was not faced with the same problem as British-mandated Iraq. The French were able to pursue a more traditional policy of divide and rule. The old Ottoman Turkish province of Lebanon, with its Christian majority, would be extended to form the state of Greater Lebanon. However, the area of Christian Maronite concentration lacked any resources so Sunni and Shiite sections were stitched together to form the current Lebanese state that would retain a Christian majority at the time of creation. Areas inhabited by the Druze and Alawi minorities were formed into the states of Jebel Druze and Latakia, while the former province of Alexandretta, with its Turkish population, was granted autonomous rule.[2]

Syria was originally divided into two states, Damascus and Aleppo; it was reunited in 1925 partly as a result of Nationalist pressures and civil unrest. *Syria: A Country Study*, published in 1979 by the U.S. Government Printing Office, contains this excerpt describing the politics of the period:

> Sheikh Salih ibn Ali led the Alawis; Sheikh Ismail Harir rebelled in the Hawran; and in the Jebel Druze, Sultan Pasha Al-Atrash, kinsman of the paramount chief of the Druze, led continual resistance, most notably in 1925 calling for unity. On February 9, 1925, to pacify these factions, the French permitted the nationalists to form the People's Party. This party was led by Faris Al-Khuri and demanded French recognition of eventual Syrian independence. After the Nazi defeat of France in May-June 1940, French authorities in Syria recognized the Vichy Government of Field Marshal Philippe Petain and appointed a new Syrian cabinet headed by Khalid Al-Azm, a son of the Ottoman Minister of Religious Affairs and member of a wealthy Damascus family, as acting President and Prime Minister.[3]

Syria assumed vital importance in the link between Turkey and the British position in Palestine and Egypt. It therefore became necessary for the Allies to gain control of the Levant. The question was raised regarding how this would play out. The British did not have enough troops to do it themselves, and they did not want the Turks to intervene for fear of offending the Arabs in Syria and elsewhere. The Free French movement in the mandate was, in the words of a Middle East command appreciation, "virtually dead from repression and lack of internal leadership."[4]

A possibility was to stir up the native population, citing that many tribal leaders, especially Druzes, had offered to cooperate with the British and, like most Nationalists, hoped for British intervention to remove French control. The former governor of French Indochina, General Georges Catroux, suggested that the best way to gain Arab support was to issue a Free French declaration, promising Syrian and Lebanese independence—simultaneously safeguarding French interests—along the lines of the Anglo-Egyptian Treaty. Catroux was the most senior French general to side with the Free French and de Gaulle. The British and Free French were in touch with General Maxime Weygand, Vichy's proconsul to the North African colonies, in an attempt to induce him to join the Allied cause. It was agreed at a meeting between General Catroux and Wavell and British high commissioner in Cairo Sir Miles Lampson that "no definite conversations with the Syrian national leaders in Iraq are expedient until question of Gen Weygand's attitude is cleared up, as any attempt to negotiate now might provoke trouble against the present French authorities in Syria and against Weygand."[5]

Vichy French and the Syrian Cabinet after June 1940

After the fall of France in 1940, Britain's predicament in the Near East was increasingly unstable when the French authorities in Syria and Lebanon aligned themselves with the new Vichy government. The British, already outnumbered by Italian forces and uncertain of Arab loyalties, now found their northern flank controlled by men susceptible to Axis demands.[6] The Vichy French sphere of influence over Syria provided safe passage and refueling for Luftwaffe planes that were en route to aid in an Iraqi revolt that began in April–May of 1941 and was suppressed by the British that same year. Vichy France allowed Germany and Italy full landing and provisioning rights in Syria; the right to establish a Luftwaffe base at Aleppo; and permission to use ports, roads, and railways for transport of equipment to Iraq and train Iraqi soldiers in Syria with French weapons.[7]

Major General Sir Edward Louis Spears was a close friend of Churchill's who had served as liaison officer between the British and French military commands during the First World War and whose British liaison mission frequently placed him in de Gaulle's company; he strongly supported the view that "it was essential to ensure that the Vichy Government did not . . . allow the Germans to get a grip on the Middle East."[8] Throughout April and May 1941 it was Spears who had gone above and beyond to support de Gaulle's and Catroux's demands for a joint Anglo–Free French move into the Levant. As late as July 19, 1941, de Gaulle had written to Oliver Lyttelton, British minister of state in Cairo, expressing his satisfaction at the appointment of Spears as head of the British liaison mission in Syria. Wavell was not unaware of this issue, but with many demands on his resources he saw no option but to encourage the neutrality of Vichy French Syrian high commissioner Henri Dentz.[9]

The Vichy French high commissioner and commander in chief of the Armée du Levant (army of the Levant) General Henri Dentz was convinced by Admiral Jean-François Darlan, minister of the Navy, to allow German and Italian aircraft an air base for logistical support and refueling. Darlan was a French naval officer and senior figure of the Vichy France regime, a man close to Field Marshal

Pétain. The French admiral rose to commander of the entire Vichy French navy after the dismissal of Pétain's deputy, Minister of Foreign Affairs Pierre Laval, for ordering the entire fleet to French North Africa. This decision was a major mistake that allowed the British fleet to shell and destroy the Vichy fleet at anchor at the Algerian port of Oran. Darlan was also made minister of the interior, minister of defense, and minister of foreign affairs.[10]

The destruction of the Vichy French fleet that occurred during Operation Catapult by the Royal Navy at Mers-el-Kébir near Oran, Algeria, in July 1940, combined with the slaughter of French sailors and the decision to deprive the Axis of additional valuable warships, aroused anti-British sentiments among Vichy French officials.[11] This resulted in the furthering of Vichy Franco-German military cooperation. On May 9, 1941, Churchill telegraphed General Wavell:

> You will no doubt realize the grievous danger of Syria being captured by a few thousand Germans transported by air. Our information leads us to believe that Admiral Darlan has probably made some bargain to facilitate the Germans. In face of your evident feeling of lack of resources, we can see no other course open than to furnish Catroux with the needed transport and let the Free French do their best at the moment they deem suitable, the RAF acting against German landings. Any improvement you can make on this would be welcome.[12]

Axis Manipulation of Syrian Governments at Will

Vichy high commissioner Henri Dentz forced the resignation of neutral Syrian president Emile Iddi and appointed pro-Vichy president Alfred Naqqash. On May 8, 1940, it was reported to Berlin that French representatives had agreed to the following concessions from the Naqqash government: (1) The Naqqash government was to make available stocks of French arms under Italian control in Syria for arms transport to Iraq. (2) The Naqqash government was to forward arms shipments of other origin to arrive in Syria by land or sea for agitation in Iraq. (3) The Naqqash government was to grant permission to the Luftwaffe, destined for Iraq, to make intermediate landings and to take on gasoline in the Levant. (4) The Naqqash government was to provide for operations in Iraq for Axis reconnaissance pursuit planes and bombers, and the Vichy Air Force was to be permitted to operate from Syria in support of Axis operations in the region. (5) The Naqqash government was to provide an air base in Syria for Axis use and render technical assistance to German planes making intermediate landings.[13]

Having witnessed the events that led to the installation of a pro-Axis Syrian government, the British imposed an economic embargo on Syria in November 1940 that contained pro-Axis French actions along the eastern Mediterranean. The U.S. State Department opposed any restrictions on Syria, fearing that such an action would draw Syria even closer to the Germans and cause further repercussions on relations with neighboring Arab states.[14] Prior to the blockade, Syrian-German wartime trading succeeded in obtaining Syrian wool and silk, as well as casings, via the Turkish route for the manufacture of parachutes needed for the Luftwaffe and German paratroopers. The vitality of Syrian military trading with Germany was a crucial aspect of the Axis war effort.[15]

By late 1940 Nazi Germany had sent Arab affairs expert Werner Otto Von Hentig to Syria. His instructions were as follows:

> To report on the political and military situation in Syria and, so far as possible, the neighboring areas. Does England constitute a serious threat to Syria by way of Palestine? Are the resources of France adequate for defense? What progress is being made by the De Gaulle movement? What are the methods that British propaganda is operating and what success does it have?
>
> To gather relevant data for our policy toward the Arab states.
>
> To observe Germany's own interests of an economic and cultural nature and to report on them.[16]

This was to implement Hitler's objectives to inevitably use the Levant as a staging area for the assault on Mosul's oil fields in Iraq and the Suez Canal in Egypt. Von Hentig met with several influential leaders of the Syrian Nationalist factions, including future president of Syria Shukri al-Quwwatli (governed 1943–1949). After showing his credentials to General Dentz, Von Hentig energetically wooed local political and social leaders, showing them a film on the fall of France and reportedly inviting Muslim views on the formation of an Arab empire. They envisaged the convening of an Islamic congress at Damascus and inciting of extremists against Britain over the Palestine question. In addition, they discussed increasing German-Syrian economic cooperation and plans to undermine Allied influence in the Levant. The British consul general in Damascus reported in February 1941 that the Syrians were excited by Von Hentig's visit and Syrian nationalist leaders proclaimed their support to the advancement of the German cause.[17]

With the Axis juggernaut in the Balkans, Rommel's Afrika Korps in the Western Desert, and the Gaylani coup in Iraq, Syria was not among Britain's top priorities in early 1941. In April 1941, however, Free French leader General Charles de Gaulle arrived in Cairo for consultations with General Georges Catroux and the Allied Middle East command based in Egypt; on the agenda of the Free French was Syria. After the successful Allied landings in North Africa, code-named Operation Torch, Catroux was appointed commander in chief of Free French forces in the Middle East. At the Cairo conference, de Gaulle proposed the capture of Beirut, Damascus, and the tactically strategic Vichy French air base at Rayaq, located approximately forty-five miles east of Beirut, using Free French troops. However, the British were reluctant because of the heavy losses inflicted on the Western Desert, and did not want to risk thinning the battered Allied front against Axis positions in Libya against Rommel.[18]

De Gaulle suspected the British of moving into Syria themselves and creating a British mandate in Damascus. No doubt those fundamental differences emerged during the Anglo–Free French invasion of Syria and were marred by rash political tactics, poor liaison, and bad diplomacy; no doubt, too, they precipitated personal antagonism between Churchill and de Gaulle. Such was the legacy of the race for colonies started in the latter part of the eighteenth century. The bitter conflict over who exercised spheres of influence in the Middle East characterized Anglo-French relations preceding the 1916 Sykes-Picot Agreement that carved out the modern Middle East among the Allies.[19]

Vichy war minister General Charles Huntziger (who led the delegation that signed the capitulation of France at Forest of Compiègne in 1940) sent a message on May 4, 1941, to Dentz, Vichy high commissioner in Syria: "It is not impossible that you may shortly be faced with a German attempt to give assistance to Iraq. If formations of German aircraft should seek to land on your airfields or should fly over your territory, it would be expedient to consider that France is not in the position of a neutral power with respect to Germany. It is not possible to treat the armed forces of Germany as hostile, but you would naturally oppose with force any intervention by the British forces."[20] This was followed on May 6 by an order from Admiral Darlan to give German aircraft en route to Iraq every means of assistance to continue their journey. Darlan flew to Berlin for consultations with Hitler and Von Ribbentrop on May 12. The discussions ended with Darlan resolved to take a clear course of entering the war against Britain. Darlan was acting under the conviction that a Nazi victory was imminent. Winston Churchill, eager as ever for action, cabled Wavell:

> You will no doubt realize the grievous danger of Syria being captured by a few thousand Germans transported by air. Our information leads us to believe that Admiral Darlan has probably made some bargain to help the Germans to get in there. In face of your evident feeling of lack of resources we can see no other course open than to furnish General Catroux with the necessary transport and let him and his Free French do their best at the moment they deem suitable, the RAF acting against German landings. Any improvement you can make on this would be welcome.[21]

Future Nazi agreements with Darlan were foiled on December 24, 1942, when a twenty-year-old French anti-Nazi royalist, Ferdinand Bonnier de La Chapelle, waited for Darlan near his headquarters in Algiers and assassinated him. De La Chapelle was executed by firing squad two days later. Darlan was replaced as high commissioner by another French flag officer, General Henri Giraud.[22]

German aircraft had been operating from Syrian airfields since April 1941 to support a revolt against the British in Iraq. By the end of May 1941 there were 120 Axis planes (100 German and 20 Italian aircraft) operating in Syria that was a base of attack toward the British-controlled Suez Canal as well as opening the potential for air raids on the oil refineries at Abadan in the northern Persian Gulf. On May 14 the RAF was authorized to act against Axis aircraft in Syria and on French airfields. The Luftwaffe, operating from the Axis-held Dodecanese Islands and Crete, seized an opportunity to bombard Egypt and prepare to airlift German airborne troops from bases in Crete to reinforce Vichy Syria. Of note, the airlift of German troops to Syria never occurred. Italian bombing raids were also conducted on Haifa, Jaffa, and the Island of Bahrain that were from the Dodecanese Islands in October of 1940 utilizing Syrian air space. In August 1940 German agents arrived with ample support to arouse Arab Nationalism and anti-British and anti-Zionist feeling in Syria.[23]

Axis agents spread rumors through an extensive system of collaborators and informants that Nazi Germany was in favor of Syrian independence. In consequence, riots broke out in Damascus. The pro-Axis coup in Iraq began to threaten British interests in the region and hence brought Syria ever closer to Axis influence. Just a modest investment in information operations by the Germans led to what arguably was a successful diversion of Allied (mainly British) resources in Iraq. These are lessons applicable to the current conflict between the United States and Iran, whereby Tehran pursues multiple diversionary fronts short of outright war to weaken American objectives in the Middle East. The American consul in Beirut, Cornelius Van Engert, warned Syrian Nationalists of the harm that would befall their country if Syria fell into German hands. Syrian Nationalist leader, Fakhri Al-Baroodi, stated "[I]n the past, the fate of the Arabic speaking countries had been in the hands of London and Paris and the results had not been happy either."[24]

The Vichy French authorities dispatched weapons from Aleppo to Baghdad in support of Iraq's pro-Axis Rashid Ali Al-Gaylani's Revolt. The magnitude of the complicity of Syria in the Iraq revolt so heightened Allied distress that the American ambassador to England, John Gilbert Winant, was reported to have said, "[I]f however, this use by the Germans of Syrian territory for military purposes continues, it is evident that the results will be very serious indeed."[25]

The Vichy French further complicated the Allied situation by sending war materiel through neutral Turkey and conducting an Axis buildup on the Turkish southern frontier. From a strategic perspective, this meant Turkey's lines of communication could be cut off geographically from British India, as the Axis was now dominant in Greece and Syria, and was fomenting instability in British Iraq. All these Axis tactical, overt, and covert operations would erode Allied lines of communication with neutral Turkey.[26]

British foreign secretary Anthony Eden thought it

essential that we should make plans of our own and that we should take
the Turks to a large extent into our confidence; if once the Germans are able
to establish themselves in any strength in Syria and succeed in organizing
a part of the Arabs against us, Turkey will be effectively surrounded and it
would indeed be difficult then to count upon her enduring loyalty . . . taking
a long view, there is this further consideration: if, as a result of her isolation,
Turkey were to cave in and allow passage of German troops into Syria,
Germany would presumably be able to accumulate in due course important
armored forces in the Middle East. These forces would not be limited by
the difficulties of communication and supplies, which hamper any forces
advancing on Egypt from the west, and a more formidable German Army
could then be maintained and employed from Syria than from Tripoli. The
only way to stop this is for Turkey to hold fast, and that could only be
achieved at the earliest possible moment with the situation in Syria.[27]

The British agreed with de Gaulle's plan to wrest the Levant from the Vichy
French, and on May 20 indicated

Catroux's request was to be granted;

The Free French were to be given not only the transport they wanted but as
much military and air support as possible;

An immediate Free French declaration of independence for Syria and
Lebanon would be backed by Britain;

Entering these two territories (Syria and Lebanon) was to be regarded as a
political coup rather than a military operation.[28]

Vichy forces had postured themselves in positions where they clearly intended
to defend Syria against any British or Free French invasions. Allied Middle East
commander General Archibald Wavell cabled London that he was

moving reinforcements to Palestine and after full discussion with my colleagues because we feel we must be prepared for action against Syria, the
whole position in the Near East is governed mainly by air power and air
bases. Enemy air bases in Greece make our hold of Crete precarious and
enemy bases in Libya, Crete and Syria would make our hold on Egypt difficult. The object of the army must be to force the enemy in Cyrenaica as far
west as possible, to try to keep him from establishing himself in Syria, and
to hang on to Crete and Cyprus.[29]

This shows the central strategic position the Axis enjoyed in Syria, but at the
same time Arab politicians in Syria seemed enamored by German Nationalism,
hoping to duplicate this in the Arab experience.[30]

As hopes to hold on to Crete became impossible for the British, the possible Axis threat to Syria commanded great attention. Despite the approval of Operation Exporter, it almost did not take place as planned owing to a combination of military and political factors. On the military side, there were some last-minute doubts as to the wisdom of proceeding in Syria with Wavell's imminent counteroffensive in the Western Desert. On the political side, a bitter dispute arose between the British and the Free French over influence in Syria.[31]

The Free French regarded the Arab Nationalists in the mandate as a matter for their exclusive concern, regarding British attempts to influence them as part of a design to exclude France from the Orient altogether. The National Defense Research Committee endorsed the decision; this was an organization created under the aegis of the Council of National Defense to coordinate, supervise, and conduct scientific research on the problems underlying the development, production, and use of mechanisms and devices of warfare in the United States from June 27, 1940, until June 28, 1941. Churchill decided to take on both Crete and Syria. The counteroffensive in the Western Desert failed miserably, largely due to the decision for a simultaneous invasion of Syria. Meanwhile, Dentz took one more step to try to prevent the Allies from having a pretext to invade Syria. On June 6, 1941, Vichy aircraft dropped leaflets over various cities in Palestine that denied allegations that Syria was controlled by the Luftwaffe. The Vichy leaflets insisted that only a few Axis aircraft were permitted to pass through Syria en route to Iraq and that within a few days none of them would remain. Despite Dentz's attempts, Allied forces launched their invasion of Syria on June 8.[32]

To some extent, the possibility of an effective Vichy resistance in the Levant depended on Turkish involvement. The issues of reinforcements and war materiel were of great concern if the Levant army was to carry on fighting with little aid from Berlin, especially in regard to aviation fuel, since the Vichy armies were consuming an average of 200,000 liters (about 52,834 gallons) every day. Before the fighting commenced, Dentz urged for petrol supplies from his government and for aircraft, including anti-aircraft and armor-piercing weapons. Turkey's role occupied a major position in this respect. A good portion of German petrol had been stored in Turkey since early June of 1941, for which the Turkish government negotiated with the Germans and Vichy French for its transit to Greece and from European ports through Turkey and into Vichy Syria. The discussions agreed to seven trainloads of munitions, military personnel, and petroleum to cross from the European continent to Thessaloniki, Greece, by June 17; they then would proceed to Turkey by sea and end in Syria. However, this plan never materialized for the Axis since Ankara declined the Vichy French request and Turkey agreed to only petrol transport and not to the transit of war materiel and combat troop personnel.[33]

Preparations for Operation Exporter

General Archibald Wavell, commander in chief of the Middle East, aimed at gathering the largest possible force to occupy Syria at the earliest date. The Allied ground forces would be made up of the 1st Australian Corps (7th Australian Division and 6th Division: constituent brigades); 5th Indian Brigade; Free French Division with the use of twelve H-39 light tanks; and Iraqforce (the Allied force occupying Iraq, including the Indian 10th Infantry Division, the British 4th Cavalry Brigade, and the Arab Legion) and the 10th Indian Division. In all, 18,000 Anzac, 9,000 British, 5,000 Free French, and 2,000 British Indian troops participated in the operation. The RAF comprised twelve Fulmar, seventeen Swordfish, and four Albacore. General Wavell sent an outline of his plan for the invasion of Syria, code-named Operation Exporter, to London. On May 21, 1941, Wavell ordered the 7th Australian Division to be ready for deployment to Palestine and ordered General Henry Maitland "Jumbo" Wilson, who had assumed command of Palestine and Transjordan, to prepare a plan for an advance on Syria. On May 25, Wavell telegraphed his outline plan for Exporter.[34]

General Maitland Wilson saw active duty in the Second Boer War and World War I. In June 1939 Wilson was appointed commander of the British and Commonwealth forces tasked with the defense of Egypt and the Sudan. He planned a three-pronged advance: one each for Beirut, Rayaq, and Damascus, with possible diversionary raids on Tripoli in Lebanon and Homs in Syria. Wavell wondered aloud to senior British military officials if the Turks could be convinced to aid the Allies and thrust into Aleppo, which is only twenty miles from the Turkish border.[35]

Churchill seemed to mirror General Wilson's view of a Turkish thrust into Syria, commenting, "The defense of Egypt from the west and from the north under the increased weight of the air attack from Crete presents the standard military problem of a central force resisting two attacks from opposite quarters. In this case the choice seems clearly dictated by the facts . . . the attack through Turkey and/or through Syria cannot develop in great strength for a good many weeks."[36]

The British ambassador in Ankara approached the Turkish foreign minister, Mr. Sukru Saracoglu, on June 2. Saracoglu brought up the question of Syria in a conversation with Von Papen. Von Papen stated, "Turkey was afraid here of an English attack on Syria, which would perforce place Turkey under the necessity of taking the Baghdad railway and the area around Aleppo for the strategic protection of her position." Von Ribbentrop replied, "[W]e have no reason whatever to give any additional assurance beyond these advantages offered Turkey [in the treaty of non-aggression and friendship], with regard of Syria, which we cannot do in any case because of our relations with France."[37] Saracoglu conveyed to Britain that his government could not accept any Allied proposal to occupy Northern Syria, as this might involve it in war with France and, possibly, Germany. The Allied ground forces comprised the 7th Australian Division headed by Major General John Dudley Lavarack; the 5th Indian Infantry Brigade group led by Brigadier General Herbert William Lloyd; Free French Forces led by General Paul Le Gentilhomme (comprising six battalions and a company of tanks, and called Gent Force, named after Gentilhomme). Allied Air Force strength for Operation Exporter would consist of twenty-eight aircraft operating from Palestine and Cyprus.[38]

In reserve were the British 6th Infantry Division, the Australian 17th Brigade, and the Iraqforce (the Allied force occupying Iraq, including the Indian 10th Infantry Division, the British 4th Cavalry Brigade, and the Arab Legion). Hitler sent little support to the Levant, as his attention was diverted in Russia, the Balkans, and Britain, as well as in sustaining Axis forces in North Africa. Therefore, Allied forces would face primarily Vichy ground forces comprising the French Foreign Legion under General Dentz made up of eighteen battalions with 120 guns and 90 tanks—35,000 men in all, mainly Senegalese, Algerian, and Moroccan; 2,000 horsemen and motorized infantry with a few armored cars; an air force of about ninety aircraft; and a naval task force of two destroyers and three submarines based in Beirut.[39]

Allied Movements in the Levant

Plans called for the 21st Australian Brigade to advance north, from Palestine, along the Lebanese coast toward Beirut. The 25th Australian Brigade's objective was Rayaq Airfield, while the 5th Indian Brigade supported by Free French forces marched on Damascus. Upon completion of that phase, the next phase required these combined units to direct their efforts against Tripoli, Homs, and Palmyra.[40]

On the eve of the invasion, Churchill sent a telegram of goodwill to General de Gaulle:

> I wish to send you my best wishes for success of our joint enterprise in the Levant. I hope you are satisfied that everything possible is being done to provide support to the arms of Free France. You will, I am sure, agree that this action, and indeed our whole future policy in the Near East, must be conceived in terms of mutual trust and collaboration. Our policies towards the Arabs must run on parallel lines. We have sought no special advantages in the French Empire, and have no intention of exploiting the tragic position of France for our own gain. I welcome therefore your decision to promise independence to Syria and the Lebanon, and, as you know, I think it essential that we must not in any settlement of the Syrian question endanger the stability of the Near East. But subject to this we must both do everything possible to meet Arab aspirations and susceptibilities. At this hour, when Vichy touches fresh depths of ignominy, the loyalty and courage of the Free French save the glory of France.[41]

The Allied invasion of Vichy French Syria began on June 7, 1941, and met with strong opposition. The Vichy French resisted along all three of the Allied routes of advance. On June 8, while the 21st Australian Brigade crossed the Litani River on the coastal road heading for Beirut, two columns advanced from Jordan. On the Lebanese coastal section, fierce fighting occurred at the banks of the Litani River two days after the invasion to capture key bridgeheads along the river. The 21st Australian Infantry Brigade passed through the area. Sea bombardment of the Lebanese port of Sidon resulted in easy occupation on June 15. On the central route, Merdjayoun, located in southern Lebanon, was captured on June 11. On June 12 Wilson decided to transport the bulk of the Allied forces to Merdjayoun to take part in the coastal advance, via a mountainside route that passed through Jezzine. A rapid progress was made by the Indians and Free French forces toward Damascus but was halted within ten miles of the capital.[42]

Wavell called on the reserves of the 6th British division to advance on Palmyra, and two brigades of the 10th Indian Division in Iraq were ordered to march up the Euphrates River on Aleppo. On June 21 the Syrian capital fell to a combined Indian, British, Anzac, and Free French force. Fighting escalated in Lebanon, however, as the Allies struggled to take the important coastal center of Damour, located twelve miles south of Beirut, which the Allies secured on July 9.[43]

Allied concentration on Jezzine and coastal areas commenced. British forces headed north to Beirut and were within a few miles of the Lebanese capital by July 10. General Dentz's forces were diminishing and only one-fifth of his air force remained. At 8:30 a.m. on July 12, Vichy envoys arrived to negotiate for the armistice, which was signed at Acre on July 14 (Bastille Day), under the direction of General Maitland Wilson, which brought Syria into the Allied fold.[44] The Armistice of Saint Jean d'Acre was signed by both Dentz and his second in command, Lieutenant General Joseph Raoul de Verdillac, who represented the Army of the Levant during the Armistice signing ceremony; this concluded the Syria–Lebanon campaign. Vichy troops, auxiliaries, and equipment were handed over to the British. In January 1945 Dentz was sentenced to death for aiding the Axis, but de Gaulle reduced his sentence to life imprisonment.[45]

Allied Endgame

The British transferred the mandate administration to Free French forces, appointing General Catroux as delegate general and plenipotentiary. With orders from de Gaulle, General Catroux selected Taj Al-din Al-Hasani as president of Syria on September 12, 1941.[46] The French-appointed Syrian leader was to manage Arab Nationalist sentiment and help finance the war effort in return for an immediate end of the French mandate and Syrian independence.

Six hundred Palmach (infant Israeli Haganah) units participated in the invasion of Syria, alongside the Allies, conducting sabotage of transportation and communication networks. Among the famous members of the Palmach who participated in Operation Exporter were future Israeli chief of staff, minister of defense, and minister of foreign affairs General Moshe Dayan, and future Israeli prime minister General Yitzhak Rabin. Dayan received the British Distinguished Service Order (DSO) for his actions in the campaign while attached to the Australian 7th Division; he was in command of reconnaissance units of the Palmach sent to secure a bridge across the Litani River. Dayan's binoculars were hit by a French sniper's bullet as he surveyed the bridge. It is here Dayan lost his left eye, earning him his trademark eye patch.[47]

According to Churchill's memoirs, Operation Exporter "greatly improved our strategic position in the Near East. It closed the door to any further attempt at enemy penetration eastwards from the Mediterranean, moved our defense of the Suez Canal northwards by 250 miles, and relieved Turkey of anxiety for her southern frontier. The occupation and conquest of the Levant ended the German advance towards the Persian Gulf and India."[48]

The Palmach unit was established by the British on May 15, 1941, to aid in the protection of Palestine from Nazi threat. After the British victory at El-Alamein in 1942, the British ordered the dismantling of the Palmach unit. The whole organization instead went underground, combining military training with agricultural work, making the Palmach self-sufficient and self-funding. The Palmach placed heavy emphasis on training field commanders. Later, their military training by the British came to haunt the British position in Palestine. From the summer of 1945 until the end of 1947, when the British administration suppressed the Jewish settlement movement and blocked Jewish immigration into the country, the Palmach brought ships with tens of thousands of Jewish refugees and Holocaust survivors from Europe illegally. As British positions withdrew from Palestine in May 1948, the Palmach emerged to influence and contribute to Israel's military initial architecture. Upon the declaration of the state of Israel on May 15, 1948, the Israel Defense Forces was established. It was founded on the infrastructure of the Haganah and its striking force, the Palmach. The Palmach unit was dissolved after the formation of the Israel Defense Forces. During the war of independence of 1948 the Palmach units held the Jewish settlements of Gush Etzion, Kfar Darom, and Revivim against Arab militia.[49]

As far as the Levant was concerned, the British policy took the form of unrelenting pressure upon the Free French to implement their pledge of independence for the two countries, Syria and Lebanon. This naturally encouraged Nationalists and led to periodic confrontations between them and the French authorities. Continuing pressure from Syrian Nationalist groups forced the French to evacuate their troops in April 1946, leaving the country in the hands of a republican government that had been formed during the mandate.[50]

Pro-Axis Syrian leaders continued to misread the British victory of El-Alamein in Egypt. This, coupled with successful landings of Allied forces in Northwest

Africa, led to the belief that the tide was turning for the Axis. So immersed were Nationalist Syrian leaders in uniting Arabs using German Nationalist models perfected after the Franco-Prussian War of 1871 (which led to two world wars), that they misread the beginnings of what was a massive Russian counteroffensive against the Germans. Thus began the change in tide in 1942 that began to favor the Allies.[51] On the Allied side, the pacification of Syria and Iraq would absorb much needed Indian reinforcements that would have been used in Malaya or even to reinforce Egypt. In October 1940 Churchill and his foreign secretary Anthony Eden complained that Iraq tied down an entire corps (25,000 to 50,000), with Basra alone absorbing a division (10,000 to 15,000) in protection duties, and the suppression of riots.[52] This should remind us of General Eric Shinseki's 2003 wise Congressional testimony in the lead-up to Operation Iraqi Freedom, in which he stressed that the problem would not be invading Iraq, but the stabilization of the country that will require a half million troops.[53] It is among the "what ifs" that inhabit my own thinking, that had Shinseki been armed with this history in his remarks, would this have made a more convincing argument? I shall leave the reader to ponder this question.

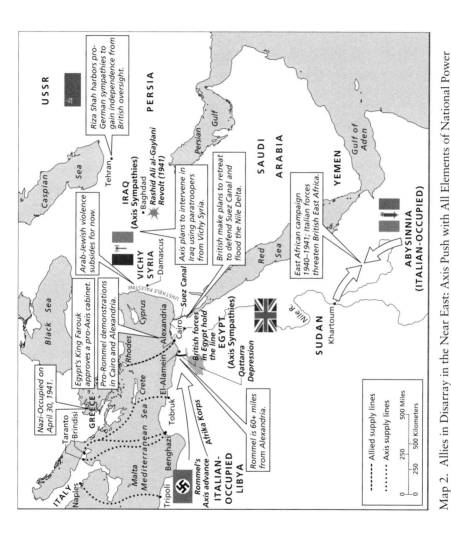

USSR

Riza Shah harbors pro-German sympathies to gain independence from British oversight.

PERSIA

Caspian Sea

Tehran

IRAQ
(Axis Sympathies)
• Baghdad
Rashid Ali al-Gaylani Revolt (1941)

Persian Gulf

SAUDI ARABIA

Black Sea

Arab-Jewish violence subsides for now.

Axis plans to intervene in Iraq using paratroopers from Vichy Syria.

VICHY SYRIA
Damascus

British make plans to retreat to defend Suez Canal and flood the Nile Delta.

YEMEN

Gulf of Aden

Egypt's King Farouk approves a pro-Axis cabinet.

Pro-Rommel demonstrations in Cairo and Alexandria.

Cyprus

UNSTABLE PALESTINE

Suez Canal

Red Sea

East African campaign 1940–1941; Italian forces threaten British East Africa.

ABYSSINIA
(ITALIAN-OCCUPIED)

Nazi-Occupied on April 30, 1941.

Rhodes

Cairo

British forces in Egypt hold the line

EGYPT
(Axis Sympathies)

Nile R.

SUDAN
Khartoum

GREECE

Crete

Alexandria

El-Alamein

Qattara Depression

Taranto
Brindisi

Afrika Korps

Mediterranean Sea

Tobruk

Rommel is 60+ miles from Alexandria.

ITALY

Naples

Malta

Benghazi

Rommel's Axis advance

ITALIAN-OCCUPIED LIBYA

Tripoli

------ Allied supply lines
‥‥‥‥ Axis supply lines

0   250   500 Miles
0   250   500 Kilometers

Map 2. Allies in Disarray in the Near East: Axis Push with All Elements of National Power

CHAPTER 5

Iran

Operation Countenance

Would His Highness kindly abdicate in favour of his son, the heir to the throne? We have a high opinion of him and will ensure his position. But His Highness should not think there is any other solution.

—Commonly understood among Iranians to be an ultimatum, given to Shah Reza Pahlavi by the British in 1941

Following Operation Barbarossa, the massive German assault on the Soviet Union on June 22, 1941, the struggling British swiftly gained a crucial ally against the Nazi war machine. The suppression of Gaylani's coup in Iraq and the removal of the pro-Nazi Vichy French control in Syria left Iran open to Allied intervention regarding supply lines for the Soviet Union. Iran would become a vital supply route of materiel and resources to Russia from the British position in the Persian Gulf and through the Caucasus as land routes. It would be the start of developing what the Allies would later call the Persian Corridor, a vital lifeline to Joseph Stalin. This corridor would see American Lend-Lease supplies flow to the Soviets facing the onslaught of the Wehrmacht. Operation Barbarossa would see war on a colossal scale from 1941 to 1944.

The Anglo-Soviet invasion of Iran is an important and often neglected chapter of World War II history. Those truly immersed in a lifelong study of the conflict find it to be a vital link to keeping the Soviets supplied with American Lend-Lease aid. The U.S. Army Center for Military History at Fort McNair has an entire volume of its multivolume *United States in World War II* series devoted to the Persian Corridor, entitled, "The Persian Corridor and Aid to Russia." The volume is the work of American military historian T. H. Vail Motter.[1] It became crucial to keep Iran free from Axis influence because Iran possessed massive petroleum reserves. Since Germany had invaded the Soviet Union and begun

100

its thrust toward the Crimea, the Allies saw Iran as the key to supplying them with much-needed petroleum, as well as a vital Allied logistics base leading to the Soviet Union. The Nazis were desperate to create additional fronts to divert the British from concentrating their efforts in conjunction with the Soviets. Both Allied and Axis leaders in 1941 saw Iran geostrategically as the objective of two massive German-led pincers from Russia: the Caucasus and Turkey on one end; and North Africa, Egypt, and Syria on the other end. The overriding concern among Allied strategists was the convergence of two Axis armies upon Iran. If successful, this would have enabled the European Axis powers to successfully overwhelm remaining opposition and link up with Imperial Japanese forces based in India.[2] Great Britain's key interest was maintaining steady petroleum supplies, which had been a strategic interest since World War I.[3]

Upon the discovery of oil reserves in Persia in 1908, the British Royal Navy, under the leadership of First Lord of the Admiralty Winston Churchill, vigorously pursued a policy of converting the fleet from coal- to oil-burning engines.[4] Upon completion of this project in 1912, the need to secure key positions in the world's oil market became of paramount concern within the British government.[5]

Persian oil prospects led to the establishment of the Anglo-Persian Oil Company (APOC; later the Anglo-Iranian Oil Company, which became British Petroleum) in 1909. The British government maintained majority stock in APOC.[6] Furthermore, given the growing threat to North Africa, the British were concerned that they might lose a main source of oil refining and transportation— Egypt—to the advancing Afrika Korps.[7]

The primary goal of the British and the Soviet Union joining forces in invading Iran was to secure the Abadan Oil Refinery, with an output of 8.6 million tons in 1940 and owned by the Anglo-Iranian Oil Company; it was vital that Iran's oil not fall to the Axis or that the Allied be deprived of Iranian oil.[8] Abadan's location was in close proximity to the Iraqi border. Iraq and its neighbor Syria were heavily influenced by German agents. Though much of the pro-Axis agitation was thwarted, it was still possible for the Axis to continue waging a propaganda war and sabotage the Allies by using the Arab population as pawns. The Nazis capitalized on anticolonial feelings. Through the Iraqi government under Rashid Ali Al-Gaylani, as well as the grand mufti, the Nazis did their best to curry favor among the world's Arab leaders, as described previously in this book.

Anglo-Soviet Policy: A Prologue

The existence of British and Soviet involvement in Persia predates both world wars. In 1800 Captain John Malcolm, a representative of the British East India Company, was sent to Persia to gain friendship with the Qajar shah, Fat'h Ali (ruled 1797–1834). This was to counter the ruler of neighboring Afghanistan, who displayed a propensity to attack British interests in India. Within a decade, an agreement between Persia and the British was reached. The agreement allowed Britain to train Persian troops in an effort to aid in containing Afghan tribes, who were becoming a challenge to both Persia and British India.[9]

Soviet interests in Persia, by contrast, had existed since the days of Tsarist Russia, which focused on building its landmass, as well as military and economic control over not only Eastern Europe, but also Central Asia. This naturally brought Russia into conflict with other European powers. As European influence spread to the Ottoman Empire, Russia believed it needed to assert itself in the region. Persia was east of the Ottoman Empire and, like the Ottoman Empire, had a land boundary with Tsarist Russia. It is at this time, during the late nineteenth and early twentieth centuries, that Russia placed economic and diplomatic pressure on Persia.[10]

Eventually, both British and Russian desires for Persian economic influence converged. Without prior consent of Persian officials, Russian and British authorities under the guise of the Anglo-Russian Convention of 1907 divided control of the region into three sections. The agreement gave control of the northern area to the Russians, and the southeast area to the British; the west and central sectors remained neutral. The Anglo-Russian Convention declared that the British and Russian governments had exclusive rights over the natural resources contained within their respective spheres of influence.[11]

Allied Course of Action in Iran

When World War II broke out in Europe, Iran officially declared itself neutral; at the same time, however, in order to break the continuous Soviet and British domination, Shah Reza Pahlavi (ruled 1925–1941) chose to establish economic ties with a rival power—the Germans. By this time, summer 1941, the Nazis had successfully campaigned against the Soviet Union, and Britain believed that its interests were threatened by Iran's neutrality and continued economic relationship with Nazi Germany. This provided the newly allied Soviets and the British with the impetus to invade Iran. The two allies rationalized the need to invade Iran, saying it was necessary in order to protect Allied oil interests and to prevent Iran from capitalizing on German technological ties that may undermine them in the Persian sphere that stretched from Iraq, to Afghanistan, to British India.[12]

In addition, Iran was ripe with Nazi propaganda. The word "Iran" means "Land of Aryans," and this point was not missed by Goebbels' propaganda machine. The Nazis, as part of their racial philosophy, searched for the origins of the Aryan peoples and thus blurred history and etymology to enhance Iranian–Nazi ties.[13] Shah Reza Pahlavi decreed in 1936 that all foreign nations refer to his nation as Iran (Land of the Aryans). Iran's military that was made up of 40,000 men in 1926 had swelled to 126,000 by 1941, to include fourteen divisions and five independent brigades comprising armor vehicles provided by the Czech firm

Skoda, which had been under Nazi control since 1938. Iran's air force consisted of two hundred obsolete British biplanes and a small navy of mainly coastal patrolling ships.[14]

The military strength of Iran's armed forces consisted of fourteen divisions and deployed nine divisions of troops. The Allies deployed the 44th, 47th, and 53rd Soviet armies along with the 8th and 10th Indian Infantry Divisions, the 21st Indian Infantry Brigade, the 2nd Indian Armored Brigade, and the 9th Armored Brigade for the Persian campaign. Hence, the shah's army was ill prepared against such an invasion.[15]

Another objective for the Allies, beyond the creation of a supply route, was the abdication and exile to Mauritius of Shah Reza in favor of his son, the young Mohammed Reza (ruled 1941–1977), who signed the Tripartite Treaty of Alliance in January 1942 between Britain, the Soviet Union, and Iran. This agreement reasserted Iranian sovereignty only after World War II, and in essence constituted one of three successful attempts at overt regime change in Iraq in 1941, Iran in 1941, and Egypt in 1942. The Soviets and the British, having several decades of almost unquestioned influence in Iran, sought to keep it that way, especially during World War II. Even during the Agreement's enforceability dates, the Soviets supplied Iranian separatists to prolong their influence over Iran after World War II.[16]

The Anglo-Iranian Oil Company had valuable concessions in Iran's Khuzestan Province; Moscow criticized the oil concessions between Iran and the British due to their proximity to the Soviet sphere of influence. In addition, with increasing American involvement in Iran, both London and Moscow saw a development they did not approve of—the encroachment of American oil companies into Iran in 1944.[17]

This resulted in friction between the Western Allies and the Soviet Union. Finally, the Soviets were defiant regarding the withdrawal of their troops. In March 1946 some Soviet troops were still occupying Iran and justifying this position under Article Six of the Russo-Persian Treaty of Friendship signed on February 26, 1921. Article Six stipulated

> If a third party should attempt to carry out a policy of usurpation by means of armed intervention in Persia, or if such Power should desire to use Persian territory as a base of operations against Russia, or if a Foreign Power should threaten the frontiers of Federal Russia or those of its Allies, and if the Persian Government should not be able to put a stop to such menace after having been once called upon to do so by Russia, Russia shall have the right to advance her troops into the Persian interior for the purpose of carrying out the military operations necessary for its defense. Russia undertakes, however, to withdraw her troops from Persian territory as soon as the danger has been removed.[18]

Iranian Ties with Nazi Germany

Shah Reza Pahlavi had fostered close economic and cultural ties with Germany since the Weimar Republic in 1921. Richard Stewart's excellent book, *Sunrise at Abadan: The British and Soviet Invasion of Iran*, is the definitive book on the subject. It details the depths of German–Iranian economic ties during the lead-up to World War II. Iran's trade with Germany rose from 8 percent to 60 percent of both combined import and export activity. Persian exports of cotton, barley, wood, rice, silver, gold, and other goods attracted the Germans. In exchange, Germany supplied Iran with industrial equipment, machinery, and motor vehicles. The Iranian railroad system boasted 2,100 bridges and 224 tunnels. The nine-hundred-mile railroad stretched from Bander-e-Shahpur on the Persian Gulf to the northwestern city of Mianeh close to the Russian border. The Iranian airline system was organized by German capital, equipment, and personnel. German engineers, builders, technicians, and architects composed the majority of the expatriates in Iran. In 1936 and 1937, Germany was Iran's largest trade partner.[19]

German diplomacy was considerably active in the region. During the late 1930s Nazi officials conducted goodwill trips to Middle Eastern capitals. Dr. Hjalmar Schacht, minister of economics (German), paid official visits to Istanbul and Tehran in 1935 to promote economic ties. Nazi propaganda continued to emphasize and reinforce the Aryan connections between Iran (land of the Aryans) and Nazi Germany. Iran and Afghanistan were the two countries of the Near East that Germany most actively sought to further their influence. Since British power and influence in Iran and Afghanistan were not as strong as in other parts of the Arab world or India, which at the time included modern-day Pakistan, the Axis was challenging Britain's position in North India. German aims were less likely to encounter British opposition. Hitler ordered the promotion of close economic ties between Germany and both Iran and Afghanistan in late 1936. By 1939 German political and economic influences in both countries had grown considerably. Between 1936 and 1939 both states would be provided sizeable amounts of armaments from Germany.[20]

There existed in Iran an active element of the Abwehr. Its primary mission was to gather intelligence about Soviet oil installations and military activities in the Caucasus. Another goal of these German agents was to infiltrate labor and government circles, thereby inciting the sabotage of British oil interests in Abadan. A military agreement between Britain and Iran was nonexistent in the event of a threat to Abadan refineries; however, the British could invoke the Anglo-Iraqi Treaty and land forces in nearby Basra. Interestingly, a contingency plan was drawn up code-named Trout. The objective was to dispatch a division of Indian troops to Basra for the purpose of securing vital Iraqi oil fields and Iranian oil installations that bordered Iraq. (It is worthwhile to note that the main threat envisaged during initial planning in March of 1940 was from the

Soviet Union.)[21] Many of these German agents operated under the direction of
Ambassador Grobba, the Nazi envoy in Baghdad, who had moved his office to
Tehran after the outbreak of the war. British intelligence and Sir Reader Bullard,
London's minister in Tehran, estimated the spy network of Germans in Iran at
around three thousand. Agents were constantly infiltrating the Soviet border on
surveillance missions.[22]

Iranian Foreign Policy during World War II

At the outbreak of the Second World War the Iranian government explained the
country's stance to German intelligence agent Bernhard Schulze-Holthus:

> You must understand the situation in this land [Iran] properly. For decades
> we have been living in a high tension field of international politics between
> Russia and England. The Russians have exploited our earlier weakness
> and have taken the Caucasus from us . . . the British . . . [act like] white
> lords who look upon us as colonials and treat us with unbearable arro-
> gance . . . what remains to us then, except to play the one off against the
> other? The Russians against the British and vice versa. But today we are
> expecting a great deal from a third power, which can be either the USA or
> Germany.[23]

Iran declared neutrality on September 4, 1939. A British naval blockade
took effect immediately, and German merchant shipping was barred from the
Persian Gulf port of Bandar-e-Shahpur. The economy of Iran relied heavily on
continued trade with Germany. On September 28, 1939, German goods were
passed to Iran via the Soviet Union; both Berlin and Moscow were signatories to
the Soviet-German Non-Aggression Pact. The inner circles of the shah's cabinet
urged him to wean Iran from increasing reliance on German sources of economic, technical, and material exchange.[24]

The Iranian government expressed its concerns to the United States over
the Soviet invasion of Finland in November 1939, and hastily constructed for-
tification lines along its northern border. Six Iranian divisions were stationed
along Iran's northern border, but they were still ill equipped to handle a potential
Soviet attack. Middle East command in Cairo, headed by General (Sir) Archibald
P. Wavell, presented to the British War Office in London a detailed analysis of
the Soviet threat to Iran and recommended British countermeasures. Wavell
advocated deploying one division and a fighter squadron to defend the Iranian
oil fields and the port of Basra in Iraq. The War Cabinet agreed with Wavell's
proposal and issued a policy: "At the first sign of Russian aggression against
Iran, British forces would provide internal security and air defense of the Anglo-
Iranian oil fields and the port of Basra."[25]

On July 7, 1940, Italian foreign minister Count Ciano presented Hitler with
Mussolini's plan for reorganizing the Near East, summarized as follows:

- Egypt and the Sudan: Italy to take over Britain's politico-military, juridical position. Elimination of the Suez Canal Company and the establishment of a special regime for the Canal Zone
- Independence for Syria, Lebanon, Palestine and Transjordan; Italian occupation of strategic points; treaty of exclusive alliance with Italy
- Military joint occupation of Aden, Perim, and Socotra (islands strategically located near the southern entrance into the Red Sea off the southwestern coast of Yemen and Somalia)
- Cession of British Somaliland and Djibouti to Italy
- No mention made about Iraq or Iran in Mussolini's plan, and which would be allocated to the German sphere and which to the Italian[26]

The Soviet and British governments focused on the German presence in Iran following the German attack on the Soviet Union. Richard Stewart details the flurry of diplomatic activity among the Allies after Operation Barbarossa. On June 26, 1941, the Soviet ambassador in Tehran, Alexei Smirnov, delivered a note to the Iranian foreign ministry stating that his government had "serious evidence" of a planned German coup d'état.[27] The U.S. ambassador to Tehran, Louis G. Dreyfus Jr., replied to a query from Washington, DC, that neither he nor the British possessed reliable information on the internal organization of a Nazi fifth column in Iran. Britain's ambassador to Tehran, Sir Reader S. Bullard, informed his government in June 1941 that "Iranians generally are delighted at the German attack on their ancient enemy Russia."[28]

As Nazi successes in the Soviet Union accelerated, Iranians gathered in Tehran's Sepah Square to cheer loudly each time the media announced the fall of a Soviet city. In June 1941 the German High Command in Berlin ordered that after the collapse of the Soviet Union, if plans were drawn to address the British presence in the Near East they would be subject to a concentric attack that included a mechanized advance through Iran. The German vice consul in Iran, Major Bernhard Schulze-Holthus, was warned of the inevitable attack on the Soviet Union three months earlier by Abwehr chief Canaris. Schulze-Holthus, while he held the rank of major, was also the chief German military intelligence agent in northwestern Iran. Canaris instructed Schulze-Holthus to gather intelligence on the Soviet oil facilities and military activities in the Trans-Caucasus. He quickly established a network of collaborators consisting of pro-German Iranians and anti-Soviet Russian émigré underground organizations who routinely dispatched agents across the Soviet border to reconnoiter the Soviet air base at Kirovabad.[29] In addition, Hitler read intelligence reports from the Forschungsamt (FA; the Nazi Party's signals intelligence unit); this unit was headed by Herman Goering and specialized in monitoring telephone and radio traffic. The FA collected intercepts from the British ambassador to Tehran on his interview with the Iranian prime minister that concerned an alliance among Great Britain, the Soviet Union, and Iran. Hitler read this with intense interest in April 1941, and also examined an FA report on the Allied diplomatic and military situation in the Middle East. The FA, for instance, revealed Admiral Jean-François Darlan's willingness to negotiate with the Allies in late 1942 for the surrender of Algeria to Allied forces.[30] Aside from the FA, the German foreign office cryptanalysts in Personal Z Sonderdiensts (sometimes referred to as Pers Z) solved the codes of thirty-four nations; the Turkish intercepts provided a treasure trove of Soviet strategic intentions. Pers Z cracked the code for one U.S. State Department encryption method, reading the traffic of American diplomat Robert Murphy, who was part of the delicate negotiations for the surrender of French North Africa.[31]

In Cairo, General Claude Auchinleck's Middle East command drafted plans to address a potential German breakthrough of Turkey or the Caucasus by defending northern Iraq and Iran from advancing Axis forces. Details of this plan against Iran were leaked to both German intelligence and the shah by King Farouk, Egypt's anti-British king. Contacts between Berlin and the Egyptian monarch began as early as October 21, 1936, with a letter of condolence from Hitler on the death of King Fuad I (ruled 1917–1936) and congratulations to King Farouk on his succession to the throne. The Egyptian monarch made secret contacts with Berlin through his father-in-law Zoulfikar Pasha, Egyptian ambassador to Tehran. In April 1941 Zoulfikar Pasha approached Erwin Ettel, German minister in Tehran. In his meeting with the minister, he conveyed Farouk's sympathy and respect for Hitler and wished him well on his success on gaining additional Egyptian self-determination from the British. Additionally, he expressed a desire that someday soon German troops might liberate Egypt from the yoke of British oppression. Ribbentrop assured King Farouk that the fight was not directed toward Egypt or any Middle Eastern country but against Britain. Farouk stated that he possessed intelligence concerning British plans to occupy the Anglo-Iranian oil fields near the Persian Gulf, to include Kermanshah. The British staff commented that it required two months to prepare an invasion and requested half a million men to conduct this operation. Farouk relayed this message to Germany's minister in Tehran, Erwin Ettel, "as proof of an attitude of candor and good faith toward Germany."[32]

The German minister to Iran, Erwin Ettel, was approached in the summer of 1941 by the Egyptian ambassador to Iran. On orders of King Farouk of Egypt, the ambassador was to pass along information to the Germans, such as British plans and intentions to occupy Iran and secure its oil fields and Persian Gulf ports, three weeks before Soviet and British forces physically occupied the northern and southern halves of Iran.[33] The British were pressuring Shah Reza Pahlavi to remove Germans from Iran. The shah stalled as Hitler urged him to resist the British until German forces pushing through the Soviet Union could rescue him. Two days after Reza Shah's communications with Hitler, Russian and British forces occupied Iran. In August 1941 Reza Shah was deposed, sailing off first to the island of Mauritius in the Indian Ocean.[34] Ultimately, Reza Shah spent his last days in exile in South Africa; he died in July 1944. Of note, Arabs who study this period make much of the marriage of Crown Prince Mohammed Reza Shah's (the future shah of Iran) to King Farouk's sister Princess Fawzia, and that the two monarchs may have colluded to find ways to undermine Britain's position in the region. There has been no direct evidence of the Reza Shah, his son Mohammed Reza, or King Farouk cooperating in this fashion, however; the conjecture probably represents a perceived concern at the time, at least until Reza Shah was deposed in 1941.

The German foreign minister created an independent intelligence service focused exclusively on the Middle East and North Africa, independent of the Abwehr and SD. Ribbentrop charged Minister Martin Luther to organize this unit, referred to as Information Post III (Inf III). Its primary mission was to decrease reliance on military sources of intelligence, but Luther was charged specifically with spreading disinformation and propaganda throughout the Middle East.[35] On one day alone (December 1, 1941) Ribbentrop forwarded the Inf III reports to Hitler concerning political and military developments in Egypt and Iran.[36] The Oberkommando der Wehrmacht (OKWs; supreme command of the German armed forces) code breakers named Egypt as one of the priority countries because of the rich traffic environment combined with anticolonial sentiment directed against the British among Egyptian officials and military officers.[37] One of the successes of Chiffrierableitung (Chi; code breaker units of the German armed forces) was the capture of the Black Code, the American encryption used by military attachés worldwide, and used to aid Rommel in his early victories in North Africa.[38] The Luftwaffe code breakers provided clear reports of Allied logistical activity from the United States to Britain via Egypt; while Hitler's policy declared Cairo an open city, this did not stop analysis of tonnage requirements needed to sustain British forces in Egypt, nor the development of target acquisition for German bombers and U-boats.[39]

The Abwehr operative Schulze-Holthus wrote an extraordinary memoir that has been translated into English and published in 1954 as *Daybreak in Iran*. It offers an Abwehr agent's view of division between the Nazi foreign office, diplomats, and members of the German military. Schulze-Holthus' mission was to foment anti-British groups into a rebellion. Operating from Tabriz in northern Iran, he interacted with several Azerbaijani underground Nationalist groups who were both anti-British and anti-Soviet. They included Dashnak-Zakan, who was anti-Soviet; the Milli Mudafai, who were classified as a petit bourgeois pro-Fascist group; and the Musawad, another underground group that played off the powers for Azerbaijani independence. The Milli Mudafai were social revolutionaries whose ideal was Hitler's Reich.[40]

In July 1941 the British evacuated their citizens in preparation for the precautionary partition of Iran between the Soviets in the north and the British in the south. German ambassador Ettel, on orders from Berlin, announced any German abandoning Persia would be viewed as a traitor; Schulze-Holthus describes this as a prestige policy designed to show German resolve and to stiffen Iranian resistance.[41] Abwehr agents disobeyed the German foreign office and attempted to escape to Afghanistan. German agents, sponsored by anti-British officials of the Iranian government and military, were provided papers describing them as architects, engineers, and building contractors.[42] Schulze-Holthus' account demonstrated the level of activity that German agents were involved in inside Iran and resulted in the Allied decision to implement Operation Countenance, details of which will be discussed in this chapter.

With the Afrika Korps poised on the Egyptian frontier, Farouk attempted to undermine the British in Egypt. British chiefs of staff were concerned that the Wehrmacht might reach the Caucasus by mid-August; at that point it would be possible for the Germans to deny British use of its airfields in Iraq. If this occurred, Iran might begin cooperating with the Germans and allowing them use of their airfields. The British planners estimated the Germans might launch a land offensive against Iraq from either Iran or southern Turkey utilizing four divisions from Tehran and one division from Tabriz. They stated that such an attack was most likely to develop before April 1942. On July 10, 1941, General Wavell stated his view: "It is essential to the defense of India that the Germans should be cleared out of Iran now. Failure to do so will lead to a repetition of events, which in Iraq were only just countered in time. It is essential that we should join hands with Russia through Iran, and if the present Government is not willing to facilitate this, it must be made to give way to one which will. To this end the strongest possible pressure should be applied forthwith while the German-Russian struggle is in doubt."[43]

The British War Cabinet agreed on July 22 to prepare for a joint Anglo-Soviet military action. American minister to Tehran, Dreyfus, emphasized that

> I do not minimize the Fifth Column danger. I am convinced, however, that the British are using it as a pretext for the eventual occupation of Iran and are deliberately exaggerating its potency as an isolated arm. I have come to the conclusion that the British and Russians will occupy Iran because of overwhelming military necessity no matter what reply the Iranians make to their demands. I must add emphatically to avoid misunderstanding that I am in full agreement with the British action and believe it to be vitally necessary for the furtherance of our common cause.[44]

Wavell instructed the general officer commanding in Iraq, General Edward P. Quinan, to be prepared to occupy Iran, securing the Abadan, Khuzestan, and Naft-e-shah oil fields and refineries. Quinan's contingency plan was code-named Operation Countenance.[45]

Waffen-SS Commandos Dropped into Persia

The Germans saw an opportunity to incite resistance against British occupation of southern Iran, and Russian occupation of the north. Schulze-Holthus himself was operating in Iran under diplomatic cover before the Iran's occupation by the Allies in 1941, after which he went underground until his capture in 1944. His memoirs describe the British tactic of buying all the rice and corn of a region in which Qashgai subtribes failed to be subdued. This step was undertaken to deprive pockets of Persian resistance in the mountains of food for the winter months and so starve them.[46]

Schulze-Holthus describes how the SS entered the operation by parachuting an officer and two NCOs into Qashgai territory with bags of gold, explosives, and letters from Berlin to tribal chiefs. Nasr Khan, the main leader of the Qashgai, received a letter and a gift of a gold revolver from Hitler; two of Nasr Khan's brothers were living in Germany. The SS dropped commandos in Iraq, Syria, Palestine, and Iran in an effort to energize resistance against the Allies. Among the plans to be undertaken was the sabotage of oil pipelines and pumping stations. These clandestine operations were orchestrated by Himmler and Kaltenbrunner, with the SS taking over the work started by the Abwehr.[47]

As the Third Reich faced imminent collapse, the Nazis saw in these covert operators a means to prolong the destruction through acts of sabotage throughout the Middle East and Persia. Schulze-Holthus achieved the perception of threat to the Baku Oil Fields by inciting the Qashgai tribes. In addition, serious British counterintelligence efforts were undertaken to capture Schulze-Holthus and the SS commando teams operating clandestinely in Iran. In 1944 Schulze-Holthus was caught by the Iranians and was surrendered to the British Consulate in Shiraz, along with incriminating papers. Schulze-Holthus would be exchanged in 1945 for a British agent.[48]

Reinforcing Schulze-Holthus' account of SS commandos deployed to incite conflict in the Middle East is the *Official History of British Intelligence in World War II* by Hinsley. The five volumes reveal that in May 1941 a flood of German "tourists" arrived in Syria as a result of Iraqi leader Rashid Ali's appeal to Hitler for assistance against British plans to reinforce Iraq. The operating procedure of the Abwehr and SS was that these were a part of an advance party to be followed by German airborne troops. Hitler personally ordered German personnel in Syria and Iraq to volunteer, and all German aircraft display Iraqi markings, in an attempt to recreate the Spanish Civil War in Iraq.[49]

Abwehr activity in Iraq and Syria led to a report that was drafted by MI-14 (British Military Intelligence Section 14, specializing in German operations) in the Hinsley volumes entitled, "Possible German Action in Syria and Iraq," dated May 2, 1941. It predicted that the Germans would utilize Syria or Cyprus as ideal staging areas for operations in Iraq. This allowed the Germans options to support Iraqi army rebellions in Mosul and Baghdad and capture Rabtah cutting oil pipeline links.[50] Supporting the Abwehr in Syria were the Italians under the cover of the Italian Disarmament Commission in Syria that worked to gather intelligence for an eventual German airborne landing in Damascus, Homs, and Palmyra airfields. According to MI-14, the Axis occupation or dominance of Syria and Iraq had the potential to cause a geostrategic shift in Turkey's ability to remain neutral while allowing Axis forces with overland access to German forces in the Caucuses to enter Syria and Iraq.[51] Also German troops could be landed in Syria from the German-occupied Dodecanese Islands. The Vichy French had stockpiles of bombs and weapons in Syria that would be effective in any Axis bid to destabilize Iraq.

Operation Countenance

The August 22, 1941, *New York Times* front page headline declared, "British and Russians Poised to Move into Iran." Iran attempted on several occasions to persuade the U.S. government to invoke its respected moral authority. The Iranian minister to Washington, Mohammed Shayesteh, cited how U.S. secretary of state Cordell Hull and other U.S. officials proclaimed the principles of peaceful international relations. The Iranian minister asked what the U.S. government planned to do to prevent the imminent British invasion of Iran. Hull replied, "British military authorities plan all of their strategy without any consultation with officials of the American government." Hull warned that the Germans had no respect for neutrality and would hurl any state into "serfdom and semi-slavery." Shayesteh replied in meek desperation, "[I]f your government would say but one word to the British, I believe they would not invade Iran."[52] Reza Shah appealed directly to American president Franklin Roosevelt using the Atlantic charter as leverage: "On the basis of the declarations which Your Excellency has made several times regarding the necessity of defending principles of international justice and the right of peoples to liberty, I beg Your Excellency to take efficacious and urgent humanitarian steps to put an end to these acts of aggression. This incident brings into war a neutral and pacific country which has had no other care than the safeguarding of tranquility and the reform of the country."[53] President Roosevelt replied,

> Viewing the question in its entirety involves not only the vital questions to which Your Imperial Majesty refers, but other basic considerations arising from Hitler's ambition of world conquest. It is certain that movements of conquest by Germany will continue and will extend beyond Europe to Asia, Africa, and even to the Americas, unless they are stopped by military force. It is equally certain that those countries which desire to maintain their independence must engage in a great common effort if they are not to be engulfed one by one as has already happened to a large number of countries in Europe. In recognition of these truths, the Government and people

of the United States of America, as is well known, are not only building up the defenses of this country with all possible speed, but they have also entered upon a very extensive program of material assistance to those countries which are actively engaged in resisting German ambition for world domination.[54]

Likely shaped by the British, and bowing to strategic short-term expediency, the United States understood which Middle East regimes were pro-Axis and took no steps to aid in their appeals to stop or hinder British intervention.

Operation Countenance began with an attack by the British warship HMS *Shoreham* on the harbor at Abadan that destroyed the Iranian sloop *Palang* on August 25, 1941. The Allied plans were carefully worked out to conform to the historic spheres of influence of the 1907 Anglo-Russian Entente. From the west and southeast, concentrated at Basra, the British Iraq Command known as Iraqforce, renamed Paiforce (Persia and Iraqforce), was under the command of Lieutenant General Quinan. Paiforce comprised the 8th and 10th Indian Infantry Divisions, the 2nd Indian Armored Brigade, the 9th Armored Brigade, and the 21st Indian Infantry Brigade, plus one bomber and a fighter squadron. The Soviets came from the north with their 44th, 47th, and 53rd armies. The Persian army mobilized nine of its fourteen infantry divisions.[55]

The objective was to seize the oil refinery at Abadan, fifty miles downriver from Maqil. Local Iranian troops, armed with the heavy caliber Skoda artillery, lacked sufficient morale and were ill trained. The refinery was captured without damage and few casualties. The 10th Indian Division, under the command of Major General Sir William Slim, entered Khanaq from the west, six hundred miles from Tehran, and thrust toward the center of the country. By August 27 Iranian troops had retreated at the sight of Blenheim bombers overhead. On August 28 Tehran called for a truce. British casualties amounted to seventeen killed and forty-two wounded. The Russians in the northwest encountered even less resistance. A mechanized column from Tiflis (Tbilisi) and another from Baku converged on the towns of Qazvin, Bandar-e Pahlavi, and Maku on the Caspian coast, north of Tehran. The Russian army was opposed by the Iranian army.[56]

At 3:00 p.m. on August 31 Iranian prime minister Foroughi informed the British and Soviet legations that his government accepted the Allied terms. The British and Soviet armed forces converged in Tehran on September 17; the oil fields were safeguarded and the strategic Trans-Iranian Railway was in Allied hands. The shah and his family boarded a British steamer first for the Indian Ocean island of Mauritius and then to Johannesburg, South Africa, where the shah died in 1944.[57] On September 17, 1941, his son, Mohammed Reza, ascended the throne and took a pro-Allied stance for the duration of the war, ensuring war materiel supply routes were conveyed to Russia through this Persian Corridor.[58]

The Persian Corridor

With Iran firmly in the hands of the Allies, a supply route to the Soviet Union was now an option for the Allied war effort. The importance of an Anglo-American supply route to the Soviet Union through the Persian Corridor was accurately anticipated as early as the spring of 1942 by a German study prepared for Hitler. It reads, in part, as follows:

> In their endeavor to support Soviet Russia, Great Britain and the United States will make every effort during the coming weeks and months to increase shipment of equipment, materiel, and troops to Russia as much as possible. In particular the supplies reaching Russia on the Basra-Iran route will go to the Russian Caucasus and southern fronts. All British or American war materiel which reaches Russia by way of the Near East and the Caucasus is extremely disadvantageous to our land offensive. Every ton of supplies which the enemy manages to get through to the Near East means a continuous reinforcement of the enemy war potential, makes our own operations in the Caucasus more difficult, and strengthens the British position in the Near East and Egypt.[59]

By this point, U.S. neutrality was increasingly a myth, in view of U.S. warships convoying non-U.S. merchantmen as far as Iceland, and the United States establishing a presence in Iran on the basis of a presidential directive of September 13.[60]

The September planning of the Persian Corridor, in its early and tentative stage, appeared in a memorandum prepared for Secretary of Commerce and Diplomatic Adviser to President Roosevelt Harry Hopkins, stating, "[T]he entrance of Russia into the war has given the Iranian theater urgent priority. The demands of the new theater are tremendous—250,000 ship tons, of railroad material in one project, more than the total shipments to the Near East to date, requiring from 50 to 75 ships, with the distance so great that only three trips a year can be made. A big automotive project is superimposed on the railroad project. Diversions of material destined for Egypt are being made to the new theater."[61] Requests for war materiel from Moscow began as early as July 30, 1940, when Hopkins arrived in the Soviet capital to obtain a detailed statement of Russian supply needs.[62]

The threatened collapse of the Soviet Union following the German invasion in June of 1941 ultimately resulted in Soviets' formal eligibility into the Lend-Lease program on November 7, 1941. Code-named Operation Typhoon, the invasion of Moscow by the 3rd and 4th Panzer Armies, comprised over 1 million men. President Roosevelt sent special envoy in London on materiel aid, Ambassador W. Averell Harriman, to the Soviet capital to meet with Soviet foreign minister Molotov and British minister of supply Lord Beaverbrook. The conference produced the signing of the First Moscow Protocol, which was described as a "binding promise by this Government to make specific quantities of supplies available for shipment to Russia by a specific date."[63]

The Moscow Protocol was the first of four similar protocols of aid to Russia. It called for a supply of roughly 1.5 million tons from the United States. The Washington Protocol, signed October 6, 1942, promised 3.3 million tons via the Arctic route and 1.1 million via the Persian Gulf route until July 1, 1943. The London Protocol, signed October 19, 1943, and running until June 30, 1944, promised 2.7 million tons via the Pacific route and 2.4 million tons through the Arctic or Persian route. The Ottawa Protocol, signed April 17, 1945, promised 2.7 million tons via the Pacific route and 3.0 million tons via the Persian Gulf and the Black Sea until May 12, 1945.[64]

The terms imposed in September 1941 by Britain and the Soviet Union were designed to secure an area essential to the survival of the Soviet Union. They renounced any designs against the territorial integrity or independence of Iran. The occupying powers promised withdrawal once the military situation improved. A key clause in the Tripartite Agreement was this: "[T]he forces of the Allied Powers shall be withdrawn from Iranian territory not later than six months after all hostilities between the Allied Powers and Germany and her associates have been suspended by the conclusion of an armistice or armistices, or on the conclusion of peace between them, whichever date is the earlier." Iran agreed to its neutrality and to abstain from any act contradicting Allied interests. These provisions were incorporated into a Tripartite Treaty of Alliance signed on January 29, 1942. The treaty provided for withdrawal from Iran of Allied troops six months after the termination of hostilities against the Axis. Iran's contribution was to be restricted only to internal security. Iran granted the Allied powers "the unrestricted right to use, maintain, guard and, in case of military necessity, control in any way that they may require, all means of communications throughout Iran, including railways, roads, rivers, aerodromes, ports, pipelines, and telephone, telegraph and wireless installations."[65]

The same clause agreed to "establish and maintain, in collaboration with the Allied powers, such measures of censorship control as they may require for all the means of communication."[66] Iran's eligibility for Lend-Lease was declared on March 10, 1942; two American military missions were established on September 24, 1942. The first mission was to advise the country on Army matters and military supply; the second mission was to advise and reorganize the country's imperial gendarmerie. Both missions were commanded under Gen. Clarence S. Ridley and Col. H. Norman Schwarzkopf Sr. Coincidentally, Colonel Schwarzkopf's son, who died in December 2012, followed in his father's footsteps, making his mark on the Middle East five decades later in Operation Desert Shield and Operation Desert Storm.[67]

With the clearance of Axis positions in the Mediterranean by 1943, cargo convoys passed through the Suez Canal and debarked on the ports of the Persian

Gulf. The main ports for incoming supplies to Iran were Bandar-e-Shahpur, Bushehr, Basra, and Umm Qasr in the southwestern coast. The overland routes were through Tehran bound to Baku, Azerbaijan; or Ashkhabad, Turkmenistan. The other land route from Basra was bound for the northwest town of Qazvin in Iran or from Jolfa in northern Iran to Beslan in the North Ossetia-Alania region of Russia.

Approximately a sum total of 8 million metric tons of ship-borne supplies from the Allies were unloaded in the Persian Gulf, either bound for Russia or for support of British forces under the Middle East command. The tonnage figure does not account for warplane transfers via Persia nor cargo delivered via air.[68]

In September 1943 Iran formally declared war on Germany. The shah hosted the Big Three on November 28 of that same year at the Tehran Conference (code-named Eureka). The Persian supply operation route was an experiment in Allied cooperation without historical precedent. Iran, forcibly occupied by long-standing rivals Britain and the Soviet Union, served as a highway while another nation, the United States, delivered supplies to one of those rivals, now by the fortunes of war instantly becoming an ally.[69]

Iran's Outcome: The American Perspective

In 1953, under Operation Ajax, the United States orchestrated a coup backed by the CIA under Kermit Roosevelt Jr., at the behest of British Secret Intelligence Service (SIS, or MI-6) against Mohammad Mosaddeq, the popular and democratically elected Iranian prime minister, whose efforts led to the nationalization of the country's oil industry. Interestingly, the CIA sent Gen. H. Norman Schwarzkopf Sr. to convince the exiled shah of Iran, Mohammad Reza Pahlavi, to return and seize power. Schwarzkopf (Senior) went on to organize and train the security forces to support the shah's SAVAK, Iran's national intelligence and security organization, that became VEVAK (the ministry of intelligence and security of Iran) after the 1979 revolution. Almost fifty years later, former U.S. secretary of state Madeleine Albright acknowledged the central role that the United States played in the coup, coming closer than any other American diplomat to apologize for the intervention. Secretary of State Albright said during a speech at the American-Iranian Council on March 17, 2000, "The Eisenhower administration believed its actions were justified for strategic reasons. . . . But the coup was clearly a setback for Iran's political development. And it is easy to see now why many Iranians continue to resent this intervention by America in their internal affairs."[70]

Iranian president Mahmoud Ahmadinejad made a press conference broadcast on Danish State television in December 2009 requesting reparations be paid to Iran for its Allied occupation, stating, "I will write a letter to the UN Secretary-General [Ban Ki-moon]. We will seek compensation for World War II damage. A team has been assigned to calculate all the damages (inflicted on Iran) in the

Second World War. This will be an invoice they [Allies powers] must pay to the Iranian nation."[71]

With its hand in the development of atomic energy and its growing nuclear program, originally supported and encouraged by the United States under Eisenhower's Atoms for Peace program, and as the chief financier of Hezbollah, Iran has now become a major player in the grand political arena of the Near East that the United States can no longer afford to ignore.

CHAPTER 6

Turkey
Balancing Neutrality

The Research Office sent me background material on a number of political matters of some interest. Relations between Turkey and the Soviet Union have worsened very much. In his private talks, the Turkish Foreign Minister, Saracoglu, used strong expressions of antagonism to the policies of the Soviets. The English are trying to calm him down. But Moscow has certainly provoked the Turkish Government.

—Joseph Goebbels diary entry, May 16, 1942

Early Stages of Turkish Policies in World War II

Mustafa Kemal Atatürk had said in 1931 that "the Treaty of Versailles has not removed any of the causes that led to the First World War. Quite to the contrary, it has deepened the rift between the former rivals." Seven years after making that statement, Mustafa Kemal advised his followers that "a World War is near. In the course of this war international equilibrium will be entirely destroyed. If during this period we act unwisely and make the smallest mistake, we will be faced with an ever graver catastrophe than in the Armistice years."[1]

The strategic importance of Turkey at the onset of the Second World War made it inevitable that the infant republic would be the target of interest from the European powers. Turkish neutrality during the Second World War remained one of the most important aspects of diplomacy during the period for both the Allies and the Axis. Turkey was able to position itself into a state of neutrality where it possessed a formal treaty of assistance with Great Britain as well as a friendship and nonaggression pact with Nazi Germany. It was a balancing act worthy of study by those interested in national security, and can offer a classic case study in balance of power politics—only this time the balance of power was between the Allies and the Axis. In discussing this with men and women of the armed forces, the authors recommend Selim Deringil's excellent volume, *Turkish Foreign Policy during the Second World War: An Active Neutrality* published in 2004 by Cambridge University Press. Deringil's phrase "active neutrality" is particularly insightful, as it demonstrates the flexibility of neutrality in war. The true purpose behind the "neutrality" between the Germans and Turkey before and during the Second World War demonstrated that the new government of the Turkish president, Ismet Inönü, was anything but neutral in the true sense. Although Turkey was technically a neutral participant during World War II, it had leanings toward Nazi Germany. The two governments formed a basis of shared confidence and genuine friendship, having full authority from their respective heads of state. German ambassador to Turkey Franz von Papen met with Turkish foreign minister Sukru Saracoglu regularly. Von Papen would remain at his post in Ankara from 1939 to 1944 and would be a key architect of the German-Turkish Treaty of Friendship and Non-Aggression signed in the Turkish capital on June 18, 1941, just four days prior to the German invasion of the Soviet Union, Operation Barbarossa. The treaty drew up several articles of agreement and accords such as binding both parties to respect the integrity of their territories and to ensure that no measure be taken that is aimed directly or indirectly against one other; communicate with each other on all questions affecting their common interests to bring about mutual considerations on the treatment of such questions; and dispatch economic cooperation between the two governments.[2]

Von Papen wrote to Berlin: "[I]f the position we occupy in Turkey, is taken over in the future by Britain and France, our relations with the countries lying beyond Turkey, namely Iraq, Iran and the Arabian world will be mortally hit." Von Papen realized that "the neutralization of the fifty Turkish divisions is a military requirement which can for the present be achieved only in the diplomatic field."[3]

Ismet Inönü declared Turkey a nonbelligerent state soon after the German occupation of France in 1940, even though Turkey was tied to the Tripartite Alliance of October 1939 with France and Britain. According to Franz von Papen's *Memoirs* published in 1952, with the American edition published a year later, Hitler sent an official letter addressed to President Inönü establishing the terms of Germany's adherence to Turkish neutrality. It stated that German troops would be allowed no closer than twenty-two miles from the Bulgarian-Turkish border. This showed a high level of diplomatic activity designed to further the goals of the Wehrmacht.[4]

Turkish Mistrust of Italy

One of the threats to Turkish security in the mid-1930s was Italy, with its heavily fortified Dodecanese Islands just off the Turkish coast and the concern over Mussolini's cries of "mare nostrum" (our sea). Turkish dislike of Italian policies dates back to the Italo-Turkish War of 1911–1912, and the Italian invasion of Libya and seizure of the Dodecanese Islands. After the brief conflict, Italy maintained its occupation of the islands until the Dodecanese were formally annexed by Italy as stipulated in the Treaty of Lausanne. During the First World War, the islands were used as a military base and a staging ground for several campaigns against Turkey, most famously the disastrous landing at Gallipoli.[5]

Turkey, in balancing its neutrality with the Axis, had had to contend with the Italians since 1934, constructing military bases on the Dodecanese Islands, and using these islands as a center to beam Radio Bari propaganda into Turkey.[6] Following Mussolini's invasion of Albania on April 8, 1939, Turkey began to tilt its neutrality toward Britain. Turkey signed a Treaty of Mutual Assistance with Great Britain and France on October 19, 1939. When Italy declared war on June 10, 1940, this activated Turkey's obligation to aid Britain and France through Clause I, Second Article of the treaty, which states, "[I]n the event of an act of aggression by a European Power leading to war in the Mediterranean area in which France and the United Kingdom are involved, Turkey will collaborate effectively with France and the United Kingdom and will lend them all aid and assistance in her power."[7]

Turkish Neutrality Declaration

Some in the Turkish Assembly believed that Italy's entry into World War II on the side of the Germans gave rise to an immediate state of war between Turkey and Italy, but the majority of legislators favored caution and advocated neutrality. Turkey applied Protocol 2 of the Tripartite Treaty with Moscow, which absolved Turkey of any action that might lead to war with the Soviet Union. It resolved to "absolve Turkey of taking any action which might involve her in a war with the Soviet Union." In addition, this Turkish, French, and British treaty went against Soviet-Turkish agreements and Joseph Stalin's desires. The Soviet leader insisted on this clause limiting Turkish aid to Great Britain, as follows: "Moreover, these engagements cannot oblige Turkey to support Great Britain and France if these countries go to war with the Soviet Union. In this case for the duration of the war, the Anglo-Franco-Turkish Pact would remain inactive."[8] Stalin wanted an exclusion clause that would absolve Russia from intervention to aid Turkey if Turkey were attacked by Germany. At the time of the Soviet-Turkish discussions over treaties and protocols, the Soviets had signed the Soviet-German

Non-Aggression Pact, which ended only when the Germans invaded the Soviet Union in June 1941. Deringil's book reveals the kind of triangular diplomacy Turkey conducted to maintain neutrality and therefore flexibility in its foreign policy. By linking Soviet treaties to British and German protocols, Ankara was able to triangulate that declaring war on Germany, then an ally of the Soviet Union, would provoke Moscow and violate Turkish agreements with the Soviets.

On June 26, 1940, Turkey issued its declaration of nonbelligerence: "The Government of the Turkish Republic has considered the situation which has arisen from Italy's entry into the war and have decided on the application of Protocol 2. Turkey will preserve her present attitude of non-belligerency for the security and defense of our country. While continuing on the one side military preparations, we also have to remain more vigilant than ever. We hope by this position of watchfulness and by avoiding any provocation, we shall preserve the maintenance of peace for our country and for those who are around us."[9]

Even though the British were disappointed by Turkey's decision to declare itself a nonbelligerent, events later showed that the Turkish decision to maintain neutrality coupled with its strategic location provided the new republic far greater autonomy and flexibility in foreign policy. However, as the full extent of the damage witnessed from the collapse of France and threats to Britain's colonies became apparent, Turkey's value as a neutral crossroad became increasingly crucial to the Allies as well as to the Axis.

Estimates from the British War Cabinet determined that the Germans could conquer Turkey and reach the Iraqi border in sixteen weeks once units crossed the Bosporus Strait. Hence, the British were forced to change their thinking, and to adopt the position that the treaty had little value inasmuch as it denied Turkey to the Germans. The British foreign office stated that it "had hardly expected Turkey to do otherwise, when it declared its non-belligerency and recognizing the difficult dilemma in which she found herself."[10]

It was concluded by British war planners that any other attitude would only throw Turkey into the arms of Germany and that London had to maintain a delicate balancing act. The War Cabinet Chiefs of Staff Committee agreed that to force Turkey would "be counter-productive and might jeopardize Turkey's own security and through Turkey, our whole position in the Near East."[11]

Turkish Relations with the Third Reich

Anticipating a quick defeat of the Soviets, Hitler planned to occupy Turkey. However, in planning Operation Barbarossa, the German leader realized that a neutral Turkey would secure Axis shipments in the eastern Mediterranean, vital for Germany's war economy. A trade agreement between Turkey and Germany was signed in October 1941. The agreement meant that Turkish metals, chromium in particular, were exchanged for German weapons. Approximately

135,000 tons of chromium ore was delivered to Nazi Germany between 1941 and 1944, making up for the loss, after Hitler's invasion of the Soviet Union, of Soviet raw materials that had been shipped to Germany.[12]

The constant flow of chromium ore to the Third Reich was so crucial that German minister of munitions and armaments Albert Speer dispatched a letter to Hitler in 1943 stating that "should supplies of chromium from Turkey be cut off, the manufacture of tanks, U-boats and other war machines would cease, the current reserve would be sufficient only for 5–6 months."[13] Speer sent a candid memo to Hitler and OKW chief Alfred Jodl in September 1944; it details the extent of how the war was grinding to a halt not due to a lack of nickel ore from Finland, but rather due to the ending of chromium ore shipments from Turkey.[14] Though considered neutral waters, the Bosporus Strait, linking the Black Sea to the Mediterranean, allowed German merchant ships carrying needed war materiel and ore access to the Black Sea. Turkey's liberal interpretation of its responsibilities to monitor and enforce neutrality of the strait under the terms imposed by the 1936 Montreaux Convention enabled German ships to have access in and out of the Black Sea.[15]

One of Turkey's political themes since the days of the Ottoman Empire was the idea of pan-Turanism (a political movement for the union of all Turkic peoples stretching from the Volga to China, sometimes referred to as pan-Turkism). As the Nazi juggernaut conquered more areas of Soviet soil that were inhabited by Turkic peoples, a few Turkish leaders were tempted to join up with the Nazis to crush the Soviet Union as Germany took further control of the Caucasus. Senior Turkish military officials believed that the opportunity to attack the southern areas of Russia should be exploited, and President Ismet Inönü maintained official contact with Berlin over this issue while awaiting results of the Nazi war on the eastern front.[16]

Deringil's book has an excellent exposé of the discussions Turkish military and political leaders had about the survivability of Joseph Stalin under the weight of a Nazi onslaught. Germany actively encouraged pan-Turanism, in which Turkey would gain influence over all Turkic peoples beyond Anatolia and into the Caucuses. Franz Von Papen reported in July 1941 that Turkish interest was illustrated by the Turks residing in Azerbaijan and the area currently controlled by Stalin. A committee of German experts on Turkish affairs had been formed. In several instances, the German general staff hosted a tour of the eastern front for General Ali Fuat Erden and General Emir Erkilet. The Turkish generals tried on several occasions to convince President Inönü and foreign minister Saracoglu that the eastern front had in fact been won by Nazi Germany. In a report dated August 8, 1942, Von Papen stated that he had spoken with Saracoglu, who said that as a Turk he was completely in favor of the defeat of Soviet Russia. Ribbentrop commented that Germany must "promote and keep alive the hitherto somewhat dormant Turkish imperialist tendencies."[17] In World

War I, Germany stimulated the impulses of pan-Islamism against the British and French, and in World War II, the Germans looked to pan-Turanism to agitate anti-British and French sentiments.

The British kept tabs on pan-Turanism activities in Turkey, and became concerned over the potential for greater activity and influence by Germany when their forces entered the Crimea.

From Tehran to Berlin: The Turkish Route

Preparations for the Eastern campaign against the Soviet Union in 1941 coincided with the weakening of German activity in the Arab world. More energy and effort was expended for the massive invasion of the Soviet Union. After the unsuccessful pro-Axis coup in Iraq and the Anglo–Free French occupation of the Levant, it became more difficult for Berlin to maintain communications with Arab Nationalists. German attempts were made to bring both Al-Husseini and Al-Gaylani to Axis-dominated Europe. On August 13 German undersecretary of state Woermann ordered his consul in Haifa, Wilhelm Melchers, who also acted as chief of the Report Section Pol VII (the section directing Middle East intelligence operations for the German foreign ministry) to invite the Jerusalem mufti, the Iraqi Nationalist, and other prominent Arab leaders to Berlin. The mufti and the Iraqi Nationalist Al-Gaylani would both be located in Tehran; their situation within Iran had become unstable following Hitler's invasion of the Soviet Union in June 1941. With British and Soviet pressure mounting on Iran, and the shah and his government dodging accusations that they were permitting enemies of Great Britain to operate in Iran, both German and Italian diplomats in Iran competed in offering asylum to the two Arab leaders within their respective nations. Berlin calculated that the only way to get them safely to Berlin was through neutral Turkey. However, Turkey was reluctant to grant transit visas to both Gaylani and Husseini, whose pan-Arab views did not meet with Ankara's approval. London aimed to prevent the freedom of movement to the troublesome pair. The British made strong attempts when, to pressure the Turkish government to place the mufti and ex–Iraqi prime minister under house arrest. However, German intervention led the demand for Turkey to finally grant visas to the mufti and Gaylani.[18] Al-Gaylani's escape from Turkey would hit a snag in Istanbul, in which German intelligence intervened, to ensure that Berlin would not be deprived of two valuable persons for their anti-British propaganda efforts.

Al-Gaylani received his Turkish visa in mid-July and left Iran on July 20, crossing the Iranian border on July 22. The Turks, however, neglected to provide him a transit visa and later refused to allow him to leave the country and proceed to Germany. However, he was promised confidentially by Ankara that he would not be prevented from leaving the country secretly. Under these circumstances, the Abwehr made preparations to get him out of Turkey safely. He then flew from Istanbul in a German plane on November 21 under the cover of a supposed member of a German press delegation, which on Turkey's invitation came to Istanbul on Ribbentrop's plane. German officials informed Turkey that the delegation comprised eight members, but only seven arrived. When the delegation departed, Gaylani was passed off as the eighth member. His arrival in Germany was kept secret. Later sources speculated that he had managed to escape from Turkey via the Black Sea to Bulgaria by his own efforts.[19]

Difficulty in transporting the mufti was compounded by the fact that numerous countries were curious as to his whereabouts. Italy had long maintained financial support for him, and Great Britain was also interested in luring him away from Axis influence. He was not given a Turkish visa. The British and Soviet invasion of Iran ended on September 17 and the Allies certainly did not want the mufti and his entourage to leave Iran. Among those who managed to escape out of Iraq to Iran were his cousin Jemal Al-Husseini and one of the mufti's assistants, Amin El-Tamimi. They were both arrested by the British and interned in Southern Rhodesia. Osman Kemal Haddad, the mufti's private secretary, and members of the Golden Square who led the Iraqi uprising were also seized. Al-Husseini managed to seek refuge at the only remaining safe consulate in Tehran, the Japanese legation, the same day the Allies demanded that Iran close German, Italian, Hungarian, and Romanian legations and expel the diplomatic representatives.[20] He later managed to escape to Turkey and from there, dressed as the servant of the Italian envoy, to Rome, where he arrived in the middle of October. His flight was organized by Italian intelligence. Thus, the two prominent pro-Axis Arab Nationalists were in Europe by November 1941.[21]

Political Encirclement

The developments of mid-1941 that highlighted the delicacy of Turkey's position were the volatile situation in Vichy-controlled Syria and the anti-British revolt in Iraq. If Turkey were attacked from either the Balkans or the Caucuses, Syria would be the vital route, with the British position being isolated in Palestine. Similarly, if Iraq were to fall to the Axis, Turkey would be surrounded and cut off from its supply route in Basra. Ensuring Turkish loyalty was an important factor in British strategy to secure various crises in the Middle East. British foreign secretary Anthony Eden emphasized to Churchill that in order for Turkey to hold fast, it was essential that it avoid encirclement by the Axis in Syria and Iraq. Britain, he said, had to deal at the earliest possible moment with the situation in these areas.[22]

The Vichy French further complicated the political landscape by asking permission to send war materiel through Turkey. Saracoglu refused on the grounds that this would be helping one of Turkey's allies against the other. The Turks found themselves in a paradoxical situation. They did not desire to see Iraq occupied by the Axis or blockaded by Britain. Germany was quick to approach them with offers of frontier rectification in Western Thrace and in the hinterland of Edirne, both territories ceded by Turkey in the First World War. On May 5 Turkey offered to mediate between Iraq and Britain. Whereas General Wavell was in favor of accepting Turkish mediation, Churchill overruled him, deciding for military intervention in Iraq to eliminate German involvement. Although the Turks ended up allowing some war materiel to reach Iraq from the Axis in mid-May, they stalled long enough to enable the British to reestablish control.[23]

The situation in the Levant was potentially more dangerous. On June 3 Saracoglu told Von Papen that for strategic reasons Turkey considered occupying the Baghdad railway up to Aleppo. Ribbentrop refused the suggestion. Meanwhile, Turkish troop concentrations along the Turkish-Syrian frontier in eastern Anatolia were directed not against the Axis, but against the Soviets. Von Papen was not convinced. As in the Iraqi case, the Turks again offered their services as mediators between the Gaullist and Vichy forces, but London refused.[24]

Another development in 1941, ominous from the Turkish point of view, was the British-Soviet invasion of Iran in August. It was obviously a question of Iran simply being the only feasible supply route for British and American supplies to the Soviets. To the Turks, the British worry about German fifth column activities in Iran was nothing but a pretext to gain military control of the country. Churchill wrote to Roosevelt on September 1 that Iran served in "encouraging Turkey to stand as a solid block against German passage into Syria and Palestine." British and Soviet ambassadors delivered notes to the Turkish government on August 11 promising to safeguard Turkish territorial integrity, which had the added assurance of being an Anglo-American-Soviet guarantee as the tides of war were turning against the Nazis.[25]

Turkey's Final Position

Another aspect of Turkish foreign policy with the Third Reich was its ability to procure quantities of armaments as well as financial aid from Germany. In the summer of 1942 Turkey was offered a loan for arms shipments. On April 29, 1942, Hitler instructed Italian leader Benito Mussolini that Turkey was moving gradually but assuredly toward the Axis sphere. As Nazi armies froze in the Russian winter and the Red Army reversed the tides of defeat, Turkey declined to take the step toward becoming an Axis partner. However, Inönü had made clear Turkey's position by stating, "We have taken all our precautions. Our decisions for the future are open and clear. We will strive to stay out of the war. We will order our business and if it proves impossible to avoid war, we will do our duty honorably."[26] Even by 1943, during the meeting between Churchill and Inönü at Adana on January 30, Inönü suggested, "Turkey need not come into the war to be sure of a place at the peace table; the Atlantic Charter takes care of that."[27] Churchill's comeback: "If you enter the war you can be sure of a place at the peace table. If you remain neutral you may have to be content with standing room."[28] It was not until February 23, 1945, that Turkey declared war on Germany and Japan to preserve a seat at the United Nations Conference. Later, when Turkey was criticized for its position during the war, Inönü responded, "I would now like to respond to the criticisms leveled at Turkey beginning at the end of 1943 and show here in your presence the injustice of the allegations against us. We were criticized for having concluded a treaty of Non-Aggression with the Germans. But with what right could anyone expect us to do anything else at the time when the Germans were at the gates of Istanbul, Britain feared invasion of the British Isles, Russia had a Non-Aggression Pact with Germany, and the United States was not in the war."[29]

This little-discussed aspect of the Second World War demonstrates the importance of behind-the-scenes diplomacy, weapons sales, and grants in the management of a neutral government that occupies strategic territory. The Allies had, through coopting King Farouk of Egypt, denied the Axis use of the Suez Canal. It was vital for Hitler not to see the Bosporus Strait denied to German shipping in the same way. German manipulation of Turkish national sentiment uncovered the irrational exuberance Nationalism had on a nation's foreign policy. Turkish leaders almost fell into the abyss of joining the Axis that seemed at the time the rational choice, given their loathing of Stalin, who controlled Soviet republics with a large population of Turkic peoples.

Turkish foreign policy remains one of the major feats of diplomatic intrigue in the annals of international relations. The country managed to position itself in such a way that it had a formal Treaty of Mutual Assistance with Great Britain and a Friendship and Non-Aggression Pact with Nazi Germany. Completely encircled by Axis and Soviet forces, Turkey succeeded in averting the devastation that surrounded it. The current Islamist Justice and Development Party (known as AKP) that has dominated Turkish politics for over a decade currently maintains a delicate regional balance between Iran, Iraq, and Syria. It also balances its membership in NATO, with ways to engage the European Union, which itself is undergoing serious structural economic problems. Understanding how Turkey balanced crisis in the past may offer a window to the types of compromises it will make on the international stage in the future. The neutrality that Turkey maintained for the better part of World War II is a case study in balancing competing interests and powers.

CHAPTER 7

Axis Efforts in the Arabian Peninsula

Drop by drop makes an inundation.

—Bedouin proverb

T he end of World War I introduced radical political changes in the Arabian Peninsula. During the 1930s Saudi Arabia's relations with the great powers of Europe entered a tense phase, as it was the only formally independent Arab state not linked to Britain or France via treaty, unlike Egypt, Iraq, Iran, and Syria. No British military bases existed on Saudi soil. With the expansion of the Third Reich, the Nazis expressed strategic interest in the Arabian Peninsula. As caretaker of two of Islam's holy cities, Mecca and Medina, King Abdul-Aziz Ibn Saud (ruled 1925–1953) initially regarded a policy of neutrality as the most prudent course for the newly created country in the event a regional conflagration erupted. The kingdom of Saudi Arabia came into being in 1932, and was only seven years old when World War II broke out in 1939. Although mistrustful and cautious of both sides, Saudi Arabia eventually found itself having to maintain a delicate balance of collaborating with both Axis and Allied interests. This brief historical overview should shed light on the little-examined aspect of World War II, the competition for influence in the Arabian Peninsula. A most excellent find that details the extent of German attempts to penetrate and influence the infant Saudi government is Lukasz Hirszowicz's *The Third Reich and the Arab East*, published in translation from Polish in 1966, which will be heavily utilized in this chapter.[1] It is a volume used by the authors when discussing or teaching aspects of Saudi political-military history to U.S. military officers and civilian Defense Department personnel. It is a definitive volume on Axis influence in the Middle East, and a treasure found only in select libraries since it has been out of print since its publication five decades ago.

Portions of this chapter were first published in the September 2008 edition *Foreign Area Officer Journal* in an essay entitled, "The Political Influence of Axis Collaborative Efforts in Saudi Arabia," by Basil Aboul-Enein and Faisal

126

Aboul-Enein.[2] The resulting discussion and questions from foreign area officer association members allowed for the expansion of ideas into this book's chapter.

Saudi Dissatisfaction with Great Britain

Unsatisfied with the quality and quantity of arms supplied by the British government, Ibn Saud looked elsewhere for the purchase of arms and expressed his readiness to establish diplomatic relations with Nazi Germany. During his stay in Baghdad in November 1937, the king's private secretary, Sheikh Yusuf Yasin, and other confidential agents, asked Otto Wolff, a major German steel industrialist, if he would supply the king with 15,000 rifles on cash credit. This was a time when the U.S.–Saudi oil subsidy of $170,000 per year was only six years old. In 1937 Ibn Saud's personal physician, Syrian-born Sheikh Medhat Al-Ardh, contacted the Außenpolitische Amt (APA; NSDAP office of foreign relations separate from German foreign ministry) in the king's name. During this time, German officials invited Saudi representatives to its party rally in Nuremberg. It is possible that a cautious attitude was imposed on the APA by the adverse position taken up by the Auswärtige Amt regarding the various arms deals in the Near East proposed by Alfred Rosenberg's office.[3] Tensions and differences in policy outlook within and among Nazi institutions would plague Hitler and his leadership, and be among the many flaws that led to Germany's defeat.

It is possible that the Germans wished to avoid taking any steps that might have increased Ibn Saud's reputation, especially since Ibn Saud sought a leadership role in the Arab world as well as to stake a claim in representing issues of the Jewish question in Palestine. This could have undermined Gaylani and the grand mufti, two Arab national leaders cultivated by the Nazis. In addition, support of Ibn Saud might be viewed as unwanted meddling in internal Arab disputes. As a case in point, political leaders of other Arab counties, particularly in Iraq, warned the Germans against Ibn Saud, whom they charged with being in the pay of the British. Iraqi leaders maintained that the Saudi king's opposition to the formation of a Jewish state in Palestine was disingenuous. Furthermore, in accordance with its entire policy toward the Arab countries, Berlin did not wish its contact with Saudi Arabia to worsen relations with Britain or arouse Italian suspicions in the lead-up to war.[4]

Early in 1938 Khalid Al-Hud Al-Qarqani, a Libyan adviser to the Saud family, visited Berlin, where he conducted general negotiations with several German firms (with the foreign relations office serving as intermediary); his objective was to purchase arms for the al-Sauds. Al-Hud proposed to buy rifles and automobiles, and to place an order to build an ammo cartridge factory in Saudi Arabia. He also relayed the Saudi king's desire to employ the assistance of German engineers and specialists for the purpose of building roads. Although Al-Hud obtained some promises to supply arms, these pledges remained unfulfilled until late 1938, when the Saudi vice minister for foreign affairs, Fuad-bey Hamza, arrived in Berlin. As a result of this visit, the Germans concluded that King Ibn Saud was interested in an exchange of diplomats between Berlin and Arabia; all ambassadors in Saudi Arabia operated not from the capital Riyadh, but from the seaport town of Jeddah.[5]

Fuad-bey Hamza stressed to the Germans Ibn Saud's limited freedom of action, particularly in relation to challenging British regional power. He maintained that his monarch could not afford to be drawn into a conflict with Britain, and that Saudi Arabia could be compelled to cooperate with Britain under certain circumstances. He further discussed the question of Saudi-Italian relations, and complained that the Italian shipment of arms had improved, but that Ibn Saud suspected Italian designs on Arabia. Fuad-bey also expressed to Berlin his king's hope that Germany harbored no imperialist goals in the Arabian Gulf.[6]

Agreement was reached with the OKW on the provision of arms to the Palestinian rebels using Saudi Arabia as a conduit, as well as providing sums of money for the Palestinian cause, but the money apparently never reached its destination. The Germans were uncertain whether Saudi Arabia would really remain neutral in the event of war; thus, the supply of arms on credit at the end could not be justified. Berlin also feared that Ibn Saud desired closer relations with Germany in order to play the British and Italians against each other and thereby extract ore material concessions.[7]

In the end, Ibn Saud's appeals for military and economic aid compelled the German government to arrive at a decision, because they were concerned that by ignoring him they would throw Saudi Arabia solidly into the camp of the Allies. German party officials, particularly those from the APA, pressed for aggressive involvement in Arab affairs. When the Nazis annexed Czechoslovakia in September 1938, the APA demanded a decision on relations with Saudi Arabia. The German foreign ministry decided not to conclude any agreement on credit for provision of arms, but only to establish diplomatic relations with Saudi Arabia so that, in case of war, Germany's Baghdad envoy, Ambassador Grobba, could withdraw to a neutral country in the event the pro-Axis Iraqi government were to change.[8]

In the meantime, the German foreign ministry took the shrewd action of informing its envoys in Egypt and Iraq that even if those governments were compelled under British pressure to sever diplomatic relations with Nazi Germany and take measures against German citizens, the Reich would not retaliate. At first this decision was of little significance since evidence suggests that the Germans still had little confidence in Ibn Saud, especially in light of potential intelligence suggesting that Fuad-bey Hamza might be serving as a paid British agent. In particular, two German transports were prepared for the Palestinian rebels; one of them was to be shipped through Saudi Arabia and the other by agreement with Baghdad was to be held up by British authorities.[9] Reading

Hirszowicz, one gains a real sense of German frustration in dealing with Ibn Saud and his retainers.

German Diplomacy in Jeddah

Nevertheless, in January 1939 the German government proceeded to establish official diplomatic relations with Saudi Arabia. On January 17 the German envoy to Baghdad, Ambassador Grobba, flew to Jeddah via Cairo to serve as a dual envoy accredited to Jeddah and Baghdad. For the Saudis the question of full diplomatic relations with Germany was one of great significance, as only a very small diplomatic corps (consisting of British, French, and Italian envoys) was accredited to Saudi Arabia. The Dutch, Turks, and Iraqis maintained a permanent chargé d'affaires. Despite this meager presence, much of the activity of these diplomatic representatives was concerned solely with Muslim *hujjaj* (pilgrims) conducting their pilgrimage to Mecca and Medina. The British had many Muslim subjects in their empire who required consular services, and the Dutch maintained a consular presence for their Muslim subjects in Indonesia visiting the holy shrines.[10]

Not surprisingly, the British envoy possessed the greatest political influence among the diplomats in Arabia. Great Britain already possessed treaties, signed in the nineteenth century, with the eastern and northern coastal states that granted Great Britain the responsibility for their foreign affairs; Britain used these treaties to indirectly limit Ibn Saud's contact with the outside world.[11]

In February 1939 Grobba had two audiences with the Saudi king and three with Sheikh Yusuf Yasin, Ibn Saud's foreign minister. From Germany, Saudi Arabia expected moral, technical, and materiel aid, mainly in the form of weapons deliveries. Ibn Saud also considered it essential to obtain German support for the Arabs on the Palestine issue. In return Ibn Saud proposed a permanent treaty of friendship and a limited trade agreement. In addition, he requested German diplomatic support in regard to several territorial claims on the Red Sea coastal town of Aqaba in Transjordan and the disputed city of Najran on the frontier with Yemen. Earlier in 1934 a brief war between Yemen and Saudi Arabia broke out that was sparked when the Idrissi of Asir withdrew his previous allegiance to Ibn Saud and fled to Yemen to join Imam Yahya.[12] The war soon ended, with the Saudi seizure of the provinces of Asir, Jizan, and Najran. Ibn Saud strong-armed the imam into making no territorial concessions and permitted a reversion to the prewar status quo. Thereafter, foreign affairs ceased to be a dominant concern, and Imam Yahya directed his attention mostly to Yemen's stabilization. The war officially ended on May 20, 1934, with the signing of the Treaty of Taif between Ibn Saud and Imam Yahya.[13]

The Saudis also revealed their lack of confidence in Fascist Italy and its dissatisfaction with the Anglo-Italian agreement regarding certain African territories bordering the Red Sea. Ibn Saud was feeling gradually encircled and encroached upon by too many European powers. The Saudi king earlier protested against that agreement, issuing a statement challenging its validity. It is likely that Ibn Saud turned to the notion of establishing relations with Germany because he feared the political division of Africa's horn would limit his ability to maneuver politically. Saudi politicians also made it clear to Grobba that, if confronted with a choice between Britain and Italy, the Arabs would favor the British. However, in return for German political support and materiel, Ibn Saud and his advisers promised neutrality in the anticipated war.[14] Of note, according to the noted Princeton Middle East academic Bernard Lewis, British military intelligence had intercepted the communications of the Saudi ambassador to Vichy France, which allowed the Allies an understanding of the progress of German penetration efforts in Arabia. Lewis served in World War II as a linguist and intelligence analyst.[15]

Despite pressure on Saudi Arabia to side with Great Britain in the Abyssinian conflict, the Ibn Saud refused to consider sanctions against Germany's ally, Italy, even going so far as to sell food, sheep, and camels to the Italians. In March 1937 Ibn Saud recognized Italy's annexation of Ethiopia and received the Italian envoy as the representative of the king of Italy and emperor of Ethiopia. In return, Italy sold Ibn Saud arms and furnished aircraft, and trained Saudi pilots.[16]

The Saudi king pretended to remain an ally of Great Britain, all the while despising the British and dealing with the Axis. Having stressed previously the necessity of Arab unity to German war strategy, Ambassador Grobba intensified his efforts to interject Germany into Arab affairs as a means of eroding British influence. As a result of his talks with Ibn Saud and other Arab leaders, Grobba was convinced the Germans provided greater opportunities to Saudi Arabia and other Arab nations than did Italy, which the Arabs considered weaker than the British despite Italy's increasing political influence in the Red Sea region and the Horn of Africa.[17]

Hirszowicz reveals the differing opinions within the German leadership over how to manage relations with Ibn Saud. Although Division Pol(itik) VII (political division 7), the political section of the German foreign ministry, began to engage in Middle Eastern affairs, the German foreign ministry as a whole as well as various senior military leaders, did not share Grobba's views on strengthening relations with Ibn Saud. They insisted that Germany should not establish closer ties with the Saudi king because of his previous close relationship with Britain. Moreover, Germany could not undertake efforts to supply Saudi Arabia with arms since the countries of the Arabian Peninsula were within the Italian sphere of interest. For example, Germany attempted economic links with Yemen, but its efforts were opposed by the Italians who considered this region their sphere of influence. By April 1939 the majority opinion prevailed in the German foreign ministry that any change of policy toward increased support to Saudi Arabia would be out of the question.[18]

The situation soon changed to such an extent, however, that Germany stopped hesitating about committing itself in the Arabian Peninsula. That same month Otto Von Hentig, director of Division Pol VII, visited Palestine and Iraq. This trip effected a radical change in Berlin's views toward strengthening relations with Saudi Arabia, and Grobba repeated his argument regarding Ibn Saud's basic hostility to Great Britain and discussed the possibility of Germany using strategically vital Saudi territory in the coming war.[19]

This attitude change in Berlin toward Saudi Arabia was felt when Khalid Al-Hud Al-Qarqani visited Berlin in June 1939. This time the Saudi king's adviser engaged not only with the Abwehr, but also with the Reich's top leaders, such as German foreign minister Ribbentrop. They discussed the shipment of rifles, anti-aircraft guns, and armored vehicles to Saudi Arabia, as well as the building of a munitions plant in the port city of Jeddah. Ibn Saud's emissary emphasized the king's desire to ease his dependence on Britain for materiel and military supplies. Ribbentrop expressed Germany's sympathy for the Arabs and delegated Von Hentig to conduct additional arms negotiations.[20]

On June 17, 1939, Hitler received Al-Hud at his mountain retreat, the Obersalzberg. Al-Hud delivered a personal letter from Ibn Saud to the German dictator, and the führer expressed his sympathy for the Arabs that he claimed began in his childhood, and declared he would provide assistance to the Saudis. By this time German policy makers no longer cared about endangering relations with Britain unnecessarily, but had to reckon more with the Italians in their gambit to engage Ibn Saud. The Germans contemplated future expansion in the Arabian Peninsula an open question, although they were convinced that they had to contact Rome before actually cooperating with Ibn Saud. During Italian foreign minister Count Ciano's visit to Berlin on the occasion of the signing of the Pact of Steel on May 22, 1939, Ernst Woermann, chief of the German foreign ministry's political department, informed Italian ambassador Gino Buti that Saudi Arabia had made countless attempts to buy arms from Germany, and they discussed the advantages of friendly relations with Ibn Saud in the event of the outbreak of war. Hirszowicz offers extraordinary details gleaned from multiple archives of the former Axis countries, which offer lessons in the use of materiel and military aid coupled with diplomacy in the pursuit of national objectives.[21]

Arms Assistance from Germany

According to Ambassador Grobba, Ibn Saud was in contact with the mufti in 1938 and 1939, and wanted to use Saudi Arabia as a base for smuggling weapons into Palestine. Nevertheless, in German negotiations with Al-Hud, Berlin showed a willingness to please Ibn Saud. In opening talks, Germany offered a 1.5 million reichsmarks credit line for the purchase of 8 thousand rifles, 8 million rounds of ammunition, and the construction of a small cartridge factory in Jeddah. In the Saudi counter-request, the Saudi representative asked for a 6 million reichsmarks credit line and privileged discounted prices on arms. As a compromise, the OKW offered Ibn Saud the rifles as a gift and a credit line of 1.5 million reichsmarks. The Abwehr also attempted to have small quantities of arms delivered to Arab insurgents in Palestine via Saudi Arabia and Iraq in 1938, though this attempt proved unsuccessful, as shipments came up short or not at all. According to Von Hentig, Fuad-bey Hamza and Rashid Ali Al-Gaylani proposed to smuggle German arms into Palestine through Saudi Arabia and the Persian Gulf. It was hoped this would incite Palestinians against the British. In a note to Undersecretary of the Political Office at the Foreign Ministry Ernst Woermann in May of 1939, Ambassador Grobba referred to money that Germany had sent to the Arab movement in Palestine via Saudi Arabia: "On behalf of King Ibn Saud, I was asked confidentially by his adviser, Sheikh Yusuf Yasin, about our relations with Fuad Hamza, and further, if we had given him the financial means for the Palestinian matter, and, when I answered that we had, I was given to understand that we should discuss matters regarding Palestine only with people whom the Grand Mufti designates as his agents."[22] The whole scheme failed because Fuad-bey Hamza was also collaborating with the British: he was a double agent.

A deal was submitted on July 17, 1939, in the form of a letter to Al-Hud, sent on a plain sheet of paper without signature. It contained three points: (1) a declaration of Berlin's readiness to express its sympathy for Saudi Arabia by supplying Ibn Saud with goods; (2) a gift to Ibn Saud of four thousand rifles of the latest construction, as well as two thousand cartridges; and (3) an agreement for the Saudi king to order war materiel on credit from German firms to the value of 6 million reichsmarks, with payments to be made in seven annual installments.[23]

This deal was never fully implemented since World War II broke out a month later, making it extremely difficult to transport arms to Red Sea ports in Saudi Arabia, due to the limitations on the use of the Suez Canal and a lack of coordination between the Germans and Italians in Red Sea operations. No shipments left Germany since it was decided in Berlin that Fuad Hamza was no longer trusted to keep the secret from London. The Abwehr arms shipments for Palestine via Saudi Arabia and Iraq were cancelled and never rescheduled. Moreover, Saudi attempts to obtain German weapons that began in 1937 took on added significance in mid-1938 with Saudi plans to transfer some German arms to Palestine, a plan Berlin rejected late in the autumn of 1938. German policy at that stage did not include arming Palestinians against the British. The German foreign ministry, the economics ministry, Ferostaal A.G. (the firm tasked with negotiating with the Saudis), and the OKW had all come out against selling arms to Ibn Saud.[24]

The German agreement to ship arms to Saudi Arabia was one of the few preliminary approaches by the Third Reich to establish a diplomatic mission in Saudi Arabia. Allied attempts came to fruition as the presence of American oil corporations in the region expanded, bringing to the forefront the possibility of diplomatic relations being established between Saudi Arabia and the United States. Encouraged by the California-Texas Oil Company (Caltex), which had purchased extraction concessions from Saudi Arabia, the U.S. government sent an envoy to Saudi Arabia. As the number of Americans in the region increased considerably, Saudi Arabia was brought firmly into the Allied fold, thus removing permanently any further economic or political penetrations by the Axis powers for the duration of the war. Saudi Arabia severed diplomatic contacts with Germany on September 11, 1939, and with Japan in October of 1941.[25]

Japanese Collaboration and Trade Contact in the Muslim World

Japan's global ambitions in Asia were not entirely devoid of Islamic manipulation and intrigue. Propaganda directed toward the Muslim community presented Japan as a liberator of Muslims from Western imperialism in the Pacific and Indian Oceans, and marketed itself as religiously tolerant. Prior to World War II, Japanese Nationalists displayed an Asian face to the world's Muslims, whom they wanted to befriend as potential collaborators in the development of a new Asia under Japanese domination. The 1905 Battle of Tsushima and defeat of Russia by the Japanese before World War I did not go unnoticed by the world's anticolonial leaders in Asia. The rise of Japan presented itself as a destabilizing factor that fascinated Muslim activists who desired to collaborate with Tokyo against the European empires, with the aim of establishing themselves as a regional power much like Japan. This caused accelerated contacts between Tokyo and the Muslim world in Eurasia and North Africa. During the Tokyo Trials, Shumei Okawa, the major intellectual figure of pan-Asianism and an Islamic scholar, justified Japan's mission to liberate Asia from Western colonialism by war if necessary and saw Islam as the means to achieve it. In the late 1930s and early 1940s, the relationship transformed into a military strategy as Tokyo began to implement its Islam-oriented policy by mobilizing Muslim forces against Britain, the Netherlands, and China.[26]

During 1938 the Japanese government started to implement its Islam-oriented policy by creating Dai Nippon Kaikyo Kyokai (DNKK; the greater Japan Islamic league) with the support of the Gaimusho (Japanese foreign ministry), the army, and the navy. The DNKK was the official Islamic organization set up by Japan during World War II. Its primary objective was to undertake propaganda work to undermine British and Dutch influence in East Asia among the Muslim population. The DNKK's side objective was to promote Islamic studies, introduce Islamic culture to the Muslim world, develop mutual trade ties, promote cultural exchange, and foster policy research. Tokyo's adoption of an Islam policy was part of its pan-Asian foreign policy, which was characterized by a Tokyo mosque that was opened in 1938 in the neighborhood of Yoyogi-Uehara. The opening ceremony publicly exposed Japan's Islam-oriented policy on the eve of World War II, just as the Imperial Japanese were contemplating expansion beyond China and Korea and into Malaya, Indonesia, and the eastern Pacific islands.[27]

During the 1942 South Seas invasion of the Dutch Indies, Japanese Muslim agents organized the local Muslim leaders and communities to aid the initial entry of Japanese forces. One of the prominent Muslim collaborationists was Abdul Rashid Ibrahim, a Russian Tatar journalist and respected Ottoman pan-Islamist intellectual. His activities sowed the seeds of training Japanese agents to be sent to the Muslim countries under Muslim identity, a tactic that the military authorities were to use during the Second World War. Ibrahim began broadcasting war propaganda on behalf of Japan to the Indonesians. His rhetoric was fully in keeping with a warlike interpretation of jihad that the Nazis hoped to incite in French and British possessions in the Middle East, India, and Asia. A sample of Ibrahim broadcasts included, "Japan's cause in Dai Toa Senso [the Great East Asia War] is a sacred one and in its austerity is comparable to the war carried out against the infidels by the Prophet Muhammad in the past."[28] This became the core of Imperial Japan's position toward Muslims that momentarily made it acceptable to Indonesians who were hoping for emancipation from Dutch colonialism.

As Japan's relations with the United States steadily deteriorated toward the end of the decade, oil became more and more important for Japan's increased military demands. Southeast Asia, particularly the Dutch East Indies, was of the greatest interest to Japan, which also directed its interest toward Middle Eastern oil. In fact, certain quantities of Bahrain's crude oil were exported to Japan in the 1930s. Moreover, in 1939 MTC (Mitsubishi Trading Company) made a purchase agreement for 200,000 tons of Iranian crude oil with APOC, but only 40,000 to 50,000 tons were actually shipped to Japan in 1941.[29]

In May 1938 the Saudi minister in London, Sheikh Hafiz Wahaba, traveled to Japan to attend an opening ceremony of the Tokyo mosque. While he was in Tokyo the minister told Mr. Inoue, the head of the Euro-Asian bureau in the Japanese foreign ministry, that the Saudi government was ready to offer Japan oil concessions. The Japanese minister to Egypt, Masayuki Yokoyama, traveled to Riyadh, and a negotiation for an oil concession took place between the Japanese minister and Sheikh Yusuf Yasin on April 6, 1939, in Jeddah. However, they did not reach an agreement. The Saudis made a proposal to Japan for a concession for the areas around Dahna Desert, Wadi Sirhan, and the Saudi-Kuwaiti Neutral Zone. However, during the Saudi-Japanese talks in Jeddah, the Saudis replaced the Neutral Zone proposal with the western half of the Rub' al-Khali Desert. But the Japanese were convinced that there was no oil in the other areas and were only interested in the Neutral Zone. Moreover, they were forbidden to travel around and make a preliminary survey of these areas. The Saudis requested that they sign a concessionary agreement and pay the Saudi government an initial concession fee of £200,000 in gold. The Japanese minister rejected the Saudi terms and turned the offer down.[30]

Japan's trade with the Middle East was not immediately interrupted with the outbreak of the war in September 1939. However, with the fall of France in June 1940 and the war's spread to the Middle East, the Suez Canal was closed to Japanese shipping, and only limited quantities of Japanese goods could be imported into various parts of the region through the port of Basra. In 1941, Egypt, Iraq, and Iran broke diplomatic ties with Tokyo. All representative offices of Japanese trading companies such as MTC closed down in Beirut, Baghdad, Tehran, and Alexandria. Even if Japan had been granted the oil concession, it could not have made good use of it during the war. It is noteworthy that as early as 1939 has Japan made such attempts in far-distant Saudi Arabia, with whom Japan had no diplomatic relations.[31]

Kuwait, the Ottoman Empire, and Imperial Germany

Germany envisaged a network of railroads that connected the Central Powers and the Near East as a strategic tool, a profiting venture, and a stabilizing factor for their Ottoman allies. However, suspicious of these penetrations and hoping to prevent its European rivals access to the Gulf, London concluded a covert agreement with the ruler of Kuwait, Sheikh Mubarak bin Al-Sabah (ruled 1896–1915), in January 1899. London intelligence learned that Germany wanted to extend the Berlin–Istanbul railroad from Basra to the Kuwaiti port of Kazima. After a visit with the Kuwaiti sheikh from the German railway commission in September that same year, Sheikh Mubarak bin Al-Sabah refused such a rail line through Kuwait as per his agreement with British political resident Malcolm John Meade.[32]

The Germans, however, felt that the Kuwaiti ruler could be persuaded. As one German official stated, "There are 25,000 inhabitants residing in Kuwait. Their Arab ruler, Sheikh Mubarak, is only a nominal subject of the Ottomans. There is no doubt that the port of Kazima belongs to the Ottomans. And it would be easy for them to realize their interests by force."[33] Since London's main concern was the growing German presence in the Near East, the Kuwaiti ruler's worry was that such a railway would allow the Ottomans to further exert their influence in Kuwait. The Ottoman administration in Basra considered Kuwait as an integral section of its sphere of influence.[34]

By 1913, through an effort by British Persian Gulf resident Sir Percy Cox, the Anglo-Ottoman Convention was signed; it recognized Kuwait as an autonomous entity, by which the British were able to secure potential oil fields in Kuwait. Britain recognized Kuwait as an independent state under British guardianship on November 3, 1914.[35]

Following the First World War, the British invalidated the Anglo-Ottoman Convention of 1913 that initially defined Kuwait as an autonomous *qad'a* (district) of the provincial subgovernment of the Ottoman Empire under Sheikh Mubarak bin Al-Sabah. The British declared Kuwait to be an independent sheikhdom under British protectorate after the collapse of the Ottoman Empire. The Uqair Protocol of 1922, held by London's high commissioner in Iraq, Sir Percy Cox, met with Ibn Saud and British political agent to Kuwait Major John More at Al-Uqair on November 2. It is here Cox defined the boundaries between Iraq, Kuwait, and Nejd (Central Saudi Arabia), with Kuwait losing part of its land to the Saudis, and a neutral zone established between the three countries.[36]

Kuwaiti Scrutiny over Axis Political Maneuvering

The Kuwait Oil Company was established in 1934, jointly owned by Anglo-Iranian Oil Company and Gulf Oil Corporation; with the discovery of oil on February 23, 1938, it established the Al-Burqan oil fields. The country's economy was revolutionized as a valuable asset to Britain. The Axis powers, in particular Berlin, saw Kuwait as a very secondary area for its policy, unlike Iraq, Iran, and Saudi Arabia. In 1941, on the same day the Germans began their invasion of Russia, the British took total control of Kuwait. Nevertheless, contacts between the Germans and Kuwaitis were attempted. Dr. Grobba closely followed developments in Kuwait and, in 1938 he reported the aspirations of some Arab tribes to establish the Vereinigte Arabische Scheichtum (United Arab Sheikhdoms) as a union of the smaller states under Saudi leadership. In 1938 broadcasters from Radio Bari boasted about the friendship of Italy and the emir of Kuwait Ahmed al-Jaber al-Sabah (ruled 1921–1950), a regular listener to Radio Bari and keen reader of Italian publications. The Saudi idea of getting the British to intervene in addressing Italian influence operations in Kuwait was rejected by London, much to Ibn Saud's disappointment. The Saudi leader saw Italian interference in Kuwait as upsetting the balance of power among the Arab sheikhdoms, and Saudi Arabia's hegemonic position on the Arabian Peninsula.[37]

In April of 1938 Britain continued to search for evidence to persuade the Iraqis that Iraq, under King Ghazi (ruled 1933–1939), had no legitimate claim to Kuwait. Foreign minister Tewfik Suweidi had indicated in 1932 that Iraq was raising the question to seek an "extension of the Iraqi railway to Kuwait Bay, in order to provide Iraq with a port on the Persian Gulf."[38] Tewfik Suweidi made a speech before the Iraqi parliament stating Kuwait was an inseparable part of Iraq because it was Iraq's natural outlet to the sea. In Geneva on September 28, 1938, Suweidi gave the British parliamentary undersecretary for foreign affairs R. A. Butler a draft, stating, "The Iraqi government, as successors of the Ottoman government in the Wilayats [provinces] of Basra, Baghdad, and Mosul, considers that Kuwait should be incorporated in Iraq. If incorporations should take place, Iraq would agree to maintain the local autonomy of Kuwait."[39] Shortly thereafter, the British embassy in Iraq presented Iraq with the following response: "The Sheikhdom of Kuwait was for a considerable period in an anomalous state of semi-independence on the Ottoman Empire, His Majesty's Government have nevertheless been in treaty relations with the Sheikhs since 1841, and Kuwait finally became completely independent of Turkey and Kuwaiti nationality finally came into existence on the same date as Iraq and Iraqi nationality."[40]

As the Germans received reports on the situation in Kuwait, so Kuwaitis were informed on the developments of the Nazis' diplomatic attempts with Ibn Saud and Gaylani. While in Berlin, the pro-Axis Iraqi figure Rashid Ali Al-Gaylani had asked that Kuwait be annexed as an Iraqi territory. For this purpose he had his own radio station in the Al-Zuhoor Royal Palace, established by King Ghazi I of Iraq (d. 1939) in 1936. King Ghazi promoted Iraq's claim to Kuwait incessantly, openly expressing his disdain for the 1922 Uqair Accords as the British imposing artificial borders upon Iraq. This inevitably brought Kuwait firmly into the arms of the Allies for the remainder of the war. On December 24, 1942, Ambassador Grobba received orders from Berlin to no longer engage in Arab politics, officially ending all further German exploitations of Arab Nationalist movements in the Middle East.[41]

Historical evidence and the authors delving into numerous volumes turn up no political or military attempts by the Axis toward the neighboring Arab gulf state of Qatar. With the discovery of oil in 1939–1940 in the Dukhan fields and a treaty with the Al-Thani royal family that gave London virtual control over Qatari foreign policy, Qatar was practically untouched by any Axis intrigue before or during the war.

Arabia Felix

Yemen was the only country on the Arabian Peninsula that to some extent broke away from the general pattern of British regional dominance. Prior to the First World War, the imam of Yemen signed the Treaty of Daan with the Ottoman presence in Yemen in 1911, supporting the Ottomans during the upcoming war. The treaty allowed for recognition of his rule over North Yemen. With British realization of the gradual dissolution of the Ottoman influence in the Hijaz coast, including Yemen, the British began a gradual diplomatic and military infiltration aimed at controlling major ports in Yemen, which included the strategic port of Aden.

The ever-growing British presence in India made the Gulf an area of strategic importance. Constant piratical threats to British merchant shipping to and from British India ended in the 1839 landing of Royal Marines at Aden to occupy the territory. The Treaty of 1886 signed by the nine Bedouin chieftains with the British government created the Aden Protectorate (later to become the People's

Democratic Republic of Yemen); the Colony of Aden was to be governed by British India. In exchange for British protection, rulers of the adjacent territories concurred to cede no territory or agree to any other foreign power's diplomatic attempts without direct British consent. By the end of the First World War the control of the Aden Protectorate was relocated from British India to the British foreign office.[42]

With foreign and domestic aggravation in the Near East at an all-time high after the implementation of the 1916 Sykes-Picot Agreement, after World War I Britain established an RAF presence in Aden, called Aden Command, headed by Captain William G. S. Mitchell, to safeguard the protectorate from potential foreign aggression. The RAF Base Khormaksar was established in 1917. Coastal reconnaissance flights and antisubmarine patrols were its main duties through the war. It played an active role during the East African campaign; testimony to the success of its work is that only a small number of ships were lost in the Red Sea and Gulf of Aden. Aden served as fuel depot and convoy route to British India and the Persian Corridor, and for logistical convoys sailing into the Red Sea from the Cape of Good Hope. Aden Command was reestablished later in 1936, as British forces remained in Aden for the remainder of the Second World War. The Colony of Aden was detached from the governing body of British India under the Government of India Act of August 2, 1935, to be established as the capital of the British Crown Colony of Aden.[43]

Anglo-Italian Diplomacy in Yemen

Overall, Yemen experienced very modest Axis infiltration, and seldom did Germany make efforts toward Yemen such as they made toward the Saudis. German efforts at extending economic aid to Yemen were met with suspicion, mainly by Italy. The Italians proposed to take over the role of Britain in Southern Arabia, and were suspect of any German encroachment. With Italian Somaliland and Eritrea draining the resources of Rome, Mussolini sought potential economic prospects on the opposite side of the Red Sea seeing that Arabian oil might rescue Italy's losing colonial venture in the Horn of Africa. The Italian principle was that the increased ties with Yemen might increase trade with Italian East African colonies and bring Southern Arabia under the Italian sphere of influence. In spite of conflicting Anglo-Italian aims, relations between Rome and London remained relatively undamaged until the Ethiopian crisis of 1935. The image of Rome was of a power whose interests were inimical to those of Britain but that lacked the economic and military means to pose a serious threat. In 1921 Italian attempts to obtain oil and mineral concessions from the Idrissi leadership in southern Yemen intensified. Large quantities of arms and ammunition were intended to induce the Idrissi tribal coalition to abandon its alliance with Britain and establish a preferential partnership with Rome. It is important to understand the Idrissi. The Italians were pressing for permission to open a consulate in Hodeidah, to create a local branch of the Marittima Italiana shipping line, and to be granted concessions in the Farasan Islands. The Idrissi sheikh, Syed Ali, however, was unwilling to endanger his relations with the British.[44]

In September 1926 Fascist Italy signed a Treaty of Amity and Economic Relations with the imam of Sanaa, Amir Yahya Muhammad Hamiduddin. The treaty recognized Yahya as king of all Yemen. This provoked serious complications in Anglo-Italian relations, for the British government interpreted this as Italian recognition of the imam's claims to sovereignty over Aden, the protectorate, Hadramawt, and Idrissi territory. Britain therefore made attempts to obtain recognition by the Italian government of the limitation of the Yemeni frontiers. Rome scrutinized provisions of the 1917 Anglo-Idrissi Treaty by which Britain undertook to defend the coast of Asir (Southern Arabia) in the event of foreign attack. With his desire to secure control over the Aden protectorate, Yahya began acquiring weapons and military supplies from Rome. Italian assistance to Yemen commenced with supplies of telegraph equipment, medical staff, arms, ammunition, and planes. In 1927 Yemeni troops, armed by Italy, steadily advanced into the territory of Asir. This incursion incited the intervention of Ibn Saud, whose forces saved the Idrissi sheikh from being decimated by the Italian-equipped Imam Yahya, and a Saudi governor took over the administration of Asir in accordance with the Mecca Agreement that the Idrissi signed with Ibn Saud in 1926, a year before the escalation of tensions brought on by Italian regional meddling.[45] Conversations with Rome had already been held on the question of the supply of arms to Yemen, which German firms wanted to undertake as part of their diplomacy to influence the region. In these conversations, Rome stressed that Yemen was in Italy's sphere of influence; as a result, Germany ceased negotiations with Yemen despite serious reservations about Italy's ability to sway the Arab leaders toward the side of the Axis. This lack of trust between Germany and Italy over managing affairs in the Middle East would be a consistent theme that would be a weakness when compared to Allied relationships, particularly those between Britain and the United States. Italian munitions were landed in Yemen's port cities of Mocha and Hodeidah. These landings were followed by the formation of an Italian-Arabian company for the export of petroleum products to Yemen. The Italo-Yemeni Treaty of 1926, also known as the Treaty of Sanaa, was followed in mid-1927 by the visit to Rome of an official Yemeni delegation. The Italians arranged a program for their visitors, emphasizing Italian strength in the fields of naval, air, and army activity. The imam approached the Italian authorities in Eritrea for anti-aircraft as well as light and heavy guns. In January 1928 the Italian gunboat *Lugnano* was placed at the disposal of the imam for patrolling the coast. Arrivals of arms continued throughout 1928. In January 1929 nine Yemeni officers traveled to Italy for pilot training and returned as fully qualified pilots. It would be interesting to study those nine officers and if their exposure to Italian military training changed their sociopolitical outlook, but this is a subject for future study. Imam Yahya also established diplomatic relations with the Soviet Union in 1928.[46] British diplomat Sir Victor Alexander Louis Mallet suggested that Italian interest in Yemen was stimulated by the possibilities of oil in the Farasan Islands, thirty miles from the Arabian coast city of Jizan. Italian aspirations over the Red Sea islands of Farasan and Kamaran were not new. Italian claims on the islands had been considered during the 1919 Paris Peace Conference.[47]

The British foreign office was beginning to understand just how important the imam was and the growing significance and deepening of his relationship with Italy. The prospect of the Italian-Yemeni treaty was of considerable concern to the British, which was viewed as a potential interference to British interests in trade around Aden and Somaliland. Sir Mallet stated that "we do not want Italy playing at politics anywhere in Arabia, and sooner or later we shall have to tell her so."[48] Italian senator Jacopo Gasparini, the mastermind behind the commercial and political intervention and member of the Italian colonial ministry and governor of Eritrea, was the driving force behind Rome's insistent presence toward Yemen and the Arabian Peninsula. Gasparini believed that for Eritrea to be an effective instrument of influence in the Red Sea, it had to play as a springboard for radiating influence throughout Arabia. He immediately dispatched agents and merchants to the opposite shore of the Red Sea with the goal of seeking economic advantages at the expense of the British.[49]

Although the British foreign office differed in its views to the colonial office with regard to the imam, the latter being rather more jaundiced in its interpretation of his activities, British concern over Italian activity was shared. Major General John M. Stewart, a British resident of Aden, stated regarding the Red Sea Isles that it is "most undesirable that any foreign power should obtain a position in this group of Islands which to the best of my belief would make an excellent submarine base on a vital trade route."[50] Although the British colonial office suggested military action to occupy areas under the imam's sphere of influence, Britain's foreign secretary Austen Chamberlain sent chief secretary in Palestine Sir Gilbert Clayton to meet with the imam. The meetings with the imam proved futile and the imam refused to recognize the protectorate treaties signed decades ago with the British.

With Italy now gaining momentum on the eastern side of the Red Sea, Rome increased its supply of war materiel to the imam. The tension between Ibn Saud and the imam had in fact driven the imam to seek Italy's military assistance. At the beginning of 1932 a conspiracy involving attacks on Hijaz from the north and the south attracted the attention of the newly appointed governor of Eritrea, Riccardo Astuto. The aim was the overthrow of Ibn Saud and the reestablishment of the Hashemite House. Rome, however, repeated its directives to conduct a policy of strict neutrality and, hence, Astuto's plan did not go beyond providing initial shipments of arms to the imam.[51] Britain sought to preempt Italian intrusion in the Farasan Islands by allowing APOC to bid for the oil concessions. The British foreign office began supplying arms to the imam's pro-British counterpart, the Idrissi of Asir. The worsening situation prompted Prime Minister Chamberlain to state, "[W]e are engaging in a covert war with Italy, she under the Imam's Flag and we under the Idrissi."[52] The Italian and Yemeni governments agreed to renew their Treaty of Amity and Economic Relations on October 15, 1937, for a period of twenty-five years.

On April 16, 1938, Italy and Britain arrived at an understanding whereby they mutually agreed not to acquire "privileged positions of a political character" in Saudi Arabia and Yemen.[53] The Anglo-Italian accord agreed to preserve the status quo in the eastern Mediterranean and the Red Sea. In return for British acceptance of Italian conquest in Ethiopia and a preponderant role in Yemen, Italy agreed to end its anti-British propaganda in the Near East. British delegations paid a number of successful visits to Sanaa during the Second World War and persuaded Imam Yahya to close two Axis broadcasting stations and break off diplomatic relations with Germany.[54] Chamberlain's characterization of a covert war was spot on, and a little-studied aspect of Allied and Axis competition in Yemen. Controlling Yemen meant not only control of resources, but mainly vital sea lanes of communications and strategic port facilities linking Europe and Asia, as well as denial of shipping from and to the Suez Canal.

Axis Naval Activity in the Arabian Sea

The Red Sea Flotilla was established in June of 1940 by the Italian Royal Navy and was based in Massawa, Eritrea. Its primary mission was the interdiction of naval traffic coming from the Indian Ocean and directed to North Africa and the Near East, disrupting Allied shipping in the Red Sea. The Italian naval task force was situated to intercept Allied convoys in the Gulf of Aden through the Suez Canal. This was a critical resupply route for British forces operating from Egypt. It comprised seven *Belva-* and *Patrioti*-class destroyers, eight submarines, five torpedo-armed motorboats, and auxiliary ships.[55]

The Regia Marina (Italian navy) fleet constantly harassed Allied shipping in the Red Sea and the Arabian Gulf. The Italian submarine *Torricelli* was on patrol in the Gulf of Aden on June 23, 1940, when she was intercepted by the destroyers HMS *Kandahar*, HMS *Khartoum*, HMS *Kingston*, and the sloop HMS *Shoreham*. The *Torricelli* was unable to dive but fought a gun and torpedo battle before scuttling herself. A shell from the Italian submarine hit HMS *Khartoum*, which suffered a fire resulting in an ammunition explosion sinking the ship. The Italian submarine *Galileo Galilei* was dispatched to patrol the coast of Yemen. *Galilei* sank the Norwegian freighter *James Stove* off the coast of Djibouti, and HMS *Khartoum* and *Shoreham* were damaged beyond repair.[56] The offensive capacity of the Red Sea Flotilla slowly declined with its diminishing fuel supplies, however. Attempted raids on the Suez Canal and Port Sudan by the 3rd and 5th Italian Destroyer Divisions ended in Italian losses of all seven destroyers either sunk or scuttled. With British forces nearing Asmara and with the fall of Massawa on April 8, 1941, the Allied victory of the East African campaign sealed all future Italian naval interdictions along the Arabian coastlines and the Suez Canal. A few Italian naval units managed to survive the campaign. The submarines *Guglielmotti, Galileo Ferraris, Perla*, and *Archimede* sailed to Bordeaux, France. Two colonial armed merchant cruisers, *Eritrea* and *Ramb II*, were able to reach Kobe, Japan.[57]

Germany's navy dispatched the auxiliary cruiser *Atlantis* along with U-boats to the North Indian Ocean and the Arabian coast. In late January 1941, off the eastern coast of Africa, *Atlantis* sank the British ship *Mandasor* and captured the British ship *Speybank*. Then, on February 2, 1941, the Norwegian tanker *Ketty Brøvig* was relieved of her fuel, which was used not only for the *Atlantis*, but also to refuel the German cruiser *Admiral Scheer* and the Italian submarine *Perla*, which was making its way from the port of Massawa around the Cape of Good Hope to Bordeaux.[58]

The German U-boats sunk HMS *Ocean Honor* off the coast of the Socotra archipelago in the Gulf of Aden in September 1942. By April 8, 1942, the Japanese had formally agreed to dispatch submarines to the east coast of Africa. The *Ocean Vintage* was sunk by Japanese submarine *I-27* south of Ras al-Hadd off the coast of Oman near Masirah Island in November of the same year. Japanese naval presence reached as far as Muscat Harbor, sinking the Norwegian merchant liner *Dah Pu* while unloading cargo in Muscat Harbor on June 28, 1943. On June 24, 1943, the British tanker *British Venture* was sunk by the Japanese submarine *I-27* about thirty-five miles south of the Iranian port town of Jask. On May 7, 1943, the *I-27* torpedoed, shelled, and sank the Dutch freighter *Berakit* in the Gulf of Oman. On June 3, 1943, the *I-27* torpedoed the American freighter *Montanan* 150 miles south of Masirah Island. Utilizing its aircraft-borne submarines, Japan dispatched *I-30* for reconnaissance operations in the Hadramawt region of Northern Yemen.[59]

A convoy of tankers proceeding toward Aden sighted German *U-188* off Masirah Island. The German U-boat moved along the coast toward the Gulf of Oman and torpedoed the Norwegian tanker *Britannia* as she headed toward the Persian port city of Bandar Abbas. Axis submarines had come within seventy miles of the Straits of Hormuz but were unable to pass through due to intense Allied air station patrols. Although Axis submarines persisted to maneuver along Arabia's coasts, the Royal Navy chose to suspend convoys in the Gulf of Aden and the Arabian Sea, such was the impact of Japanese operations in this sector.

The Bahrain Archipelago

Located twenty miles off the Arabian coast, the island of Bahrain was not immune to the ravages of the Second World War. In the late 1920s and early 1930s, American oil company Standard Oil Company of California (SOCAL) expressed keen interest in Bahrain, signing a concession agreement with Sheikh Hamad bin Isa Al-Khalifa (ruled 1932–1942) creating a subsidiary known as Bahrain Petroleum Company Limited (BapCo) and began drilling on June 1, 1932. In 1935 SOCAL joined with its Texas counterpart to form Caltex. With the discovery of oil in 1932, the construction of Royal Air Field Muharraq, and an establishment of the British naval installation HMS *Juffair* in Manama by April 13, 1935, Bahrain under Sheikh Hamad declared war on Nazi Germany on September 10, 1939. Bahraini forces fought under British command for the duration of the Middle East theater.[60] Of note, the HMS *Juffair* naval installation was leased by the U.S. Navy after Bahrain's independence in 1971; it is home to the U.S. Fifth Fleet.

Apart from food rationing, the war had little impact on the island with the exception of a long-range bomber raid by Fascist Italy. Bahrain became a strategic Allied archipelago safeguarding oil supplies in the Persian Gulf. With the ongoing East African campaign that began in June 1940, Italy was being pressed by British forces from Italian Ethiopia through British Somaliland. From July through September 1940 Rome bombed the island of Perim located at the southern entrance of the Red Sea, and Tel Aviv and Haifa. Their proximity to Palestine enabled Italian planes to be dispatched to bomb strategic targets. In July of 1940 the port of Haifa was targeted with the intention of demolishing both ports and refineries. Residential neighborhoods in Tel Aviv were targeted by the Italian air force. Civil defense measures and blackouts were instigated in most major cities in Palestine, including Acre and Jaffa.[61]

Italian Air Raids on Haifa and Manama

One of the unexplored events that occurred in Palestine during the Second World War was the series of bomber raids on civilian and military targets in Palestine by the Axis air forces of Italy, Germany, and Vichy France. Although these attacks caused considerable damage in the major cities of Tel Aviv and Haifa, they failed to alter the course of the war in the Near East. During the Italo-Ethiopian War, the Regia Aeronautica (Italian air force) began examining targets for bombardment in Egypt, Palestine, and Cyprus, among other areas of the eastern Mediterranean. To prepare for these contingencies, they upgraded their military preparedness in the Dodecanese Islands—the only Italian territories within reach of the eastern Mediterranean coast. In April 1936 General Pietro Pinna, deputy chief of staff of the Regia Aeronautica, inspected the Dodecanese Islands and submitted detailed plans that turned their airfields into forward operating bases with the ability to support offensive operations in the eastern Mediterranean. His recommendations were implemented, and on March 1, 1937, the Comando Aeronautica dell'Egeo (Aegean air force command) was established.[62] This demonstrated the importance of islands in the eastern Mediterranean for the projection of air and sea power in the Middle East and North Africa.

Italian military intelligence took an interest in Haifa, focusing on their oil refineries and British naval base. The Italian navy chief of staff, Domenico Cavagnari, noted that the Allied navies were heavily dependent on oil that reached Haifa and Tripoli through the Iraqi Petroleum Company pipeline. In January 1938 Axis plans, code-named PR 12, were drawn up to strike Alexandria, Port Said in Egypt, Haifa in British Palestine, and Beirut in French-controlled Lebanon as targets of major importance in the eastern Mediterranean. However, with the Easter Accords signed between Britain and Italy in April 1938, these plans were tabled in favor of a focused assault on the Balkans. Though Italy produced one of the best-known air power theorists of the early twentieth century, Guilio Douhet, the Italians were ill equipped to carry out strategic bombings because most of their aircraft were outdated and technologically inferior compared to British and French aircraft. For example, the SM-81 fighter, first flown in 1935, was considered obsolete by the time Italy entered World War II five years later.[63]

British and municipal authorities in Haifa, Palestine, prepared for defensive measures in September 1939 when war broke out in Europe. As the likelihood of Italy joining the war increased, evacuation plans were drawn to move women, children, and the elderly from the city. After the fall of France in June 1940, Mussolini pushed for an Italian offensive against the British in Egypt. Before Italy's attack on Egypt got under way in September 1940 under Marshal Rodolfo Graziani, army chief of staff and commander of Italian armed forces in Libya, the Regia Aeronautica had an opportunity to attack British strategic positions in the Near East and shipping in the eastern Mediterranean. De Vecchi, Italian governor in Rhodes, was fairly free to select targets for his aerial units that were eager to see action.[64]

Italian aircraft took off from the Dodecanese Islands in July and August 1940, bound for Palestine and raids on the port and oil refineries of Haifa. The first raid took place on July 15 with five Italian aircraft commanded by Major Ettore Muti, general secretary of the Fascist Party. The aircraft approached Haifa and dropped more than fifty bombs on and near the Iraq Petroleum Company installation. Oil tanks and power stations were severely damaged, resulting in a temporary interruption of the city's electricity supply. The second raid on July 24 aimed for the oil refineries and storage facilities. Most of the casualties worked at the Shell Oil Company installation. Many American citizens working in these oil refineries left Haifa as a result of these air raids. Mussolini induced Graziani finally to launch a ground offensive against Egypt. By September Italian air raids in the eastern Mediterranean had intensified. From July 1940 until September 1942 a total of approximately twenty-seven Axis air raids were conducted in Palestine, fourteen of them Italian, nine German, and four Vichy French, killing two hundred civilians, damaging infrastructure and property, and temporarily disrupting the work of the oil refineries in Haifa. Target cities included Tel Aviv, Jaffa, Ramla, and Acre. However, militarily and politically the attacks failed to achieve any considerable gains for the Axis.[65]

The Regia Aeronautica, realizing that it lacked strategic bombers, decided to transform several three-engined transports into planes capable of conducting strategic bombing raids. Of all air raids made by Fascist Italy during the war, such as the bombing of Port Sudan, Gibraltar, and the Suez Canal, the air raid on Bahrain may have been the most futile. At the beginning of October 1940 the command of the Regia Aeronautica decided that a group of newly fitted SM-82 bombers led by Lieutenant Colonel Ettore Muti should be transferred from Rome to the airport of Gadurrà in the Dodecanese Islands. Lieutenant Colonel Muti was later indicated to be a participant in one of the bombings of Haifa and the Battle of Britain. The Italian Command planned to utilize the special SM-82s to bomb the Allied BapCo oil refinery plants at Manama. Mussolini had approved the plan developed by Regia Aeronautica captain Paolo Moci to show the potential ability of Regia Aeronautica to inhibit a steady supply to the British Navy. This mission, involving a 2,983-mile flight, was conducted by Ettore Muti and his comrades.[66]

En route they would have to avoid RAF patrols out of Iraq, bomb the oil refinery, cross Arabia, and land in Eritrea. The Italians decided that the highly dangerous flight of returning back to the Dodecanese Islands on the same route was too risky, fearing interception by the RAF based in Cyprus, Palestine, or Iraq. As a precaution, the Italians equipped the flotilla with a homing beacon and ordered another SM-82 cargo plane to stand by at Massawa airfield in Eritrea filled with gasoline to refuel the mission in case the raiders were forced to land in the Arabian Desert. In command of the first aircraft was Lieutenant Colonel Muti, assisted by Major Giovanni Raina and Captain Paolo Moci. Lieutenant Colonel Fortunato Federici, Captain Aldo Buzzaca, and Lieutenant Emanuele Francesco Ruspoli were on the second aircraft, while Captain Giorgio Meyer, Lieutenant Adolf Rebex, and Warrant Officer Aldo Carrera were on the third plane. The fourth plane was piloted by Captain Antonio Zanetti assisted by Lieutenant Vittorio Cecconi and Warrant Officer Mario Badii.[67]

For security purposes, Lieutenant Colonel Muti decided that radio communications cease. The planes carried more than 1,300 gallons of fuel each as they took off. The Mediterranean sky was clear as the planes traveled over Vichy French Syria. Over the mountains of Lebanon, Lieutenant Colonel Muti lost visual contact with one of the planes. The other planes continued on their mission early that morning of October 19, 1940. As they flew over the Kuwaiti coast, they dropped to three thousand feet, banking toward the northern coast of Bahrain. The refinery was unprotected with clear visibility.[68] Unaware they were the target, Allied ground control was surprised by the sight of SM-82s and assumed they were friendly aircraft. The Italians released their bomb loads on the refinery as they banked toward Ethiopia to report back to Rome on the destruction of the refinery. The plane lost over Damascus surprisingly appeared over Dhahran, dropping its bombs on the Arabian city's crude oil separator plant and heading to Massawa Airport, reaching Eritrea with forty gallons of fuel to spare. Interestingly enough, the RAF decided to bomb Massawa Airport that day and so, through radio, Lieutenant Colonel Muti guided the formation to nearby Zula.[69]

The Italian formation had flown fewer than 1,865 miles in more than fifteen hours. They then returned to Rome through Benghazi, on the way bombing a British harbor installation in Port Sudan. The pilots learned later that the refinery was unharmed despite optimum conditions. The Italian flight commander received poor intelligence and the bombs fell harmlessly onto a petroleum coke pile. In Dhahran one bomb merely cut a water main and punctured an oil line as the rest fell in a sand pile. The raid on Manama, though unique for its time, gained the Axis very little except for Italian propaganda value. The RAF placed a squadron of fighters close to the refineries and some batteries of antiaircraft guns for the remainder of the war. Moci and Muti were later decorated by Mussolini. The Italian air raid distinguished itself as possibly one of the first to hold a World War II record for a long-distance strategic bombing run before the advent of the U.S. B-29s.[70]

Allied Ties with the Sultanate of Oman

During the 1930s the United States renewed its trade relationship with Oman, sending to Muscat the American envoy to Baghdad, Mr. Paul Knabenshue, in 1934. With Knabenshue went a letter from President Franklin D. Roosevelt, marking the centennial celebration of the 1833 Treaty of Amity and Commerce between the United States and Oman. This 1833 treaty was considered the first bilateral accord between the United States and an Arab Gulf state. The U.S. envoy was welcomed by Omani ruler Sayyid Sa'id bin Taymur, and Knabenshue presented an official invitation to the Omani ruler from President Franklin Roosevelt to tour the United States in 1938. In that year bin Taymur visited Washington, DC, and was greeted as an honored guest by Secretary of State Cordell Hull. Joseph Kechichian has an excellent account of America's diplomacy in Oman in his RAND study *Oman and the World*. During the war, the Omani ruler proved a reliable supporter of the Allies, providing base access between Europe, Africa, and Asia.

The British provided Oman military and financial support toward the defense of Muscat, sending Major L. B. Hirst and the 10th Gurkhas to the sultanate as trainers and advisers. In return the British received use of the airfields at Salalah, Al-Masirah, and Ras al-Hadd. The sultan made available to U.S. aircraft bound for the Far East the British RAF facilities at Salalah, in the Dhofar province of Oman, and the facilities on Masirah Island. A small number of U.S. Army Air Force maintenance personnel would be stationed at these British RAF facilities servicing transiting aircraft; they would also undertake the upgrading of both Ras al-Hadd and Masirah airfields.[71]

The competition for the Arabian Peninsula in World War II between the Axis and Allies would see an aggressive use of economics, propaganda, diplomacy, and espionage to ensure the loyalty of tribes, emirs, and religious imams. Competition in the region would continue as World War II was coming to a climax when Churchill and Franklin Roosevelt argued about postwar oil policy in 1944. Roosevelt privately worried, "I am disturbed by the rumors the British want to horn in on Saudi Arabian oil reserves."[72] It makes for an excellent discussion among America's military planners today as we confront the challenges of the region in the twenty-first century. As has been seen, Italy almost gained control of Yemen by sponsoring Imam Yahya against all other Yemeni leadership factions. The struggle to influence tribes continues to this day.

CHAPTER 8

Afghanistan and the Third Reich
Fomenting Rebellions

We resist British Imperialism no less than Nazism. If there is a difference, it is in degree. One-fifth of the human race has been brought under the British heel by means that will not bear scrutiny. Our resistance to it does not mean harm to the British people. We seek to convert them, not to defeat them on the battle-field. Ours is an unarmed revolt against the British rule. But whether we convert them or not, we are determined to make their rule impossible by non-violent non-co-operation.

—Part of a letter from Mohandas K. (Mahatma) Gandhi to Adolf Hitler appealing for peace, December 24, 1940

The Interwar Period

Mohammed Zahir Shah (ruled 1933–1973) was proclaimed king of Afghanistan after the assassination of his father, Mohammed Nadir Shah (ruled 1929–1933), on November 8, 1933. The Afghan armed forces were incapable of producing or acquiring sufficient arms to defend themselves against potential external threats and decisively joined the League of Nations on September 24, 1934, as a means of deterring perceived external aggressors. Afghanistan was not completely immune from the Second World War and would be locked into the intrigues of Britain, the Germans, the Italians, and the Soviets. Britain's fear of the collapse of the Soviet Union under the weight of the German blitzkrieg in June 1941 was such that the British equipped the Khyber Pass linking Afghanistan to British India with anti-tank mines in the event of a German panzer breakthrough emerging from the Caucuses.[1] Such was the level of fright the new German tactics instilled in the first few years of World War II. Major Charles Davidson, assistant instructor at the Gunnery School in Kakul, the current site of the Pakistan Military Academy in Abbottabad, was called on to survey the Khyber Pass and set up kill zones. The concerns of the British in India were that the mechanized nature coupled with the air power used in the invasions of France and Poland meant that timetables had to be revised because armies would not ride on horses and pack animals to threaten the northwest frontiers.[2] This line of reasoning is incredible in hindsight because it presupposes that, once the German armies defeated Russia, they would have the capabilities in men and materiel to make it through the Khyber Pass, and that their equipment could endure the rigors of mountain fighting. The British authorities in India realized their folly in preparing for an imagined threat from the Germans coming from the east, through Afghanistan, and by late 1941 began to address the real tactical threat coming from Imperial Japanese forces, threatening India from Burma and the Bengal.

Afghanistan sought to create neutral buffers surrounding the country with the signing of the Saadabad Non-Aggression Pact with Turkey, Iran, and Iraq at the palace of Reza Shah Pahlavi in Tehran on July 8, 1937. This pact lasted for five years. This Oriental entente was considered the predecessor and some argue the model for the Baghdad Pact of 1955 that marked the first effort to develop a Middle Eastern security pact.[3] The Saadabad Pact was intended as a regional alliance at the League of Nations; as part of the agreements, Turkish and Iraqi military missions were established in Kabul.[4]

Afghanistan's armed forces were expanded and modernized with the aid of the RAF, which supplied a small number of aircraft. Afghan pilots were trained and instructed by Italy. Artillery and ground equipment were supplied by Czechoslovakia. Afghanistan's continued requests to the British foreign office to supply further ammunition and update its air force were met with little interest by Britain, which declined to help arm Afghanistan. This was possibly due to border disturbances caused by Afghan guerrilla leader Mirza Ali Khan, famously known as the faqir of Ipi. The faqir, along with another religious leader, the Shami Pir, would be used by Axis agents to attempt to foment an insurgency from Afghanistan on British India, which at the time included modern-day Pakistan.

In 1935 Afghanistan turned to the Third Reich for economic military upgrades and as a counterweight to British imperial interests and threats over Soviet invasion. Ambassador Grobba had already established the first German diplomatic mission in Kabul on December 16, 1923. In 1936, with Afghanistan sending a hockey team to the Berlin Olympics, Germany sent war materiel to and increased commercial operations in Kabul. In 1938 Lufthansa established a direct air link between Berlin and Kabul. Germany's civil and military engineering group was labeled by the Germans as Organization Todt, after its organizer Fritz Todt, who was responsible for providing technical assistance in Kabul. Major projects to upgrade Afghanistan's airfields, bridges, and industry, as well as the joint exploration of mineral deposits, were undertaken while the Wehrmacht trained Afghanistan's military. By the end of 1939 Afghanistan and

Iran were the Reich's only suppliers of cotton and wool. Between 1939 and 1940 Afghanistan's armed forces reached 100,000 men in nine army divisions, one artillery division, and an air force with one hundred pilots. In 1939 an economic and credit agreement assured Berlin of deliveries of vital Afghan raw materials in exchange for German finished goods. This represented a tenfold increase of foreign trade within two years. Germany was involved in the entire educational and vocational training system of Afghanistan, likely shaping a segment of the Afghan population toward its worldview.[5]

The British minister in Kabul, Sir Kerr Fraser-Tytler, asked the unavoidable question of how menacing German influence could become to British interests and security:

> [S]o long as the world is at peace the assistance rendered by Germany to progress of Afghanistan is to our advantage . . . but in the event of war in which Great Britain was involved the position would be far different. It is probably true that the German penetration of this country is aimed primarily at Russia, and that the Germans see in Afghanistan the focal point in Central Asia where they might link up with Japan against the Soviet Government; but what is true of Russia is also true of India. In any way involving Great Britain and Germany, the latter would certainly attempt to make use of Afghanistan . . . to harass the Frontier . . . and to tie up as much as possible of the Army and Air Forces in India.[6]

One of the most definitive volumes on the Third Reich's efforts to undermine the British in India was written by Milan Hauner and published by the London-based German Historical Institute. This chapter relies on Hauner's work, which in turn is derived from German World War II archives. In a discussion group that Commander Aboul-Enein led at the National Defense University at Fort McNair, the commander introduced a few students to Hauner's work, both his book and an excellent essay; these works prompted discussions on looking at Afghanistan geostrategically among the powers during World War I, World War II, and in the current conflict in the twenty-first century.

Axis Elements in Kabul

German penetration into Afghanistan began in 1914 when Imperial Germany dispatched German diplomats Werner Otto Von Hentig and Oskar Von Niedermayer to Kabul with the purpose of winning over the Afghan government under Emir Habibullah Khan (ruled 1901–1919) for a subversive scheme to incite the Afghans in British India in World War I. Von Hentig, a diplomat who had served in Iran, and von Niedermayer, an Imperial German army captain, along with an Ottoman Turkish officer, two Indian revolutionaries, and a number of Pashtuns released from a POW camp, made up the Hentig-Niedermayer expedition. Although the expedition did not achieve its objectives, it marked the first diplomatic contact between Afghanistan and Germany. Afghanistan and Iran were countries in which Germany actively sought to strengthen its political influence throughout the 1930s. This was because there was less likelihood of running into British opposition since British power and influence was weaker in Afghanistan than it was in the Arab countries.[7]

The steady German infiltration of Afghanistan was observed throughout the entire interwar period. The resurgence of Germany under Hitler, with its imposing industrial might and strident militarism, was an attractive factor that the Afghan educated class could not ignore. The Afghan delegation was impressed by the display of German superiority and displays of national confidence exhibited during the 1936 Olympic Games. Germany was willing to grant generous credits at substantial discounts with terms that were free from humiliating conditions that would have placed Afghanistan in the position of some Indian princely states in negotiating their own relationship with the British.[8]

In October of 1936 Hitler ordered closer economic ties between Germany and both Iran and Afghanistan; these ties grew between 1936 and 1939. Rosenberg's foreign policy office in the NSDAP, in spite of reservations from Grobba and the foreign ministry, initiated a program whereby Germany undertook the training and equipping of the Afghan army and police. With the outbreak of the war, Afghanistan came under pressure from Great Britain and the Soviet Union to expel the German advisers and technicians and proclaim Afghan neutrality. King Zahir Shah and his advisers understood that in the near term their relationship with Germany was not worth a potential conflict with these two powers that were geographically so close to Afghanistan. Zahir Shah declared Afghanistan's neutrality on September 6, 1939. Because of the state's ties to the Axis powers, he relented and developed a compromise in the expulsion of Axis personnel. In an effort not to alienate the Germans, the king ordered the nondiplomatic personnel of all the belligerents, including the Allies, out of Kabul. Zahir Shah also initiated a *loya jirga* (grand council of tribal chiefs and notables) that confirmed support for his policies toward these combatants, both Allied and Axis. Rosenberg and his foreign office initiated a fifth column in Kabul, however, with the support of Abdul Majid Zabuli, Afghanistan's minister of national economy. However, Von Ribbentrop supported the notion of overthrowing Zahir Shah and installing the exiled former anti-British king Amanullah (ruled 1919–1929), who was in exile in Switzerland. With the signing of the Molotov-Ribbentrop Pact, the British proposed a defensive plan to shield India from a potential Soviet invasion of Afghanistan.[9] Such was the concern of British officials regarding the implications of the newly signed pact between Hitler and Stalin.

The British Indian plan made more prescient with the 1939 Soviet-German Non-Aggression Pact, suggested one armored division with five infantry brigades respond to a Soviet incursion into Afghanistan. The Germans tried to influence the Soviet Union to take countermeasures against the concentration of British and French troops in the Near East and north India by creating a danger to the frontiers of British India using Afghanistan as a base. Differences developed on this between the APA, which had contact with the existing Afghan government, and the German foreign ministry, which favored a coup and replacement on the Afghan throne with the exiled king Amanullah, who had been forced to abdicate in 1929 because of his pro-Western policies. As a result of Rosenberg's intervention, Hitler finally turned down this plan, and in July 1941, when the matter gained renewed interest in connection with Operation Barbarossa, Hitler officially gave his support to a coup plot involving Abdul Majid.[10]

Pro-Axis Sentiments in the Afghani Leadership

In May–June 1940, shortly after the German–French armistice, Abdul Majid notified Hans Pilger, the German minister in Kabul, that for the purpose of active participation in the German interest, Kabul was "ready to mobilize all opportunities arising from sentimental and religious ties."[11] Abdul Majid began inciting Afghan tribal leaders to take up arms and elicit border skirmishes against British India and in support of the Axis cause. Pilger was reported to have announced with absolute confidence that by the middle of August 1940 Hitler would be in London. The Nazi fifth column operatives in Afghanistan notified Berlin in anticipation of Afghanistan's readiness in joining the Axis in return for German support in annexing Soviet territory in its northern frontier and a portion of British India, areas of what is now northern Pakistan. The arrival of Indian anticolonialist leader Subhas Chandra Bose in Kabul on February 1, 1941, after evading British arrest, would allow Berlin to provide a chartered plane to Germany with the assistance of the Afghan minister Abdul Majid. Bose was to join the Iraqi ex-prime minister Gaylani and Grand Mufti Hajj Amin al-Husseini in German anti–British propaganda efforts. At the beginning of April 1941, when the position of the pro-Axis government in Iraq appeared strong, Abdul Majid advocated an extended Berlin-Baghdad-Kabul Axis.[12]

With the early successes of the pro-Axis coup in Iraq, Abdul Majid voiced his support to the Iraqi prime minister Rashid Ali Al-Gaylani in his effort to evict the British from his country. To bypass Turkish neutrality, which hindered direct Axis land support by rail to Iraq, Germany sent armaments to Iraq that supposedly were destined for Kabul: the Iraqi army could intercept and seize such transports and Abdul Majid could benefit from plausible deniability. Abdul Majid was in favor of this plan; after visiting Berlin at the beginning of March, he made it clear he was ready to help Iraq. A transport through Turkey, camouflaged as goods and merchandise destined for Afghanistan or Iran, required the cooperation of the Afghan or Iranian authorities. Abdul Majid invited his country's ambassador to Ankara, Faiz Muhammad Khan, to Budapest for a meeting on orchestrating assistance to the Iraqis and to discuss the question of Afghan assistance to the Germans. The ambassador warned that his monarch Zahir Shah must be informed of any plans to ship to Iraq transports destined for Afghanistan. German operatives of the Abwehr continued supplying Kabul with finances and arms, and even contacted Mirza Ali Khan, the faqir of Ipi, who waged continuous skirmishes against the British in Waziristan, providing him payments and materiel aid from the Axis. Some voices alleged that the faqir of Ipi's incredible capacity to throw in his *lashkar* (military camp) whenever he liked was largely due to his receiving Italian and German materiel support.[13]

In a case of truth being stranger than fiction, the faqir of Ipi would capitalize on a single incident in 1936 to inflame passions among the administered districts and catapult himself to notoriety. At the time, a Hindu girl had allegedly converted to Islam, and married a Pashtun in the frontier area of Bannu. The family of the girl accused the Pashtun of kidnapping and forced conversion, and argued that the marriage was illegal since the girl was a minor. A British Indian jurisdictional court ruled that since no evidence of abduction or legal consent to enter into a marriage could be determined, it was ordered that the girl live with a third party until she reached the age of majority, at which time she could choose her husband and religion. The Muslim community in Bannu saw this as a ruling in favor of the Hindus. The faqir of Ipi called a *jirga* and, finding sympathy among the mullahs, rallied tribes to jihad against British garrisons in North Waziristan starting with the Khaisora region.[14] No thought was given to the Quranic verse, "Let there be no compulsion in matters of religion" (Quran 2:256). This is not the point for the faqir; his aim was using a chaotic situation to amass influence and power. The British, to their credit, had studied, consulted, and codified various expressions of Islamic (using mainly the Hanafi Sunni School of Islam) and Hindu personal law to aid in the administration of India. Capitalizing on emotions to gain power and influence is not new in the human course of events, nor is it restricted to the Afghanistan-Pakistan border. The purpose is not rationality but manipulation.

Hauner introduces a few of the headlines that appeared in the British press that must have gratified the Germans and Italians; these newspapers would exaggerate the extent of Axis influence in Southwest Asia. The *Daily Herald* claimed on its front page of April 16, 1937, that "Mussolini was behind the revolt in North Waziristan."[15] The *Sunday Chronicle* on February 26, 1939 implied that a radio link between the faqir of Ipi and the Italians had been established. The article added, "Meanwhile Hitler is active in Kabul . . . where more and more German airmen are being sent as instructors."[16] Concerns of Axis meddling in Afghanistan had finally reached the British media from 1937 to 1939; the above is just a sampling of concerns reported in the press. Immediately after the start of the Russian invasion, Barbarossa, Ribbentrop issued instructions to Von Hentig to go to Kabul. His task was to actively support "the national independence movements in Iran and Afghanistan, particularly in so far as these are connected and cooperate with one another." Von Hentig was also instructed to "ascertain British strength and position both in India and Afghanistan, to coordinate all German agents and experts available at the time in Afghanistan, with the purpose of using them, if necessary, against the government in power."[17] He received orders to establish direct links with the frontier tribes; in the lead would be the faqir of Ipi.

Hentig never reached Kabul due to combined Anglo-Soviet diplomatic pressures on the Afghan government. This pressure also brought about in November the expulsion of Axis nationals from Afghanistan. It was in fact Pietro Quaroni, Italian ambassador in Kabul, who was the driving force in establishing contact with the faqir of Ipi. In June 1939 he was reported to have declared that the frontier tribes should be incited and in case of war, directed to fight the British, saying in reference to Afghanistan, "We could not defeat Great Britain in a war in those areas, but seriously injure her; we possess inadequate instruments for the purpose."[18]

One month later Quaroni told the Germans in Kabul that the Axis powers should coordinate their political activities in Afghanistan with a view to using the exiled king Amanullah as well as promoting unrest among the tribes. In Quaroni's detailed testimony provided to the British after the Italian surrender in 1943 he recounted how it had taken Axis agents a whole year after the outbreak of the war to establish contacts with the faqir of Ipi with the first payment being sent to the faqir in March 1941.[19]

Hauner describes how Quaroni also helped Subhas Chandra Bose, the anti-British Indian Nationalist, acquire an Italian passport when he was in Kabul in February 1941. Bose viewed the Afghan tribal territory as an important staging area in his plan to harass British India; Bose discussed these plans personally on his visit to Berlin. Isolated insurgent attacks, such as those carried out by the faqir of Ipi, were to become part of an ambitious plan to combine propaganda and subversion against the British Empire at what was considered to be a vulnerable spot. The Axis, however, proved incapable of establishing a strong propaganda operation on the northwest frontier, and never attained any capability to airlift commando units to support an insurgency in Afghanistan. The Axis legations in Kabul received the following monetary requests from the faqir: £25,000 to be paid bimonthly, according to Hauner's research, and double the sum if tribal unrest should be extended to other areas. In the event of a general uprising on the frontier the sum would be increased three times the original amount, not including supplies of weapons and ammunition that the faqir also required urgently to sustain the revolt.[20]

Hauner provides many details in an excellent chapter contributed to a book on the Second World War edited by the noted scholar Walter Laqueur. In it he describes how the German minister in Kabul admitted that the faqir's annual requirements amounted to around half a million reichsmarks; it would have been quite a cheap price considering the cost to the government of India. It was not so much the problem of forwarding foreign banknotes to Kabul (which the Axis did not find difficult as long as the Soviet territory remained open for traffic to and from Afghanistan), but that of converting sterling pounds and U.S. dollars into currencies like afghanis or Indian rupees. Indian intelligence received evidence in June 1941 that links between the Axis and the faqir existed for some time after the arrest of the interpreter to the Italian legation in Kabul. According to Quaroni's statement, several Italian agents visited the faqir between 1939 and 1941 with supplies of money and weapons, including machine guns, radio transmitters, and a receiving set.[21]

The Germans also wanted to establish their own link with the faqir. But unlike the Italian improvisation, theirs had to be on a truly grandiose scale. Oberleutnant Dietrich Witzel-Kim, chief of the Abwehr branch in Kabul, was ordered with his Afghan and Indian agents to take charge of contact arrangements with the faqir and to seek out a landing strip in the operating area of the faqir of Ipi. A full-scale uprising among the frontier tribes was among the schemes dreamt of by the Axis, to occur on September 1941 when Barbarossa (the German invasion of the Soviet Union) was expected to be completed, thereby facilitating the expected Japanese advance on India from Burma and achieving a link between German and Japanese forces.[22]

Hauner reveals how the Axis powers were implicated in another unusual incident that occurred in 1938 on the northwest frontier known as the Shami Pir Affair. Muhammad Saadi al-Keilani, otherwise known as the Shami Pir, was a holy man from Syria who claimed direct descent from Prophet Muhammad through the Sufi sheikh Abdul Qadir al-Keilani. The Shami Pir was the spiritual leader of one of the most influential Islamic Sufi orders, Al-Qadiriyya, founded in the twelfth century. Muhammad Saadi studied in Germany where he had married a daughter of a senior police officer from Potsdam. Through his extended Afghan lineage, he was also first cousin of the former queen, Souriya, Amanullah's wife. During the latter's rule, he had visited India and Waziristan where he spent time among his religious adherents. He openly denounced King Zahir Shah as a usurper and acclaimed Amanullah as the legitimate king of Afghanistan.[23] By 1938 both the faqir of Ipi and Shami Pir would find common cause in agitating and opposing British influence along the Afghan border with British India, currently the Afghan-Pakistan border.

The British administrator in India, Sir Olaf Kirkpatrick Caroe, was convinced that the Shami Pir's activities were part of a greater effort at Axis intrigue designed for the whole of the Middle East, of which the grand mufti of Jerusalem was the chief proponent and that British Indian intelligence failed to uncover. Another intriguing concern for Caroe was the Gaylani brotherhood in the Muslim world and whether there were contacts between Shami Pir and Gaylani of Iraq. Such speculations and proposed linkages were frequently proposed during the war, especially since the British learned that the German foreign office and the Abwehr had made contact with the Shami Pir. However, little evidence has shown that he had been recruited by Berlin prior to or during the war as a pro-Axis agent for the planned restoration of Amanullah as king. British intelligence learned after the war that the Shami Pir admitted in a private conversation that the German authorities expressed displeasure with regard to his failure to restore Amanullah to the Afghan throne. It is possible that he was in contact with von Hentig, head of the Oriental section in the political department. Von Hentig was considered by the British a most competent and dangerous expert on Islamic countries. In January 1941, while the Shami Pir was in Damascus, he was visited by the Abwehr agent, Rudolf Roser, in the company of von Hentig, who was said to have pressured the Pir to continue stirring up a pro-Amanullah rebellion. The Pir, however, refused to continue with the Axis plans to replace Zahir Shah with Amanullah.[24] He was bought off by British agents, and retired to Damascus.[25]

With the failure of the Shami Pir affair in 1938, the Axis missed the last possible chance on the eve of World War II to exploit the Afghan tribes against the Allies. Furthermore, during the war, there were unique opportunities in Waziristan and the Northern Frontiers to foment anti-British rebellions, along what is now the Afghanistan and Pakistan border. Had the Axis managed the faqir of Ipi and the Shami Pir affair differently and fought a long-term war on the periphery instead of direct attacks on France and the Soviet Union, the conflict would have evolved differently. Hauner's work is relevant today as U.S. combat forces plan for a December 2014 withdrawal and the various insurgencies and tribal rivalries in Afghanistan reassert themselves. Hauner's book and in particular his essay, "One Man against the Empire," demonstrates the potency of low levels of investment in fighting proxy wars along the Afghan-Pakistan frontier.[26]

With the Axis successes in Operation Barbarossa and the Allied accomplishments in Operation Countenance, the Allies demanded that Afghanistan expel Germany's fifth column from the Afghan capital and halt Axis infiltration of the tribal areas. Zahir Shah, witnessing the deposed Reza Pahlavi of Iran and the victory of Operation Sabine in Iraq, could not disregard the demands of the Allies and ordered all Axis personnel to leave Kabul by October 1941. Plans were in preparation during the winter of 1941 to follow up Operation Barbarossa. By the end of February Hitler ordered plans drawn up for the invasion of Afghanistan, Persia, and India, with the conquest of the Soviet Union as the precondition. Specially trained armored, motorized infantry and mountain divisions were formed and assigned operational group forces to Spanish Morocco, Egypt, Anatolia, and Afghanistan. Interestingly, Zahir Shah never officially declared war on the Axis and maintained diplomatic contact with Berlin.[27] The efforts of the Germans to agitate Afghan tribes were not lost on Churchill and are reflected in two encrypted telegrams sent in September and October 1941. The first telegram, dated September 14, 1941, is from His Majesty's Representative in Kabul Sir Francis Wylie to Churchill, Anthony Eden (foreign secretary), and L. S. Emery (secretary of state for India and Burma). In paragraph three of this long telegram, Wylie writes of "Germans marching through Afghanistan to invade India."[28] This is incredible analysis, as the Germans would have to fight their war through the Russians, then mountainous terrain, and over tremendous logistical distances. Churchill would show his annoyance at Wylie's assessment by writing to Eden and Emery, "This telegram like all Indian messages is windy and wordy. The writer's estimate differs from the facts in our possession and leads to mere procrastination."[29] Churchill's response, sent on October 19, 1941, was to offer underhanded praise to Wylie and then complain of the 6,639 cipher groups (messages) he sent in panic from September 11 to October 17.[30] These events also demonstrate how a small investment in subversion, propaganda, and the intelligence activities of the Abwehr caused the British ambassador such concerns that he overinflated the threat to the prime minister.

There is much to learn from these events. For one, the British agitated the Waziristan tribes throughout the 1930s by using RAF planes to bomb *lashkar* formations they deemed a threat. This indiscriminate bombing inflamed passions among the Pathan tribes and reminded the authors of the current controversy surrounding unmanned combat aerial vehicles (UCAVs, known popularly as drones). Controlling the Northwest Frontier Province using the RAF was insufficient and the British were left with no choice than to establish a ground presence. The Wazir and Mehsud tribes were angry at the size of their subsidy and resentful of army garrisons and roads being built on their tribal lands. These tribes and the region are the same area of concern to NATO coalition forces and elements of the Pakistani government.[31]

The British were not reticent, while the Germans agitated in Afghanistan anti-British sentiment, to use, among other tools, religious imagery. George Cunningham, the governor of the Northwest Frontier Province worked through his political agent Kuli Khan to get more mullahs (religious leaders) in the tribal areas to speak out against Bolshevism, and then the Axis countries as enemies of Islam. Among the descriptions used against the Japanese was *but-parasti* (Urdu, idol worshipper), a term the British knew was also used by Muslims to describe Hindus in occasional bouts of sectarian flare-ups. In a case of expediency they used it against the Japanese and the allies of the Germans who would restrict the practice of Islam.[32] The British would have too much explaining to Pathan tribal elders, when they concluded an alliance with Stalin and the Soviet Union, as well as when the Germans signed a nonaggression pact with Turkey, a Muslim nation. Such news could no longer be hidden among the valleys of the Afghan–North Indian border (current-day Pakistan), with the proliferation of more and more radio sets. In the twenty-first century this has been replaced by the mobile app, the Internet, and hundreds of satellite channels. Researching this chapter, the authors were struck by the common themes, tribes, geography, and personalities found in pre– and post–World War II Afghanistan/Pakistan and the problems encountered today. While not an exact model, it does offer some insight into how the human terrain will unfold along the Afghan-Pakistan border. We hope the faqir of Ipi, Shami Pir, tribesmen, mullahs, accusations of abduction, British military and civilian officials, as well as German operatives stimulate your thoughts on Afghanistan and Pakistan today. The best part of researching this book is discussing this history with men and women who have deployed to Iraq and Afghanistan.

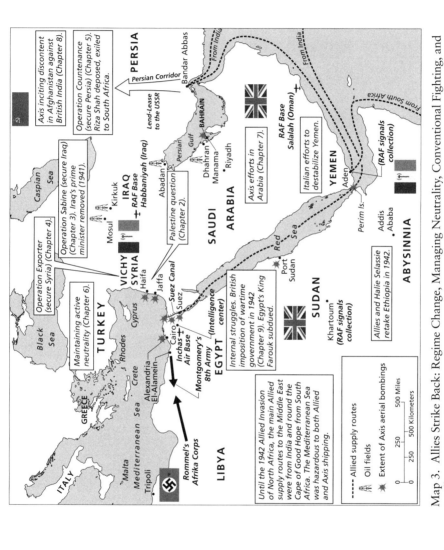

Map 3. Allies Strike Back: Regime Change, Managing Neutrality, Conventional Fighting, and Intelligence Operations

Axis inciting discontent in Afghanistan against British India (Chapter 8).

Operation Countenance (secure Persia) (Chapter 5). Riza Shah deposed, exiled to South Africa.

PERSIA

Bandar Abbas

From India

Persian Corridor

Lend-Lease to the USSR

BAHRAIN

Persian Gulf

Dhahran
Manama

Abadan

•Riyadh

Axis efforts in Arabia (Chapter 7).

SAUDI ARABIA

RAF Base Salalah (Oman)

Italian efforts to destabilize Yemen.

YEMEN

Aden

(RAF signals collection)

From South Africa

From India

Perim Is.

Addis Ababa

ABYSSINIA

Allies and Halie Selassie retake Ethiopia in 1942.

Caspian Sea

Operation Sabine (secure Iraq) (Chapter 3). Iraq's prime minister removed (1941).

•Kirkuk

Mosul•

IRAQ
RAF Base Habbaniyah (Iraq)

Palestine question (Chapter 2).

Red Sea

Port Sudan

SUDAN

Khartoum•
(RAF signals collection)

Operation Exporter (secure Syria) (Chapter 4).

VICHY SYRIA

Haifa
Jaffa

Maintaining active neutrality (Chapter 6).

TURKEY

Rhodes
Cyprus

Suez Canal
Suez

Black Sea

GREECE

Crete

Cairo
Inchas
Air Base

(Intelligence center)

Internal struggles. British imposition of wartime government in 1942. Egypt's King Farouk subdued.

EGYPT

Alexandria
El-Alamein

Montgomery's 8th Army

ITALY

Mediterranean Sea

•Malta

Tripoli

Rommel's Afrika Corps

LIBYA

Until the 1942 Allied Invasion of North Africa, the main Allied supply routes to the Middle East were from India and round the Cape of Good Hope from South Africa. The Mediterranean Sea was hazardous to both Allied and Axis shipping.

- - - - Allied supply routes

Oil fields

Extent of Axis aerial bombings

0   250   500 Miles
0   250   500 Kilometers

CHAPTER 9

Egypt's Internal Struggle
To Declare War or Not?

I venture to think the Allied declaration that [they] are fighting to make the world for freedom and for democracy sounds hollow so long as India and Africa are exploited by Great Britain.

—Part of a letter from Mohandas K. (Mahatma) Gandhi to President Franklin Delano Roosevelt, July 1, 1942

The 1936 Anglo-Egyptian Treaty

Among the seminal documents that culminated the tug-of-war between Egypt and Britain over Egyptian sovereignty was the 1936 Anglo-Egyptian Treaty. This agreement is important in order to understand Anglo-Egyptian relations in the Second World War. Although it covers many aspects of the political relationship between the two nations, in the end Britain retained highly intrusive controls over Egypt's fiscal, foreign, and defense policies. There were specific impacts on the Egyptian military that included these:

- British troop presence in the Suez Canal Zone was downsized to 10,000.
- The percentage of Egypt's defense budget was gradually increased from 1938 to 1950.
- The office of chief of staff for the Egyptian armed forces was finally created in April 1938 with General Mahmoud Shukry the first Egyptian chief of staff.
- An Egyptian general staff began taking shape with operations, intelligence, and logistics heads.
- A Higher Army Council was established that gave the defense minister oversight over the armed forces service chiefs, four field army commanders, and the chief of staff.

- The Egyptian 7th Infantry Regiment was allowed to reenter the Sudan, thirteen years after the assassination of British *sirdar* (senior military representative) Sir Lee Stack.
- Egyptian military education was expanded with technical schools established in 1937 and 1938, and the Egyptian Staff College established in 1940; the Infantry School and Artillery School would be established in 1941.
- The first regularly published professional military journals made their appearance in 1938 and military production was examined through a special office of the army inspector general.

This administrative, diplomatic, and restrictive history between Egypt and Britain explains the inherent distrust Egyptians have for formal agreements between militaries and wariness of any agreements that grant special privileges to a foreign power or ally. Understanding this history is key to unlocking the tenor of any future negotiations with any Egyptian political entity in power. The knee-jerk reaction of many Arab policy makers today against such agreements as status of forces agreements (SOFAs) or the exercise of specific diplomatic notes covering the legal protection of forces during a major military exercise coordinated with U.S. forces must be understood in the context of the history of agreements between Arab leaders and European powers. Entities like the U.S. Office of Program Manager in various countries in the region have arrangements by which Arab militaries that purchase U.S. military equipment would be subject to monitoring and light restrictions on use. This brings back memories of European colonial intrusion, and a defiant assertion of national sovereignty. It would be wise to look back and study this history. Discussions about Anglo-Egyptian relations from 1882 to 1952 serve as part of what Commander Aboul-Enein teaches at the National Defense University and National Intelligence University in Washington, DC.

The 1936 Anglo-Egyptian Treaty also did not clearly specify that Egypt would declare war on British adversaries. This lack of clarity, some argue, was caused partly by problems in translation and interpretation of Arabic, French, and English meanings that would lead to the crisis between Egypt and Britain in declaring war against Nazi Germany and Fascist Italy.[1] Another agreement that left Egyptian nationalists seething was the 1937 Montreaux Convention for the Abolition of the Capitulations in Egypt (named after the Swiss city where the agreement was signed) that sought to do away with mixed courts. In essence, since the nineteenth century Egypt had two independent courts systems and therefore two standards of justice: one for Egyptians and another for Europeans. This extraterritorial legal system afforded protections to Europeans living, visiting, and working in Egypt, which meant Europeans could commit serious crimes or ignore contractual obligations and then come under immunity from Egyptian law. In addition, Egyptians had to petition these separate capitulations courts if legally injured by a European. In 1937 it was agreed that this system would be phased out in twelve years, by 1949. This did not please those wanting an immediate end to the system of mixed courts, and it would become a source of resentment among Egyptians and the British, particularly when abuses of Egyptians by Europeans, generally with little recourse, would make headlines.

The Collapse of the Ali Maher Pasha Government

A shift of attitude in the ruling political circles toward the British would cause major distress in Egypt, which was threatened with an imminent Axis invasion and the real possibility of the eviction of British forces from the country. British demands for a declaration of war on Italy was disregarded by Egypt. The government of Ali Maher Pasha agreed only to the dissolution of diplomatic ties; the Italian envoy to British Palestine and Egypt, Serafino Mazzolini, remained at his post. The general atmosphere of the British authorities toward Egyptian delays in taking measures against the advancing Italians would be a source of frustration to London. Even before Italy's entrance in the war Ali Maher stated that in the event Britain engaged in conflict with Italy his government would discharge all obligations under the 1936 treaty, but it would not declare war on Italy unless directly attacked. Ali Maher relayed this message to Mazzolini. The government wanted to abstain from any measures that might endanger Egyptian neutrality. When the Italians entered the war in 1940 Egyptian authorities severed diplomatic ties with Rome on June 12. However Prime Minister Ali Maher proclaimed at a closed session of Parliament a statement that would be reiterated in a note to Rome stating Cairo's position, as follows:

- Egypt would remain loyal to its treaty with Britain and would render all necessary aid only within the country's borders.
- Egypt would not join hostilities unless Italian troops encroached upon Egyptian territory.
- Should Egyptian cities be bombarded, or military installations attacked by (Axis) air forces, it would leave no choice but for Egypt to join in hostilities against Italy.[2]

According to the note submitted to Italy, a land attack on British military installations only was not regarded as an act of aggression against Egypt itself. This declaration was later tested when Italians raided Sollum and Marsah Matruh; the attack inside Egyptian borders resulted in many Egyptian casualties. Ali Maher stated that these clashes should be regarded as border incidents that could be settled via diplomatic efforts.[3] The Egyptian government of Ali Maher was doing all it could to not side against the Axis, and this was a result of the discomfort many Egyptians felt with sacrificing Egyptian lives to preserve the British status quo quasi-occupation of Egypt, the Sudan, and the Suez Canal Zone.

The British believed that King Farouk and Ali Maher were adopting a policy of appeasing Italy. The British war cabinet applied diplomatic pressure on Farouk with Britain's ambassador, Sir Miles Lampson. Both Lampson and General Wavell recommended an immediate change of government and instructed King Farouk that "the vacillation of Ali Maher Pasha was neither in accordance with the spirit of the Anglo-Egyptian Treaty nor representative of the feelings of the Egyptian people."[4] The king accepted Ali Maher's resignation on June 23 and appointed Hasan Sabri Pasha as prime minister. On September 13, 1940, Italian forces crossed the Egyptian border advancing toward Siddi Barrani, deeper into Egypt than the attack on Sollum, again testing whether Egypt would declare war or stick to its previous proclamation. Egypt, in response, declared a state of emergency. However, the Egyptian government evaded declaring war on the Axis and appeared reluctant to cut diplomatic ties with Axis satellites, whose officials provided Egypt with important back channels of communication with Berlin and Rome.[5]

Egyptian Military Policy in World War II

Egyptian policy makers understood their commitment as not to declare war on Britain's enemies, but rather to offer materiel support to British forces fighting the Axis. Egyptian politicians made several arguments for resisting British pressure to declare war on the Axis outright, such as the following:

- A widespread Egyptian view that Axis powers in 1939 to 1942 were unstoppable and that they could rid Egypt of British influence over Egyptian policy once and for all.
- The British never provided Egypt with enough military capability to expand its armed forces and thereby they did not possess enough forces to be an effective partner in a global war.[6]
- The British saw in an unconditional Egyptian declaration of war against the Axis as important to its interests due to Egypt being the leading Arab nation to declare war on the Axis powers; concerns about Egyptian commitments to provide materiel support to its forces; and tactical concerns of British military units fighting the Italians and Afrika Korps in the west and dealing with insurrections in the Nile Delta, thereby trapping its forces in urban warfare in Egypt while at the same time facing a modern mechanized army approaching from the east.[7]

British ambassador Sir Miles Lampson was determined to rectify this precarious situation. In 1940 he demanded the withdrawal of Egyptian troops from the Western Desert and the assumption of its defense by British forces with Egypt paying the expense of this defense; and the removal of both General Aziz Masry, the chief of staff, and General Abdel-Rahman Azzam, his inspector general of the army, for pro-Axis sympathies.

These demands led to a compromise whereby General Maitland Wilson would command Egyptian forces in the Western Desert and forces defending such Egyptian towns in the region such as Siwa, and Anglo-Egyptian forces would defend the city of Siddi Barrani. Lampson also sweetened the offer by indicating that if Egypt declared war against the Axis, Egyptians could assume the partial defense of the Suez Canal and place more Egyptian troops in the Western Desert. However, the Egyptians did not accept this offer, viewing it as a nonconcession of trading the privilege of defending Egypt contingent on declaring war against the Axis.[8] The Lampson offer only reminded Egyptian military leaders of British control over its defense policies. The British had reason to worry: aside from Rommel's Afrika Korps, German bombers raided Alexandria harbor, and conducted aerial reconnaissance of Alexandria, as well as the entire length of the Suez Canal at 37,500 feet beyond the range of British anti-aircraft guns and fighter ceiling.[9]

This brazen diplomacy by Lampson culminated on February 4, 1942, a date that created the conditions for a revolution that within ten years led to the establishment of the First Republic in 1952.[10] On that day Lampson, fed up with the wavering of King Farouk, surrounded Abdeen Palace and dictated that Prime Minister Nahas Pasha was to be appointed in place of the recently dismissed Sirry Pasha, in what would be described an emergency wartime government. Farouk was engineering a return of the Axis-sympathetic Ali Maher, and did not learn from what had happened to Ali Rashid Al-Gaylani in Iraq and Reza Shah in Iran, the year before, that the British were serious about regime change. The reasons for British insistence on Mustafa Nahas are not completely clear, but it is thought he was the only person capable of bringing internal control of the Egyptian populace during a critical phase of the war in North Africa. Nahas was anti-British and believed in gradual independence for Egypt and the Sudan.[11] The British seemed to settle for an Egyptian nationalist leader who could bring calm until the end of the Second World War, after which the terms of the British status in Egypt and the Sudan could be negotiated.

The personal life of King Farouk became an exercise of satisfying his every whim both in public and in private. When he assumed the throne in 1936, he was sixteen years old, and was regent for two years. When he became king he was determined to make up for a childhood in which he was subjected to his harsh and domineering father King Fuad I (ruled 1917–1936), and for his mother's (Princess Nazli Sabri) control of the regency. He later came under the influence of his court chamberlain Ahmed Hassanien Pasha, who was allegedly engaged in a long-term illicit affair with Farouk's mother. It was Hassanien Pasha who provided Farouk with an early introduction into the world of gambling and womanizing. By providing this diversion, Hassanien retained power over the institution of the monarchy for himself and for Farouk's mother. It was Hassanien who accompanied Crown Prince Farouk to London; the two enjoyed avoiding security details, leading them on wild chases. The other chaperone during the London trip was the military martinet General Aziz al-Masri. The young Farouk had been ill prepared by his father King Fuad for rule; the king had refused to enroll the crown prince in Egyptian schools, and barred him from playing with Egyptian children. Egyptians in the royal court treated Farouk with formality, and so he sought emotionalism from European auto mechanics and palace workers. The king in waiting had no experience with the people he was to govern.

The Transition from King Fuad I to Farouk I:
Axis and Allies Position Themselves

In 1935 the British wanted to firm up their geostrategic position in Egypt, seeing the Suez Canal as a vital access point for its empire in Asia, and specifically in India. British planners viewed with concern the rise of Hitler, and worked to conclude basing and transit rights in Egypt, Iraq, and the Arabian Peninsula. Ideally, the British wanted an Egyptian government that had popular support, while securing access to Egypt as a logistical base and transit point from east to west in case of the outbreak of war. London's prayers were answered with the election of Prime Minister Nahas Pasha and the Wafd Party in 1935. A year later Nahas concluded the 1936 Anglo-Egyptian Treaty. The treaty was an attempt by Nahas to form a coalition of Nationalists, parliamentarians, and the British to contain the king's power. King Fuad died in 1936, and Farouk was named regent for two years until he reached the age of eighteen in 1938. Upon ascending the throne in 1938, King Farouk removed Nahas from power, less than a year before World War II broke out. From 1939 to 1942 Axis forces marched into France and were at the gates of Moscow, and General Erwin Rommel's Afrika Korps combined with Mussolini's legions stood poised to take Alexandria. The Committee of Imperial Defense, the equivalent of the Joint Staff today, created the Middle East Intelligence Center in Cairo in June 1939. Its role was to coordinate and furnish intelligence to the Joint Planning Staff in the Middle East for preparing combined plans, and to the Joint Intelligence Subcommittee in London for consumption by the British government. British signals intelligence collection in the Middle East was diffused in Baghdad (RAF), Cairo (Army), and Malta (Royal Navy). The Royal Navy moved its signals intelligence operations in 1939 from Malta to Mersa Matruh on the Egyptian Mediterranean coast to consolidate intelligence with collection activities already present in Egypt. By 1940 the RAF had increased signals intelligence collection in Cairo and added intercept stations in Khartoum, Sudan; and Aden, Yemen.[12]

In Cairo and Alexandria an aggressive pro-Axis propaganda campaign was under way by the Germans and Italians. The Abwehr not only had agents in Egypt, but also had crafted a public perception campaign inciting Egyptians to overthrow British colonial tyranny. A string of anti-British Egyptian political leaders surrounded King Farouk; among those seeking appointment as prime minister included Ali Maher Pasha, the former prime minister and now royal court chamberlain, and Hussein Sirri Pasha, who served as foreign minister. Farouk had ample reason to believe Britain was in decline as he observed the withdrawal of 150,000 troops from Dunkirk, the Italian occupation of Somalia and Eritrea, and Japan's lightning success against British possessions in Malaya, Burma, and Singapore. These events, coupled with Neville Chamberlain's appeasement policies for Hitler, led Ali Maher Pasha to advise the king that the British Empire's days were numbered. Italian intelligence had infiltrated the king's palaces and collected information on Allied troop movements and morale in North Africa and the Middle East, sending wireless signals to Axis intelligence handlers in Libya, Italy, and Vichy French Syria. Unlike in Afghanistan with Sir Francis Wylie, in Egypt Churchill recognized the threat of espionage and anti-British propaganda, coupled with an advancing Afrika Korps. Churchill wrote to Sir Alexander Cadogan (permanent under-secretary for foreign affairs) and R. A. Butler (president of the board of education in World War II and former under-secretary for foreign affairs) on April 5, 1941: "Encourage Sir Miles Lampson to take the stiffest line with the Egyptian government to prevent espionage and tale-bearing for the benefit of our enemies by foreign and neutral diplomat(ists) in Egypt."[13]

How Close Were the Axis Powers to Taking Egypt? The British in Crisis

So precarious was the British position in Egypt that a little over 50,000 Allied troops faced off against 215,000 Italian troops deployed in Libya when Il Duce (Mussolini) declared war on France and Britain in June 1940. These expeditionary forces were under the command of Field Marshal Rudolfo Graziani, and he stood poised to simply seize the British naval base at Alexandria and from there the Suez Canal. On April 7, 1941, Churchill remarked to his war cabinet, "The loss of Egypt and the Suez Canal would be a disaster of first magnitude to Great Britain second only to the successful invasion and final conquest of the Home Island."[14] The 50,000 British and Allied forces in Egypt, designated the Army of the Nile, were made up primarily of untrained and administrative military personnel; reinforcing this army after the withdrawal from Dunkirk was out of the question. In September 1940 Graziani attacked General Wavell's forces, leading to a further retreat into Egypt. Wavell could not possibly request troops from Churchill, as Britain faced Hitler's Operation Sealion (the German invasion of the British Isles).[15] The only solution was to deceive Graziani as to the strength and intentions of the Army of the Nile and its commander, General Wavell. The British commander in Egypt charged Colonel Dudley Clarke to conduct an elaborate deception scheme with hundreds of tanks, artillery, and trucks made of rubber. He wanted to feign an attempted encirclement of Marshal Graziani's forces by deceiving Italian aerial reconnaissance. Clarke had dummy roads constructed and tank tracks carved in the desert. Perhaps his most innovative deception was to pay large groups of Arab Bedouins to have their camels, horses, and donkeys drag large planks kicking up sand. Seen from the air, the enormous clouds would look like concealed mechanized armor or a tank column on the move. Part of the deception hinged on British anti-air batteries keeping Italian aerial probes above a certain altitude. Wavell allowed Graziani glimpses into British communication by having him intercept messages of a large relief force being organized for the Army of the Nile, communication based partly on fact. What Graziani did not know was when or if this large force had arrived. Graziani, fearing a mass assault on his right flank, dug in, preferring to get a clearer picture of the Army of the Nile's order of battle before attacking. This pause by Graziani at Siddi Barrani saved Alexandria and the Suez Canal from falling into Axis hands. By the time the Italian field marshal realized he was deceived, reinforcements had arrived in force from Britain via the Cape of Good Hope, a distance of 14,000 miles and 50 days by ship.[16] The April 28, 1941, war cabinet meeting, convened by Churchill, saw Egypt as the main discussion point. Following are excerpts from the minutes to understand the strategic with the operational context of Churchill's view on Egypt:

> The Prime Minister emphasized the necessity for fighting for every inch of the way in Egypt.
> Nothing would be more ignominious than to be driven out of Egypt.[17]

William Manchester wrote in his posthumous biography of Churchill, "The Battle of Britain and the Battle for Egypt were two sides of the same coin. Neither would survive if the other fell."[18] Manchester's statement is an excellent summation of the importance of the Middle East to the global strategy of the Allies.

At least two members of Hitler's inner military circle understood the importance of the desert campaign but failed to truly persuade the führer, who was obsessed with Stalin. Oberkommando des Heeres (OKH; supreme high command of the German army) chief, Frantz Halder, and the navy chief, Admiral Raeder, advocated the dismemberment of the British Empire before America entered the war. The two proposed that this could be accomplished by starting in the Mediterranean, from Gibraltar to Egypt. They understood controlling these two access points, and harassing remaining British forces in Egypt, Iraq, and Persia would leave these formations cut off from both Britain and India. They also proposed a grand strategic operation that, coupled with a Japanese attack on Hong Kong and Singapore, would drive the British out of Asia.[19]

Understanding the Efficiency of German and Italian Intelligence: Rommel's Source

To understand the extent of the intelligence compromise King Farouk's entourage and palace retainers presented, it is useful to discuss General Erwin Rommel's source that led to his early stunning victories in the Desert War. Aside from Rommel's tactical skill in desert warfare, which is well known, few realize his success was due in large measure to an Italian spy who provided the Desert Fox with a wealth of information. Rommel's source was employed in the U.S. embassy in Rome. An agent of SIM, Italy's military intelligence, he falsified papers in order to gain employment with the U.S. embassy and worked his way to the office of the U.S. Defense Attaché in Egypt. The source was recruited for his abilities as an expert locksmith; he took advantage of access to the office of U.S. military attaché Col. Norman E. Fiske.[20] From Fiske, the Italian source copied the Black Code, a secret cipher used by U.S. military attachés worldwide. However, it was only when Col. Frank Fellers assumed his duty as U.S. military attaché in Cairo and was ordered to keep the War Department informed of British diplomatic and military activities from October 1941 to August 1942 that Rommel's source paid off. Fellers wired information concerning the command structure, commander's abilities, tactical prowess, warship deployments, logistics, troop and naval positions, as well as the serviceability of mechanized forces. Feller sent his information encoded using the compromised Black Code from the Egyptian telegraph office in Cairo. This joint intelligence effort by SIM and the Abwehr provided Rommel with the clearest picture of Allied intentions and capabilities. The compromise of the Black Code extracted intelligence of the following quality in 1942 that Rommel had access to:

January 23: 270 aircraft being withdrawn from North Africa to reinforce the Far East

January 29: Complete rundown of British armor, to include numbers, unit efficiency status, and numbers damaged

February 1: Forthcoming commando operations, efficiency ratings of British units, report that American M-3 tanks could not be used until mid-February

February 6: Location and efficiency of 4th Indian Division, and 1st Armored Division, and British plans to dig in along the Acroma-Bir Hacheim Line

February 7: British units stabilized along the Ain-el-Gazala-Bir Hacheim Line

June 12: British sabotage plans directed against Axis airfields allowing Rommel to warn his airfields[21]

British skepticism followed by an investigation uncovered the compromise of the Black Code. Fellers continued to transmit disinformation in Black Code, reinforcing it through the use of a Nazi double-agent code-named Kondor; this deception helped to defeat Rommel's Afrika Korps and helped the Allies outfox the Desert Fox. General Bernard Law Montgomery benefited from an ever-increasing improvement of Enigma decrypts, which allowed him to gain insights into Rommel's intentions. In researching this book, the astonishing case of Col. Truman Smith, USA, came to light. Smith was a protégé of General Marshall, but as a former U.S. attaché posted to Berlin in the 1930s he had acquired a pro-German and anti-Roosevelt attitude. As chief analyst and adviser to Marshall on German affairs, he would continue to provide politicized intelligence advocating that the United States should seek accommodation with Germany and stay out of the war. Smith would work with prominent isolationists such as Charles Lindbergh in plotting antiwar strategies and furnishing military information. In mid-April 1941 War Secretary Henry Stimson grew frustrated with Smith's pessimistic reports about British losses in Greece and the Middle East, even saying that Smith's rumors and attacks were undermining the security of the United States. Marshall and Stimson got into verbal blows over Smith and the war secretary's concerns over pro-German influence within Army intelligence and senior civilians calling for Smith's court-martial. Smith's pro-German–tinted intelligence likely shaded how America's senior military leadership digested events in the Middle East from 1939 to late 1941.[22] It is an abject lesson into the damage done by intelligence that is politicized, containing personal biases. Smith is also an excellent case study in the problems created by a senior intelligence officer violating the sanctity of civil-military relations that is a cornerstone of America's democracy. Lindbergh, Smith, and supporters of the America First Movement would wither into political oblivion after Japan bombed Pearl Harbor and Hitler declared war on the United States four days after the Japanese attack in December 1941.

The British requested that King Farouk dismiss his Italian retainers from his palace. The Egyptian monarch and his advisers sought an exchange: the removal of the pro-Axis palace retainers and a declaration of war against the Axis in exchange for a pledge to evacuate all British forces from Egypt and the Suez Canal Zone at the conclusion of World War II. In addition, the Egyptian monarch insisted that the British ambassador dismiss his Italian agent, which was a reference to Lady Lampson, who was of Italian origin. At a time when Britain alone confronted the Axis, there was little tolerance for negotiating troop withdrawals or insults aimed at the British ambassador. In December 1941 the Italian submarine *Scirè* deployed six frogmen along with their human-guided torpedoes inside Alexandria Harbor, inflicting damage to the battleships HMS *Valiant* and HMS *Queen Elizabeth*, as well as the tanker *Sagona* and destroyer HMS *Jervis Bay*. The Italian sailors who deployed the limpet mines were captured, but the audacity of the attack added a psychological dimension to the war in North Africa. This was the environment that led to the showdown between King Farouk and Sir Miles Lampson in February 1942.

World War II Egyptian War Minister Offers Insights

In his memoirs, General Mohammed Saleh Harb (1889–1968) of Egypt discussed his time as war minister from 1939 to 1940, offers a previously unknown aspect of World War II. He joined the second cabinet of Prime Minister Ali Maher Pasha. Harb's memoirs were compiled in a single volume by Dr. Ahmed Hassan Mohammed al-Kinani (hereafter Kinani), and published in 2009 by the General Cultural Commission, a subdivision of Egypt's cultural ministry.[23] It has remained undiscovered for four decades, and this book represents the first time Harb's memoirs have been highlighted in the English language. Mohammed Saleh Harb (1889–1968), who started his military service as a member of the Egyptian Frontier Guard, was involved in the Senussid Revolt along the Libyan-Egyptian border resisting first the Italians, and then both the Italians and the British. General Harb would rise to become commander in chief of Senussid forces in Libya, begin a British revolt in 1915 in the Western Desert, and fight alongside Mustafa Kemal Atatürk (1881–1938), the founder of modern Turkey. Harb represents many Egyptian leaders of the period who would be torn about serving the military of an Egypt that was a British protectorate until 1922. Harb was sentenced to death in absentia by the British, but would return to Egypt when a new government and constitution pardoned Egyptians serving Ottoman forces after World War I. The 1915 Revolt in Libya represents the tactics of Lawrence of Arabia and the 1916 Arab Revolt against the Ottomans in reverse, and one year before the better-known revolt in Arabia. As one reads Harb's memoirs, one cannot help but think that the Senussid Revolt planted the seeds among British military planners in Cairo for the revolt in Arabia that made T. E. Lawrence a household name. Harb would become chief of Egypt's coastal defenses, and would be war minister from 1939 to 1940 under the second government of Prime Minister Ali Maher Pasha. Harb's desire for Egyptian independence led him to possess pro-Axis leanings, a sentiment nurtured by Nazi and Italian aggressive anti-British propaganda campaigns.

Upon taking over the war ministry in early 1939, Harb inquired about defensive plans against the Italian army led by General Rudolfo Graziani. He discovered, much to his chagrin, that plans for defense were not implemented because of the British military who believed their duties were confined to training the Egyptian military and therefore played no part in the actual defense of the

Nile Valley. Harb was the first Egyptian official who concerned himself with the threat to Libya. His persistent inquiries before Britain declared war on Germany in 1939 led to a briefing of King Farouk I at Muntaza Palace in Alexandria. The meeting was attended by Harb, Prime Minister Ali Maher, Foreign Minister Aziz al-Masri, and General Maitland Wilson. Here are excerpts of Harb's discussion with British general Wilson:

Harb: Is your presence in Mersa Matruh necessary for [Egypt's] defense?

Wilson: Yes, and its port is absolutely necessary.

Harb: Your defense is concentrated along the coast. Who will protect the flank from an attack from the desert?

Wilson: Armored units will respond.

Harb: If the enemy occupies Siwa [Oasis], your right will face continual harassment and threats of envelopment.[24]

Discussions took place using a large map of the Western Desert. Wilson, convinced by Harb's argument, requested that the king, prime minister, and senior British officers travel to Siwa with him to personally inspect the terrain. While Wilson and the king traveled by plane, Harb decided to take a car to inspect the ground he had been intimately familiar with as a young officer. He assessed that the Mersa Matruh to Siwa road was unsuited for long-range armor support, and recommended three routes to mass forces for a defense of Siwa: the Dabaa to Siwa route; the Wadi Natrun to Siwa route; and the route from Fayyum Oasis to Bahariya Oasis and on to Siwa.[25]

With proper road construction, these three approaches, in addition to the Siwa to Mersa Matruh route, could quickly bring force to bear in order to prevent envelopment against Allied forces defending the Egyptian coastline. Harb recommended that supply and fuel depots be built along the three routes, and Wilson was entirely convinced by Harb's tactical analysis. War Minister Harb was quoted in a May 13, 1940, *Time* magazine article, "Power Politics: Fleets to the East": "The military preparations for defense of the country today reached maximum perfection."[26]

Despite these discussions among Egyptian and British military leaders over the Axis, both Berlin and Rome recognized that a segment of Egypt's leadership was seduced by Axis propaganda and thereby incited calls for the eviction of the British from Egypt. It is at this stage that the elements of government, the military, and the Muslim Brotherhood coalesced to form a loose network in order to take advantage of a crisis and potentially gain Egyptian independence. In hindsight, these Egyptian factions were shortsighted. On the one hand, the British remained entrenched in their belief in maintaining the status quo and refused to negotiate for gradual self-determination, while on the other hand few Egyptians had read, let alone understood, the deeper racial messages contained within *Mein Kampf*, and that Egypt most likely would become a vassal state of

Italy or Germany. Harb described how British officials initiated an aggressive campaign to discredit both the Egyptian prime minister and Harb, alleging the two harbored Axis sympathies. The British also falsely accused them of divulging secrets to the enemy when they discovered copies of the Siwa defense plans on captured Italians. This is ham-fisted diplomacy, and incredible on the part of the British to accuse Harb. As a young officer, Harb spent several years fighting the Italians in Libya before and during World War I, and his ideas for the defense of Egypt against an invasion from Italy clearly demonstrated that he was more concerned about Italian occupation than the current quasi-occupation of Egypt. It is an example of wanting to conduct a regime change at all costs and install a pro-Allied government in Egypt that would unconditionally declare war on the Axis. Harb's memoirs recount how the British complained to King Farouk that his government was not honoring the 1936 Anglo-Egyptian Treaty. The treaty maintained Egypt's quasi-protectorate status for another twenty years and placed British troops along the Suez Canal Zone. In exchange, Britain agreed to train and equip the Egyptian army and help defend them in time of war. The document was negotiated and signed by the Anglophile government of Prime Minister Mustafa Nahas Pasha.

Discussions between Egypt's Cabinet and British Officials

In 1939 Prime Minister Ali Maher called the British ambassador to Egypt, Sir Miles Lampson, and proposed that Egypt declare war on the Axis. However, the declaration was contingent on Britain's willingness to renegotiate four restrictive clauses, thereby relinquishing their control over Egypt's defense and foreign policies and allowing Egypt to participate as an independent and sovereign partner in the alliance against Germany. Furthermore, Maher petitioned for withdrawal of British forces from Egypt and Sudan upon the conclusion of hostilities. The prime minister added that the provisions of the 1936 treaty only sanctioned an Egyptian declaration of war if Egypt was attacked. War Minister Harb met with General Maitland Wilson, and Wilson asked why Harb's government was being obstinate on the issue of declaring war against Germany. Harb recollects the discussion in his memoirs:

> Harb: Our government [Egypt] does not have to declare war by the provisions of the 1936 treaty.
>
> Wilson: No?
>
> Harb: Why do you [the British] insist on a declaration of war?
>
> Wilson: For our mutual friendship.
>
> Harb: Is this a friendship for your convenience or our convenience? Why don't you agree to an evacuation of British forces from Egypt and the Sudan after the war, and negotiate a new treaty to replace the

1936 agreement? What will I say to an Egyptian officer or soldier preparing to lay down his life? Shall I tell him to die for the British Empire; can you [Wilson] imagine they will accept this sacrifice? You are sacrificing for your country and freedom; allow us to do the same?[27]

Wilson was impressed with this line of argument, but the British continued to pressure the government of Egypt. Analyzing the discourse between the two individuals illuminates the need to understand the importance of historic details, given the fact that the discourse permeates the collective psyche of the decision makers residing in the Middle East today. From Churchill's side, this is what he wrote to Anthony Eden on January 20, 1941: "History will regard Egypt as having been shamed by the pusillanimous, cowardly manner in which she allowed her frontiers to be invaded and her cities bombed, without ever daring to make a declaration of war against the aggressor."[28] When you line up Harb's conversations with that of Churchill, you see the two sides talking over one another regarding the preservation of a British veiled or quasi-protectorate status over Egypt, and the need for full Egyptian self-determination.

General Maitland Wilson remains one of the least known of Churchill's generals, having been eventually sent off to Persia to ensure that American Lend-Lease made its way through the Persian Corridor to the Soviets.[29] The Persian Corridor was a logistical triumph for the American and British military leaders: the port of Abadan along with thousands of miles of paved roads and rail links had to be built from scratch, linking the Soviets to much-needed war materiel. One of the most enlightening parts of researching this book was reading the archive of the U.S. Army Center for Military History that details the effort that went into constructing this vital logistical link, and obtaining the official records to study.

The British ordered the search, arrest, and removal of Axis diplomats and their pro-Axis palace advisers and courtiers. However, the Egyptian governments argued against such actions and instead declared them persona non grata and sent them back to their respective countries according to the customs of diplomacy. Egyptian ministers, including Harb, refused British authorities' dictating terms and conditions to King Farouk. Frustrated and concerned with Axis meddling in Iraq, the pro-Axis Vichy government in Syria, and the unstable conditions in Palestine, the British foreign minister sent a cable to King Farouk calling for the removal of Prime Minister Ali Maher. Upon discovering this request, Harb urged Maher to publish the cable in the press to inform the public and display his resolve against British pressure to enter the war. Why Maher did not choose this option is not understood. Perhaps he was concerned about rioting and violence.

Harb wrote that the Halifax demand for the removal of Prime Minister Maher triggered an emergency session between Harb and Egypt's leaders.

Discussions centered on the outrage of British interference in Egypt's internal politics. After much deliberation, the king withdrew from discussions and Prime Minister Maher stepped down from office.[30] However, the British had opened a Pandora's Box, enabling a series of much more virulent anti-British leaders to assume the prime ministership of Egypt from 1940 to 1942, to include Hassan Sabry Pasha and Hussein Sirri Pasha. The British government, fed up with the king and various governments' refusal to cooperate with their plans to thwart the Axis, launched an armored assault against Abdeen Palace dictating terms to the Egyptian government through force of arms in February 1942. The British called for the exile of Harb for organizing demonstrations among his Muslim Youth organization, of which he was leader, in 1942. After discussing several options, it was decided to relocate him to Aswan in Upper Egypt, where he remained until 1945. Meanwhile, Prime Minister Ali Maher was exiled to Alexandria where, according to Harb, he spent his time deliberately attempting to scatter former cabinet members to various locations in Egypt. The expulsion of the Egyptian cabinet and forcible installation of an emergency wartime government under Nahas Pasha by the British military was so painful to discuss amongst Egyptians that Harb merely referred to it in his memoirs as "the "1942 Incident."[31] This event humiliated the Egyptian army and caused a young major to form the Free Officers Association, later mentioned in his book, *The Philosophy of the Revolution*.[32] The young major was Gamal Abdel Nasser. This incident would lead to the radicalization of the Muslim Brotherhood and toward the path of colluding with elements within Egypt's military to organize resistance to British rule. Hussein Tawfiq formed an insurgency cell in 1942, targeting British soldiers and pro-British Egyptian politicians, a cell that would be supported by Anwar Sadat.[33] In his memoirs, Sadat writes about his support of Tawfiq's group as a "task of removing the men who had supported the British, those led by Mustafa al-Nahas." Wasim Khalid, one of the conspirators in the failed attempt on Nahas, wrote that Sadat provided the arms and explosives for the operation.[34] Beginning in 1942 and increasing after the 1948 Arab–Israeli War, Egypt would suffer from a rash of assassinations and attempted assassinations; they include the killing of Judge Ahmed Khazindar (Bey) (1948), Prime Minister Nokrashi Pasha (1948), and the founder of the Muslim Brotherhood, Hassan al-Banna (1949). The latter was likely killed by government agents in retaliation for the first two being murdered by the Muslim Brotherhood Jihaz al-Khass (special apparatus), a group of assassins organized during World War II as part of the wave of secret societies opposing the British in Egypt and wanting to restore the lost pride brought about by the forcible imposition of Nahas Pasha as prime minister by British armored forces in 1942; more on that later in this chapter. The Muslim Brotherhood entered its violent phase during World War II, and would not emerge from it until arguably 1971.

Added Pressure: The Clergy Weigh In against the British

The cleric of al-Azhar Rectory (the Sunni world's most influential religious establishment) in Cairo declared from his pulpit, "Egypt cannot enter in the side of any belligerent of the war, without assurances of its [Egypt's] independence."[35] Radio Berlin announced that Germany and Italy would consider Cairo a free and open city due to its historic significance. The desire was to agitate anti-British sentiment in Egypt, as Britain continued to use Cairo and its rail station to provide military logistics and off-load Lend-Lease equipment to counter the Axis in North Africa. The British ambassador to Cairo, Sir Miles Lampson, pressured Prime Minister Hassan Sirri Pasha to rein in the clerics. The prime minister met with the chief cleric of al-Azhar, who refused to stop his line of preaching; the cleric reminded the prime minister that the British were on the verge of defeat, and that Britain gave Egypt no quarter when it stood indebted and economically defeated. The cleric was referring to the mortgaging of Egypt by King Farouk's ancestors, the Khedive Tewfik (ruled 1879–1892) and Ismail (ruled 1863–1879), who drove Egypt into receivership and eventual protectorate of the British in 1882. The cleric also reminded the prime minster of British efforts to thwart Egyptian aspirations for self-determination after World War I and only granted Egypt quasi-independence in 1922.[36] Between the establishment of the British protectorate over Egypt and the Sudan in 1882 and the assassination of pro-British prime minister Boutros Ghali in 1910, the Egyptian Secret Service Bureau documented twenty-six known secret societies that ranged from the Nationalist to secular to Islamist.[37] This statistic should provide the reader with an appreciation of the toxic atmosphere of Anglo-Egyptian relations.

Anti-British Egyptian Leaders and the King's Hit Squad

War Minister Saleh Harb Pasha was one in King Farouk's cabinet who was fiercely anti-British and pro-Axis. Added to this was the prospect of Ali Maher becoming prime minister in 1942. Maher was also pro-Axis; leaving Egypt governed by anti-British ministers and an anti-British prime minister was intolerable for Allied interests. Sir Miles Lampson surrounding Abdeen Palace in February 1942, as previously discussed, demanded Farouk reappoint Nahas Pasha as prime minister and declare an emergency wartime government. The king facing the choice of appointing Nahas or the prospect of forcible removal acquiesced to British demands. Farouk's personality changed after the 1942 incident, and he reserved special hatred for Nahas Pasha, and for the Egyptian people, whom he viewed as unsupportive. The king spent World War II drawing up target lists of Nahas Pasha protégés, and was actively engaged in plotting their assassination; a cabal of officers selected by the king was nicknamed "the Iron Guard." Members of the palace associated clandestinely with Trotskyites, who viewed Stalin as betraying Communism by joining the Allies.

One of the king's fantasies was to recreate the Hashashin Sect, an eleventh-century Sufi order that used hashish-affected assassins to undermine such figures as Saladin. Amin Uthman, Nahas Pasha's conduit to the British ambassador, was the first to be killed. Then a car laden with dynamite exploded in front of Prime Minister Nahas' home. The prime minister was not injured, and after another failed attempt on Nahas the king broke up the cell, and attempted to create a new hit squad. It is during this time the Muslim Brotherhood created its own hit squad known as the Special Apparatus that targeted pro-British Egyptian politicians. Under the guise of Muslim Brotherhood Boy Scouts, they conducted military training in sport camps. This armed militia became active after World War II and, in particular, during and after the 1948 Arab–Israeli War. Aside from the Muslim Brotherhood receiving a boost from the British undermining the authority of the king, the seed of the 1952 revolution and Nasser's Free Officers Association that overthrew Farouk and established the Egyptian Republic was planted on February 4, 1942.

A prime example that revealed the adversarial relationship between the British and Egyptians was the visit to the region by American presidential contender Wendell Willkie. The Republican leader witnessed firsthand the haughty behavior exhibited by British officials toward the locals while staying at the Shepheard's Hotel in Cairo.[38] Reports such as this make it easy to understand the plight of the Egyptians and the ability of the Germans to take advantage of the situation. Added internal stressors that were influenced by a saturation of Fascist propaganda in the Middle East were how Egypt's political parties began to organize themselves: for instance, members of Misr al-Fatat (Young Egypt) marched around Cairo and Alexandria in "green" shirts, a takeoff from Mussolini's "black" shirts. This meant most Egyptian political parties of the 1930s needed to have a group of young enforcers, so the Muslim Brotherhood, which became politically active in 1932, organized its Muslim Brotherhood Youth with uniforms to counter Misr al-Fatat in violent street brawls.

German Forces Conquer Russia and
Drive into the Middle East: A Real Debate?

To understand why Britain took drastic measures in Iraq, Egypt, Iran, and Syria, one must delve into British official histories of World War II intelligence. The Joint Intelligence Subcommittee of the chief of staff in 1941 speculated that a defeated Russia meant a German drive through an acquiesced Turkey and into Syria and Iraq. The valid concern over the possibility of the Afrika Corps and the German Army in the Caucasus linking up to threaten British oil interests in the Persian Gulf was shared amongst the British imperial staff. Coincidentally, their concern mirrored plans envisaged by the Germans who anticipated the conquest and subjugation of Russia.[39]

Führer directive of June 11, 1941, and an amended OKW directive of June 30, 1941, planned for the eventual consolidation of the Soviet Union while simultaneously pressuring Turkey, Vichy France, and Spain. Part of the discussions between Churchill and Roosevelt at Placentia Bay in August 1941 concerned containing the Germans in North Africa and the occupation of Iran by British and Soviet forces as a precautionary measure, as five thousand Germans in Iran represented a fifth column that had already stimulated a pro-Axis rebellion in Iraq.[40]

Iran was also a topic of debate between the British foreign office and the defense committee. The foreign secretary asserted the Germans in Iran had little influence, as they were unable to get Mohammed Reza Shah to support the Rashid Ali coup in Iraq. Military intelligence dismissed rumors of an Axis-sponsored coup by the Iranian army. We now know that the Abwehr collected intelligence on Iranian oil fields and refineries, and an Italian Intelligence Center was formed in Tehran, laying the groundwork for an Iranian coup against British interests, installations, and forces to be deployed should German forces reach the Caucasus. Generally, British leaders in Whitehall and Cairo agreed that if Russia collapsed under the German onslaught it would be followed by a Middle East offensive. They disagreed on timing, and the Joint Information Center of the general staff issued two studies and reported that German forces were likely to go through Turkey to access Syria and Iraq by November 1941 at the earliest, if the Germans continued to meet no resistance from Soviet forces. Factors for a Nazi push into Iraq were the collapse of the Soviet Union and Turkish acquiescence. Russian resistance in the Battle of Stalingrad began to reassure the Allies that a German advance into Turkey was unlikely.[41] Additionally, Mussolini's strategic blunder in Greece resulted in a military quagmire requiring German assistance, and thereby diluted Rommel's efforts to advance into Egypt from Libya. Rommel and Admiral Raeder, German navy chief, saw the valuable opportunity to sweep the British from the eastern Mediterranean. Raeder drew up plans to attack Alexandria and Suez from the sea jointly with Rommel. They argued for a diversion of a fourth of the forces allocated for Barbarossa to deal a final blow against the British in Egypt. Hitler was too focused on the threat of Judeo-Bolshevism, a case of the German dictator believing his own slogans and propaganda, to appreciate tactical practicalities.[42]

What Did Egypt Contribute to World War II?

Considerable sums of money, around $30 million to $40 million per year, were paid by the Egyptian government from 1939 to 1945 to subsidize British forces in Egypt. There was also a tremendous logistics trail the Egyptian military and transportation sector provided to the British 8th Army, leading to the defeat of Rommel. This included the transportation of tons of food, fuel, and supplies on various forms of transport. The Egyptian military manned coastal and anti-aircraft batteries and was credited with downing several Axis aircraft. Large cities such as Alexandria and Cairo served as major supply hubs and therefore endured attacks from Axis bombers while their populace assisted in the support of Great Britain's eventual triumph against Rommel's vaunted Afrika Korps at El-Alamein in 1942. The Egyptian military was also responsible for preventing entrance to the Suez Canal by Axis shipping, accomplishing all this with a mere force of 1,000 officers and 24,500 troops.

The Egyptian government formally declared war against the Axis in 1945, with the government of Prime Minister Ahmed Maher (no relation to Prime Minister Ali Maher) now in support of the Allies.[43] Prime Minister Ahmed Maher would be assassinated on February 24, 1945, the very day he made the announcement of a formal declaration of war in parliament against the Axis. Maher engineered this declaration of war so that Egypt could be part of the UN. His killer, Mustafa al-Issawi, was a young lawyer who thought that Maher had betrayed Egypt by siding with the British. Issawi murdered the prime minister outside parliament minutes after his declaration of war.[44]

Egypt also provided a logistical base for the Allied liberation of Ethiopia. Sudanese historian Saleh Muhammad Ali Omar delves into the Sudanese role in restoring Emperor Haile Selassie I of Ethiopia (ruled 1930–1974) to his throne following his eviction by Italian forces in 1935. Omar's Arabic work *Al-Dawr al-Sudani fee Tahrir Ethiopia wa Irjaa Ibratur Haile Selasie ila Arshu (1935–1941)*, translated as *The Sudanese Role in the Liberation of Ethiopia and Restoration of Emperor Haile Selasie to his Throne (1935–1941)*, demonstrates the importance of relations between Sudan and Ethiopia in ridding the Horn of Africa of Mussolini's dominance. The book contains maps, statistics, tactical descriptions, and strategic decisions depicting how Ethiopia maintained a robust army in exile in Sudan that harassed conventional Italian forces. In addition, it details logistical bases, routes, and the Sudanese forces provided in collaboration with Ethiopian forces to attack Italian army units. The book culminates with Haile Selassie's six months in Khartoum and the final entrance of the Ethiopian emperor. Arabic works on little-known operations of World War II offer new venues for academic exploration, and show that while leaders like the grand mufti of Jerusalem collaborated with the Nazis, others fought against them in Egypt, Libya, and Sudan despite the tensions created by a history of French and British colonialism.

One of the more interesting Axis espionage operations was orchestrated by Rommel's spy Johannes Willi Eppler (aka John W. Eppler, Hussein Gaffer, and numerous other aliases). A German raised in Egypt, before his capture in July 1942 he had recruited escorts, belly dancers, and anti-British Egyptian officers (including Sadat). His handler, Laszlo Almasy, was an even more intriguing spymaster who provided intelligence on Egypt and Libya for the Germans. The

Eppler cell would operate from a Nile houseboat in Cairo, and frequent the Kit Kat Club to access loose talk from drunken British officers and Allied military personnel seeking female company. The cell collected information and used counterfeit banknotes; their lifestyle gave Eppler and his team away, coupled with counterintelligence surveillance. They were arrested in their Nile houseboat from which they also transmitted encrypted Morse messages to their German handlers. Laszlo Almasy spent the rest of the war in Turkey scheming to foment an anti-British revolt in Egypt, which never materialized. Operation Salaam/ Kondor, an attempt to infiltrate Cairo eyes and ears for Rommel's Afrika Korps, led to prison sentences for Eppler and his female acquaintance the belly dancer Hekmet Fahmy, as well as members of the Egyptian military who aided the cell.[45] Anwar Sadat mentions the cell and cryptically his involvement with the Eppler ring in his book *Revolt on the Nile*.[46]

Middle East Operations: Foundation of Modern British Intelligence Organization and Tradecraft

The British delayed integrating intelligence data into the daily briefing of the minister of state for the Middle East and the commander in chief until the middle of 1942. Consequently, this action enabled senior military and policy makers based in Cairo to assess and coordinate their actions. In addition, the SIS operations in the Middle East were integrated with British Army unit signals intelligence and these were tied into the British 1/8 Armies in Egypt by a special liaison unit. This integration and fusion of intelligence from the policy makers to the field commanders, and across intelligence disciplines, integrated all sources of intelligence and disseminated this upward and downward from the strategic leaders in London to the operational leaders in Cairo. This combination of operations and intelligence came just in time for the Allied invasion of North Africa, Operation Torch.[47] The breaking of the Enigma code allowed for the reading of German intelligence, but what is little known were the problems processing the volumes of information derived from Enigma. High-grade intercepts in the Middle East were forwarded to the Government Communications and Cypher School in Bletchley Park for exploitation; this took up to five days if transmitted by wireless, and three weeks if by air. At Bletchley Park messages took a month to decipher.[48] Despite efforts to remain current, events in the Middle East outpaced analysis. In April 1941 the cypher office in Cairo was so swamped by intercepts from the Middle East that 1 million intercepts were destroyed simply to clear the backlog. This problem was not solved until the United States' entry into the war, and the integration of Americans into British intelligence gathering and processing.[49] From 1941 to 1942 the coordination of various intelligence units was undertaken. In addition, British Intelligence (MI) insisted that traffic analysis must be undertaken in close proximity to Enigma traffic and decoding.

This, in effect, allowed the gatherers and analysts of data to rely on one another in the effort to produce actionable intelligence. The Royal Navy created a watch center specifically designed to fuse all sources of intelligence to evaluate the maritime situation in the Mediterranean. Among his best decisions, commander in chief of British forces in Egypt, General Wavell, brought his old subordinate from his Palestine command, Brigadier General Dudley Clarke, to orchestrate an elaborate deception operation called A-Force. It was Clarke who would gather together a team of eccentrics and safecrackers and place them under the charge of the famous and flamboyant magician Jasper Maskelyne. His large-scale visual deception and camouflage is the stuff of legend, debate, and controversy. Clarke's theory that every operation should have a complimentary deception was validated when he was tasked to plan the deception for the D-day landings in Normandy. Although Maskelyne and Clarke are not the subject of this volume, you may wish to read Nicholas Rankin's *A Genius for Deception* and Rick Stroud's *The Phantom Army of Alamein*.[50]

The organization designated to handle and interrogate prisoners of war underwent its most rapid expansion in the Middle East. As Italians surrendered in North Africa, each service maintained an interrogation center, as well as the Combined Services Detailed Interrogation Center—Middle East. However, it was not until 1942 when an interrogation staff was dispatched from the commander in chief (Middle East) that coordination between the three services became a reality. POW intelligence focused on tactical and operational intelligence. More valuable POWs, like General Wilhelm von Thoma (German), who was captured at the Battle of Alamein, were incarcerated and interrogated in Britain. In 1943 intelligence from interrogations between the United States and Great Britain were amalgamated into the Allied Captured Intelligence Center located in Algiers. The photo intelligence was processed at the Central Interpretation Unit headquartered in Cairo; they received input from army and air force photographic interpretation units forward deployed in the Western Desert.[51]

The information provided by Enigma indicated that the Germans were in short supply of men and equipment. The weaknesses revealed by Enigma enabled the Allies to further restrict resupply of Axis forces from once every three days down to once every ten days; however, this information also proved a source of contention between Churchill and General Wavell, his commander in chief in Egypt. Arguments for and against an immediate attack against Rommel revolved around his army's dwindling fuel supply. By July 29, 1942, estimates revealed the Afrika Korps had enough petrol for only two days, yet the dilemma remained that the British lacked sufficient armor for a counterattack. This intelligence architecture that fused tactical, operational, and strategic intelligence organizations not only within the British military, but also between the British and Americans, was a secret to the success of the Allies in World War II. Such a level of fusion and intelligence sharing would have been unthinkable by the Axis powers, as a dictatorship naturally breeds distrust and competition among organizations to please the dictator. There was a level of contempt between Germany, Italy, and Japan that precluded the type of intelligence sharing described that brought about the defeat of the Afrika Korps.

In researching this book, the authors were reminded that deputy führer Rudolf Hess, born in 1894 and educated in Alexandria, Egypt, had spent his formative years there.[52] Before his flight to Scotland in the Spring 1941 in a delusional one-man peace mission, it is unknown the extent of his discussions with Hitler over the importance of maintaining pressure in the Middle East and North Africa, instead of Hitler undertaking the invasion of Russia. What is known is that among Hess' many fears was Germany engaging in a two-front war. The great counterfactual histories would be a coalition made up of Raeder, Halder, and Hess advocating a secondary effort in the Mediterranean and the Middle East and possibly dissuading Hitler from the Russian invasion in 1941. What is also unknown is the extent to which Hess shared his views on the Middle East during the long hours spent in Landsberg Prison after the 1923 Munich Beer Hall Putsch. The two were close at this time, with Hitler dictating to Hess what would be the manuscript of his book, *Mein Kampf.* Hess' mental stability has been the subject of much discussion in the lead-up to and during the Nuremburg Trials. Some feel he was truly mentally ill, other argue he feigned illness to escape the death penalty for his role as deputy führer and chief signatory of the racial Nuremburg Laws. His fanaticism and obedience to the person of Hitler more than likely blinded any candid advice he could provide the German dictator; before his flight to Scotland he was increasingly marginalized among other Nazi leaders, chiefly Goering and Himmler.

In conclusion, it should be noted that America's civilian and military leaders also recognized the importance of the Middle East to achieving ultimate victory. Less than two weeks after Pearl Harbor, Gen. George Marshall summoned Brig. Gen. Dwight D. Eisenhower to Washington, DC. Marshall asked Eisenhower, What should be done in the Pacific and the Atlantic? Eisenhower asked for time and the next day prepared a paper for Marshall outlining the prioritization of America's strategy. Aside from recommending that the Philippines should be abandoned and that the new line of defense should be Australia, Eisenhower outlined to Marshall three primary objectives: "the security of England, the retention of Russia in the war as an active war ally, and the defense of the Middle East."[53] Eisenhower worried about a Japanese-German linking in Iran, but more importantly Eisenhower passed a key strategic test for Marshall and went on to make his contribution as supreme allied commander in Europe. Perhaps it is best to end this chapter with an excerpt from FDR's notes: "The Middle East must be held in order to prevent the joining hands between Germany and Japan and the probable loss of the Indian Ocean."[54] When understanding the mind-set of FDR, Marshall, and Eisenhower in late 1941 to mid-1942, is it any wonder one would be at least tempted to consider trading short-term gains (defeat of the Axis) for long-term problems such as the radicalization of politics and a distrust of Western powers in the Middle East? Understanding this empathetically will allow us to better operate in the region, as the political landscape changes once again in light of the events of the Arab Spring.

CHAPTER 10

Conclusion

Dictatorship naturally arises out of democracy, and the most aggravated form of tyranny and slavery out of the most extreme liberty.

—Plato

A rabism emerged as a significant factor during the years before the outbreak of World War I. The war made it possible for some Arabs, with the encouragement of their new British ally, to revolt against the Ottoman Empire. For some Arab historians, the 1916 Arab Revolt was the symbolic touchstone and the most significant expression of Arab Nationalism. Other Arab historians interpret the 1916 Arab Revolt as the manipulation of European powers that led to the ultimate demise of the last Islamic powerhouse, the Ottoman Empire. Arab Nationalist politicians saw the rise of Nazi Germany and Fascist Italy as their most suitable—yet illusory—occasion to strike out for Arab liberation similar to the Arab patriotic intellectuals of 1915–1916. The events of pre– and post–World War I, however, were never far from the minds of those who saw in the Fascists a means of striking against the colonial powers of France and Britain. Decades of discontent with colonial domination and the British sponsorship of Zionism, and through such events as the 1916 Sykes-Picot Agreement and the 1917 Balfour Declaration, caused the Arabs to reason using the classic cliché *'adu 'aduwi sahbi* (enemy of my enemy is my friend). The Arab Nationalist movements were attracted to superficial sound bites such as the Nationalist fervor of the German NSDAP movement and its resolve to remove the inequities of the post–World War I settlement or *diktat*, if you were a German living at the time. This sense of humiliation and victimization shared by the Germans held considerable appeal for Arab Nationalist leaders who saw in their own plight victimization by France and Britain. In his interviews with German leaders, the mufti outlined the basis for collaboration by emphasizing the community of interests that constituted the link in German–Arab affairs. He

183

asserted that the Arabs trusted Germany since they had no colonial ambitions for asserting control over Arab territories and both (Arabs and Germans) shared common enemies (i.e., Britain, the obsession with international Jewish conspiracies, and the Soviets). The mufti feared that a Bolshevik victory might hinder his intentions to include the Muslim populations of the Soviet Union in the grand formation of an Arab state, however, and had delusions that he spoke for all Muslims, including those under Stalin. But this is not the entire picture between Hitler and the mufti: as discussed in chapter 2 of this book, on a November 28, 1941, meeting between the two, Hitler assured the mufti, "When Germany triumphed in the Middle East, it would support Arab liberation. . . . Germany's objective would then be solely the destruction of the Jewish element residing in the Arab sphere under the protection of the British power."[1] It is unknown how the mufti thought about the practicalities of Hitler's grotesque plan not only for the destruction of Jews in Europe, but also beyond, or even if the mufti would be able to convince other Arab leaders to be a partner to Hitler's genocide. For instance, Sultan Mohammad V of Morocco refused to turn over Jews to the Vichy French who were demanding their return to almost certain death at the hands of the Nazis. This view of global genocide against the Jews was also captured by Ambassador Grobba, who was in the meeting between the mufti and Hitler. He recounts Hitler saying, "Germany had no interest there [the Middle East] other than the destruction of the power protecting the Jews."[2]

In the Palestine mandate, as elsewhere in the Arab world, Arab Nationalism turned toward Germany during the interwar years for diplomatic and materiel support in their own struggle against the British and the emerging Zionist movement. This effort gathered momentum as many Arabs interpreted the anti-Jewish and the anti-British sentiment of the Nazi regime as a partnership in a common struggle. Even the realization that Nazi Germany was responsible for the increase in Jewish immigration into Palestine after 1933, due to their persecution of Jews, failed to dampen Arab enthusiasm for Hitler's Germany, such is the power of sound bites versus actual consequences of actions.

In spite of its alliance with the Ottoman Empire during World War I, the Arab world harbored no ill will toward Germany. From the Arab perspective, Germany was considered a fellow victim of the post–World War I settlement and the only major European power seen as being without imperial ambitions in the Middle East. Hence, Germany was not an object of suspicion and hostility among the Arabs during the interwar period. The Arabs interpreted past German policy of non-imperial intervention in the Arab world as a sign of goodwill. The Arabs had sympathy for an aggrieved Germany in regards to the events and treaties that followed World War I. The Arab world was subject to active German involvement that predated Hitler. From Curt Prüfer and Alois Musil, to von Hentig and Grobba, German intervention was common in the Middle East before the advent of Hitler, as an arena for its competition with Britain and

France. Historical evidence exposes German intrigue at the beginning of a global creation of a German-made political Islam exported to and adapted in the Arab world as part of a coordinated campaign set within Germany's and later Nazi grand strategy.

Though Germany supported the post–World War I status quo in the Middle East, Hitler accepted both the preeminence of British power in the Near East as well as some form of a Jewish national home under British authority, both concepts embodied in the mandate system and the Balfour Declaration. Hitler accepted the postponement, delay, and rejection of Arab national self-determination and independence initially, but as the clouds of war loomed over Europe he began to alter his views and the potential of inciting various Arab, Persian, and Afghan movements to undermine the Allied position in the region. There can be no question that the Nazis reflected on past German efforts in World War I to incite a Muslim revolt, even creating an Office of Jihad in the foreign ministry. Moreover, few Arab leaders at the time realized that NSDAP ideology placed the Semitic Arabs at the bottom of the racial hierarchy. It is with a degree of sadness that we realize no Arab author or intellectual, even in hindsight, has reflected on what Egypt or Syria would be if the Nazis had marched on Cairo or Damascus. Would the Gestapo or being a Nazi vassal state be a better alternative to the arrangement with the British? It would be interesting to have a member of the Arab literati or historian write an alternate history of what Egypt or Iraq would have been like under the Fascists.

Arab sympathies for Germany were strengthened since the Arabs viewed the Germans as partners during World War II against French and British domination over the Arab territories. Since German blood had been shed on Arab soil, notably in North Africa, the Fascist propaganda machine portrayed this sacrifice as helping to rid the region of Anglo-French domination. With regards to the Arab leaders themselves, they were under no illusions concerning the limitations and ambiguities from the Axis powers, since they were well aware that the success of the Arab movement depended on an Axis victory and Germany's willingness to honor their wartime commitments, a question that could only be answered with the defeat of the Allies.

German official statements spoke of liberation of the Arab world, without detailed reference to any goals for the future. The German attitude toward Arab Nationalism was one of indifference. This indifference was enough to sustain the hopes and aspirations of Arab Nationalists such as Iraqi prime minister Rashid Ali Al-Gaylani and Palestinian grand mufti of Jerusalem Al-Husseini. It seemed too many in the Arab world, like many in the global economic depression of the 1930s, were in search for easy models for swift development. Arabs like other nations yearned for a developed, united, and militarily strong autonomous state. Nazi Germany was perceived as a nation that triumphed over the effects of the economic depression, widespread unemployment, and a challenge that the colonial powers, Britain and France, could not afford to ignore. Hitler's consistent references to the "infamy of Versailles" provided a natural attraction for the Arabs, who were trying to liberate themselves from colonial structures imposed on them by France and Britain. Also, the anti-Semitic policies of the Nazi Party seemed ideologically comparable to the emerging Arab resistance against Zionism and what was seen as the growing Jewish colonization of the Palestine mandate. Arab national aspirations and anticolonial movements sought to challenge Zionism in Palestine, whereas Nazi ideology was bent on conducting genocide against the Jews. Hitler's plans took on Wagnerian epic proportions of political evil in which all subhumans (those deemed non-Aryans) were actors and props in the opera, elements to be disposed of.

The political scientist Bruno De Cordier and certain opinion makers affiliated with the far right wing and extremist Zionists have attempted to present the existence of Muslim units in the Wehrmacht and the SS and the behavior and alliance of Al-Husseini as proof that Islam and Muslims have a weakness for Fascism, and they eagerly use this page of history to demonize Islam.[3] While this may be intellectually gratifying and might maintain the fallacy of Islam versus the West, it does not examine the complex human conditions and how the contributions of both ideology and political actions taken by Western powers helped to shape radicalism in the region today. After all, simple arguments of black and white despise complexity. Ideologically, it is important to note that Arab agendas and passions of that period were more Nationalist and anticolonial than religious. Given the nature of the interwar geopolitical order, the Arab Nationalist circles that engaged with one imperialist or totalitarian to fight another were nothing more than pawns in a game that was viewed by many as not theirs.

Arab Nationalism brought a sense of dignity after the long years of colonization, a set of words and phrases that allowed them to narrate their own history and to reinvent themselves. Previously, Arabs had languished under foreign control, suffered the sense of unremitted inferiority, and naturally looked for political remedies. This political remedy came in the shape of Hitler's Germany; Arab Nationalists intended to maximize this new movement in Europe for their own goals and aspirations. With the end of World War II and the defeat of Nazi Germany, pan-Arabism had to reinvent itself, and part of this reinvention would be tied up with the creation of Israel in 1948. The Arab Nationalist movement during World War II had, in turn, divided into nothing more than a shapeless, fragmented, counterposition to the British, and a tool for German and Italian propagandist aspirations.

The toxic, self-pitying disease that swept through Germany that gave rise to Nazism fermented the same brew of self-pity in the Arab world following World War I. This syndrome manifested itself through symptoms of anti-Semitism, a self-perceived form of victimization, and a defective atavistic version of pan-Arabism. According to historian Jeffrey Herf, "The history of Nazism beyond its Eurocentric limits pointed to the European dimensions of Arabic nationalism and Islamic radicalism of the early and mid-twentieth century."[4]

The Middle East clandestine campaigns in Iraq, Iran, Syria, and Egypt during World War II were, on the whole, overshadowed by the more immediate offensive against Rommel's Afrika Korps in the Western Desert. It is important not to write off these vital but lesser-known operations as mere sideshows; their effects had repercussions far greater than those of the North African campaigns. Churchill constantly complained to his generals of the wasted troops used for policing action in Egyptian cities, the Suez Canal, and Palestine. British wartime generals in the field understood they were not only fighting the Axis, but also bolstering an unpopular British colonial policy being stoked by the Axis. Churchill blamed this on "slackness of the Middle East Command," and not on the genuine appeals of Arab leaders, like Egyptian war minister Harb, for complete independence.[5]

OKH leader Field Marshal Walther von Brauchitsch developed a concept for a North African campaign as early as July 1940. This staff work, later to be called Operation Sunflower, was designed to break the strategic stalemate for Operation Sealion.[6] It would have put the British in the position of having to choose whether to maintain control of the Mediterranean or defend the Home Island. Hitler's focus on initiating a Russian offensive in 1941 would detract from the opportunities presenting themselves in North Africa and the Middle East. With the expulsion of Rommel from Tunisia, the Allies shaped political initiatives throughout the Near East, including non-Arab countries like Iran and Turkey, from Morocco to Iraq and Syria to Yemen. Britain initiated attempts to create an Arab bloc aimed politically against Russia and the United States in an effort to win the support of the Arab ruling circles. The Arab League arose in 1945 as a result of these efforts; it later was to become nothing more than an Arab "country club." In writing this book, the authors uncovered interesting surprises relevant to America's involvement in the Middle East today. The Axis was faced with the same dilemma of acquiring sufficient numbers of translators fluent in Arabic, Chinese, and Hindustani required for their expanding propaganda, analysis, and translation needs.

Operation Husky (the Allied invasion of Sicily) in August 1943 was compromised when a British officer in Cairo sent his uniform to the laundry service with the battle plans in the pocket. The laundry used several pages found in the uniform to write out invoices; somewhere in Cairo were person(s) with pressed clothes, and a bill with the Allies' most secret invasion plans.[7] Another compromise of Husky occurred when a British colonel left a top secret cable that gave the time and date of the invasion on the terrace of Cairo's Shepherd's Hotel. The cable was missing for two days before the Egyptian hotel manager returned it to military authorities. In North Africa, *The Soldier's Guide to Sicily* was prematurely published and distributed weeks before the commencement of the Sicily landings.[8] Such gross violations of security probably aided the grand deception plan, Operation Barclay, which had been designed to convince the Germans that the target of Allied preparations in North Africa was Greece, and not Sicily.

A corpse carrying a map showing clear desert routes was placed in a blown-up scout car before the Battle of Alam Halfa in 1942. In reality, the map was a deception designed to guide Rommel's tanks into soft sand.[9] The seeds of such deception operations as Mincemeat (the infamous "man who never was" or the corpse that was dumped off the coast of Spain with secret plans used to deceive the Allies), Barclay (grand deception on the Allied intent to invade Sicily), and ultimately Fortitude (the grand deception plan for the Normandy invasion) were arguably formulated through trial and error in the sands of the Middle East during the two world wars.

The postwar period deeply affected Arab Nationalist thinkers such as Sati al-Husri, Michel Aflaq, Salah al-Din al-Bittar, and Gamal Abdel Nasser. This saw the development of two major pan-Arab movements in the Near East: the Arab Socialist Ba'ath Party and, to a lesser extent, the Nasserite movement. Arab Nationalism, in its heyday, brought a sense of dignity after the long years of colonization, a set of words and phrases that allowed them to narrate their own history. For too long the Arabs had languished under foreign control, suffering the sense of unremitting inferiority; they naturally looked for political remedies. It was not until the Arab Nationalist tide that swept through during the 1950s and 1960s that the Arabs would acquire the confidence for which they searched. However, Arab Nationalism was used by the Axis and Allies to gain an advantage against one another in their titanic struggle of World War II, and left much bitterness in the Arab imagination toward Western powers.

Arab Nationalism would be in the ascendency until 1961, and then a series of declines would follow, coupled with the inability of Arab Nationalism to remedy the Palestinian question, while cloaking itself in resonant rhetoric. There was a steady erosion of the credibility of secular pan-Arabism, starting with the dissolution of the United Arab Republic in 1961 (the political unification of Nasser's Egypt and Quwwatli's Syria). This erosion continued with Nasser's military involvement in the quagmire of the Yemen War in 1962, referred to as Egypt's Vietnam; this erosion of pan-Arabism lasted until the June 1967 War.

The 1967 Six-Day War thoroughly discredited Arab Nationalism generally and Nasser specifically. As a result, thousands sought refuge in Islamist politics of various forms, from political activism to the militancy of fringe jihadist groups. By the end of the twentieth century, there was little left of the goal of pan-Arabism but a string of broken promises, demoralized masses, and a shattered state of affairs. Yet the language of Fascism found its way into twentieth- and twenty-first-century militant Islamist ideology through the demonization of Jews and the tactic of societal control under the guise of promoting virtue and preventing vice. When the Taliban enforced morals using this Quranic injunction and ruthlessly beat those not observing their perceived Islamic norms of behavior, it was not for the morality of the individual being beaten, tortured, or humiliated but for the silent spectator, the intimidated majority. It is a subtle message—"What are you going to do about this?" "Nothing!" This is reminiscent of how the Nazis operated and demonstrates a subconscious link between Nazism and the Taliban, the manipulation and intimidation of the populace. This connection is revealed in a subconscious strand of thought in the writings of the Egyptian militant theorist Sayyid Qutb, who came of age during World War II and was influenced by the events described in this book. Qutb went on to influence many militant Islamist organizations who attempted to operationalize his theories—including al-Qaida. This history matters, and should be discussed and reinterpreted in light of America's current challenges.

In spending time amidst the declassified al-Qaida archives at the Conflict Records Research Center at the National Defense University, the authors found captured al-Qaida manuals used to train operatives on a variety of operational tradecraft, with a specific focus on intelligence and counterintelligence. In one section the manuals make references to World War II intelligence mistakes, deceptions, and operations, to include the interception by Franco's Fascist intelligence arm of the location of the 1943 Casablanca conference, which was mistranslated and passed on to the Germans with the meeting occurring in the White House instead of in Casablanca, Morocco.[10] The same captured document also makes references to America's effort in World War II to break the Japanese code, although the al-Qaida manual lacks specifics and is inaccurate, referring to those who broke the code as the CIA, for instance. It was actually Naval Intelligence that broke the code; the CIA did not exist until 1947. This situation does show, however, a thinking enemy who reflects on aspects of American military history.

The narrative matters in the Middle East and part of the narrative in the twenty-first century is derived from the past. The period leading to World War II had the Italians and Germans bequeathing the Arab masses the language of Fascism through the introduction of the first popular Arabic broadcasts in 1932 and 1933, at a time when many Arabs had access to a radio. The language of Fascism prevalent among post–World War II pan-Arabists and militant Islamists of the late twentieth century can be linked to the creation of an anti-British hostile environment before and during the war. The British decision for regime change, whether it was in Iraq in 1941, Persia that same year, or the Egyptian prime minister in 1942, would have unintended consequences in the form of humiliated military officers turning to conspiring to achieve a revolutionary coup, secret cells being organized to carry out attacks on British troops, espionage, or the narrative leading to further radicalization through the use of fragments of religion. During World War II the United States took its cue from the British, and planned to replace the Vichy French prime minister of Tunis with OSS director General "Wild" Bill Donovan allocating $50,000 to the plot, which was never executed. This would be among several OSS plans to incite the local population against the Vichy in North Africa.[11] Colonel Robert Solberg and Colonel William Eddy established a special operation section, which coordinated information collection dedicated to implementing subversive activities in the region, beginning in the spring of 1942.[12] OSS commanders in Cairo ran arms and supplies to Greek and Yugoslav Communist partisans during World War II.[13] The United States did not have a free hand in subversive operations against the Axis in the Middle East, mainly because of troubled relations with the British SIS that viewed the Americans as amateurs and did not want them meddling in their sphere of influence. For instance, OSS director Donovan wanted to create an organization "Expedition 90" to work with Arab countries in undermining the Axis. The British downsized the operation from active clandestine operations to collection.[14] Likely another reason for the lack of enthusiasm by the British for American intelligence efforts in the region was their fear of further inflaming anticolonial sentiment and developing Arab partisans who would later turn to overthrow the British after the war.

Perhaps the most important lesson to be learned is this: before undertaking war, it is vital to know the region, the area of operation, your nation's place in it, and previous armies that have fought in the area. Get inside the history of the region; walk around between perception, conspiracy, and fact to gain a true understanding of those fighting alongside you, and against you. What are the real lessons to be learned regarding the regime change that occurred via the Allies in Iraq, Iran, and Egypt? How has this change shaped perceptions, and are the tactical necessities of the war and the sacrifice of our democratic values worth the short-term gains? In the long term, Egypt, Iraq, Iran, Syria, and Palestine would develop narratives of conspiracy and distrust fueled in part by the actions by the Axis and Allies in World War II. Situational awareness of the human terrain is a matter of life and death in any field of war; ignore it and your army will be wearing the label of other armies that have marched through the same terrain, neighborhoods, and cities. We owe a thorough net assessment and information superiority to our troops, making them more aware of the region's history than the adversary. This net assessment starts with a grounding of the historical narratives that drive the psychology of the area of operation and its surroundings. This effort will require a multidisciplinary, as well as ever-more-complex, analysis as the events of the Arab Spring and the changes it has wrought are occurring at the speed of wireless Internet. Understanding this military-political history allows us to better understand how the Middle East rationalizes decisions. We are fortunate in the United States to be able to harness the intellectual diversity of our citizens, and from this diversity we derive the talent to achieve information superiority in current and future conflicts. Since this is a war of the intellect and information, the United States and our allies have the capacity to understand the narrative better than our adversaries who attempt to manipulate it; an open democracy allows for this advantage. We have encountered many fellow

Americans who have spent decades studying various cultures, religious narratives, and the origins of ideas in the Middle East and beyond. It is our hope that this book has, in some way, taken you along our own intellectual journey of exploring the secret war for the Middle East. This book represents a decade of thinking, writing, and publishing in such journals as *Infantry*, and the *Foreign Area Officer Association Journal*. Perhaps the best part was the interaction with dozens of men and women within the Defense Department and our armed forces who read books with us and explored ideas to develop a deeper understanding of the region beyond unhelpful sound bites and quick slogans. We can only end by saying to our fellow men and women of the U.S. Armed Forces, "Thank you for educating us both!"

APPENDIX 1

Excerpts from *The Goebbels Diaries, 1942–1943*[1]

January 30, 1942: It is interesting to observe what importance the clever exploitation of religion can assume. The Tatars at first had a less-than-gratifying attitude to the German Wehrmacht. But they changed completely when permitted to sing their religious chants from the top of the minarets. Their change of attitude went so far that Tatar auxiliary companies which fought actively against the Bolsheviks could be formed. Our efforts there were supported by our propaganda companies who distributed a picture showing the Grand Mufti of Jerusalem [Haj Amin al-Husseini] visiting the führer. That was extremely successful.

While following Rommel, Hitler's inner circle followed Egyptian politics as reflected by Goebbels Diary entries:

February 7, 1942: Nahas Pasha has issued a pro-British declaration, stating that the Anglo-Egyptian Treaty will be carried out both in letter and in spirit. We don't place great hopes in Nahas Pasha; nevertheless one must not forget that he simply had to make such a declaration because he and his government are under the thumb of the English and he can't afford in any way to oppose the pro-British course.

February 8, 1942: The reconstruction of the Egyptian government has brought no sensational changes. Nahas Pasha declared that he intended to carry out the treaty with England without any reservation. He was clever enough, however, to obtain authority to dissolve Parliament. That, undoubtedly, is right. We [the Nazis] did the same thing in February 1933. He must first get parliamentary backing before he can bring about fundamental changes. I will hope he [Nahas] may act more favorably for us than we are inclined for the present to assume.

February 9, 1942: A serious explosion in Tangiers. The Secret Service is badly compromised. [Writes of giant anti-British demonstrations in Tangiers, not physical explosion.]

February 26, 1942: An attempt was made at Ankara to assassinate Ambassador von Papen and his wife. . . . The origin of this attempt is perfectly clear. It was without a doubt prepared by the [British] Secret Service in collaboration with the [Russian] GPU.[2]

March 17, 1942: The Viceroy of India assembled the Indian princes about him and abjured solemnly to rally to and remain on the side of England. The Indian people haven't much to expect of these princes. They are, for the most part, corrupt and bribed characters, who will go with the English as long as they receive money there. The Indian people will have to look to other quarters for their liberation.

March 19, 1942: The Turkish foreign minister, Saracoglu, has given an interview to an Italian newspaper in which he favors absolute neutrality towards the Axis as well as the Anglo-Saxon powers, but nevertheless uses turns of speech to which we haven't been used hitherto. His attitude is typical for Turkey. Ankara no doubt has the intention of deciding in favor of one side or the other only when victory for that side is absolutely sure. [Skukri Saracoglu was Turkish foreign minister from 1938 to 1942 and from 1944 on, the Nazis worked feverishly to draw Turkey into the Axis sphere to at least maintain their neutrality.]

March 27, 1942: The Wafd party has achieved a glorious victory; let's not question with what means, but it did gain 216 out of 264 seats. That makes it possible for Nahas Pasha to act. Of course not much is to be expected of him, as he has probably been a satellite of the English for some time already.

April 6, 1942: Gandhi has broken into print. He published an interview against British exploitation, but can offer nothing as a countermeasure except passive resistance, which naturally can't cause the English much trouble. Gandhi's policies have thus far brought nothing but misfortune to India. Had these four hundred and fifty millions of people been led by an energetic nationalist, Indian politics, and especially the Indian freedom movement, would undoubtedly be further along than they are today.

May 16, 1942: The Research Office sent me background material on a number of political matters of some interest. Relations between Turkey and the Soviet Union have worsened very much. In his private talks, the Turkish foreign minister, Saracoglu, used strong expressions of antagonism to the policies of the Soviets. The English are trying to calm him down. But Moscow has certainly provoked the Turkish Government.

APPENDIX 2

Lessons from the 1941 Anglo-Iraqi Revolt: The Writings of the Late Iraqi Army Officer and Military Historian Mahmood Al-Durrah[1]

Among the problems of the Saddam Hussein regime was the downfall of Iraqi scholarly thought and publications. Many Iraqi historians, political scientists and writers within Iraq, were reduced to publishing works that did not contain true analysis and discussions of the problems facing Iraq's modern history, instead the focus was on slogans of Ba'athism and praising the regime. As a reader of Arabic books on military and political history, it is my earnest hope that among the fruits of Operation Iraqi Freedom is the re-awakening of the true scholarly potential of Iraqi intellectuals. The late Iraqi officer Mahmood Al-Durrah served as an army lieutenant in World War II. When you say 1941 to an American soldier or sailor they remember Pearl Harbor, for Iraqis it is the invasion of Iraq by British forces to suppress the pro-Axis government of Prime Minister Rashid Ali, who was installed as prime minister in a military coup that swept aside the Iraqi Hashemite monarchy. Al-Durrah wrote *Al-Harb Al-Iraqiyah Al-Britaniah* (The Iraqi-British War, 1941) in 1969, which offers a comprehensive study of the strategy and tactics of British and Iraqi forces. It discusses how the British secured the port Basra and fought its way to Baghdad. The book although in Arabic, gives perspectives on operational and tactical decisions made by Iraqi senior officers in confronting new British combined armor, infantry and air tactics. It also offers lessons into how the Iraqi military entered Arab political life.

As U.S. forces become involved in the positive evolution of Iraq as well as battling the Iraqi extremist insurgency, it is vital to study Arabic works written by Iraqis. These works not only should be read by American students of warfare, but need to be rediscovered by Iraqi security forces who have sadly endured two decades of devolution in Iraqi military thought. As an example, one of the better Arabic books on the tactics of the Iran-Iraq War was written by former Egyptian defense minister Abdel-Haleem Abu-Gazallah. Iraqis now must be given the self-confidence of past military historians and tactical writers; it also offers valuable lessons on how Iraqi senior officers have encroached upon civil authority. Durrah's book was published in Beirut, Lebanon by Dar-Al-Taleeah Printers and is 478 pages.

The chief cause of the 1941 Anglo-Iraqi conflict lay in the very structure by which modern Iraq was created. After World War I, during the 1921 Cairo Conference British officials such as Winston Churchill, T. E. Lawrence as well as the Hashemite family of the Hijaz (western Arabia) that led the Arab Revolt gathered to stitch together modern Iraq from the Ottoman provinces of Mosul, Baghdad, and Basra. After Prince Feisal was ejected by the French in 1920 and denied kingship of Syria, it was in Iraq that the British would find a convenient monarchy to install Feisal. It also provided the British with a method of giving their mandate in Iraq the veneer of Arab governance. The installation of Feisal as King of Iraq represented many negative images to the average Iraqi including being:

- a Sunni ruling over a Shiite majority nation;
- a British-inspired monarch;
- a western Arabian (Hijazi) with no connection to Iraq.

The Iraqi monarchy and constitution was created from 1921 to 1923 with British oversight. This was a time when many Arab officers demobilized or simply defected from the Ottoman armies and were experimenting with ideas of nationalism, self-determination, and even fascism. The Iraqi constitutional monarchy was created to primarily preserve British basing and oil interests in Iraq. This was further cemented by the 1930 Anglo-Iraqi Treaty that ensured favorable terms for the British and control of strategic military bases, primarily the Habbaniya Air Base, and valued oil fields. The terms of the 1930 treaty led to the suicide of Iraq's prime minister Abdel-Mohsen Saddoun who could not endure the humiliation of the terms dictated by the British.

The 1930 treaty led to mass demonstrations including an infamous riot orchestrated by General Yassin Hashimi, who would become prime minister in 1935. In this climate, Iraqi officers dreamt of being the next Kemal Atatürk or Reza Shah, both military officers, the first founded modern Turkey and the latter the Pahlavi Dynasty in Iran. Other Arab officers in Iraq also saw solutions in the militant fascism of Hitler and Mussolini who created a façade of order and industry using hidden violence and suppression of civil and political life. The book highlights how Iraqi officers discussed their nation being the Arab Prussia that would create a greater Arab state.

Among the most influential military officers that infused the army into Iraqi politics was not a field commander but an instructor in Iraq's military academy. Colonel Tawfik Hussein taught military history and injected ideas that inspired not only the author of the book but a string of Iraqi military leaders who would orchestrate a series of military coups. Hussein laced his history lesson with images of King Feisal betraying the aspirations of Iraqi, Syrian, and Palestinian officers who left the Ottoman service to fight against the Turks in the Arab Revolt in the hope of establishing an independent Arab state. He argued that the Iraqi army has a duty to undertake political action to realign the direction of the nation. In 1929, Hussein began teaching and by 1934, he had influenced over 70 key officers and attracted the attention of the Muslim Youth Group who yearned to reestablish the Caliphate in Iraq. Two of the four generals in charge of the army and who understood they held the key to maintaining internal order for King Feisal, were followers of Hussein's rationale. In addition, Lebanon became a haven for Iraqi officers who published pamphlets as well as anti-monarchy and anti-British articles in the Lebanese press. More importantly, Lebanon offered a location to hold meetings with Islamists, communists and nationalists all committed to ridding Iraq of British influence.

The 1936 Bakr Sidqui Military Coup

It is important that all Arabs study what would become the first incidence in modern Arab political history of army officers staging a successful military coup in October 1936. The climate to create the perfect conditions for this military coup included the bulk of the Iraqi army being deployed on annual summer maneuvers, the army chief of staff being out of the country in London for military talks, and the cooperation of a flight commander who controlled five bombers all under the leadership of General Bakr Sidqui. Events unfolded on the night of 26/27 October 1936 that began with a shock and awe of bombers under the command of Ali Jawad screaming over Baghdad at 1130. They dropped four bombs in front of the Council of Ministers building, the central post office, parliament, and the Dakhla River leading to seven casualties. More importantly this was the first time aerial bombardments were used in a military coup. The officers in revolt swore fealty to King Ghazi and sent a proclamation to the king indicating they were purging the corrupt ministers around him. Communists led by lawyers in and around Baghdad asked the people to rise up against the government and in the ensuing chaos War Minister Jafar Al-Aksary was murdered by several officers sent by Sidqui. General Sidqui imposed Prime Minister Hikmat Sulayman on King Ghazi and Iraq would be ruled by unconstitutional means for a year. The book laments the decision to execute Jafar Al-Askary who dedicated his life to Arab nationalist causes and was a competent warrior having distinguished himself fighting the Ottomans in the Arab Revolt, he also fought the French in Syria. General Sidqui's dictatorship would last less than one year and he would be killed in an assassination plot hatched by military officers.

Iraqi politics after Sidqui would see the return of Prime Minister Nuri As-Sa'id, for his fourth time as prime minister. Prime Minister Sa'id attempted to remove Iraq's chief of staff General Amari. Instead of having General Amari capitulate to the wishes of civilian authority, it was Amari and thirty senior officers who removed Nuri Sa'id from power and imposed Rashid Ali Gaylani as prime minister. For added measure, the thirty senior officers all yearning to return to the Sidqui dictatorship deposed the war minister Taha Hashemi. Only one encampment, the Wishash barracks, remained loyal to civil authority. The dictatorships of Generals Fawzy and Amari along with Prime Minister Rashid Ali Gaylani began in 1940 and would last until the end of the Anglo-Iraqi War in late May 1941.

World War II Iraq

During World War II, Iraqi officers and cadets saw a Britain that was on its last legs of empire. Many senior Iraqi generals and Arab nationalists assessed the situation and found:

- Britain stood alone;
- the Wehrmacht rolled over France, Poland and Czechoslovakia;
- Hitler signed a non-aggression pact with Stalin;
- Iran's Reza Shah was pro-Axis;
- Turkey's Kemal Atatürk remained neutral;
- Haj Amin Husseini, the Mufti of Jerusalem, allied himself fully with the Nazis and was offering religious sanction for Arab officers to throw off their governments that enabled British colonization; and
- London requested that Baghdad abide by the provisions of the 1930 Anglo-Iraqi treaty and declare war on Italy and Germany.

Iraqi officers questioned why Iraq should continue its pro-British policies and have British oversight in policy matters when it was losing to the Germans. In a compact with Prime Minister Gaylani and the senior generals it was decided that Iraq's policy was to gain full independence for itself, Syria, Lebanon and Palestine to form a Greater Arab State. These five also formed a government that favored militarism. What entered in their calculus to stall on declaring war on the Axis were the following:

- the Axis recognized Arab self-determination;
- the Axis announced it has no colonial ambitions in Egypt and Sudan and recognizes their independence;
- the Axis recognized the need for Arabs to be linguistically and culturally linked; and
- the Axis were vehemently anti-Zionist.

There was a selective memory about Axis efforts to colonize Arab and African nations, for instance the Italians colonized Libya in 1911, and began an invasion of Ethiopia in 1935. From 1940 to the start of hostilities between British and Iraqi forces a series of negotiations were undertaken to get Baghdad to:

- first, declare war on the Axis;
- second, to allow access through Iraq for British forces; and
- finally, London wanted extra Iraqi security in and around two strategic British air bases at Habbaniyah and Baghdad.

The book contains American diplomatic urgings for Iraq to cooperate with Britain as a means of asserting its right to full independence. This was the same line of reasoning the United States urged with Morocco, that Allied forces would after World War II work towards self-determination and independence of protectorates, mandates and colonies. The Iraqis in turn wanted Britain to assert the independence of Syria and Lebanon once it was liberated from the Vichy French, and demanded a just and lasting settlement of the Palestinian problem (then as it is now the Palestinian question was an agenda item of Arab governments). The British were in no mood for negotiation and expected the Iraqis to abide by the provisions of the 1930 Anglo-Iraqi Treaty. Finer points of disagreement over the Iraqis and British governments dealt with unimpeded access to Iraqi facilities versus the landing of British forces only with the consent of Baghdad. Such Iraqi indecisiveness in times of war would lead to the May 1941 British invasion of Iraq. What gave Britain's Iraq policy a sense of urgency was the successful invasion of Greece by Nazi forces in April 1941. This made German bombers and transports within easy range of the Middle East.

It is important to pause and understand the state of the Iraqi monarchy in 1940–1941. First King Ghazi had died in a car crash in 1938. In the world of conspiracies the Iraqi street blamed his death on a British plot. In his place King Feisal II was too young to assume the throne and a regency under his uncle Prince Abdal-Illah was declared. Prince Abdal-Illah saw the controversy between Prime Minister Gaylani and the army versus the British as a means of wresting more power for the monarchy with British support.

British and Iraqi negotiations became crucial when Nazi forces solidified their hold on Greece and were moving on strategic islands such as Rhodes and Crete. The government of Prime Minister Gaylani agreed to allow British forces to land in Basra but attached many conditions as to the size, use of roads by these forces and follow-on forces. The issue of follow-on British forces would be the spark that ignited conflict in May 1941. In the last week of April, British air, land and naval forces were making their way to Iraq from Bahrain, India, and Palestine. The bulk of these ground forces would land in Basra regardless of what Iraqi generals and ministers thought about follow-on forces. The stage was set for conflict.

The Rashid Ali (Gaylani) Revolt or Anglo-Iraqi Conflict

Before delving into the tactics and operational aspects of this conflict, it is important to reflect on the choices that Iraqi leaders made versus how Morocco attained independence as a result of World War II. Iraq saw in British weakness in the early years of the war (1939–1941) an opportunity to defy London and assert its sovereignty. Morocco, a French protectorate, and its monarch King Mohammed V, chose to throw their lot with the Allied cause, contributing troops in the hope that the removal of its status as a French protectorate would be the natural outcome after the liberation of France and the victory of the Free French. The outcome for Iraq would be a chaotic government after World War II leading to the demise of the monarchy in 1958; for Morocco it would lead to independence in 1956 with little skirmishes with French forces and a relatively easier removal of its protectorate status. In Iraqi memory the 1941 British landing would signify the second time English troops occupied Iraq, the first being 1914 to 1918. Little attention is paid to the reasons and geo-strategic issues that drove London to send troops both times. For the Iraqis, including Durrah's book, it is enough to say the British occupied Iraq twice in the twentieth century without a real comprehension of the historic or millennial geo-strategic background of Mesopotamia.

The Military Balance of Forces and Disposition

Iraq commanded approximately 46,000 active and 280,000 reserve army officers and troops in 1941. Add to this number, under 13,000 policemen. The Iraqis possessed a mixed number of Italian, British and American warplanes and transports and one armored group composed of a mixture of antiquated tanks and armored personnel carriers. Unique to Iraqi forces is a riverine force of four armored patrol craft of 70 tons displacement armed with machine guns. Iraqi forces were divided into three security regions:

- 1st and 2nd Army Groups headquartered in Baghdad with garrisons in Fallujah, Baquba, Ramadi and Habbaniya Air Base (one of two in the country).
- The 3rd Army Group headquartered in Mosul.
- 4th Army Group headquartered in Basra with garrisons in Nasiriya, Diwaniyah, Amarah and Al-Shuayba Air Base (second of two in the country).

Why Iraq's Military Fate Was Sealed

Despite the British landing a superior force both technologically and militarily, the main reason Durrah attributes to the total defeat of Iraq was what Durrah calls the governance of five (the four military generals and Prime Minister Gaylani), the four senior officers (one general and three colonels) were: Salah-al-din Sabbagh, Fahmy Said, Mahmood Suleiman, and Kamel Shabeeb. Each was in command of an Army Group and each with his own political ambitions and tribal groups to protect. As there was no overall command and control of Iraqi forces their military fate was sealed. An example highlighted in Durrah's book is the Iraqi general staff drawing up contingencies for the defense of Basra, but this was completely ignored by field commanders who took their orders from General Salah-al-Din Sabbagh the military governor of Basra. The first wave of British forces were granted access into Basra by Prime Minister Gaylani and landed on 18 April 1941. They were composed of:

- the 20th Infantry Brigade;
- an artillery regiment;
- an anti-tank battery;
- an engineering company; and
- a civil affairs/humanitarian group.

Their mission was to secure the port of Basra for follow-on forces that were to arrive 27 April.

It is this second British contingent which in which Prime Minister Gaylani refused to grant access, adding that British forces cannot exceed one Brigade in Iraq. On April 29, 1941, the British considered this refusal an abrogation of the Anglo-Iraqi Treaty of 1930 and tantamount to war. London refused to tie-in any political concessions on such issues as Palestine and its mandatory status over Iraq to the landing of British troops in Iraqi soil during a time of war and national survival against Axis powers. General Sabbagh of the Basra Military District remarked that by allowing this initial force unopposed into Basra that the battle for this strategic port city had been lost. Another problem of the Iraqis was no clear objectives were provided to Army Group Commanders except to be prepared to defend their regions. The British had clear objectives that included securing Basra first and secondarily the airfield at Habbaniya.

The Strategic Importance of Habbaniya Air Base

To demonstrate the importance of the Habbaniya airfield and its airport Sin Al-Zuban, a secret communiqué from Berlin was dispatched by Mufti Kamal Haddad guaranteeing Axis support to Iraqi Prime Minister Gaylani should war break out with the British. In addition, it stated that it would provide an air bridge of re-supply from the island of Rhoades but pressed for the Iraqis to occupy Sin Al-Zuban Airport and Habbaniya airfield as well secure sources of highly refined airplane fuel for German transports and fighter escorts. This Axis air bridge offered an important supply option for Iraqi forces since Basra was closed to them. The Colonel Haqi Abdel-Karim, Commanded elements of the Third Army Group, took the initiative and laid plans for moving his group to secure Habbaniya Air Base. His forces would take positions around the base and attack once hostilities began with the British. Colonel Abdel-Karim worried about British air superiority in strafing his ground forces and breaking a siege of Habbaniya air base. Among Abdel-Karim's plan was to amass several artillery pieces across the Euphrates River overlooking Habbaniya air base and begin bombarding the base while conducting an infantry assault.

On April 30, the British base commander of Habbaniya awoke to find a massing of Iraqi troops around the perimeter and occupying the strategic heights of Talul overlooking the entire base. Immediately the base was placed on alert and mobile armored vehicles with Vickers mounted machine guns began taking positions along the perimeter. The Iraqis pushed forward a tank, armored, machine gun, and mechanized infantry companies that were supporting the 4th infantry brigade that arrived from Kirkuk. They also reinforced this assault force with anti-air, and engineering companies. British reconnaissance patrols revealed that the 1st Infantry Brigade had moved from Baghdad to Ramadi to cut any reinforcements for the British from Jordan. The Iraqis also moved their 11th Infantry Regiment from Baghdad to Fallujah by train, to act as a reserve force that could respond using the village's central location with its rail and river connections. The Iraqi generals and colonels then debated about whether to make the first move and attack Habbaniya Air Base or wait for the British to strike first. The British continued their reconnaissance flights in the Baghdad, Fallujah, and Habbaniya sectors.

Capitalizing on Airpower: A New British Realization

The Anglo-Iraqi War of 1941 saw a maximum use of airpower by British forces, and their Iraqi counterparts, as well as their Axis allies. At 0500 May 2nd, British bombers took off from Al-Shuayba Air base near Basra and from the surrounded Habbaniya Air base in the center of Iraq. Their target would be Iraqi units surrounding Habbaniya Air base that were not within artillery range. The British had prioritized their target list in the following order of priority:

- artillery;
- tanks;
- armored carriers;
- trucks; and
- infantry formations.

Iraqis responded by shelling Habbaniya Air base starting at 0550 and sending up anti-air flak directed at British warplanes. The British aerial attack lasted 19 hours and targets were drawn against Iraqi military assets in Baghdad, as well as Iraqi planes at the Rashid Ali airstrip and troop barracks in Qurna. Four Wellington fighters decimated Iraqi warplanes on the ground at the Rashid Ali airstrip. Sensing an imminent attack and by observing the mass takeoffs of British warplanes, the Iraqis sent up their own fighters and bombers that downed one Royal Air Force (RAF) fighter at Salman Pak and attacked British-held Sin Zuban Airport at Habbaniya before making an emergency landing at Fallujah. After the attack on the Rashid Ali airstrip, the Iraqis dispersed their planes to airstrips at:

- Baquba;
- Khan Bani Saad;
- Dilli Abbas; and
- Mikdadiyah.

However good reconnaissance alerted the British to these other airstrips and they were attacked by aerial sorties one of which scored a direct hit on the precious airplane fuel storage facility in Baquba. By May 4th, only 7 out of 69 Iraqi warplanes remained and the only time the Iraqis would enjoy any air support was when Nazi Messerschmitt fighters and Henkel bombers flew to Iraq from bases in Rhodes and Syria (then controlled by the Vichy French). Iraqis and Germans could not coordinate Axis airpower with Iraqi ground operations against British forces. Instead Axis warplanes stumbled on RAF fighters over Iraq.

The British employed a new tactic of keeping Iraqi units pinned in location using continuous aerial bombardment. Iraqis were unable to maneuver and support forces surrounding the British air base at Habbaniya. RAF planes located an infantry group traveling from Baghdad to Fallujah and strafed it. After almost two days of relentless RAF aerial bombardment against Iraqis surrounding Habbaniya, a combined air and land force went to the Talul Heights with infantry and armored Vickers machine gun regiments to mop up the concentration of Iraqi artillery and infantry forces surrounding the air base. Large British transports disgorged heavy artillery pieces at Habbaniya which began shelling Iraqi artillery positions across the Euphrates River overlooking Habbaniya Air Base. On May 6th and 7th a combined British and Indian expeditionary force landed in Basra that made up two infantry brigades. These forces would be critical in bringing civil order in Basra.

The Axis Enters the Fray

Perhaps the most important lesson to be learned from the 1941 Anglo-Iraqi conflict is the impact outside powers had on the outcome of warfare in Iraq, whether Vichy French Syria, Germany and Palestinian guerillas in 1941 or Syria, Iran and non-Iraqi Islamist extremist terrorist groups today. The Germans used Vichy French Syria to shuttle supplies and conduct air attacks in support of the Iraqis; also used were bases in Mosul, which offered the added benefit of access to fuel supplies. On May 14 and 15, the British had had enough and launched air attacks on Mosul and Irbil in Northern Iraq and struck at airstrips and air bases in Damascus, Halab, and Rayan in Syria. The British also maintained two remote fuel depots labeled H3 and H4 along the Jordan, Rabta, and Baghdad roads. This would aid General Glubb Pasha's Arab Legions and British forces in Palestine to quickly access Iraq during this crisis in support of British units.

Another item eerily similar to the 2003 Iraq War is the use guerillas to harass regular forces. In this case, the guerillas and so-called mujahideen from Syria, Iraq and Palestine joined the irregular force led by Palestinian leader Al-Kaukji.

On 19 to 22 May British generals in Basra focused their efforts on Fallujah because the village at the time offered a crossroads as well as rail and river links to Syria, Jordan and Palestine. The British staged a diversionary attack on Ramadi to deceive Iraqis into committing forces in that sector while the main thrust on Fallujah began at 0500, 19 May with bombardment from 57 fighter-bombers. The Iraqis failed to stop an advance of combined artillery, infantry and mobile armored vehicles mounted with Vickers machine guns and Fallujah fell. An Iraqi truck laden with dynamite that was to destroy the iron bridge linking Fallujah and Baghdad was strafed by sheer luck by a RAF fighter.

Hitler realized the importance of unfolding events in Iraq and signed a directive on 23 May authorizing military aid, advisors, weapons, intelligence sharing and communications with Iraqi resistance forces to bog down the British in Iraq. Hitler's preoccupation with Operation Barbarossa and his eventual invasion of Russia sapped the effectiveness of Axis assistance to Iraq.

The Fall of Baghdad and Conclusion

Durrah's book ends with a criticism of the way in which Baghdad would fall. Iraqi generals and colonels did not overcome and adapt to British tactics using combined air, ground and artillery forces along with the effective armored machine gun vehicles. Instead the Iraqi regular forces fought predictably a defensive action. Durrah compares the plan for the defense of Baghdad as almost identical to the defense of Fallujah. The book describes how the defensive plans of Baghdad collapsed as soon as it came into contact with British regiments and aerial bombers. Generals and colonels, who were confident of British defeat and support of the Axis almost a year before, were now fleeing towards Mosul. The British returned the regency of Prince Abdal-Illah and many of these generals and colonels were rounded up and then subjected to an Iraqi military tribunal. Thus ended the reign of Prime Minister Rashid Ali Gaylani and his four generals that ran Iraqi affairs for a little over a year. They were replaced by Prime Minister Nuri Sa'id who would become prime minister for a fifth time. The war would assert the Iraqi monarchy's executive authority until the revolution of 1958 that violently ended Hashemite rule in Iraq and brought Colonel Abdel-Karim Qassem into power.

This book offers American military planners an understanding of why Iraqis mistrust foreign intervention and in particular why Iraqi leaders are highly sensitive to foreign basing rights. That is why routine agreements governing status of forces protections that enable a military exercise today are resisted and sometimes viewed with suspicion by many Arab governments. The challenge is to understand the history and keep reassuring Arab friends that such agreements are not designed to impinge on sovereignty and unlike the European colonial, mandatory and protectorate experiences that crafted documents to subjugate a region, current civilized nations and global powers are working together to empower Arab countries in dealing with its security challenges.

Just as America's military students spent much time studying Russian works during the cold war, today's conflict demands a comprehensive study of Arabic works like Durrah's. It also offers a tactical view of Iraq in conflict and more geo-political issues that have swept Iraq's history. Durrah's main contributions to Arab military thought were his over ten books on Arab warfare, Iraqi military history, the Iraqi conflict with the Kurds, as well as early Islamic tactics of the seventh century.

Published by Cdr. Aboul-Enein in U.S. Army *Armor Journal* 1, no. 6 (2008 November/December): 5–10. This essay was part of a collection prepared to provide deploying units in support of Operation Iraqi Freedom a better understanding of Iraq's political-military history.

NOTES

Preface

1. Winston S. Churchill, *The Second World War*, vol. 1, *The Gathering Storm* (Boston: Houghton-Mifflin, 1948), 55.
2. Winston S. Churchill, *The Second World War*, vol. 2, *Their Finest Hour* (Boston: Houghton-Mifflin, 1949), 418.
3. Robert L. Baker, *Oil, Blood and Sand* (New York: D. Appleton-Century Company, 1942), v–vii.
4. Leigh White, "Book Review of Robert L. Baker's *Oil, Blood and Sand*," *New Republic* 107, no. 10 (September 1942): 292. See also Robert Gale Woolbert, "Book Review of Robert L. Baker's *Oil, Blood and Sand*," *Foreign Affairs*, January 1943.

Background

1. Wolfgang Schwanitz, *Germany and the Middle East, 1871–1945* (Princeton, NJ: Markus Weiner Publishers, 2004), 4–6.
2. Sean McMeekin, *The Berlin-Baghdad Express: The Ottoman Empire and Germany's Bid for World Power* (Cambridge, MA: Harvard University Press, 2010), 16.
3. Donald McKale, "Germany and the Arab Question in the First World War," *Middle Eastern Studies* 29 (1993): 236–253.
4. A mufti simply refers to a cleric and person educated enough to issue *fatwas* (religious opinions). A grand mufti is a cleric in charge of a major Sunni Islamic center like the mosques in Mecca, Cairo, or Jerusalem. During the early Caliphate, the mufti was a researcher who helped an Islamic *qadi* (judge) write legal opinions and render judgments Islamically.
5. Robert Melka, "Max Freiherr von Oppenheim: Sixty Years of Scholarship and Political Intrigue in the Middle East," *Middle Eastern Studies* 9 (1973): 81–93.
6. McMeekin, *The Berlin-Baghdad Express*, 192.
7. McKale, "Germany and the Arab Question in the First World War," 236–253.
8. Palestine and Iraq were British mandates, and Syria was a French mandate. The mandate system was created after World War I to appease Woodrow Wilson, who called for the self-determination of peoples; this enabled the British

and French to create new colonies without calling them such. A mandatory power would oversee the eventual independence of the mandated state, but the date of independence was never clearly defined, leading to constant tension.

9. Francis Nicosia, "Arab Nationalism and National Socialist Germany, 1933–1939: Ideological and Strategic Incompatibility," *International Journal of Middle East Studies* 12 (1980): 351–372.

10. David Fromkin, *A Peace to End All Peace: The Fall of the Ottoman Empire and the Creation of the Modern Middle East* (New York: Avon Books, 1990); Margaret MacMillan, *Paris 1919: Six Months that Changed the World* (New York: Random House, 2001).

Chapter 1. Introduction

1. Published in the Egyptian government weekly magazine *al-Musawwar* 1510 (September 18, 1953).

2. The Italian colonization of Libya lasted from 1911 to 1943.

3. Churchill, *Second World War*, vol. 2, *Their Finest Hour*, 459.

4. "Lord Caldecote, U.K. Secretary of State for Dominion Affairs to Sir Geoffrey Whiskard, U.K. High Commissioner in Australia; Circular cablegram Z168 LONDON, 3 July 1940, 5.10 p.m.; IMPORTANT MOST SECRET." National Archives of the Commonwealth of Australia. http://www.info.dfat.gov.au/info/historical/HistDocs.nsf/2ecf3135305dccd7ca256b5d007c2afc/a82c80d0ba6833aeca256b7e00055326?OpenDocument.

Chapter 2. The Palestine Question

1. Albert Speer, *Inside the Third Reich: Memoirs* (New York: Macmillan, 1970), 96. Note: Albert Speer was discussing this topic with Hitler at the Obersalzburg, the führer's mountain retreat; these events might have occurred if Islam had absorbed Europe, according to Hitler's alternative history, as recounted by Speer.

2. The title sherief is an honorific given to those claiming descent from Prophet Muhammad's family.

3. Nahum Sokolow, *History of Zionism 1600–1918*, vol. 2 (London: Longmans, Green, 1919), 83.

4. Pankaj Mishra, *From the Ruins of Empire: The Intellectuals Who Remade Asia* (New York: Farrar, Strauss and Giroux, 2012). Read the chapter on Jamal al-Din al-Afghani in Mishra's work to begin to unlock the origins of pan-Islamism.

5. Aaron Klieman, *Foundations of British Policy in the Arab World: The Cairo Conference of 1921* (Baltimore: Johns Hopkins University Press, 1970), 260.

6. Stefan Wild, "National Socialism and the Arab East between 1933 and 1939," *Die Welt des Islams* 25 (1985): 128.

7. Ibid., 143.

8. Yunus al-Bahri, *Huna Berlin! Hayyi l-'arab* (Beirut, Lebanon: Dar al-Nashr lil-Jami Tiyin, 1955).

9. Lukasz Hirszowicz, *The Third Reich and the Arab East* (London: Routledge and Kegan Paul, and Toronto, Canada: Toronto University Press, 1966).

Originally published in Polish as *III Rzesza i arabski Wschod* (Warsaw: Ksiazka Wiedza, 1963).

10. Nicosia, "Arab Nationalism and National Socialist Germany, 1933–1939."

11. Jeffrey Herf, *Nazi Propaganda for the Arab World* (New Haven, CT: Yale University Press, 2009), 16. See also Basil H. Aboul-Enein and Youssef Aboul-Enein, "Axis and Allied Strategic Posturing in Palestine: Hidden Lessons from World War II," at http://www.benning.army.mil/armor/eARMOR/Heritage.html. This is part of the U.S. Army e-Armor Heritage Collection and was first published in the U.S. Army *Armor Journal* in the winter of 2009. This chapter is an expansion of this essay, which stimulated discussion among U.S. Army readers.

12. Nicosia, "Arab Nationalism and National Socialist Germany, 1933–1939."

13. Herf, *Nazi Propaganda for the Arab World,* 39.

14. Francis Nicosia, *The Third Reich and the Palestine Question* (Piscataway, NJ: Transaction, 2000), 86. Originally published, Austin: University of Texas Press, 1985.

15. Ibid., 87.

16. Ibid., 91.

17. Ibid.

18. David Kahn, *Hitler's Spies: German Military Intelligence in World War II* (New York: Macmillan, 1978), 275.

19. Norman H. Baynes, ed., *The Speeches of Adolf Hitler*, vol. 2, *April 1922–August 1939* (New York: Oxford University Press, 1942), 1497.

20. Ibid., 1558.

21. Ibid., 1596.

22. Ibid., 1639. See also Louis L. Snyder, ed., *Hitler's Third Reich: A Documentary History* (Chicago: Nelson-Hall, 1981), 619, for further context and analysis.

23. Baynes, *Speeches of Adolf Hitler*, vol. 2, *April 1922–August 1939*, 1647.

24. Ibid., 1649.

25. Nicosia, *The Third Reich and the Palestine Question*, 177.

26. Manucla Williams, *Mussolini's Propaganda Abroad: Subversion in the Mediterranean and the Middle East, 1935–1940* (London: Routledge, 2006), 47.

27. Claudio G. Segré, "Liberal and Fascist Italy in the Middle East, 1919–1938," in Uriel Dann, ed., *The Great Powers in the Middle East, 1919–1939* (New York: Holmes and Meier Publishers, 1988), 208.

28. Ibid., 208.

29. "Arabs Prefer Bari," *Sydney Morning Herald*, January 10, 1938, National Library of Australia archives, http://trove.nla.gov.au/ndp/del/article/17437732

30. Sir John Hammerton, *The Second World War*, vol. 3, *Under Siege* (Naples, FL: Trident Press International, 2000), 330.

31. Callum MacDonald, "Radio Bari: Italian Wireless Propaganda in the Middle East and British Countermeasures," *Middle Eastern Studies* 13 (1977): 195–207. Radio Bari began broadcasting on May 24, 1934; Radio Cairo began a week later on May 31, 1934, and was controlled mainly by Egyptian

nationalists; Radio Algiers was controlled by the French and later Vichy French who entered the mass-media market in the region in 1935; Jerusalem on March 30, 1936; Baghdad on July 12, 1936; Ankara on July 12, 1937; Beirut (French controlled) on September 3, 1937; Tripoli (Italian controlled) on December 29, 1937. Segré, "Liberal and Fascist Italy in the Middle East, 1919–1939," 211.

32. Peter Partner, *Arab Voices: The BBC Arabic Service 1938–1988* (London: British Broadcasting Corporation, 1988), 5. See also Tamara Chalabi, *Late for Tea at the Deer Palace: The Lost Dreams of my Iraqi Family* (New York: Harper, 2011), 183. Note the author is the daughter of the highly controversial Ahmed Chalabi, whose advocacy and questionable sources brought the United States closer to undertaking what would become Operation Iraqi Freedom. The RAF, so concerned about Axis radio propaganda, set up Al-Sharq al-Adna (Near East) Radio with its transmitter in Jaffa in 1941. In two years the British Special Operations Executive had taken over the station as part of its political warfare section. See Douglas A. Boyd, "Sharq al-Adna/The Voice of Britain, The UK's Secret Arabic Radio Station and Suez War Propaganda Disaster," *Gazette: The International Journal for Communications Studies* 65, no. 6 (2003): 443–445. The first time an Egyptian king was heard on radio by his subjects was when King Farouk delivered his 1937 coronation speech.

33. Herf, *Nazi Propaganda for the Arab World*, 267.

34. The SOE was a section of British Intelligence in charge of sabotage, propaganda, and organizing resistance. It technically fell under the Minister of Economic Warfare until 1941, when it became an independent intelligence agency run under the Political Warfare Executive. The SOE was dissolved by Prime Minister Clement Atlee in 1946.

35. Martin Seth Kramer, *The Arab Awakening and Islamic Revival: The Politics of Ideas in the Middle East* (Piscataway, NJ: Transaction Publishers, 2011), chap. 5, "The Arab Nation of Shakib Arslan," 103–110.

36. Ibid.

37. Herf, *Nazi Propaganda for the Arab World*, 24–26.

38. Sean O'Neill and John Steele, "Mein Kampf for Sale in Arabic," the UK *Daily Telegraph*, March 19, 2002, http://www.telegraph.co.uk/news/uknews/1388161/Mein-Kampf-for-sale-in-Arabic.html

39. Williams, *Mussolini's Propaganda Abroad*, 88.

40. Howard Morley Sachar, *Europe Leaves the Middle East, 1936–1954* (London: Allen Lane, 1974), 167.

41. Nicosia, *The Third Reich and the Palestine Question*, 104.

42. Tom Segev, *One Palestine, Complete: Jews and Arabs under the British Mandate* (New York: Henry Holt, 1999), 360.

43. Ibid., 361.

44. Ibid., 362–363.

45. Nicosia, *The Third Reich and the Palestine Question*, 104.

46. Massimiliano Fiore, *Anglo-Italian Relations in the Middle East, 1922–1940* (Burlington, VT: Ashgate, 2010), 92–94.

47. McMeekin, *The Berlin-Baghdad Express*, 362.

48. Reeva S. Simon, *Iraq between the Two World Wars: The Militarist Origins of Tyranny* (New York: Columbia University Press), 2004, 38.

49. Shelomo Alfassa, *Reference Guide to the Nazis and Arabs during the Holocaust: A Concise Guide to the Relationship and Conspiracy of the Nazis and the Grand Mufti of Jerusalem in North Africa and the Middle East during the Era of the Holocaust* (New York: International Sephardic Leadership Council, 2006).

50. Simon, *Iraq between the Two World Wars*, 37–38. Also see James Scott, "Germany, Great Britain and the Rashid Ali al-Kilani Revolt of Spring 1941," commonly referred to as "Nazi Foreign Policy in the Middle East" (Master's thesis, Portland State University, 1995), http://www.csus.edu/indiv/s/scottjc/title.htm, 22nd para.

51. Nicosia, *The Third Reich and the Palestine Question*, 102.

52. Ibid., 103.

53. Ibid.

54. Ibid., 103.

55. Rudolf Bernhardt, *Encyclopedia of Public International Law*, vol. 12, *Geographic Issues* (Amsterdam: North-Holland Publishing Co., 1990), 156.

56. Steven M. Gelber, *No Balm in Gilead: A Personal Retrospective of Mandate Days in Palestine* (Ottawa: Carleton University Press, 1989), 100–101.

57. Salafi means a return to the pious founders; there are hundreds of Salafi groups because there is no single agreement on who constitutes the pious founders. How to recreate a society in their image? Salafis are a subset of Sunni Islam; some are benign proselytizers, others are politically active, and a minority advocate direct violent action to bring about an Islamic social order in their image. Some are reformist progressives and others are radical.

58. Beverly Milton-Edwards, *Islamic Politics in Palestine* (New York: I. B. Tauris, 1999), 24.

59. Jennie Lebel, *The Mufti of Jerusalem Haj Amin al-Husseini and National Socialism*, trans. Paul Munch (Belgrade, Serbia: Chigoja, 2007).

60. Howard Morely Sachar, *A History of Israel: From the Rise of Zionism to Our Time* (New York: Knopf, 2010), 170.

61. Sahar Hunaydi, *A Broken Trust: Sir Herbert Samuel, Zionism and the Palestinians, 1920–1925* (London: I. B. Tauris, 2001), 133.

62. Nicosia, *The Third Reich and the Palestine Question*, 104–108.

63. Ibid.

64. Ibid.

65. Philip Mattar, *The Mufti of Jerusalem* (New York: Columbia University Press, 1988), 105–107.

66. David Blair, "He Dreamed of Glory but Dealt Out Only Despair," *Daily Telegraph*, March 18, 2003, http://www.telegraph.co.uk/news/1424980/He-dreamed-of-glory-but-dealt-out-only-despair.html?pageNum=1

67. Yehuda Bauer, "From Cooperation to Resistance: The Haganah 1938–1946," *Middle Eastern Studies* 2 (1966): 182.

68. Ibid., 183.

69. Donald Neff, "Hamas: A Pale Image of the Jewish Irgun and Lehi Gangs," *Washington Report on Middle East Affairs* 25 (May/June 2006): 14.

70. Joseph Heller, "Zeev Jabotinsky and the Revisionist Revolt against Materialism: In Search of a World View," *Jewish History* 12 (1998): 54.

71. Y. S. Brenner, "The 'Stern Gang' 1940–1948," *Middle Eastern Studies* 2 (1965): 3.

72. Ibid.

73. Lillian Goldman Law Library, "British White Paper of 1939," Yale Law School, http://avalon.law.yale.edu/20th_century/brwh1939.asp

74. Brenner, "The 'Stern Gang' 1940–1948," 3.

75. Ibid., 4.

76. Joseph Heller, *The Stern Gang: Ideology, Politics, and Terror, 1940–1949* (London: Frank Cass, 1995), 97.

77. Ibid., 91.

78. Mattar, *The Mufti of Jerusalem*, 95.

79. Michael J. Cohen, "The Moyne Assassination, November, 1944: A Political Analysis," *Middle Eastern Studies* 15 (1979) 370.

80. Bernard Lewis, *Semites and Anti-Semites: An Inquiry into Conflict and Prejudice* (New York: W. W. Norton, 1999), 151.

81. Nicosia, *The Third Reich and the Palestine Question*, 104–108; "was entrusted to me," 186.

82. Hirszowicz, *Third Reich and the Arab East*, 110.

83. "Documents on German Foreign Policy 1918–1945, Series D," vol. 13 (London, 1964), 881 (both quotes). See also Fritz Grobba, *Manner und Machate im Orient: 25 Jahre Diplomatischer Tatigkeit im Orient* [Men and power in the Orient: 25 years of diplomatic activity in the East] (Gottingen, Germany: Musterschmidt-Verlag, 1967), 270 (both quotes).

84. Christopher Browning and Jürgen Matthäus, *The Origins of the Final Solution: The Evolution of Nazi Jewish Policy, September 1939–March 1942* (Lincoln: University of Nebraska Press, 2004), 406.

85. Roger Cohen, *Hearts Grown Brutal: Sagas of Sarajevo* (New York: Random House, 1998), 40–41.

86. George H. Stein, *The Waffen SS: Hitler's Elite Guard at War, 1939–1945*, trans. and published by the U.S. Goverment Printing Office (New York: Cornell University Press, 1966), 182. Derived from RFSS to SS-HA, SS-FHA, Kammerhofer and Wagner, gehe v. 6. 8. 1943, T-175/70/7128-9 from the Captured German and Related Records on Microform in the U.S. National Archives, Washington, DC.

87. Ibid.

88. Peter Longerich, *Heinrich Himmler*, trans. Jeremy Noakes and Leslie Sharpe (New York: Oxford University Press, 2012), 677. Of note, most of Himmler's personal papers are held at the Hoover Institite at Stanford University, California; many books about him reference this archive.

89. Joseph Schechtman, *The Mufti and the Fuhrer: The Rise and Fall of Haj Amin el-Husseini* (New York: Thomas Yoseloff, 1965), 139.

90. Klaus-Michael Mallman and Martin Cuppers, *Nazi Palestine: The Plans for the Extermination of the Jews in Palestine*, trans. Krista Smith (New York: Enigma Press, 2010), 100.

91. Ibid., 100.

92. Speer, *Inside the Third Reich*, 96.

93. Hirszowicz, *Third Reich and the Arab East*, 252, 264.

94. Ibid., 252.

95. Al-Umar, Abd Al-Karim, *Muzakkirat Al Hajj Muhammed Amin Al Husseini* [The memoirs of Al Hajj Amin Al-Husseini] (Damascus: Al-Ahali, 1999), 126.

96. William Breuer, *Deceptions of World War II* (New York: John Wiley, 2002), 143.

97. Nation Associates, "The Arab Higher Committee: Its Origins, Personnel and Purposes, The Documentary Record," submitted to the United Nations, May 1947, http://unispal.un.org/UNISPAL.NSF/0/FB6DD3F0E953581585 2572DD006CC607

98. Lionel Casper, *The Rape of Palestine and the Struggle for Jerusalem* (Jerusalem, Israel: Gefen Publishing, 2003), 167–168.

99. Benny Morris, *1948: A History of the First Arab-Israeli War* (New Haven, CT: Yale University Press, 2008), 123.

100. Anwar Sadat, *In Search of Identity: An Autobiography* (New York: Harper and Row, 1978), 13.

101. Ibid.

102. Nicosia, *The Third Reich and the Palestine Question*, 96–98.

103. Ibid.

104. Wild, "National Socialism and the Arab East," 143.

105. Nicosia, *The Third Reich and the Palestine Question*, 175 ("I advise the members"), 176 ("My task").

106. Williams, *Mussolini's Propaganda Abroad*, 99.

107. Nicosia, *The Third Reich and the Palestine Question*, 121.

108. Lewis, *Semites and Anti-Semites*, 144.

109. Paul Salem, *Bitter Legacy: Ideology and Politics in the Arab World* (Syracuse: Syracuse University Press, 1994), 245.

110. Alfred Rosenberg, *Mythus des Zwanzigsten Jahrhunderts* [The myth of the twentieth century] (Munich: Hoheneichen-Verlag, 1930).

111. Elie Kédourie, *Arabic Political Memoirs and Other Studies* (London: Cass Publishing, 1974), 200.

112. Wild, "National Socialism and the Arab East," 131.

113. John Entelis, *Pluralism and Party Transformation in Lebanon: Al-Kata'ib, 1936–1970* (Leiden, The Netherlands: E. J. Brill, 1974), 46.

114. Robert Fisk, *Pity the Nation: The Abduction of Lebanon* (New York: Nation Books, 2002), 65.

115. James Jankowski, "Egypt's Young Rebels: Young Egypt, 1933–1952 (Stanford, CA: Hoover Institute Press, 1975), 59.

116. Wild, "National Socialism and the Arab East," 134.

117. Ibid., 135–137, 138 ("The nation which does not excel"). This address was given to students of the Central Secondary School in 1933. It also appears in Sami Shawkat, *Hadhihi Ahda-funa* [These are our aims] (Baghdad, 1939), 1–3.
118. Wild, "National Socialism and the Arab East," 134.
119. Ibid., 138.

Chapter 3. Hashemite Iraq

1. Akeel Naseeri, *Al-Jaysh wal Sultah fee Iraq al-Malaki, 1921–1958* [The army and authority in Iraq under the monarchy, 1921–1958] (Damascus: Dar al-Hassad Publishers, 2000). Abridged translation was published by Lt. Cdr. Youssef Aboul-Enein, USN, and Basil Aboul-Enein as "Civil-Military Affairs in Hashemite Iraq: An Examination of Past Military Conduct in Iraqi Political Life," *Infantry* 95, no. 2 (March/April 2006). Youssef and Basil Aboul-Enein published this essay as a means of introducing those deploying in support of Operation Iraqi Freedom to an understanding of Iraqi political-military perspective from an Arab perspective. If you are interested in reading additional works by the author prepared for the U.S. military on Iraq's military-political history, read Youssef Aboul-Enein, *Iraq in Turmoil: Historical Perspectives of Dr. Ali al-Wardi from the Ottomans to King Feisal* (Annapolis, MD: Naval Institute Press, 2012). Al-Wardi is the father of Iraqi sociology and his eight-volume modern history of Iraq is a definitive Arabic text on the sociopolitical history of Iraq, with an entire volume devoted to engineering Prince Feisal as king of Iraq and setting up his monarchy that would become a British mandate.
2. *Hawzas* are circles of Shiite influence that competed within Shiite Islam for a following; the most influential *hawza* is in Najaf.
3. Hana Batatua, *Al-Tabaqat al-Ijtimayiah wal Harakat al-Thawriyah* [Social classes and revolutionary movements] (Beirut, Lebanon: Arab Research Center, 1989); and Naseeri, *Al-Jaysh wal Sultah*, 20–27.
4. Naseeri, *Al-Jaysh wal Sultah*, 20–27.
5. Ibid.
6. The school also took students from the Levant.
7. Ibid., 32–36.
8. Ibid.
9. Ibid., 41.
10. Ibid.
11. For more information on this period, see the author's essay published in the November–December 2005 edition of the U.S. Army journal *Infantry*, entitled "History of the Syrian Arab Army: Prussianization of the Arab Army, the Arab Revolt of 1916–1918, and the Cult of Nationalization of Arabs after World War I." It introduces readers to the Center for Military History in Damascus and the perspectives of the Syrian defense establishment on this history.
12. Al'aa Jassem Mohammed, *Jafar al-Askary wa Dawruhu al Siyasi wal Askari* [Jafar al-Askary: His political and military role] (Baghdad, Iraq: Maktabat al-Yazqah al-Arabiya, 1987).

13. Jamal Omar Nazmi, *Al-Juzoor al-Siyasiyah wal Fikriyah lil Haraka al-Qawmiyah fee al-Iraq* [Roots of political thought of the Nationalist movement in Iraq] (Beirut, Lebanon: Research Center for Arab Unity, 1984). See also Naseeri, *Al-Jaysh wal Sultah*, 30–36; and finally Aboul-Enein, "Civil-Military Affairs in Hashemite Iraq."

14. Naseeri, *Al-Jaysh wal Sultah*, 30–36.

15. Ibid.

16. Ibid.

17. Ibid.

18. Ibid.

19. Ibid.; see also T. E. Lawrence, arranged by Malcolm Brown, *The Letters of T. E. Lawrence* (New York: Oxford University Press, 1991), 163–167.

20. Naseeri, *al-Jaysh wal-Sultah*, 57–63.

21. Ibid.

22. Ibid.

23. Ibid.

24. Ibid.

25. Peter Young and Michael Roffe, *The Arab Legion: Men at-Arms* (Oxford: Osprey Publishing, 1972), 7.

26. Ibid., 8.

27. Ibid.

28. Ibid., 29.

29. Hirszowicz, *Third Reich and the Arab East*, 46.

30. Naseeri, *Al-Jaysh wal Sultah*. For an excellent read from a British perspective on the events in Iraq and Syria, read Douglas Porch, *The Path to Victory: The Mediterranean Theater in World War II* (New York: Farrar, Strauss and Giroux, 2004).

31. Edmund Ghareeb and Beth Dougherty, *Historical Dictionary of Iraq* (Lanham, MD: Scarecrow Press, 2004).

32. Ibid.

33. Daniel Silverfarb and Majid Khadduri, *Britain's Informal Empire in the Middle East: A Case Study of Iraq 1929–1941* (New York: Oxford University Press, 1986), 111.

34. Ian Playfair, *The Mediterranean and the Middle East: History of the Second World War, United Kingdom Military Series,* vol. 1, *The Early Successes Against Italy (to May 1941)* (East Sussex, UK: Naval and Military Press, 2004), 178.

35. Geoffrey Warner, *Iraq and Syria 1941: The Politics and Strategy of the Second World War* (Newark: University of Delaware Press, 1974), 35–36.

36. Playfair, *The Mediterranean and the Middle East*, 178.

37. Basheer M. Nafi, "The Arabs and the Axis: 1933–1940," *Arab Studies Quarterly* 19 (1997): 1–24.

38. Naseeri, *Al-Jaysh wal Sultah*, 30–36; and Aboul-Enein, "Civil-Military Affairs in Hashemite Iraq."

39. Robert Lyman and Howard Gerrard, *Iraq 1941: The Battles for Basra, Habbaniya, Fallujah and Baghdad* (Essex, UK: Osprey, 2006), 11.

40. Thomas Hubbard Vail Motter, *The Persian Corridor and Aid to Russia*, vol. 7, *Part 1* (Washington, DC: Office of the Chief of Military History, Department of the Army, 1952), 8.

41. *Defense of the Middle East*, text of appendix 1, Defense and Military Provisions of the Anglo-Iraqi Treaty of Alliance British Information Services (New York: British Information Services, Reference Division, an agency of the British government, Reference Division, 1954), 21; and Motter, *Persian Corridor and Aid to Russia*, 8. See also Silverfarb and Khadduri, *Britain's Informal Empire in the Middle East*, 127.

42. Foreign Relations of the United States (FRUS) Diplomatic Papers, "The British Commonwealth, the Soviet Union, the Near East and Africa" (Washington, DC: U.S. Department of State, 1940), 713; the University of Wisconsin digitized archives of FRUS, http://digicoll.library.wisc.edu/cgi-bin/FRUS/FRUS-idx?type=turn&id=FRUS.FRUS1940v03&entity=FRUS.FRUS1940v03.p0725&isize=M. Also see J. C. Hurewitz, *The Middle East and North Africa in World Politics: British-French Supremacy 1914–1945* (New Haven, CT: Yale University Press, 1979), 422.

43. Hirszowicz, *Third Reich and the Arab East*, 77.

44. Akten zur Deutschen Auswartigen Politik, 1918–1945 [Documents on German foreign policy, 1918–1945], Series D (1937–1945), vols. 5, x–xiii, London-Washington, 1956–1964, trans. and published by the U.S. Goverment Printing Office, 143; and for context see Nafi, "The Arabs and the Axis."

45. Akten zur Deutschen Auswartigen Politik, 1918–1945, 143 ("to convey to His Excellency"), 144 ("Palestine, which has for the past years"), 142 ("the future development of the political situation"), 144 ("as the Arab movement had fought Anglo-French imperialism").

46. Warner, *Iraq and Syria 1941*, 50.

47. Ibid., 52 ("public declaration" and "Apart from other").

48. Akten zur Deutschen Auswartigen Politik, 1918–1945, 261.

49. Hirszowicz, *Third Reich and the Arab East*, 80.

50. Ibid., 119.

51. Warner, *Iraq and Syria 1941*, 45. See also Majid Khadduri, *Independent Iraq, 1932–1958: A Study in Iraqi Politics* (Oxford: Oxford University Press, 1960), 223, for an excellent description of how Prime Minister Gaylani used the radio and press to agitate against Britain. Gaylani took a page from the former Iraqi monarch King Ghazi I, who had his own private radio station set up inside his palace in 1936 to rail against British policies in Iraq and the Middle East.

52. Nafi, "The Arabs and the Axis."

53. Silverfarb and Khadduri, *Britain's Informal Empire in the Middle East*; and Lyman and Gerrard, *Iraq 1941*, 113.

54. Robert Lyman, *First Victory: Britain's Forgotten Struggle in the Middle East, 1941* (London: Constable, 2006), 20; and Lyman and Gerrard, *Iraq 1941*, 12.

55. Lyman and Gerrard, *Iraq 1941*, 21.
56. Ibid.
57. Nicosia, *The Third Reich and the Palestine Question*, 184.
58. Franz Kurowski, *The Brandenburger Commandos: Germany's Elite Warrior Spies in World War II* (Mechanicsburg, PA: Stackpole Books, 2005), 140–141. This was concerning enough to Winston Churchill that excerpts of this directive made it into his multivolume history of World War II: Churchill, *The Second World War*, vol. 3, *The Grand Alliance* (Boston: Houghton-Mifflin, 1951), 264.
59. Churchill, *Second World War*, vol. 3, *The Grand Alliance*, 52.
60. Hirszowicz, *Third Reich and the Arab East*, 80.
61. Michael Bloch, *Ribbentrop* (New York: Crown Publishers, 1992), 327–328. See also David Brown, *The Road to Oran: Anglo-French Naval Relations, September 1939–July 1940* (London: Taylor and Francis, 2004), 72.
62. Porch, *The Path to Victory*.
63. Akten zur Deutschen Auswartigen Politik, 1918–1945, 936.
64. Lyman and Gerrard, *Iraq 1941*.
65. Herf, *Nazi Propaganda for the Arab World*, 61.
66. Ibid.
67. Hirszowicz, *Third Reich and the Arab East*, 84.
68. Ibid.
69. D. A. Farnie, *East and West of the Suez: The Suez Canal in History, 1854–1956* (London: Clarendon Press, 1969), 621–622.
70. Silverfarb and Khadduri, *Britain's Informal Empire in the Middle East*.
71. Alexander Greenwood, *A Biography of Field-Marshal Sir Claude Auchinleck, G.C.B., G.C.I.E., C.S.I., D.S.O., O.B.E., LL. D* (London: Pentland Press, 1990), 141.
72. Churchill, *Second World War*, vol. 3, *The Grand Alliance*, 254.
73. D. J. E. Collins, *The Royal Indian Navy, 1939–45*, vol. 1, *Combined Inter-services Historical Section, India & Pakistan* (Bombay: Orient Longmans, 1964), 71.
74. Lyman and Gerrard, *Iraq 1941*, 62.
75. Ibid., 29
76. Churchill, *Second World War*, vol. 3, *The Grand Alliance*, 259.
77. Ibid., 260.
78. Sachar, *Europe Leaves the Middle East*, 177.
79. Warner, *Iraq and Syria 1941*, 92,
80. Ibid.
81. Lyman and Gerrard, *Iraq 1941*, 39.
82. Reprinted from Aboul-Enein, "Civil-Military Affairs in Hashemite Iraq," which is an abridged translated synthesis of the Arabic work of Naseeri, *Al-Jaysh wal Sultah*.
83. Ibid.
84. Ibid.
85. Lyman and Gerrard, *Iraq 1941*, 40.

86. Ibid., 41.

87. Ibid., 43.

88. Ibid., 52.

89. Warner, *Iraq and Syria 1941*, 107.

90. John Connell, *Wavell: Scholar and Soldier* (New York: Harcourt, Brace and World, 1965), 436. In Harold Raugh's excellent book, *Wavell in the Middle East, 1939–1941* (London: Brassey's, 1993) the disagreements between Wavell and Auchinleck over the importance of Mosul and the Abadan oil fields (Auchinleck's position) over security of Egypt and the Suez Canal (Wavell's position) is discussed in great detail on pages 213–215. In essence, there can be no defense of the Suez Canal or any area of interest to Britain if it were deprived of vital oil supplies. Auchinleck's view was favored by Churchill and the chief of the imperial general staff, Field Marshall (Sir) John Dill, and the removal of Gaylani became a top priority. Field Marshall Dill would be replaced in December 1941 with Field Marshal Alanbrooke, with Dill taking charge of the British mission in the United States. Dill would die at Walter Reed Army Hospital in November 1944 and is one of the rare foreign officers buried at Arlington National Cemetery, such was Dill's influence on the American–British Combined Staff generally and on U.S. Army Chief of Staff Gen. George Marshall personally.

91. Lyman and Gerrard, *Iraq 1941*, 53. See also Aboul-Enein, "Civil-Military Affairs in Hashemite Iraq," which is an abridged synthesis of the Arabic work of Naseeri, *Al-Jaysh wal Sultah*.

92. Lyman and Gerrard, *Iraq 1941*, 21. Of note, Lyman and Gerrard, *Iraq 1941*, provide a great section containing short biographies of the Iraqi commanders of that time period.

93. Sir John Kennedy, *The Business of War* (London: Hutchinson, 1957), 137. In the war diaries of Field Marshal Lord Alanbrooke, the chief of the imperial general staff, he recounts a 6th Armored Division Conference with Churchill on April 27, 1941. In this meeting Kennedy proposes preparations for the withdrawal of British forces to the Suez Canal as a line of defense against the advancing Axis forces. Churchill was angered by such talk and labeled Kennedy a defeatist for most of the war, when prudence demanded a discussion on selecting and pre-planning lines of defense. See Field Marshall Lord Alanbrooke, *War Diaries, 1939–1945: Field Marshal Lord Alanbrooke*, ed. Alex Danchev and Daniel Todman (Berkeley: University of California Press, reprint 2001), 154. See also Scott, "Nazi Foreign Policy in the Middle East."

94. Lyman and Gerrard, *Iraq 1941*, 22–24.

95. Ibid.

96. Ibid.

97. Aboul-Enein, "Civil-Military Affairs in Hashemite Iraq," which is an abridged synthesis of the Arabic work of Naseeri, *Al-Jaysh wal Sultah*.

98. Ibid.

99. Lieutenant General (Sir) John Bagot Glubb, Pasha, would serve the majority of his career in the Middle East, and is widely credited with professionalizing the Arab Legion (also known as the Royal Jordanian Army). Glubb took

command of the Arab Legion in 1939 and relinquished command in 1956, when King Hussein dismissed him to provide distance between the British and himself during the height of Nasser's pan-Arabism. Glubb would direct Jordanian combat forces in the 1948 Arab–Israeli War, seizing the West Bank from organized infant Israeli fighting units. Glubb died in his East Sussex home in 1986, with the eulogy being delivered at Westminster by the late King Hussein of Jordan. Glubb was the author of close to twenty books from 1943 to 1983 on Islamic, Middle East, and the region's military history.

100. Lyman, *First Victory*, 119, 126.

101. Ibid., 116.

102. Barrie James, *Hitler's Gulf War: The Fight for Iraq 1941* (South Yorkshire, UK: Pen & Sword Books, 2010).

103. Hayyim Cohen, "The Anti-Jewish Farhud in Baghdad 1941," *Middle East Studies* 3 (1966): 2–17.

104. Anthony R. De Luca, "Der Grossmufti in Berlin: The Politics of Collaboration," *International Journal of Middle East Studies* 10 (1979): 125–138.

105. Ibid.

106. Ibid.

107. Ibid.

108. Ibid.

109. Ibid.

110. Akten zur Deutschen Auswartigen Politik, 1918–1945, 1015; see also Herf, *Nazi Propaganda for the Arab World*, 58.

111. Herf, *Nazi Propaganda for the Arab World*, 58.

112. Antonio Munoz, *Lions of the Desert: Arab Volunteers in the German Army* (Bayside, NY: Axis Europa, 1997), 28.

113. Ibid.

114. Hellmuth Felmy and Walter Warlimont, *German Exploitation of Arab Nationalist Movements in World War II*, Part 1 by General der Flieger Hellmuth Felmy, Section 5, Lessons Derived from the Employment of Foreign Troops, Manuscript of the U.S. Army-Foreign Military Studies Branch MS P-207, Box 145 (Washington, DC: U.S. National Archives, 1955), 39.

115. Munoz, *Lions of the Desert*, 29.

116. Herf, *Nazi Propaganda for the Arab World*, 150–151 (both letters).

117. Ibid.

118. Schwanitz, *Germany and the Middle East, 1871–1945*, 109.

119. Ibid.

120. Churchill, *Second World War*, vol. 3, *The Grand Alliance*, 236.

121. Schwanitz, *Germany and the Middle East, 1871–1945*, 98.

122. Nicosia, *The Third Reich and the Palestine Question*, 191.

123. Akten zur Deutschen Auswartigen Politik, 1918–1945, 641. See also Scott, "Nazi Foreign Policy in the Middle East."

124. Akten zur Deutschen Auswartigen Politik, 1918–1945, 689; see also Richard Stewart, *Sunrise at Abadan: The British and Soviet Invasion of Iran,*

1941 (New York: Praeger, 1988), 39, for further context of German assessment of British vulnerabilities defending the Suez Canal.

125. Hirszowicz, *Third Reich and the Arab East,* 82; see also Scott, "Nazi Foreign Policy in the Middle East."

126. Warner, *Iraq and Syria 1941,* 56.

127. Milan Hauner, *India in Axis Strategy: Germany, Japan, and Indian Nationalists in the Second World War* (Stuttgart: Klett-Cotta, 1981), 195.

128. De Luca, "Der Grossmufti in Berlin," 125–138. Weizsäcker published his memoirs six years after the end of the war, writing, in hindsight, "The German leaders, on the other hand, were living in a world of military chimeras. At first they said that they would shake hands with the Japanese in Siberia. And now they imagined that they may do the same thing via Suez or in Basra. They dreamed of a great pincer movement against Egypt, starting from Palestine and Libya. In accordance with the orders I had been given, I maintained relations with the Mufti of Jerusalem; and in doing so I derived aesthetic pleasure from the Oriental etiquette of negotiation. But I always took the view that all our combinations in the Near East went beyond our strength, and that only our political and strategic amateurs could take these things seriously." Ernst von Weizsäcker, *Memoirs,* trans. John Andrews (Chicago: Henry Regnery Company, 1951), 268.

129. Kahn, *Hitler's Spies,* 237.

130. Jak P. Mallmann Showell, *Fuehrer Conferences on Naval Affairs, 1939–1945* (Annapolis, MD: Naval Institute Press, 1990), 153; and see also Scott, "Nazi Foreign Policy in the Middle East."

131. "Nazi Conspiracy and Aggression, Volume 2, Chapter XVI, Part 15," of the digitized Nuremburg Trials made available by the Lillian Goldman Law Library at Yale University, http://avalon.law.yale.edu/imt/chap16_part15.asp

132. Ibid.; and see Nir Arielli, *Fascist Italy and the Middle East, 1933–1940* (New York: Palgrave Macmillan, 2010), 109–132, for further context of this quote.

133. Kahn, *Hitler's Spies,* 237.

134. F. H. Hinsley, *Hitler's Strategy* (Cambridge: Cambridge University Press, 1951), 199. The same page of Hinsley's book reveals Raeder's instincts on the state of the British fleet in the Mediterranean was correct. Axis mines and submarine attacks had reduced the British Mediterranean Fleet to three fully operational cruisers, the HMS *Dido, Naiad,* and *Euryalus.*

135. Warner, *Iraq and Syria 1941,* 164.

136. Ibid.

137. Gerhard Schreiber, Bernd Stegemann, and Detlef Vogel, *Germany and the Second World War,* vol. 3, *The Mediterranean, South-east Europe, and North Africa 1939–1941: From Italy's Declaration of Non-belligerence to the Entry of the United States into the War* (Oxford: Oxford University Press, 1995), 199.

138. William Shirer, *The Rise and Fall of the Third Reich: A History of Nazi Germany* (New York: Simon and Schuster, 1990), 813.

139. Ibid.

140. Showell, *Fuehrer Conferences on Naval Affairs*, 141.

141. Warner, *Iraq and Syria 1941*, 42.

142. Scott, "Nazi Foreign Policy in the Middle East."

143. "The Avalon Project, Documents in Law, History and Diplomacy, Eighty-Second Day, Friday, 15 March 1946, Morning Session," Nuremberg Trial Proceedings, vol. 9, http://avalon.law.yale.edu/imt/03-15-46.asp

144. Akten zur Deutschen Auswartigen Politik, 1918–1945, 30–31.

145. Hauner, *India in Axis Strategy*, 198.

146. Hirszowicz, *Third Reich and the Arab East*, 91.

147. Scott, "Nazi Foreign Policy in the Middle East."

148. Warner, *Iraq and Syria 1941*, 97 ("Iraq had to be helped" and "the possessions of this center"); see also Scott, "Nazi Foreign Policy in the Middle East."

149. Akten zur Deutschen Auswartigen Politik, 1918–1945, 33.

150. Churchill, *Second World War*, vol. 3, *The Grand Alliance*, 265. Churchill expounds on the strategic necessity of holding Iraq in this section of his Second World War history.

151. Schwanitz, *Germany and the Middle East, 1871–1945*, 109.

152. Ibid.

153. J. Hampden Jackson, *The Between War World: A Short Political History, 1918–1939* (London: V. Gollancz, 1947), 229.

154. W. G. Elphinston, "The Kurdish Question," *International Affairs* (Royal Institute of International Affairs) 22, no. 1 (January 1946): 91–103.

155. Amir Hassanpour, "The Kurdish Experience," *Middle East Report* 24 (1994), http://www.merip.org/mer/mer189/kurdish-experience

156. Elphinston, "The Kurdish Question."

157. Ibid.

158. Youssef Aboul-Enein, "Lessons from the 1941 Anglo-Iraqi Revolt: The Writings of the late Iraqi Army Officer and Military Historian Mahmood Al-Durrah," U.S. Army *Armor Journal* (November/December 2008). See also Mahmood Al-Durrah, *Al-Harb Al-Iraqiyah Al-Britaniah* (Beirut, Lebanon: Dar al-Taleeah Publishers, 1969).

159. Michael Eisenstadt and Eric Mathewson, eds., *U.S. Policy in Post-Saddam Iraq: Lessons from the British Experience* (Washington, DC: Washington Institute for Near East Policy, 2003).

160. Lawrence Pratt, "The Strategic Context: British Policy, 1936–1939," in Dann, *The Great Powers in the Middle East, 1919–1939*, 20.

Chapter 4. Vichy French Syria

1. Warner, *Iraq and Syria 1941*, 37. Excerpts from Youssef Aboul-Enein and Basil Aboul-Enein's essay, "The Anglo-French Intervention in the Levant June 8 to July 11, 1941," appear throughout this chapter; this essay was published in the May 2008 edition of the U.S. Army *Infantry Journal*. The essay and then this chapter were derived from lecture notes designed for delivery to U.S. military personnel deploying to Iraq in support of Operation Iraqi Freedom.

2. Understanding this history matters, as the Alawis are a subsect within Shia Islam, the faith of the current Assad regime. The Alawis represent 12 percent of today's Syria, ruling over upwards of 65 percent Sunni majority. As of this writing upwards of 70,000 to 90,000 Syrians have been killed in a sectarian war between the Assad regime and various anti-Assad groups. In many ways we are living among the last unresolved remnants created in the aftermath of World War I.

3. *Syria: A Country Study* (Washington, DC: U.S. Government Printing Office, 1979), 23.

4. Warner, *Iraq and Syria 1941*, 70.

5. Ibid., 71.

6. A. B. Gaunson, "Churchill, De Gaulle, Spears and the Levant Affair, 1941," *Historical Journal* 27 (1984): 697–713; Edward Spears, *Fulfillment of a Mission: The Spears Mission to Syria and Lebanon, 1941–1944* (Hamden, CT: Archon Books, 1977), 17.

7. Gaunson, "Churchill, De Gaulle, Spears and the Levant Affair," 697–713.

8. Spears, *Fulfillment of a Mission*; and see also N. E. Bou-Nacklie, "The 1941 Invasion of Syria and Lebanon: The Role of Local Paramilitary," *Middle Eastern Studies* 30 (1994): 512–529, for an excellent discussion of context.

9. Eugene Rogan, *The Arabs: A History* (New York: Basic Books, 2009), 241.

10. Mario Faivre, *We Killed Darlan, Algiers 1942: A Personal Account of the French Resistance in North Africa, 1940–1942* (Manhattan, KS: Sunflower University Press, 1999), 6.

11. Warner, *Iraq and Syria 1941*, 129.

12. Churchill, *Second World War*, vol. 3, *The Grand Alliance*, 323; see also Warner, *Iraq and Syria 1941*, 129.

13. Warner, *Iraq and Syria 1941*, 71.

14. Jafna Cox, "The Background of the Syrian Campaign, May–June 1941: A Study in Franco-German Wartime Relations," *History* 72 (1987): 432–452.

15. James Melki, "Syria and State Department 1937–47," *Middle Eastern Studies* 33 (1997): 92–106.

16. Robert Lewis Melka, "The Axis and the Arab Middle East: 1930–1945" (Ph.D. dissertation, University of Minnesota, 1966), 182.

17. Hirszowicz, *Third Reich and the Arab East*, 113.

18. Ibid.

19. Gaunson, "Churchill, De Gaulle, Spears and the Levant Affair."

20. Warner, *Iraq and Syria 1941*, 26; see also Aboul-Enein and Aboul-Enein, "The Anglo-French Intervention in the Levant."

21. Churchill, *Second World War*, vol. 3, *The Grand Alliance*, 323.

22. Claude Huan, "The French Navy in World War II," in James J. Sadkovich, ed., *Reevaluating Major Naval Combatants of World War II* (New York: Greenwood, 1990), 93. See also Aboul-Enein and Aboul-Enein, "The Anglo-French Intervention in the Levant."

23. Huan, "The French Navy in World War II," 93.

24. FRUS Diplomatic Papers, 1941, vol. 3 (Washington, DC: U.S. Government Printing Office, 1959), 704; see also Aboul-Enein and Aboul-Enein, "The Anglo-French Intervention in the Levant."
25. FRUS Diplomatic Papers, 1941, vol. 3, 704.
26. Selim Deringil, *Turkish Foreign Policy during the Second World War: An Active Neutrality* (Cambridge: Cambridge University Press, 1989).
27. Warner, *Iraq and Syria 1941*, 133.
28. Connell, *Wavell*, 461.
29. Warner, *Iraq and Syria 1941*, 136.
30. Churchill, *Second World War*, vol. 3, *The Grand Alliance*, 326.
31. Warner, *Iraq and Syria 1941*, 136.
32. Ibid.
33. Hirszowicz, *Third Reich and the Arab East*, 177.
34. Ibid.; see also "The History of the British 4th and 7th Armoured Brigades, The Black Rats and Green Jerboa" Web site, at http://www.desertrats.org.uk/bde/7thAB1943.htm#Bottom
35. Aboul-Enein and Aboul-Enein, "The Anglo-French Intervention in the Levant."
36. Churchill, *Second World War*, vol. 3, *The Grand Alliance*, 327.
37. Warner, *Iraq and Syria 1941*, 136 ("Turkey was afraid here"), 137 ("no reason whatever").
38. Ibid., 138.
39. Ibid.
40. Dharm Pal, *Official History of the Indian Armed Forces in the Second World War, 1939–1945* (New York: Orient Longmans, 1957), 58.
41. Churchill, *Second World War*, vol. 3, *The Grand Alliance*, 328.
42. Australian War Memorial, "Syrian Campaign," http://www.awm.gov.au/units/event_295.asp
43. Ibid.; and Aboul-Enein and Aboul-Enein, "The Anglo-French Intervention in the Levant."
44. Churchill, *Second World War*, vol. 3, *The Grand Alliance*, 330–332.
45. Ibid.; and William Watson, *Tricolor and the Crescent: France and the Islamic World* (Westport, CT: Greenwood, 2003), 83.
46. Aboul-Enein and Aboul-Enein, "The Anglo-French Intervention in the Levant."
47. Samuel Katz and Ron Volstad, *Israeli Elite Units Since 1948* (London: Osprey Publishing, 1988), 4; see also Chaim Herzog, *The Arab-Israeli Wars: War and Peace in the Middle East from the War of Independence through Lebanon* (New York: Vintage, 1983).
48. Churchill, *Second World War*, vol. 3, *The Grand Alliance*, 331.
49. "Foundations of Excellence: Moshe Dayan and Israel's Military Tradition (1880 to 1950)," by Maj. Allan A. Katzberg, USMC, Marine Corps University Research Paper completed in satisfaction for a Command and Staff College Degree, 1988, 125–132.
50. Ibid.

51. Ibid.
52. Churchill, *Second World War*, vol. 2, *Their Finest Hour*, 499.
53. Eric Schmidt, "Pentagon Contradicts General on Iraq Occupation Force's Size," *New York Times*, February 28, 2003, http://www.nytimes.com/2003/02/28/us/threats-responses-military-spending-pentagon-contradicts-general-iraq-occupation.html

Chapter 5. Iran

1. Motter, *Persian Corridor and Aid to Russia*. The Motter work is a book first printed in 1952 as CMH Pub 8-1, and this edition is still being printed by the Government Printing Office in Washington, DC. Motter, a noted military historian, spent two years in the Middle East theater during World War II before being selected to become chief of Middle East Section, Office of the U.S. Army Chief of the Military History. His personal papers covering details on the World War II Middle East and early Cold War Iran and Iraq are housed in Princeton University Library Rare Books and Special Collections Department. Motter earned his PhD at Princeton. See http://findingaids.princeton.edu/collections/C0670/#summary for more information.
2. Kahn, *Hitler's Spies*, 297. Excerpts of this chapter were taken from Capt. Basil Aboul-Enein, USAF, Faisal Aboul-Enein, and J. D. Thornton, "Axis and Allied Intervention, Collaboration in Iran," published in the U.S. Army *Infantry Journal* in November 2010.
3. Yonah Alexander, *The United States and Iran: A Documentary History* (Frederick: University Publications of America, 1980); and Elizabeth Monroe, *Britain's Moment in the Middle East: 1914–1971* (Baltimore: Johns Hopkins University Press, 1981), 23–28.
4. Sara Searight, *The British in the Middle East* (London: East-West Publishers, 1979), 269.
5. Monroe, *Britain's Moment in the Middle East*, 91.
6. Alexander, *The United States and Iran*, 23–28.
7. Parker Hart, *Saudi Arabia and the United States: Birth of a Partnership* (Bloomington: Indiana University Press, 1999), 16.
8. Jack Greene and Alessandro Massignani, *Rommel's North Africa Campaign: September 1940–November 1942* (New York: DaCapo Press, 1999), 22.
9. Steven R. Ward, *Immortal: A Military History of Iran and Its Armed Forces* (Washington, DC: Georgetown University Press, 2009), 63.
10. Alexander, *The United States and Iran*, 11–13.
11. Ibid., 457. See also Rogers Platt Churchill, *The Anglo-Russian Convention of 1907* (Freeport, NY: Books for Libraries Press, 1972; orig. pub. 1939) for detailed text of this agreement. This reprinted volume is usually available in law libraries or U.S. government repositories.
12. Stewart, *Sunrise at Abadan*, 94.
13. Abbas Milani, *The Shah* (New York: Macmillan, 2012), 60. This book contains a vivid description of the extent the Nazis propagandized mythological linkages between their Aryan master race and Iranians.

14. Stewart, *Sunrise at Abadan*, 11; and Aboul-Enein, "Axis and Allied Intervention, Collaboration in Iran."

15. Stewart, *Sunrise at Abadan*, 11–13; and Aboul-Enein, "Axis and Allied Intervention, Collaboration in Iran."

16. Stewart, *Sunrise at Abadan*, 11–13.

17. Sachar, *Europe Leaves the Middle East*, 339.

18. Hurewitz, *Middle East and North Africa in World Politics*, 241.

19. Stewart, *Sunrise at Abadan*, 10.

20. Nicosia, *The Third Reich and the Palestine Question*, 183.

21. Warner, *Iraq and Syria 1941*, 23.

22. Sachar, *Europe Leaves the Middle East*, 158.

23. Bernhardt Schulze-Holthus, *Daybreak in Iran: A Story of the German Intelligence Service* (London: Staples Press, 1954), 21.

24. Aboul-Enein, "Axis and Allied Intervention, Collaboration in Iran."

25. Stewart, *Sunrise at Abadan*, 18.

26. MacGregor Knox, *Mussolini Unleashed, 1939–1941: Politics and Strategy in Fascist Italy's Last War* (Cambridge: Cambridge University Press, 1986), 138. See also Aboul-Enein, "Axis and Allied Intervention, Collaboration in Iran."

27. Stewart, *Sunrise at Abadan*, 56.

28. Ibid.

29. Kahn, *Hitler's Spies*, 297.

30. Ibid.

31. Stewart, *Sunrise at Abadan*, 57.

32. Ibid. See also Kahn, *Hitler's Spies*, 68.

33. Stewart, *Sunrise at Abadan*, 57.

34. Ibid. See also Field Marshall (Sir) William Slim, *Unofficial History* (London: Cassell, 1959), 179–242. Chapter 2 provides details of the operation as commanding British units who along with Soviet forces forced Reza Shah from his throne in 1941.

35. Jefferson Adams, *Historical Dictionary of German Intelligence* (New York: Rowan and Littlefield Division, Scarecrow Press, 2009), 204.

36. Kahn, *Hitler's Spies*, 71.

37. Ibid., 192.

38. The definition for Chi was taken from Adams, *Historical Dictionary of German Intelligence*, 68.

39. Kahn, *Hitler's Spies*, 114.

40. Schulze-Holthus, *Daybreak in Iran*, 43–44.

41. Ibid.

42. Ibid., 152.

43. Stewart, *Sunrise at Abadan*, 59.

44. Ibid., 92. See also Aboul-Enein, "Axis and Allied Intervention, Collaboration in Iran."

45. Stewart, *Sunrise at Abadan*, 64.

46. Schulze-Holthus, *Daybreak in Iran*, 229.

47. Ibid., 250.

48. Kurowski, *The Brandenburg Commandos*, 163–164.
49. Harry Hinsley, *Official History of British Intelligence in World War II*, vol. 1 (London: Her Majesty's Stationery Office, 1979), 225.
50. Ibid., 191.
51. Götz Nordbruch, *Nazism in Syria and Lebanon: The Ambivalence of the German Option* (London: Routledge, 2008), 90–91.
52. Stewart, *Sunrise at Abadan*, 95 ("British military," "serfdom," and "your government would say").
53. FRUS Diplomatic Papers, 1941, vol. 3, 419.
54. Alexander, *The United States and Iran*, 80.
55. Stewart, *Sunrise at Abadan*, 107.
56. Ibid., 158.
57. Reza Shah's body would see much travel reflecting the events of the Middle East: during World War II it was interred at the al-Rafai Mosque in Cairo, then moved to be reburied in Iran at a mausoleum. After the 1979 Islamic Revolution, his body was again reinterred at the al-Rafai Mosque in Cairo. Ayatollah Khalkhali (Khomeini's hanging judge) would oversee the destruction of Reza Shah's mausoleum.
58. Motter, *Persian Corridor and Aid to Russia*, 10.
59. Ibid., 5.
60. Alexander Hill, "British Lend Lease Aid and the Soviet War Effort, June 1941–June 1942," *Journal of Military History* 71 (2007): 773–808.
61. Motter, *Persian Corridor and Aid to Russia*, 17.
62. Ibid.
63. Ibid., 23.
64. Ibid. Neutral Turkey had declared its alliance with the Allies on February 23, 1945.
65. Hurewitz, *Middle East and North Africa in World Politics*, 588 ("forces of the Allied Powers" and "the unrestricted right to use").
66. Ibid.
67. Federal Records of Interservice Agencies (Record Group 334) 1916–1973, 334.5.6 Records of Military Assistance Units in Iran held at the U.S. National Archives, Washington, DC, http://www.archives.gov/research/guide-fed-records/groups/334.html#334.5.6
68. Ibid.
69. Ibid.
70. Stephen Kinzer, *Reset: Iran, Turkey and America's Future* (New York: Times Books, 2010), 123.
71. Iran's Press TV Web site, "Ahmadinejad to seek UN compensation for WWII," http://www.presstv.com/detail/114112.html

Chapter 6. Turkey

1. Deringil, *Turkish Foreign Policy during the Second World War*, 1 ("the Treaty of Versailles" and "a World War is near").

2. "Treaty of Friendship between Germany and Turkey, June 18, 1941," The Avalon Project, Documents in Law, History and Diplomacy, Yale Law School Lillian Goldman Library at http://avalon.law.yale.edu/wwii/turger41.asp

3. Deringil, *Turkish Foreign Policy during the Second World War*, 74 ("the position we occupy"), 121 ("the neutralization"); see also Franz Von Papen, *Memoirs* (London: Andre Deutsch, 1952; trans. Brian Connell and printed in English, New York: E. P. Dutton, 1953). Von Papen *Memoirs* first published in German in 1952 and made available in English a year later contains details of the efforts of the German diplomat to keep Turkey neutral. Chapter 26, "Duel for Turkey" (470–484), describes a dramatic effort in 1944 to keep Turkey neutral. The effort failed and Turkey severed relations with Germany on August 2, 1944 and declared war on February 23, 1945.

4. Deringil, *Turkish Foreign Policy during the Second World War*, 121.

5. Deniz Bolukbasi, *Turkey and Greece: The Aegean Disputes: A Unique Case for International Law* (London: Routledge, 2004), 682–683. See also James Butler, *History of the Second World War: Grand Strategy*, vol. 2, *September 1939–June 1941* (London: Her Majesty's Stationery Office, 1957), for a full British perspective; and Von Papen, *Memoirs*, 25, for a German view.

6. Deringil, *Turkish Foreign Policy during the Second World War*, 72.

7. Ibid., 86.

8. Ibid. ("absolve Turkey" and "Moreover").

9. Ibid., 105.

10. Ibid., 108.

11. Ibid., 109. See also Christian Leitz, *Nazi Germany and Neutral Europe during the Second World War* (Manchester, UK: Manchester University Press, 2000), 104. See also Akten zur Deutschen Auswartigen Politik, 1918–1945, 589.

12. FRUS Diplomatic Papers, 1943, vol. 4, "The Near East and Africa" (Washington, DC: U.S. Government Printing Office, 1964), 1165.

13. Speer, *Inside the Third Reich*, 317.

14. Ibid., 405–406.

15. Bulnet Gokay, *Soviet Eastern Policy and Turkey, 1920–1991: Soviet Foreign Policy, Turkey and Communism* (London: Routledge, 2006), 54.

16. Deringil, *Turkish Foreign Policy during the Second World War*, 131.

17. Ibid.

18. Hirszowicz, *Third Reich and the Arab East*, 207.

19. Mallmann and Cuppers, *Nazi Palestine*, 89.

20. Daniel Carpi, "The Mufti of Jerusalem: Amin el-Husseini, and His Diplomatic Activity during World War II, October 1941–July 1943," *Studies in Zionism* 7 (Spring 1983): 104.

21. Herf, *Nazi Propaganda for the Arab World*, 241.

22. Nicholas Tamkin, *Britain, Turkey and the Soviet Union, 1940–45* (New York: Palgrave MacMillan, 2009), 53.

23. Deringil, *Turkish Foreign Policy during the Second World War*, 127.

24. Ibid., 126.

25. Ibid., 126 ("encouraging Turkey"), 142.
26. Ibid., 137.
27. Attilio Gatti, *Mediterranean Spotlight* (New York: C. Scribner's Sons, 1944), 94.
28. Ibid.
29. Deringil, *Turkish Foreign Policy during the Second World War*, 182.

Chapter 7. Axis Efforts in the Arabian Peninsula

1. Hirszowicz, *Third Reich and the Arab East*, 51. Excerpts of this chapter were taken from a previously published essay by Basil Aboul-Enein and Faisal Aboul-Enein, "The Political Influence of Axis Collaborative Efforts in Saudi Arabia," *Foreign Area Officer Association Journal*, September 2008, 20–24.
2. Aboul-Enein and Aboul-Enein, "The Political Influence of Axis Collaborative Efforts in Saudi Arabia."
3. Hirszowicz, *Third Reich and the Arab East*, 19.
4. Ibid., 49–51.
5. Ibid., 48–51. See also Nicosia, *The Third Reich and the Palestine Question*, 189.
6. Hirszowicz, *Third Reich and the Arab East*, 48–49.
7. Ibid.
8. Ibid.
9. Ibid.
10. Ibid.
11. Ibid.
12. The Idrissi were a cluster of northern Yemeni tribes collected around Seyyid Mohammed al-Idrissi, whose grandfather Seyyid Ahmed al-Idrissi migrated from Morocco to Arabia. The family comes from a line of Sufi religious nobles. Seyyid Mohammed gathered the northern tribes around Asir, currently above modern-day Yemen, and formed an independent Idrisid emirate sandwiched between Yemen and the Saudi coast of the Hijaz along the Red Sea from 1915 to 1934, after which it was incorporated into modern-day Saudi Arabia. In World War II he sided with the Allies and was a competitor for influence and tribal alliances with the ruler of Yemen in San'aa.
13. Schreiber et al., *Germany and the Second World War*, vol. 3, 170.
14. Hirszowicz, *Third Reich and the Arab East*, 27; and see a text of the agreement between the Germans and Ibn Saud on page 368. See also Anthony Cordesman, *Saudi Arabia: Guarding the Desert Kingdom* (Boulder, CO: Westview Press, 1997), 9. See also Christoph Wilcke, *Saudi Arabia, the Ismailis of Najran* (Washington, DC: Human Rights Watch, September 2008), 11.
15. Bernard Lewis and Buntzie Ellis Churchill, *Notes on a Century: Reflections of a Middle East Historian* (New York: Viking Adult, 2012).
16. Hirszowicz, *Third Reich and the Arab East*, 86.
17. Ibid.
18. Ibid.
19. Ibid., 56.

20. Ibid., 57.
21. Ibid.
22. Nicosia, *The Third Reich and the Palestine Question*, 186.
23. Hirszowicz, *Third Reich and the Arab East*, 58.
24. Nicosia, *The Third Reich and the Palestine Question*, 188.
25. Hirszowicz, *Third Reich and the Arab East*, 55. Ibn Saud had to balance German aid with substantial British and then Anglo-American food aid through the Middle East Supply Center to include large shipments of grains. This hidden aspect of World War II, the management and distribution of food to the Middle East then suffering from severe crop failures, famine, and drought, can be argued alleviated what could have been a worse situation for the British in their competition with the Axis in the region. See Ashley Jackson, *The British Empire and the Second World War* (London: Hambledon Continuum, 2006), 168–169.
26. Selcuk Esenbel, "Japan's Global Claim to Asia and the World of Islam: Transnational Nationalism and World Power, 1900–1945," *American Historical Review* 109 (2004): 1140–1170.
27. Ibid.
28. Use Paul Kratoska, *The Japanese Occupation of Malaya: A Social and Economic History* (Honolulu: University of Hawaii Press, 1997), 135.
29. Kaoru Sugihara and J. A. Allan, *Japan in the Contemporary Middle East* (London: Routledge, 1993).
30. Ibid.
31. Ibid.
32. Ahmed Abu Hakima, *The Modern History of Kuwait, 1750–1965* (London: Luzac and Company, 1983), 116.
33. Wolfgang Schwanitz, "German-Kuwaiti Relations: From Their Beginnings to the Reunification of Germany," *Middle East Review of International Affairs Journal* 13 (March 2009), http://www.gloria-center.org/2009/03/schwanitz-2009-03-08/
34. Hakima, *Modern History of Kuwait*, 117.
35. Peter Herbstreuth, *Along the Gulf from Basra to Muscat* (Berlin: Schiler, 2006); and Sukuru Hanioglu, *A Brief History of the Late Ottoman Empire* (Princeton, NJ: Princeton University, 2008).
36. Hakima, *Modern History of Kuwait*.
37. Ibid.
38. David Finnie, *Shifting Lines in the Sand: Kuwait's Elusive Frontier with Iraq* (London: I. B. Tauris & Co., 1992), 100.
39. Richard Schofield, *Kuwait and Iraq: Historical Claims and Territorial Disputes* (London: Royal Institute of International Affairs, 1993), 75.
40. Finnie, *Shifting Lines in the Sand*, 114–115.
41. Stephan Longrigg, *Oil in the Middle East: Its Discovery and Development* (New York: Oxford University Press, 1955); and Hakima, *Modern History of Kuwait*.
42. Tom Little, *South Arabia: Arena of Conflict* (London: Pall Mall Press, 1968).

43. Ibid.

44. Fiore, *Anglo-Italian Relations in the Middle East.*

45. Williams, *Mussolini's Propaganda Abroad.*

46. Christian Tripodi, "The Foreign Office and Anglo-Italian Involvement in the Red Sea and Arabia, 1925–28," *Canadian Journal of History* 42 (2007): 209–234.

47. John Baldry, "Anglo-Italian Rivalry in Yemen and Asir 1900–1934," *Die Welt des Islams* 17 (1976): 155–193.

48. Tripodi, "The Foreign Office and Anglo-Italian Involvement," 217.

49. Fiore, *Anglo-Italian Relations in the Middle East.*

50. Tripodi, "The Foreign Office and Anglo-Italian Involvement," 218.

51. Fiore, *Anglo-Italian Relations in the Middle East.*

52. Tripodi, "The Foreign Office and Anglo-Italian Involvement," 221.

53. Baldry, "Anglo-Italian Rivalry," 180.

54. Ibid.

55. Spencer Tucker, *World War II at Sea: An Encyclopedia* (Santa Barbara, CA: ABC-CLIO, 2012), 623 (naval operations in Red Sea), 122–124 (British Eastern Fleet), and 355 (hospital ships).

56. Jackson, *British Empire and the Second World War,* 282.

57. Jurgen Rohwer, *Chronology of the War at Sea, 1939-1945: The Naval History of World War Two* (Annapolis, MD: Naval Institute Press, 2000), 59.

58. Ibid., 61.

59. Piecing together this picture of Japanese naval action in Arabia required the use of Roger Jordan, *The World's Merchant Fleet, 1939: The Particulars and Wartime Fates of 6,000 Ships* (Annapolis MD: Naval Institute Press, 2006), 490; Jurgen Rohwer, *Axis Submarine Successes, 1939–1945* (Annapolis, MD: Naval Institute Press, 1983), 269; and Keith Dickson, *World War Two Almanac: Almanacs of American Wars* (New York: Facts on File, 2008), 213.

60. David Winkler, *Amirs, Admirals and Desert Sailors: Bahrain, the U.S. Navy and the Arabian Gulf* (Annapolis, MD: Naval Institute Press, 2007).

61. Ibid.; and John Whelan, *Bahrain: A MEED Practical Guide* (London: Middle East Economic Digest, 1983).

62. Arielli, *Fascist Italy and the Middle East,* 109–132.

63. Ibid.

64. Ibid.

65. Ibid.

66. William Mulligan, "Air Raid! A Sequel," *Saudi Aramco World Journal* 27 (1976): 2–3.

67. Ibid.

68. Ibid.

69. Ibid.

70. Ibid.

71. Joseph Kechichian, *Oman and the World: The Emergence of an Independent Foreign Policy* (Santa Monica, CA: RAND, 1995), 173.

72. Aaron David Miller, *Search for Security: Saudi Arabian Oil and American Foreign Policy, 1939–1949* (Chapel Hill: University of North Carolina Press, 1980), 102.

Chapter 8. Afghanistan and the Third Reich

1. Yair P. Hirschfeld, "The Northern Tier in European Politics during the 1920s and 1930s," in Dann, *The Great Powers in the Middle East, 1919–1939*, 317–330, for depth and context. See also Alexander Mikaberidze, ed., *Conflict and Conquest in the Islamic World: A Historical Encyclopedia*, vol. 1 (Santa Barbara, CA, ABC-CLIO, 2011), 777.
2. Victoria Schofield, *Afghan Frontier: At the Crossroads of Conflict* (New York: I. B. Tauris Paperback, 2010), 224–225.
3. The Baghdad Pact was also referred to as the Central Eastern Treaty Organization (CENTO); it included Iran, Iraq, Turkey, and the United Kingdom, and was modeled after NATO. CENTO was created as another alliance to contain the Soviet Union, but digressed into internal political squabbling between pan-Arabists and Arab monarchies. Nasser did much to undermine this alliance, seeing Cairo and not Baghdad as the center of the Arab world. Iraq withdrew during the toppling of the monarchy in 1958, Pakistan attempted unsuccessfully to solicit aid through CENTO against its 1971 war with India, Turkey would invade Cyprus in 1974, and Iran would topple the shah in 1979; the changes in the post–World War II Near East effectively doomed the CENTO alliance.
4. See D. Cameron Watt, "The Saadabad Pact of 8 July 1937," in Dann, *The Great Powers in the Middle East, 1919–1939*, 333–352, for depth and context.
5. Ibid., 330.
6. Hauner, *India in Axis Strategy*, 490.
7. Ibid.
8. Ibid.
9. Tom Lansford, *A Bitter Harvest: US Foreign Policy and Afghanistan* (Burlington, VT: Ashgate Publishing, 2003).
10. Hauner, *India in Axis Strategy*, 167–169.
11. Schreiber et al., *Germany and the Second World War*, vol. 3, 163.
12. Hauner, *India in Axis Strategy*, 217.
13. Ibid.
14. Sana Haroon, *Frontiers of Faith: Islam in the Indo-Afghan Borderland* (New York: Columbia University Press), 168–169.
15. Ibid., 214. See also Alan Warren, *Waziristan, the Faqir of Ipi, and the Indian Army: The North West Frontier Revolt of 1936–37* (New York: Oxford University Press, 2000) for a comprehensive look at this particular campaign.
16. Hauner, *India in Axis Strategy*, 214.
17. Milan Hauner, "One Man Against the Empire: The Faqir of Ipi and the British in Central Asia on the Eve of and During World War II," in Walter

Laqueur, ed., *The Second World War* (London: Sage, 1982), 374–403; 386 ("the national independence movements" and "ascertain British strength").

18. Hauner, *India in Axis Strategy*, 228 ("We could not defeat"); and ibid.
19. Hauner, "One Man Against the Empire," 388.
20. Ibid., 389
21. Ibid.
22. Ibid., 395.
23. Ibid., 383.
24. Ibid.
25. Alex Strick Van Linschoten and Felix Kuehn, *An Enemy We Created: The Myth of the Taliban-Al-Qaida Merger in Afghanistan* (Oxford: Oxford University Press, 2012), 17. In case you are curious, Shami Pir was bought off for £25,000 (approximately £1.2 million in today's money), which the British assessed was a bargain compared to the £1.5 million expended to manage the faqir of Ipi insurgency; see Warren, *Waziristan, the Faqir of Ipi, and the Indian Army*, 219.
26. Hauner, "One Man Against the Empire."
27. Winston Churchill, arranged by Martin Gilbert, *The Churchill War Papers: The Ever Widening War*, vol. 3, 1941 (New York: W. W. Norton, 1st American ed., 2001), 1217. Endnotes 25 to 27 refer to Telegram No. 308, from the British minister in Kabul, Sir Francis Wylie, on the policy to be pursued in Afghanistan.
28. Ibid., 1350.
29. Ibid.
30. Ibid.
31. James W. Spain, "The Pathan Borderlands," *Middle East Journal* 15, no. 2 (Spring 1961): 165–177.
32. Mathura Prasada Misra, *A Trilingual Dictionary Being a Comprehensive Lexicon in English, Urdú and Hindí, Exhibiting the Syllabication, Pronunciation and Etymology of English words, with their Explanation in English, and in Urdú and Hindí in the Roman Characters* (Benares, India: E. J. Lazarus, 1865), 506. With regard to incitement against the Japanese, see Haroon, *Frontier of Faith*, 174.

Chapter 9. Egypt's Internal Struggle

1. Yusri Abdel-Aleem and Ahmed Fateen Farid, *Al-Tarikh Al-Askary lil Jaysh Al-Misry min al-Harb al-Alamiyah Al-Ulaa wa hataa nihayah Al-Harb Al-Alamiyah Al-Thaniyah* [The military history of the Egyptian armed forces from World War I to World War II] (Cairo: Nasser Higher Military Academy Center for Strategic Studies, Egyptian Defense Ministry, 1993).
2. Ibid., 22–24.
3. Hirszowicz, *Third Reich and the Arab East*, 75.
4. Ibid.
5. Ibid., 76.
6. There is credence to the Egyptian view that their armed forces was in no state to participate in a global war. A British Foreign Office note concluded

"[W]e should lose no sleep over inefficiency in Egyptian higher places or the deterioration of army materiel through bad officership. So long as we can fairly place the blame on the shoulders of the Egyptians, these deficiencies are, on a long view, no loss to us" (Pratt, "The Strategic Context," 20).

7. Abdel-Aleem and Fateen Farid, *Al-Tarikh Al-Askary lil Jaysh Al-Misry.*

8. Ibid.

9. Kahn, *Hitler's Spies,* 194.

10. It is important to discuss Egypt today in terms of a First (military) Republic (1952–2011), and a Second Republic (2011–present), which as of this writing is leaning toward an Islamist illiberal democracy.

11. Abdel-Aleem and Fateen Farid, *Al-Tarikh Al-Askary lil Jaysh Al-Misry.*

12. Hinsley, *Official History of British Intelligence in World War II,* vol. 1, 278.

13. Churchill and Gilbert, *The Churchill War Papers,* vol. 3, 1941, 451.

14. William Manchester and Paul Reid, *The Last Lion: Winston Spencer Churchill, Defender of the Realm, 1940–1965* (New York: Little, Brown and Company, 2012), 342.

15. General Wavell would be dismissed by Churchill on June 21, 1941, and replaced with General Claude Auchinleck. Churchill's insistence on Wavell sending forces to Greece undermined British strength in Egypt, allowing the Axis to reinforce and press an attack leading to the loss of Allied territory in Libya, and a British retreat into Egypt. Churchill blamed Wavell for the loss of Tobruk in 1941, but in reality the two personalities never got along: Churchill was the flamboyant bold actor on the world stage, and Wavell was the calm, subdued strategic thinker. It was only after Operation Compass that Churchill realized that Wavell had written two books on the Middle East, *The Palestine Campaign* in 1928 and a biography of World War I general Edmund Allenby in 1940. Wavell was with General Allenby as a junior officer during Allenby's march into Jerusalem. Churchill could have understood Wavell's mind by reading his books and understanding the most significant role model for Wavell as a general in command was Allenby. He was not as inept as Churchill made him out to be. The Wavell-Churchill relationship in the Middle East provides an excellent discussion in civil-military relations and what civilian leaders should do prior to passing judgment on military commanders. See Carlo D'Este, *Warlord: A Life of Winston Churchill at War, 1874–1945* (New York: HarperPerennial, 2009), 494.

16. William B. Breuer, *Undercover Tales of World War II* (New York: John Wiley and Sons, 1999), 44–45.

17. Churchill and Gilbert, *The Churchill War Papers,* vol. 3, 566. In Manchester and Reid, *The Last Lion,* 224, Spanish dictator Francisco Franco had the following discussion with Hitler: if Germany took the Suez Canal and Spain given the means to seize Gibraltar, it would undermine the British strategic position. Their talks along the French-Spanish border in the Basque town of Hendaye in October 1940 yielded no results on this particular matter, due to a lack of interest on Hitler's part.

18. Manchester and Reid, *The Last Lion,* 159.

19. Ibid., 340. See also Michael Howard, *The Mediterranean Strategy in the Second World War* (London: Praeger, 1968). The noted military and Clausewitzian scholar writes this assessment: "[A]n Axis victory which drove British forces from Egypt and the Persian Gulf might make it impossible for them to carry on the war at all—a situation which Hitler's naval and military advisers were, happily, unable to make him understand" (p. 12).

20. Breuer, *Undercover Tales of World War II*, 44–45.

21. Kahn, *Hitler's Spies*, 194–195.

22. Lynne Olson, *Those Angry Days: Roosevelt, Lindbergh, and America's Fight over World War II, 1939–1941* (New York: Random House, 2013), 70, 303–304.

23. Ahmed Hassan Al-Kinani, *Dhikraya't al-Liwa' Muḥammad Ṣa'liḥ Ḥarb* [Recollections of General Muhammad Saleh Harb] (Cairo: al-Hay'ah al-'A'mmah li-Quṣu'r al-Thaqa'fah, 2009), 41.

24. Ibid., 42.

25. Ibid., 43.

26. *Time*, "Power Politics: Fleets to the East," May 13, 1940, http://www.time .com/time/magazine/article/0,9171,884027,00.html

27. Al-Kinani, *Dhikraya't al-Liwa' Muḥammad Ṣa'liḥ Ḥarb*, 44–47; 46 ("does not have to declare war").

28. Churchill and Gilbert, *The Churchill War Papers*, vol. 3, 98.

29. John Keegan, ed., *Churchill's Generals* (New York: Grove Wiedenfeld, 1991).

30. Al-Kinani, *Dhikraya't al-Liwa' Muḥammad Ṣa'liḥ Ḥarb*, 76.

31. Ibid.

32. Gamal Abdel Nasser, *Egypt's Liberation: The Philosophy of the Revolution* (Washington, DC: Public Affairs Press, 1955).

33. Abdel-Aziz Khamis, "Asrar al Kifah al-Sirri [Secrets of the underground resistance]," *Ruz al-Yusuf Magazine* 2555 (May 30, 1977): 14–15.

34. Khalid Wasim, *Al-Kifah al-Sirri Didaa al-Ingleez* [The secret resistance against the British] (Cairo: Dar wa Matabi' al-Sha'ab, 1963), 121 ("task of removing the men"), 119–122.

35. Al-Kinani, *Dhikraya't al-Liwa' Muḥammad Ṣa'liḥ Ḥarb*, 49.

36. The term "quasi-independence" is my own, as from 1922 to 1952 Egyptian politics were dominated by three spheres of influence: the king of Egypt, parliament, and overbearing British civilian and military leaders in Cairo.

37. Eliezer Tauber, "Egyptian Secret Societies, 1911," *Middle Eastern Studies* 42/4 (2006): 603–623. See also Alanbrooke, *War Diaries, 1939–1945*, which demonstrates the depth of concern regarding the loss of Egypt in 1940–1942. On September 14, 1940, Field Marshal Alanbrooke confides to his diary, "[I]s it all a bluff to pin [British] troops down in this country, while he [Hitler] prepares to help Italy to invade Egypt, etc.?" The context is dealing with Operation Sealion, the German assault on Britain along with the Italian advance through North Africa (see Alanbrooke, 108). In discussions with General Auchinleck in Cairo on August 4, 1942, he compares the loss of Abadan (Iran) to the loss of Egypt: "[The] loss of Abadan could not be made up by American [oil] resources

due to shortage of tankers; lose Persian oil, you lose Egypt, and command of the Indian Ocean" (Alanbrooke, *War Diaries, 1939–1945*, 290). The same diary captures Churchill's contempt for King Farouk of Egypt: Field Marshal Alanbrooke writes of dinner with the prime minister at the British Embassy in Cairo: "PM's best remark King Farouk wallowing like a sow in the trough of luxury!" The context was a discussion of anticolonial protests in Egypt (p. 541). These war diaries capture the feelings and emotions of the time without the benefit of more than seven decades of hindsight.

38. Walter Isaacson, *Profiles in Leadership: Historians on the Elusive Quality of Greatness* (New York: W. W. Norton, 2010), 253–256.

39. Hinsley, *Official History of British Intelligence in World War II*, vol. 1, 191–194.

40. Ibid.

41. Ibid.

42. Manchester and Reid, *The Last Lion*, 340.

43. Abdel-Aleem and Fateen Farid, *Al-Tarikh Al-Askary lil Jaysh Al-Misry*.

44. Khamis, "Asrar al Kifah al-Sirri" [Secrets of the underground resistance], 14–15.

45. Saul Kelly, *The Lost Oasis: The Desert War and the Hunt for Zerzura: The True Story Behind the English Patient* (Boulder, CO: Westview Press, 2003).

46. Anwar Sadat, *Revolt on the Nile* (New York: J. Day Company, 1957).

47. R. K. Betts, "Analysis, War, and Decision: Why Intelligence Failures Are Inevitable," *World Politics*, 31/2 (October 1978): 61–89; and Hinsley, *Official History of British Intelligence in World War II*, vol. 2 (London: Her Majesty's Stationery Office, 1981), 57–65.

48. Ibid.

49. Ibid.

50. Nicholas Rankin, *A Genius for Deception: How Cunning Helped the British Win Two World Wars* (New York: Oxford University Press, 2008); Rick Stroud, *The Phantom Army of Alamein: How the Camouflage Unit and Operation Bertram Hoodwinked Rommel* (London: Bloomsbury, 2012).

51. Stroud, *Phantom Army of Alamein*.

52. Wolf Rüdiger Hess, *My Father Rudolf Hess* (London: W. H. Allen, 1984).

53. Thomas Ricks, *The Generals: American Military Command from World War II to Today* (New York: Penguin Press 2012), 52. Note that comparing the comments of FDR, Eisenhower, Marshall, and Churchill as well as Field Marshal Alanbrooke on the Middle East with the diary of German field marshal Franz Halder, OKW chief, offers astonishing depth of insight. In notes he made on November 2, 1940, to be presented that day to Hitler, Halder wrote, "Should the English be beaten in Egypt and the Suez Canal occupied, two armored, [and] one motorized [divisions] with a large number of engineers [would be] required." Charles Burdick and Hans-Adolf Jacobsen, eds., *The Halder War Diaries, 1939–1942* (Novato, CA: Presidio, 1988), 275–276. This was based on an assumption that German divisions would be supplemented by 215,000 Italian troops in Libya and Egypt. That same day he also wrote of a plan to attack England through the eastern Mediterranean that "would be an

operation through Anatolia and Syria. It is already studied conceptually, [and] two motorized corps would be required" (Burdick and Jacobsen, 276).

54. Manchester and Reid, *The Last Lion*, 546.

Chapter 10. Conclusion

1. Browning and Matthäus, *The Origins of the Final Solution*, 406.
2. David Yisraeli, *The Palestine Problem in German Politics, 1889–1945* (Tel-Aviv: Bar-Ilan University, published by Ramat-Gan, 1974), 310. This is what Ambassador Grobba recollects Hitler said in German during the November 28, 1941 to the mufti, which still echoes Hitler's genocidal ambitions toward the Jews: "Das deutsche Ziel würde dann lediglich die Vernichtung des im arabischen Raum unter der Protektion der britischen Macht lebenden Judentums sein [Germany had no interest there (the Middle East) other than the destruction of the power protecting the Jews]" (from the Schmidt Memorandum, Yisraeli, *Palestine Problem in German Politics, 1889–1945*, 310.
3. Bruno De Cordier, "The Fedayeen of the Reich: Muslims, Islam and Collaborationism during World War II," *China and Eurasia Forum Quarterly* 8 (2010): 23–46.
4. Herf, *Nazi Propaganda for the Arab World*, 709.
5. Churchill, *Second World War*, vol. 2, *Their Finest Hour*, 500.
6. David Stone, *Genius Shattered: The Decline and Fall of the German General Staff in World War II* (Philadelphia: Casemate, 2011), 180.
7. Ben MacIntyre, *Operation Mincemeat: How a Dead Man and a Bizarre Plan Fooled the Nazis and Assured an Allied Victory* (New York: Harmony Books, 2010), 270.
8. Ibid.
9. Ibid., 21.
10. CRRC #AQ-ISNE-D-000-121, "Importance of Information, Briefing Obtained from Abu Hafs Home, Kandahar." Unknown date, estimated to be prior to 2002. Document archived at the National Defense University's Conflict Records Research Center, Fort McNair, Washington, DC.
11. R. Harris Smith, *OSS: The Secret History of America's First Intelligence Agency* (Berkeley: University of California Press, 1972), 42–43. Smith was a former research analyst for the CIA, and later taught political science at the University of California extension campuses. Chapter 5 of his book contains an excellent accounting of OSS efforts at various intelligence operations in the Middle East and North Africa, and the tensions this created with British SIS in Cairo.
12. Ibid., 41.
13. Ibid., 123–124.
14. Ibid.

Appendix 1.

1. Joseph Goebbels, *The Goebbels Diaries, 1942–1943*, trans. and ed. Louis P. Lochner (Garden City, NY: Doubleday, 1948). Associated Press

reporter Lochner was awarded the 1939 Pulitzer Prize for his coverage of Nazi Germany. He followed the Wehrmacht into Poland in 1939, and reported on the surrender of France in 1940. Lochner would interview Hitler twice: once in 1930 and once in 1933. He would be interned by the Germans in December 1941 and then released during a prisoner exchange in May 1942. Among the Americans interned by the Nazis along with Lochner was George Kennan, the father of Cold War containment.

2. Gosudarstvennoye Politicheskoye Upravlenie, or state political directorate under the Soviet NKVD. The GPU was the espionage and assassination arm both domestically and internationally for the Soviet Union.

Appendix 2.

1. "The Writings of the late Iraqi Army Officer and Military Historian Mahmood Al-Durrah," published in U.S. Army *Armor Journal*, introducing U.S. military readers to Arabic works of military significance. This article is reproduced here as it originally appeared.

SELECTED BIBLIOGRAPHY

Archives

Akten zur Deutschen Auswartigen Politik, 1918–1945. [Documents on German foreign policy, 1918–1945]. Series D (1937–1945), vols. 5, x–xiii, London-Washington, 1956–1964, translated and published by the U.S. Goverment Printing Office.

Nation Associates. "The Arab Higher Committee: Its Origins, Personnel and Purposes: The Documentary Record." Submitted to the United Nations, May 1947. http://unispal.un.org/UNISPAL.NSF/0/FB6DD3F0E9535815852572DD006CC607

National Archives of the Commonwealth of Australia. Documents on Australian Foreign Policy, 1937–49. Series A1608. File H41/1/3.

Primary Works

Al-Bahri, Yunus. *Huna Berlin! Hayyi l-'arab* [This is Berlin! Salutations to the Arabs]. Beirut, Lebanon: Dar al-Nashr lil-Jami Tiyin, 1955.

Alanbrooke, Field Marshall Lord. *War Diaries 1939–1945: Field Marshal Lord Alanbrooke,* edited by Alex Danchev and Daniel Todman. Berkeley: University of California Press, reprint 2001.

Churchill, Winston. *The Churchill War Papers*, vol. 3, *The Ever Widening War, 1941.* Arranged by Martin Gilbert. New York: W. W. Norton, 1st American ed., 2001.

———. *The Second World War*, vol. 1, *The Gathering Storm.* Boston: Houghton-Mifflin, 1948.

———. *The Second World War*, vol. 2, *Their Finest Hour.* Boston: Houghton-Mifflin, 1949.

———. *The Second World War*, vol. 3, *The Grand Alliance.* Boston: Houghton-Mifflin, 1951.

Felmy, Hellmuth, and Walter Warlimont. *German Exploitation of Arab Nationalist Movements in World War II.* Manuscript for the United States Army–Foreign Military Studies Branch (MSP-207), Box 145 (MSP.200-212). Washington, DC: U.S National Archives, 1955.

Goebbels, Joseph. *The Goebbels Diaries, 1942–1943.* Translated and edited by Louis P. Lochner. Garden City, NY: Doubleday, 1948.

Grobba, Fritz. *Maenner und Machte im Orient: 25 Jahre Diplomatischer Tatigkeit im Orient* [Men and power in the Orient: 25 years of diplomatic activity in the East]. Gottingen: Musterschmidt-Verlag, 1967.

Halder, Frantz. *The Halder War Diary, 1939–1942.* Edited by Charles Burdick and Hans-Adolf Jacobsen. Novato, CA: Presidio Press, 1988.

Kennedy, Sir John. *The Business of War.* London: Hutchinson, 1957.

Lawrence, T. E. *The Letters of T. E. Lawrence.* Arranged by Malcolm Brown. New York: Oxford University Press, 1991.

Sadat, Anwar. *In Search of Identity: An Autobiography.* New York: Harper & Row, 1978.

———. *Revolt on the Nile.* New York: J. Day Company, 1957.

Schulze-Holthus, Bernhardt. *Daybreak in Iran: A Story of the German Intelligence Service.* London: Staples Press, 1954.

Shawkat, Sami. *Hadhihi Ahda-funa* [These are our aims]. Baghdad, Iraq: Baghdad Printers, 1939.

Slim, Field Marshall (Sir) William. *Unofficial History.* London: Cassel, 1959.

Spears, Sir Edward L. *Fulfillment of a Mission: The Spears Mission to Syria and Lebanon, 1941–1944.* Hamden, CT: Archon Books, 1977.

Speer, Albert. *Inside the Third Reich: Memoirs.* New York: MacMillan, 1970.

Von Papen, Franz. *Memoirs.* London: Andre Deutsch, 1952. (Translated by Brian Connell and printed in English. New York: E. P. Dutton, 1953.)

Secondary Works

Abdel-Aleem, Yusri, and Ahmed Fateen Farid. *Al-Tarikh Al-Askary lil Jaysh Al-Misry min al--Harb al-Alamiyah Al-Ulaa wa hataa nihayah Al-Harb Al-Alamiyah Al-Thaniyah* [The military history of the Egyptian armed forces from World War I to World War II]. Cairo: Nasser Higher Military Academy Center for Strategic Studies, Egyptian Defense Ministry, 1993.

Aboul-Enein, Youssef. *Iraq in Turmoil: Historical Perspectives of Dr. Ali al-Wardi from the Ottomans to King Feisal.* Annapolis, MD: Naval Institute Press, 2012.

Adams, Jefferson. *Historical Dictionary of German Intelligence.* New York: Scarecrow Press, 2009.

Al-Umar, Abd Al-Karim. *Muzakkirat Al Hajj Muhammed Amin Al Husseini* [The memoirs of Al Hajj Amin Al-Husseini]. Damascus, Syria: Al-Ahali, 1999.

Alexander, Yonah. *The United States and Iran: A Documentary History.* Frederick, MD: University Publications of America, 1980.

Alfassa, Shelomo. *Reference Guide to the Nazis and Arabs during the Holocaust: A Concise Guide to the Relationship and Conspiracy of the Nazis and the Grand Mufti of Jerusalem in North Africa and the Middle East during the Era of the Holocaust.* New York: International Sephardic Leadership Council, 2006.

Arab Higher Committee: Its Origins, Personnel and Purposes, The Documentary Record. Submitted to the United Nations, May 1947.

Arielli, Nir. *Fascist Italy and the Middle East, 1933–1940.* New York: Palgrave Macmillan, 2010.

Baker, Robert. *Oil, Blood and Sand.* New York: D. Appleton-Century Company, 1942.

Batatua, Hana. *Al-Tabaqat Al-Ijtimayiah wal Harakat Al-Thawriyah* [Social classes and revolutionary movements]. Beirut, Lebanon: Arab Research Center, 1989.

Baynes, Norman H. *The Speeches of Adolf Hitler*, vol. 2, *April 1922–August 1939*. New York: Oxford University Press, 1942.

Bernhardt, Rudolph. *Encyclopedia of Public International Law*, vol. 12, *Geographic Issues*. University Park: Pennsylvania State University, 1990.

Bloch, Michael. *Ribbentrop*. New York: Crown, 1992.

Bolukbasi, Deniz. *Turkey and Greece: The Aegean Disputes: A Unique Case for International Law*. London: Routledge, 2004.

Breuer, William. *Deceptions of World War II*. New York: John Wiley, 2002.

———. *Undercover Tales of World War II*. New York: John Wiley and Sons, 1999.

Brown, David. *The Road to Oran: Anglo-French Naval Relations, September 1939–July 1940*. London: Taylor & Francis, 2004.

Browning, Christopher, and Jürgen Matthäus. *The Origins of the Final Solution: The Evolution of Nazi Jewish Policy, September 1939–March 1942*. Lincoln: University of Nebraska Press, 2004.

Butler, James. *History of the Second World War: Grand Strategy*, vol. 2, *September 1939–June 1941*. London: His Majesty's Stationery Office, 1957.

Casper, Lionel. *The Rape of Palestine and the Struggle for Jerusalem*. Jerusalem, Israel: Gefen, 2003.

Chalabi, Tamara. *Late for Tea at the Deer Palace: The Lost Dreams of my Iraqi Family*. New York: Harper, 2011.

Cohen, Roger. *Hearts Grown Brutal: Sagas of Sarajevo*. New York: Random House, 1998.

Collins, D. J. E. *The Royal Indian Navy, 1939–45*, vol. 1. Bombay, India: Orient Longmans, Combined Inter-services Historical Section, India & Pakistan, 1964.

Connell, John. *Wavell: Scholar and Soldier*. New York: Harcourt, Brace & World, 1965.

Cordesman, Anthony. *Saudi Arabia: Guarding the Desert Kingdom*. Boulder, CO: Westview Press, 1997.

Dalin, David, and John Rothmann. *Icon of Evil: Hitler's Mufti and the Rise of Radical Islam*. New York: Random House, 2008.

Dann, Uriel, ed. *The Great Powers in the Middle East, 1919–1939*. New York: Holmes & Meier, 1988.

Davidson, Lawrence. *America's Palestine: Popular and Official Perceptions from Balfour to Israeli Statehood*. Gainesville: University of Florida Press, 2001.

Deringil, Selim. *Turkish Foreign Policy during the Second World War: An Active Neutrality*. Cambridge: Cambridge University Press, 1989.

Dickson, Keith. *World War Two Almanac: Almanacs of American Wars*. New York: Facts on File, 2008.

Eisenstadt, Michael, and Eric Mathewson. *U.S. Policy in Post-Saddam Iraq: Lessons from the British Experience*. Washington, DC: Washington Institute for Near East Policy, 2003.

Entelis, John. *Pluralism and Party Transformation in Lebanon: Al-Kata'ib, 1936–1970*. Leiden, The Netherlands: E. J. Brill, 1974.

Faivre, Mario. *We Killed Darlan: A Personal Account of the French Resistance in North Africa, 1940–1942.* Manhattan, KS: Sunflower University Press, 1999.

Farnie, D. A. *East and West of the Suez: The Suez Canal in History, 1854–1956.* London: Clarendon Press, 1969.

Finnie, David. *Shifting Lines in the Sand: Kuwait's Elusive Frontier with Iraq.* London: I. B. Tauris & Co., 1992.

Fiore, Massimiliano. *Anglo-Italian Relations in the Middle East, 1922–1940.* Burlington, VT: Ashgate, 2010.

Fisk, Robert. *Pity the Nation: The Abduction of Lebanon.* New York: Nation Books, 2002.

Fromkin, David. *A Peace to End All Peace: The Fall of the Ottoman Empire and the Creation of the Modern Middle East.* New York: Avon Books, 1990.

Gatti, Attilio. *Mediterranean Spotlight.* New York: C. Scribner's Sons, 1944.

Gelber, Steven M. *No Balm in Gilead: A Personal Retrospective of Mandate Days in Palestine.* Ottawa, Canada: Carleton University Press, 1989.

Ghareeb, Edmund, and Beth Dougherty. *Historical Dictionary of Iraq.* Lanham, MD: Scarecrow Press, 2004.

Gokay, Bulnet. *Soviet Eastern Policy and Turkey, 1920–1991: Soviet Foreign Policy, Turkey and Communism.* London: Routledge, 2006.

Goldschmidt, Jr., Arthur. *A Brief History of Egypt.* New York: Facts on File, 2008.

Greene, Jack, and Alessandro Massignani. *Rommel's North Africa Campaign: September 1940–November 1942.* New York: DaCapo Press, 1999.

Greenwood, Alexander. *A Biography of Field-Marshal Sir Claude Auchinleck, G.C.B., G.C.I.E., C.S.I., D.S.O., O.B.E., LL. D.* London: Pentland Press, 1990.

Hakima, Ahmed Abu. *The Modern History of Kuwait, 1750–1965.* London: Luzac and Company, 1983.

Hammerton, Sir John. *The Second World War,* vol. 3, *Under Siege.* Naples, FL: Trident Press International, 2000.

Hanioglu, Sukuru. *A Brief History of the Late Ottoman Empire.* Princeton, NJ: Princeton University, 2008.

Haroon, Sana. *Frontier of Faith: Islam in the Indo-Afghan Borderline.* New York: Columbia University Press, 2007.

Hart, Parker Hart. *Saudi Arabia and the United States: Birth of a Partnership.* Bloomington: Indiana University Press, 1999.

Hauner, Milan. *India in Axis Strategy: Germany, Japan, and Indian Nationalists in the Second World War.* Stuttgart, Germany: Klett-Cotta, 1981.

Heller, Joseph. *The Stern Gang: Ideology, Politics and Terror, 1940–1949.* London: Frank Cass, 1995.

Herbstreuth, Peter. *Along the Gulf from Basra to Muscat.* Berlin: Schiler, 2006.

Herf, Jeffrey. *Nazi Propaganda for the Arab World.* New Haven, CT: Yale University Press, 2009.

Herzog, Chaim. *The Arab-Israeli Wars: War and Peace in the Middle East from the War of Independence through Lebanon.* New York: Vintage, 1983.

Hess, Wolf Rüdiger. *My Father Rudolf Hess.* London: W. H. Allen, 1984.

Hinsley, Harry. *Official History of British Intelligence in World War II.* London: His Majesty's Stationery Office, vols. 1 (1979) and 2 (1981).

———. *Hitler's Strategy.* Cambridge: Cambirdge University Press, 1951.

Hirszowicz, Lukasz. *The Third Reich and the Arab East.* London: Routledge & K. Paul, and Toronto, Canada: Toronto University Press, 1966.

His Majesty's Stationery Office. *British Vessels Lost at Sea, 1914–18 and 1939–45.* Wellingborough, UK: Patrick Stephens, 1988.

Howard, Michael. *The Mediterranean Strategy in the Second World War.* London: Praeger, 1968.

Hunaydi, Sahar. *A Broken Trust: Sir Herbert Samuel, Zionism and the Palestinians, 1920–1925.* London: I. B. Tauris, 2001.

Hurewitz, J. C. *The Middle East and North Africa in World Politics: British-French Supremacy, 1914–1945.* New Haven, CT: Yale University Press, 1979.

Ireland, Phillip Willard. *Iraq: A Study in Social Development.* London: Jonathan Cape, 1937.

Isaacson, Walter. *Profiles in Leadership: Historians on the Elusive Quality of Greatness.* New York: W. W. Norton, 2010.

Jackson, Ashley. *British Empire and the Second World War.* London: Hambledon Continuum, 2006.

Jackson, J. Hampden. *The Between-War World: A Short Political History, 1918–1939.* London: V. Gollancz, 1947.

James, Barrie. *Hitler's Gulf War: The Fight for Iraq 1941.* South Yorkshire, UK: Pen & Sword Books, 2010.

Jankowski, James. *Egypt's Young Rebels: Young Egypt, 1933–1952.* Stanford, CA: Hoover Institute Press, 1975.

Jordan, Richard. *The World's Merchant Fleet, 1939: The Particulars and Wartime Fates of 6,000 ships.* Annapolis, MD: Naval Institute Press, 2006.

Kahn, David. *Hitler's Spies: German Military Intelligence in World War II.* New York: MacMillan, 1978.

Katz, Samuel, and Ron Volstad. *Israeli Elite Units since 1948.* London: Osprey, 1988.

Kechichian, Joseph. *Oman and the World: The Emergence of an Independent Foreign Policy.* Santa Monica, CA: RAND, 1995.

Kédourie, Elie. *Arabic Political Memoirs and Other Studies.* London: Cass, 1974.

Keegan, Sir John, ed. *Churchill's Generals.* New York: Grove Wiedenfield, 1991.

Kelly, Saul. *The Lost Oasis: The Desert War and the Hunt for Zerzura: The True Story Behind the English Patient.* Boulder, CO: Westview Press, 2003.

Kinzer, Stephen. *Reset: Iran, Turkey, and America's Future.* New York: Times Books, 2010.

Klieman, Aaron. *Foundations of British Policy in the Arab World: The Cairo Conference of 1921.* Baltimore: Johns Hopkins University Press, 1970.

Knox, MacGregor. *Mussolini Unleashed, 1939–1941: Politics and Strategy in Fascist Italy's Last War.* Cambridge: Cambridge University Press, 1986.

Kratoska, Paul. *The Japanese Occupation of Malaya: A Social and Economic History.* Honolulu: University of Hawaii Press, 1997.

Kurowski, Franz. *The Brandenburger Commandos: Germany's Elite Warrior Spies in World War II.* Mechanicsburg, PA: Stackpole Books, 2005.

Lansford, Tom. *A Bitter Harvest: US Foreign Policy and Afghanistan.* Burlington, VT: Ashgate, 2003.

Lebel, Jennie. *The Mufti of Jerusalem Haj Amin Al-Husseini and National Socialism.* Belgrade, Serbia: Chigoja, 2007.

Lewis, Bernard. *Semites and Anti-Semites: An Inquiry into Conflict and Prejudice.* New York: W. W. Norton, 1999.

Lewis, Bernard, and Buntzie Ellis Churchill. *Notes on a Century: Reflections of a Middle East Historian.* New York: Viking Adult, 2012.

Little, Tom. *South Arabia: Arena of Conflict.* London: Pall Mall Press, 1968.

Longerich, Peter. *Heinrich Himmler.* Translated by Jeremy Noakes and Leslie Sharpe. New York: Oxford University Press, 2012.

Longrigg, Stephan. *Oil in the Middle East: Its Discovery and Development.* New York: Oxford University Press, 1955.

Lyman, Robert, and Howard Gerrard. *First Victory: Britain's Forgotten Struggle in the Middle East, 1941.* London: Constable, 2006.

———. *Iraq 1941: The Battles for Basra, Habbaniya, Fallujah and Baghdad.* Essex, UK: Osprey, 2006.

MacIntyre, Ben. *Operation Mincemeat: How a Dead Man and a Bizarre Plan Fooled the Nazis and Assured an Allied Victory.* New York: Harmony Books, 2010.

MacMillan, Margaret. *Paris 1919: Six Months that Changed the World.* New York: Random House, 2001.

Mallman, Klaus-Michael, Martin Cuppers, and Krista Smith. *Nazi Palestine: The Plans for the Extermination of the Jews in Palestine.* New York: Enigma Press, 2010.

Manchester, William, and Paul Reid. *The Last Lion: Winston Spencer Churchill, Defender of the Realm, 1940–1965.* New York: Little, Brown and Company, 2012.

Mattar, Philip. *The Mufti of Jerusalem.* New York: Columbia University Press, 1988.

McMeekin, Sean. *The Berlin-Baghdad Express: The Ottoman Empire and Germany's Bid for World Power.* Cambridge, MA: Harvard University Press, 2010.

Mikaberidze, Alexander, ed. *Conflict and Conquest in the Islamic World: A Historical Encyclopedia,* vol. 1. Santa Barbara, CA, ABC-CLIO, 2011.

Milani, Abbas. *The Shah.* New York: Macmillan, 2012.

Miller, Aaron David. *Search for Security: Saudi Arabian Oil and American Foreign Policy, 1939–1949.* Chapel Hill: University of North Carolina Press, 1980.

Mishra, Pankaj. *From the Ruins of Empire: The Intellectuals Who Remade Asia.* New York: Farrar, Strauss and Giroux, 2012.

Mohammed, Al'aa Jassem. *Jafar Al-Askary wa Dawruhu al Siyasi wal Askary* [Jafar Al-Askary, his political and military role]. Baghdad, Iraq: Maktabat al-Yazqah al-Arabiya, 1987).

Monroe, Elizabeth. *Britain's Moment in the Middle East: 1914–1971.* Baltimore: Johns Hopkins University Press, 1981.

Morris, Benny. *1948: A History of the First Arab-Israeli War*. New Haven, CT: Yale University Press, 2008.

Motter, T. H. Vail. *The Persian Corridor and Aid to Russia*. Washington, DC: U.S. Army Center of Military History, 1952.

Munoz, Antonio J. *Lions of the Desert: Arab Volunteers in the German Army*. New York: Bayside Axis Europa, 1997.

Nasser, Gamal Abdel. *Egypt's Revolution: The Philosophy of the Revolution*. Washington, DC: Public Affairs Press, 1955.

Nasseri, Akeel. *Al-Jaysh wal Sultah fee Iraq Al-Maliki* [The army and (political) authority in Iraq under the monarchy 1921–1958]. Damascus, Syria: Dar Al-Hassad, 2000.

Nazmi, Jamal Omar. *Al-Juzoor Al-Siyasiyah wal Fikiriyah lil Haraka Al-Qawmiyah fee Al--Iraq* [Roots of political thought of the Nationalist movement in Iraq]. Beirut, Lebanon: Research Center for Arab Unity, 1984.

Nicosia, Francis. *The Third Reich and the Palestine Question*. Piscataway, NJ: Transaction, 2000.

Nordbruch, Goetz. *Nazism in Syria and Lebanon: The Ambivalence of the German Option, 1933–1945*. London: Routledge, 2009.

Olson, Lynne. *Those Angry Days: Roosevelt, Lindbergh, and America's Fight over World War II, 1939–1941*. New York: Random House, 2013.

Omar, Ali Saleh. *Al-Dawr al-Sudani fee Tahrir Ethiopia wa Irjaa Ibratur Haile Selasie ila Arshu (1935–1941)* [The Sudanese role in the liberation of Ethiopia and restoration of Emperor Haile Selasie to his throne (1935–1941)]. Khartoum, Sudan: International University of Africa, 2005.

Pal, Dharm. *Official History of the Indian Armed Forces in the Second World War, 1939–45: Campaigns in Western Asia*. New York: Orient Longmans, 1957.

Partner, Peter. *Arab Voices: The BBC Arabic Service 1938–1988*. London: British Broadcasting Corporation Publishing, 1988.

Playfair, Ian Stanley. *The Mediterranean and Middle East, History of the Second World War, United Kingdom Military Series*, vol. 1, *The Early Successes Against Italy (to May 1941)*. East Sussex, UK: The Naval and Military Press, 2004.

Porch, Douglas. *The Path to Victory: The Mediterranean Theater in World War II*. New York: Farrar, Strauss and Giroux, 2004.

Rankin, Nicholas. *A Genius for Deception: How Cunning Helped the British Win Two World Wars*. New York: Oxford University Press, 2008.

Raugh, Harold. *Wavell in the Middle-East, 1939–1941*. London: Brassey's, 1993.

Ricks, Thomas. *The Generals: American Military Command from World War II to Today*. New York: Penguin Press 2012.

Rogan, Eugene. *The Arabs: A History*. New York: Basic Books, 2009.

Rohwer, Jurgen. *Axis Submarine Successes, 1939–1945*. Annapolis, MD: Naval Institute Press, 1983.

———. *Chronology of the War at Sea, 1939–1945: The Naval History of World War Two*. Annapolis, MD: Naval Institute Press, 2000.

Sachar, Howard. *Europe Leaves the Middle East 1936–1954*. London: Allen Lane, 1974.

———. *A History of Israel: From the Rise of Zionism to Our Time*. New York: Knopf, 2010.

Sadkovich, James J., ed. *Reevaluating Major Naval Combatants of World War II*. New York: Greenwood, 1990.

Salem, Paul. *Bitter Legacy: Ideology and Politics in the Arab World*. Syracuse: Syracuse University Press, 1994.

Schechtman, Joseph. *The Mufti and the Fuhrer: The Rise and Fall of Haj Amin el-Husseini*. New York: Thomas Yoseloff, 1965.

Schofield, Richard N. *Kuwait and Iraq: Historical Claims and Territorial Disputes*. London: Royal Institute of International Affairs, 1993.

Schofield, Victoria. *Afghanistan: At the Crossroads of Conflict*. London: I. B. Tauris Paperback, 2010.

Schreiber, Gerhard, Bernd Stegemann, and Detlef Vogel. *Germany and the Second World War*, vol. 3, *The Mediterranean, South-East Europe, and North Africa 1939–1941: From Italy's Declaration of Non-Belligerence to the Entry of the United States into the War* Oxford: Clarendon Press, 1995.

Schwanitz, Wolfgang. *Germany and the Middle East, 1871–1945*. Princeton, NJ: Markus Wiener, 2004.

Searight, Sarah. *The British in the Middle East*. New York: Athenum, 1970.

Segev, Tom. *One Palestine, Complete: Jews and Arabs under the British Mandate*. New York: Henry Holt, 1999.

Shirer, William. *The Rise and Fall of the Third Reich: A History of Nazi Germany*. New York: Simon & Schuster, 1990.

Showell, Jak P. Mallmann. *Fuehrer Conferences on Naval Affairs, 1939–1945*. Annapolis, MD: Naval Institute Press, 1990.

Silverfarb, Daniel, and Majid Khadduri. *Britain's Informal Empire in the Middle East: A Case Study of Iraq 1929–1941*. New York: Oxford University Press, 1986.

Simon, Reeva. *Iraq between the Two World Wars: The Militarist Origins of Tyranny*. New York: Columbia University Press, 2004.

Smith, R. Harris. *OSS: The Secret History of America's First Intelligence Agency*. Berkeley: University of California Press, 1972.

Snyder, Louis L. *Hitler's Third Reich: A Documentary History*. Chicago: Nelson-Hall, 1981.

Sokolow, Nahum. *History of Zionism*, vol. 2, *1600–1918*. London: Longmans, Green & Co., 1919.

Stein, George. *The Waffen SS: Hitler's Elite Guard at War, 1939–1945*. New York: Cornell University Press, 1966.

Stewart, Richard. *Sunrise at Abadan: The British and Soviet Invasion of Iran, 1941*. New York: Praeger, 1988.

Stone, David. *Genius Shattered: The Decline and Fall of the German General Staff in World War II*. Philadelphia, PA: Casemate, 2011.

Stroud, Rick. *The Phantom Army of Alamein: How the Camouflage Unit and Operation Bertram Hoodwinked Rommel*. London: Bloomsbury, 2012.

Sugihara, Kaoru, and J. A. Allan. *Japan in the Contemporary Middle East*. London: Routledge, 1993.

Tamkin, Nicholas. *Britain, Turkey and the Soviet Union, 1940–45.* New York, Palgrave-MacMillan, 2009.

Tucker, Spencer. *World War II at Sea: An Encyclopedia.* Santa Barbara, CA: ABC-CLIO, 2012.

Van Linschoten, Alex Strick, and Felix Kuehn. *An Enemy We Created: The Myth of the Taliban-Al-Qaida Merger in Afghanistan.* Oxford: Oxford University Press, 2012.

Ward, Steven R. *Immortal: A Military History of Iran and Its Armed Forces.* Washington, DC: Georgetown University Press, 2009.

Warner, Geoffrey. *Iraq and Syria 1941: The Politics and Strategy of the Second World War.* Newark: University of Delaware Press, 1974.

Warren, Alan. *Waziristan, the Faqir of Ipi, and the Indian Army: The North West Frontier Revolt of 1936–37.* New York: Oxford University Press, 2000.

Wasim, Khalid. *Al-Kifah al-Sirri Didaa al-Ingleez* [The secret resistance against the British]. Cairo: Dar wa Matabi' al-Sha'ab, 1963.

Watson, William. *Tricolor and the Crescent: France and the Islamic World.* Westport, CT: Greenwood, 2003.

Whelan, John. *Bahrain: A MEED Practical Guide.* London: Middle East Economic Digest, 1983.

Wilcke, Christoph. *Saudi Arabia, the Ismailis of Najran.* Washington, DC: Human Rights Watch, September 2008.

Williams, Manuela. *Mussolini's Propaganda Abroad: Subversion in the Mediterranean and the Middle East, 1935–1940.* London: Routledge, 2006.

Winkler, David. *Amirs, Admirals and Desert Sailors: Bahrain, the US Navy and the Arabian Gulf.* Annapolis, MD: Naval Institute Press, 2007.

Young, Peter, and Michael Roffe. *The Arab Legion: Men-at-Arms.* Oxford: Osprey, 1972.

Articles

Arielli, Nir. "'Haifa Is Still Burning': Italian, German and French Air Raids on Palestine during the Second World War." *Middle Eastern Studies* 46 (2010): 331–347.

———. "Italian Involvement in the Arab Revolt in Palestine, 1936–1939." *British Journal of Middle Eastern Studies* 35 (2008): 187–204.

Baldry, John. "Anglo-Italian Rivalry in Yemen and Asir 1900–1934." *Die Welt des Islams* 17 (1976): 155–193.

Bauer, Yehuda. "From Cooperation to Resistance: The Haganah 1938–1946." *Middle Eastern Studies* 2 (1966): 182–210.

Bou-Nacklie, N. E. "The 1941 Invasion of Syria and Lebanon: The Role of the Local Paramilitary." *Middle Eastern Studies* 30 (1994): 512–529.

Brenner, Y. S. "The 'Stern Gang' 1940–1948." *Middle Eastern Studies* 2 (1965): 2–51.

Cohen, Hayyim. "The Anti Jewish Farhud in Baghdad 1941." *Middle Eastern Studies* 3 (1966): 2–17.

Cohen, Michael J. "The Moyne Assassination, November, 1944: A Political Analysis." *Middle Eastern Studies* 15 (1979): 353–373.

Cox, Jafna. "The Background to the Syrian Campaign, May–June 1941: A Study in Franco–German Wartime Relations." *History* 72 (1987): 432–452.

De Cordier, Bruno. "The Fedayeen of the Reich: Muslims, Islam and Collaborationism during World War II." *China and Eurasia Forum Quarterly* 8 (2010): 23–46.

De Luca, Anthony R. "Der Grossmufti in Berlin: The Politics of Collaboration." *International Journal of Middle East Studies* 10 (1979): 125–138.

Elphinston, W. G. "The Kurdish Question." *International Affairs* (Royal Institute of International Affairs) 22, no. 1 (January 1946): 91–103.

Esenbel, Selcuk. "Japan's Global Claim to Asia and the World of Islam: Transnational Nationalism and World Power, 1900–1945." *American Historical Review* 109 (2004): 1140–1170.

Gaunson, A. B. "Churchill, De Gaulle, Spears, and the Levant Affair, 1941." *Historical Journal* 27 (1984): 697–713.

"German Ideas on Iraq, 1937–1938," and other excerpts of documents on German foreign policy, 1918–1945 (Washington, DC: Government Printing Office). *Middle East Journal* 12, no. 2 (Spring, 1958): 195–204.

Hauner, Milan. "Afghanistan between the Great Powers, 1938–1945." *International Journal of Middle East Studies* 14 (1982): 481–499.

———. "One Man against the Empire: The Faqir of Ipi and the British in Central Asia on the Eve of and during the Second World War." *Journal of Contemporary History* 16 (1981): 183–212.

Heller, Joseph. "Zeev Jabotinsky and the Revisionist Revolt against Materialism: In Search of a World View." *Jewish History* 12 (1998): 51–67.

Herf, Jeffrey. "Nazi Germany's Propaganda Aimed at Arabs and Muslims during World War II and the Holocaust: Old Themes, New Archival Findings." *Central European History* 42 (2009): 709–736.

Hill, Alexander. "British Lend Lease Aid and the Soviet War Effort, June 1941–June 1942." *Journal of Military History* 71 (2007): 773–808.

Khamis, Abdel-Aziz. "Asrar al-Kifah al-Sirri [Secrets of the underground resistance]." *Ruz al-Yusuf* 2555 (May 30, 1977): 14–15.

MacDonald, Callum. "Radio Bari: Italian Wireless Propaganda in the Middle East and British Countermeasures." *Middle Eastern Studies* 13 (1977): 195–207.

McKale, Donald. "Germany and the Arab Question in the First World War." *Middle Eastern Studies* 29 (1993): 236–253.

Melka, Robert. "Max Freiherr von Oppenheim: Sixty Years of Scholarship and Political Intrigue in the Middle East." *Middle Eastern Studies* 9 (1973): 81–93.

Melki, James. "Syria and State Department 1937–47." *Middle Eastern Studies* 33 (1997): 92–106.

Mulligan, William. "Air Raid! A Sequel." *Saudi Aramco World Journal* 27 (1976): 2–3.

Nafi, Basheer. "The Arabs and the Axis: 1933–1940." *Arab Studies Quarterly* 19 (1997): 1–24.

Neff, Donald. "Hamas: A Pale Image of the Jewish Irgun and Lehi Gangs." *Washington Report on Middle East Affairs* 25 (May/June 2006): 14–15.

Nicosia, Francis. "Arab Nationalism and National Socialist Germany, 1933–1939: Ideological and Strategic Incompatibility." *International Journal of Middle East Studies* 12 (1980): 351–372.

Polkehn, Klaus. "The Secret Contacts: Zionism and Nazi Germany, 1933–1941." *Journal of Palestine Studies* 5 (1976): 54–82.

Porch, Douglas. "The Other Gulf War British Intervention in Iraq, 1941." *Joint Force Quarterly* 35 (2004): 134–140.

Roshwald, Aviel. "The Spears Mission in the Levant: 1941–1944." *The Historical Journal* 29 (1986): 897–919.

Spain, James. "The Pathan Borderlands." *Middle East Journal* 15 (1961): 165–177.

Stegner, Wallace. "Discovery! The Story of Aramco then: Chapter 12: Air Raid." *Saudi Aramco World Journal* 21 (1970): 17–21.

Tripodi, Christian. "The Foreign Office and Anglo-Italian Involvement in the Red Sea and Arabia, 1925–28." *Canadian Journal of History* 42 (2007): 209–234.

Wild, Stefan. "National Socialism and the Arab East between 1933 and 1939." *Die Welt des Islams* 25 (1985): 126–173.

Wolpert, Stanley. "The Brave Law of Love." *India Today International Anniversary Issue*, Makers and Breakers of Modern India (2011): 12.

Theses and Dissertations

Flacker, Edgar. "Fritz Grobba and Nazi Germany's Middle Eastern Policy: 1933–1942." PhD diss., University of London, 1998.

Katzberg, Allan. "Foundations of Excellence: Moshe Dayan and Israel's Military Tradition (1880 to 1950)." Command and Staff College thesis, Marine Corps University, Quantico, VA, 1988.

Melka, Robert. "The Axis and the Arab Middle East, 1930–1945." PhD diss., University of Minnesota, 1966.

Scott, James. "Germany, Great Britain and the Rashid Ali al-Kilani Revolt of Spring 1941." Master's thesis, Portland State University, 1995. http://www.csus.edu/indiv/s/scottjc/title.htm

Internet Sources

Australian War Memorial. "Syrian Campaign." http://www.awm.gov.au/units/event_295.asp

Avalon Project, Documents in Law, History and Diplomacy, Eighty-Second Day, Friday, 15 March 1946, Morning Session (vol. 9, Nuremberg Trial Proceedings). http://avalon.law.yale.edu/imt/03-15-46.asp

British Broadcasting Corporation. "WW2 People's War, An archive of World War Two memories–Persia Invaded." http://www.bbc.co.uk/ww2peopleswartimeline/factfiles/nonflash/a1130121.shtml?sectionId=3&articleId=1130121

Hassanpour, Amir. "The Kurdish Experience." *Middle East Report* 24 (1994). http://www.merip.org/mer/mer189/kurdish-experience

Herf, Jeffrey. "Nazi Germany and the Arab and Muslim World: Old and New Scholarship." Presentation at the Historical Society's 2008 Conference on Migration, Diaspora, Ethnicity & Nationalism in History, Johns Hopkins

University, Baltimore, MD (June 5–7, 2008). http://www.bu.edu/historic/confer ence08/Herf.pdf

Iran's Press TV Web site. "Ahmadinejad to seek UN compensation for WWII." http://www.presstv.com/detail/114112.html

Schmidt, Eric. "Pentagon Contradicts General on Iraq Occupation Force's Size," *New York Times,* February 28, 2003. http://www.nytimes.com/2003/02/28/ us/threats-responses-military-spending-pentagon-contradicts-general-iraq- occupation.html

Schwanitz, Wolfgang G. "German-Kuwaiti Relations: From Their Beginnings to the Reunification of Germany." *Middle East Review of International Affairs Journal* 13 (March 2009). http://www.gloria-center.org/2009/03/schwanitz-2009-03-08/

INDEX

Aden, 2, 53, 137–38, 139, 140, 142, 165
Aden, Gulf of, 141–42
Afghani, Jamal al-Din al-, 6, 17, 21–22
Afghanistan: British interests in and anti-British sentiments, xxii, 148–49, 150, 154–58; German and Axis interests in, 104, 148–58; German economic and trade ties, 149–50, 151; interwar period, 148–50; Khyber Pass, 148–49; neutrality of, 151; regime change in, 151, 152; Shami Pir activities and affair, 149, 155–56, 158, 230n25
Africa: British interests and defense of, 3; colonial expansion activities, 12–13. *See also* North Africa
Afrika Korps: arrival in Libya and Egypt, 61; deception plan against, 188; defeat of, 73, 178, 181; desert combat operations, xiii, 3, 187; intelligence operations in Egypt, 166, 168–69; supplies and troops for, 9, 177, 180
Ahmadinejad, Mahmoud, xv, 115–16
Alawi, 86, 220n2
Algeria, 11, 29–30, 59, 74, 75, 88, 95, 107
Allies/Allied powers: Axis influence, actions to prevent, xiii; democratic values of, betrayal of, xiii; intelligence operations and success of, 180–81; intervention in affairs of Middle East, xv–xvi, 115–16; maps of campaigns, 99, 159; shift in course of war,

97–98; WWII operations and Arab Nationalism, xiii–xvi, 1–3
Anglo-Egyptian Treaty (1936), 48, 87, 160–62, 163, 164, 165, 172, 193
Anglo-Iraqi Treaty (1930), 45–46, 48–50, 65, 104, 196, 198, 199, 201, 202
Anglo-Iraqi War (1941): Axis assistance to Iraq, 203; British forces, 67–68; fall of Baghdad, 204; German role in, 69; guerrilla operations, 203; invasion and operations, 61–70, 200–204; Iraqi forces, 68; lessons from, 83–84, 195–204; Syrian support for, 91
anti-Semitism: anti-Zionist sentiments and, 186; German racial policy, 74; in Iraq, 36; radio and spread of, 3
Arab League, 187
Arab Legion, 29, 40, 67, 68, 69, 72, 94, 95, 203, 216–17n99
Arab Nationalism: Allies and Axis operations and, xiii–xvi, 1–3; anti-colonialism and WWI, xxii–xxiii, 6, 183–88; Arab homeland, 40; Axis influence on, xiii–xvi, 1–2, 183–84; British appeasement of Arab grievances, 54; British pledges to support autonomy and, 5–6; confrontation against mandatory powers, xxiii; decline of, 188–89; evolution of, xi; German ideology and political party development, 34–36; German support for, xiv, 1–2, 76–82, 183–87; Italian support for, xiv, 53; leadership quarrels, 70–72; origins of ideology

of, xiv–xvi, 1–3, 183–87; Palestinian movement for, 9–12; unity of Arabs and pan-Arabism, xiv; victimization narratives, 9, 183, 184, 186–87

Arab Revolt (1916), xxii, 17, 40–41, 42, 46, 183

Arab Revolt (1936), 17–21

Arabian Sea, 141–42

Arab-Israeli War (1948), 31, 216–17n99

Arslan, Shakib, 16–17

Askary, Jafar Al-, 41–42, 45, 197

Assad, Bashar al-, 42, 220n2

Auchinleck, Claude, 61–62, 63–64, 70, 107, 216n90, 231n15, 232–33n37

Axis/Axis powers: agreement between Axis powers, 2; anticolonial sentiments and interventions by, xiii–xiv, 2, 29–30; Arab soldiers serving with Axis forces, 29, 72–74; Arabian Sea naval activity, 141–42; coordination of operations, 53–54; Egyptian interests of, 32, 162–68, 193–94; influence on Arab Nationalism, xiii–xvi, 1–2; maps of campaigns, 99, 159; Palestinian and Arab Nationalism support, xxi–xxii, 23–33, 193; shift in course of war, 97–98; subversive actions against, 190; WWII operations and Arab Nationalism, xiii–xvi, 1–3, 76–82, 183–88

Ba'ath Party and Ba'athism, xiv, 34, 49, 188

Baghdad Pact (Central Eastern Treaty Organization, CENTO), 149, 229n3

Baghdad-Haifa route, 2, 84

Bahrain, 143, 145–46

Baker, Robert L., xvi

Balfour Declaration, xxii, 5–6, 9, 22, 183

BBC Arabic Service, 16, 37

Black Code, 108, 168–69

Bolshevism, 11, 20

Bush, George W., xiv

Cairo Conference (1921), 6, 23, 43, 196

Casablanca Conference (1943), 13, 189

Central Eastern Treaty Organization (CENTO Baghdad Pact), 149, 229n3

Chalabi, Ahmed, 208n32

Churchill, Winston: Afghanistan operations, 156–57; Anglo-Iraqi War, 62, 63, 65, 67, 216n90; colonial status quo, defense of, 13–14; de Gaulle, relationship with, 90; Egyptian operations, 166–67, 231n15; *The Gathering Storm*, xiv; German Middle East policy, opinion about, 76, 82; intelligence operations in Egypt, 166; Iranian oil reserve policy, 101; on *Mein Kampf* influence, xiv; Middle East as theater of war, 2; Middle East policy, 187, 196; oil policy discussions, 147; Palestine status, British support for autonomy, 6–7; strategic and tactical control of Iraqi operations, 70; Suez Canal defense, xvi, 167, 216n93; Syrian operations, 88, 92–93, 94, 97; Turkey operations and neutrality, 123, 124–25; Wavell, relationship with, 231n15

concentration camps, Arab inmates in, 74–75

Crete, 56, 60, 61, 65, 67, 79, 91, 92–93, 94

Czechoslovakia, 2, 11–12, 13, 33, 128, 149, 198

Dayan, Moshe, 97

de Gaulle, Charles, 83, 87, 89–90, 92, 95, 96

Eden, Anthony, xv, 15, 92, 98, 123, 157, 173

Egypt: Allies-Axis confrontation, 231n15, 232n19; anti-British propaganda, 1, 166, 171, 175; anti-British sentiments in, 107, 170–76; Arab soldiers serving with Axis forces, 73; assassinations in, 174, 175, 176; Axis sympathies in, 107, 171–72,

173, 175–76; British interests in, defense and security of, xvi, 2, 8, 78–79, 84, 166–68, 187, 231n17, 232n19; collapse of government, 162–63; concerns about loss of, 232–33n27; declaration of war against Axis, 178; distrust narratives in, 161, 190; expulsion of government, 174; First Republic, 164, 231n10; German and Axis powers, relationship with, 32, 107–8, 128, 162–68, 193–94; German and Axis threat to and attacks on, 59, 67, 78, 81, 166–70, 177; Harb insight on operations, 170–74; independence (quasi-independence) for, 5, 175, 232n36; intelligence operations in, 165, 166, 168–70, 178–81; Italian troops in, 233–34n53; regime change in, 3, 103, 189, 190; revolt in (1919), 5; Second Republic, 231n10; US intervention in, 78; victimization narratives, 9; WWII contributions, 177–79; WWII military policy, 163, 230–31n6

Eisenhower, Dwight D., 115, 116, 181–82, 233–34n53

Enigma code, 169, 179–80

Ethiopia, xxiii, 13, 14, 15, 17, 20, 178, 198

Farouk, King of Egypt, 30, 107–8, 109, 125, 163, 164–66, 168, 169–70, 172, 173, 175–76, 208n32, 232–33n37

Fascism: Arab Nationalism, anticolonialism, and, 6; democracy compared to, 13; Italian propaganda about, 14; militant Islamist ideology and, xiv, 186; Palestinian interest in, 9–12, 38; radio and spread of, 189

Feisal I, King of Iraq, 21, 22, 41–42, 43–46, 51, 196, 212n1

Feisal II, King of Iraq, 51, 199

Fortitude, Operation, xvi

France: alliance between Great Britain, Turkey, and, 118, 119, 125; colonial expansion activities, xxi; colonial expansion activities, xxi; colonial expansion activities, xxi; colonial

interests and influence, undermining of by Axis, xiii–xiv, 2; German invasion of, 13; mandate system and colonial expansion, 5, 205–6n8; Maysalun battle and Syria, 41–42; strength of in Mediterranean region, 14

Fuad I, King of Egypt, 164, 165

Futuwwa, 34, 35–36

The Gathering Storm (Churchill), xiv

Gaylani, Rashid Ali Al-: Anglo-Iraqi War, 65, 66; anti-British propaganda campaign, 214n51; anti-British sentiments of, 48–49; armaments for, 56–58; Axis authorities, meetings with, 2, 25; British-Iraqi negotiations, 199; early life and education of, 48; end of reign of, 204; escape from Iraq, 70; German and Axis interests in Iraq, 47, 48–49, 51–56, 63, 76, 84, 127; German opinion of Arabs, 74–75; hero status of, 70; Husseini, relationship with, 70–72; independence for Iraq, 198–99; influence of, 70–72; Iraqi government-in-exile, status as head of, 70, 71; Kuwait annexation into Iraq, 137; prime minister role, 48, 50, 77, 197–98; removal of, 54–55, 67, 69, 216n90; revolt led by, xv, 25, 47, 55–56, 59, 60, 70, 76, 77, 84–85, 91, 200, 201; transit to Germany through Turkey, 122–23

Germany: anticolonial sentiments and interventions by, xiii–xiv, 2, 183–87; appeasement policies toward, 166; Arab Nationalism, support for, xiv, 1–2, 76–82, 183–87; Arab soldiers serving with Axis forces, 29, 72–74; Arab-German collaboration, xxi–xxii, 23–33, 193; Arabian Sea naval activity, 142; armaments for Iraq, 56–61, 76, 80, 152; British interference in German possessions, xiv, 33; colonial expansion activities, xxi; declaration of war against by Turkey, 125, 225n3; economic successes of

Nazi Germany, xxii–xxiii, 185–86; Egyptian interests of, 32, 193–94; exploitation of Muslims, 27–29; ideology and Islamist militant ideology, 34–36, 38, 72, 186, 188–89; Jewish Final Solution, 26–27, 38, 184, 234n2; Middle East policy, 33–34, 67, 76–82, 218n128; nationalism and ethnic Germans, xiii; noninterference in British affairs, xiv, 8; Olympic Games in, 34–35, 36, 151; opinion of Arabs, 2, 4, 74–75, 206n1 (chap 2); Ottoman Empire relationship with, xxi; Palestinian attitudes toward Germany, 7–14; Palestinian insurgents, support for, 19; Palestinian interests of, 9–12, 22–33, 38; Palestinian policy of, 33–34; Paris Protocols, 58–59; political activity in Arab territories, 53–54; Soviet invasion by, 8–9, 59, 78, 79, 81, 100–101, 106, 176–77, 181; trade agreement between Turkey and, 120–21; Tripartite Pact, 8; victimization narratives, 4, 9, 183, 184, 186–87; WWI and instigation of Arab uprisings, xxi–xxii, 185. *See also* propaganda

Ghazi, King of Iraq, 16, 37, 47, 48, 51, 136–37, 197, 214n51

Gibraltar, 16, 78, 79, 80, 145, 231n17

Glubb, John Bagot "Glubb Pasha," 40, 67, 68–69, 203, 216–17n99

Goebbels, Joseph: diaries of, 193–94, 234–35n1; German propaganda operations, 10; pro-German and Axis sentiments in Near East, 10

Goering, Herman, 17, 56, 78, 80, 106–7, 181

Great Britain: alliance between France, Turkey, and, 118, 119, 125; alliance between Iran, Soviets, and, 103, 106–7, 114, 118, 119; Arabian Sea naval activity, 141–42; attack on, 79; challenges to Middle East interest of, xxii; colonial expansion activities, xxi; colonial interests

and influence, undermining of by Axis, xiii–xiv, 2; colonial status quo, defense of, 13–14; defense and security of Middle East interests, 2–3, 78–79, 166–68, 187–88, 231n17, 232n19; dismemberment of empire, 167–68, 232n19; food aid for Middle East, 227n25; German interference if British possessions, xiv, 33; intelligence (MI), 179–80; intervention in affairs of Middle East, xv–xvi; Iranian oil reserve policy, 101, 103, 105; mandate system and colonial expansion, 5, 205–6n8; noninterference in German affairs, xiv, 8; pledges of Arab autonomy support by, 5, 6; strength of in Mediterranean region, 14, 78, 218n134; troops positioned in Egypt, xvi; US attitude toward imperialism, 13–14; WWII and British-Iraqi negotiations, 198–99

Greece: British interests in, 169, 188, 231n15; German and Axis interests in, 8, 65, 71–72, 73, 91, 92–93, 177, 199; German-Arab units in, 73; Italian operations, 8, 177; military aid to, 61; Ottoman operations, 41; radio operations, 16, 37

Grobba, Fritz: Afghanistan interests, 149, 151; Arab independence movement, 71–72, 77; Arab interest in NSDAP, 10; German Final Solution, 184, 234n2; Iran interests, 105; Iraq interests, 49, 51, 56–57, 60, 81–82; Kuwait interests, 136, 137; Middle East role of, 19; Palestine interests, 19, 20, 25, 26, 32–33, 34; pan-Arabism, support for, 19; Saudi Arabia interests, 128, 129–32; wasted opportunities of Middle East policy, 76

Habbaniya air base, 48, 49–50, 63, 64, 65, 66–67, 68–69, 70, 196, 201–3

Haifa: Italian air raids on, 143–45; oil pipeline and refineries at, 64, 66, 84

Harb, Mohammed Saleh, xv, xxiii, 170–74, 187

Hashemite clan: British pledges to, 5, 6; Feisal as descendent in, 43; revolution to overthrow monarchy, 70; Shia opposition to rule by, 43–44

hawzas, 40, 212n2

Hijaz, xxi

Himmler, Heinrich, 27–28, 29, 110, 181, 210n88

Hitler, Adolph: appeasement policies toward, 166; Arab soldiers serving with Axis forces, 29, 72; armaments for Iraq, 56–58; Brenner Pass meeting, 61; British interests, threat to and attack on, 78–79, 80; German nationalism and ethnic Germans, xiii; German threat to neighbors, response to, 12–13; Jewish Final Solution, 26–27, 38, 184, 234n2; Judeo-Bolshevism threat, 9, 78, 177; *Mein Kampf*, xiv, 16; Middle East policy, 76, 77; opinion of Arabs, 2, 4, 206n1 (chap 2); Palestinian and Arab Nationalism support, 26; short war and need for oil, 80; Tripartite Pact, 8; views on Palestine, 11–12

human terrain, xvi, 3, 190

Hussein, Saddam, 24, 43, 70, 195

Hussein ibn Ali, 5, 6

Husseini, Amin Al-: anti-British sentiments of, 48–49, 51–52; Arab coordination committee, 52; Arab soldiers serving with Axis forces, 29, 71–72; armaments for Palestine, 131, 132; Axis authorities, meetings with, 2, 23, 25–27, 30–31, 184, 193; early life and education of, 21–22; Fascist and Nazi interests in Palestine, 9–10, 23–33, 38; Gaylani, relationship with, 70–72; German and Axis interests in Iraq, 48–49, 54, 84, 127; influence of, 21, 48–49, 50–51, 70–72; Italian support for, 17, 18–19, 25, 123; Palestinian and Arab Nationalism goals, 21, 22–31; retirement of, 31; transit to Germany through Turkey, 122, 123

Ibn Saud, Adbul-Aziz, xvi, 31, 32, 126, 127–33, 136, 137, 139, 140–41, 227n25

India: anti-British sentiments in, 8, 30, 194; army in, 8; challenge to British interests, xxii, 81–82, 84; divisions from for Middle East operations, 62–64, 98; German and Axis interests in, 104; pro-British sentiments in, 194

intelligence operations: Allied operations, xiv, 1; Allied security violations, 187–88; Allied success and, 180–81; al-Qaida manual information about, 189; Axis operations, xiv, 1; Black Code, 108, 168–69; in Egypt, 108, 165, 166, 168–70, 178–81; Enigma code, 169, 179–80; German Abwehr operations, 4, 11, 108–9, 110–11; German WWI operations, xxi; in Iran, 104–5, 106–7, 108–9, 177; in Iraq, 110–11; OSS operations, 190, 234n11; POW interrogations, 180; in Syria, 110–11

Iran: alliance between British, Soviets, and, 103, 106–7, 114, 118, 119; British interests in, 8, 100–103; British-Soviet invasion and occupation of, 69, 100–103, 107–8, 109–10, 111–12, 124; Countenance operation, 109, 111–12; declaration of war against Germany, 115; distrust narratives in, 190; foreign policy of, 105–9; German and Axis interests in, 100–101, 102–3, 104–10; German troops in, 177; influence of, 116; intelligence operations in, 177; military forces in, 102–3; Nazi propaganda in, 102, 104, 222n13; neutrality of, 102, 105; oil reserves in, 100–101, 103, 104, 105, 115; Persian Corridor supply line, 100–101, 112–15; regime change in, 3, 69, 103, 107–8, 112, 115, 189, 190; sabotage activities in, 110; Soviet interests in, 100–103; strategic importance of, 101; US and Allies

interventions in, 115–16; Western
intervention in affairs of, xv
Iranian Revolution (1949), xiv
Iraq: air bases in, 48, 49–50, 63, 64, 65,
66–67, 68–69, 70, 196, 198, 201–
3; anti-British propaganda in, 1, 48,
59; anti-British sentiments in, 48–49,
51–53, 110; anti-Jewish pogrom,
70; anti-Semitism in, 36; Arab coordination committee, 52; Arab soldiers serving with Axis forces, 73;
armaments for, 56–61, 76, 80, 152;
army forces, volunteer and con-
scripted, 45–46; army of, origins of
modern, 40–42; army officers, loyalties of, 42–44, 46; Axis sympathies in, 177; British appeasement of
Arab grievances, 54; British interests
in, defense and security of, 2, 49–50;
British invasion of, 195, 200–204;
British mandate status, 5, 21, 42–46,
48, 82–83, 85–86, 205–6n8, 212n1;
British strategic and tactical control
of operations in, 70, 82–84; British
troops in and occupation of, 8, 55,
69–70, 98; Caliphate reestablishment
in, 197; creation of, 39–40, 196; distrust narratives in, 190; foreign intervention, mistrust of, 204; German
and Axis interests in, 32, 48–49,
51–56, 63, 76–82, 84, 110–11, 127,
128; German interventions, cessation
of, 69; German invasion of, 177; government-in-exile in Germany, 70, 71;
importance of understanding political-military history of, 195–204;
independence (quasi-independence)
for, 41, 44, 46–47, 198–99; insurgency potential in, 3; Italy, relationship with, 48, 51; Kuwait annexation
into, 136–37; lessons from Axis and
Allied experiences in, 82–84; Levy
Force, 45; military coups, uprisings,
and revolts, 46–47, 55–56, 59, 60,
70, 77, 152, 196–98; military families in, 42–43, 46; monarchy and constitution, creation of, 196; Ottoman

administration of, 39–42; Paris
Protocols, 58–59; political actions
of military, 196–98; political-military history of, 39–42, 82–84, 212n1;
regime change in, 3, 103, 189, 190;
revolt in (1920), 5; Sunni officers in
army, 42–43, 46; Sunni participation
in government, 47, 82; Vichy France,
relationship with, 69; victimization
narratives, 9; WWII and British-Iraqi
negotiations, 198–99. *See also* Anglo-
Iraqi Treaty (1930); Anglo-Iraqi War
(1941)
Iraqi Freedom, Operation, 82–84, 98
Islam and Muslims: exploitation of
Muslims for Nazi purposes, 27–29;
Italian respect for Islamic religion,
14; Italian support for pilgrimages,
14; Japanese Islam-oriented policies,
133–35; military service of Muslims
with Germany, 74
Islamist militant groups: caliphate, 72;
evolution of, xi; German ideology
and development of, 34–36, 38, 72,
186, 188–89; NSDAP and worldview
of, 72
Islamo-Fascism, xiv
Israel: creation of, 97, 186; defense
forces, 97; Palestinian-Israeli dispute,
diplomatic doublespeak and, 5–6;
Palmach units, 96–97; US support for
creation of, 13
Italy: air raids on Haifa, 143–45; air
raids on Manama, 145–46; anticolonial sentiments and interventions by,
xiii–xiv, 2; Arab Nationalism, support for, xiv, 1–2, 53, 76; Arabian
Sea naval activity, 141–42; colonial
expansion interests and activities,
xxiii, 2, 17, 53, 198, 206n2 (chap 1);
freedom of action and control and
strength in Mediterranean region,
14–17, 53–54, 77, 80; German-
Arab collaboration, 25–26; image
of, improvement of, 15; Iraq interests of, 48, 51, 53–54; Islamic religion, respect for, 14; North African

operations, 8; Palestinian interests of, 14–17, 20, 38; Roman glory, recreation of, 15; Tripartite Pact, 8; troops positioned in Libya, xvi; Turkey, relationship with, 119. *See also* propaganda

Japan: attacks on British interests in Asia, 166, 169; declaration of war against by Turkey, 125; German-Japanese alliance, concerns about, 181; intelligence operations and breaking code of, 189; Islam-oriented policies, 133–35; oil needs of, 134–35; Pearl Harbor attack, 169; Saudi Arabia interests, 133, 134–35; Tripartite Pact, 8

Jews/Jewish people: German Final Solution, 26–27, 38, 184, 234n2; German racial policy, 74; global genocide, 184, 186, 234n2; homeland in Palestine for, 5–6, 8, 15, 20–21, 26–27, 33, 184, 186; immigration into Palestine, xiv, 22–25, 97, 184; Iraqi anti-Jewish pogrom, 70; settlements in Palestine, xiv

jihad and global jihad concept, xxii

Joint Intelligence Task Force for Combating Terrorism, xi–xii

Judeo-Bolshevism, 9, 20, 27, 78, 177

Kurds and Kurdistan, 45, 47, 68, 82, 83, 204

Kuwait, 135–37

Lampson, Miles, xv, 87, 163–64, 166, 169–70, 172, 175

Lawrence, T. E., xxii, 41, 44–45, 46

Lebanon: Exporter operation, 69, 85, 92–97; French mandate status, 85–86; independence for, 86–87, 92, 97, 198, 199; majority and minority populations, 86

Lend-Lease program, 78, 100, 114

Levant: Exporter operation, 69, 85, 92–97; Italian interests in, 15; sabotage activities in, 29; staging area for

Axis operations, 89; victimization narratives, 9

Levy Force, 67

Libya: anti-British insurgency in, xxii; Italian colonial expansion activities, xxiii, 2, 198, 206n2 (chap 1); Italian image in, improvement of, 15; Italian respect for Islamic religion in, 14; Italian troops in, xvi, 233–34n53

Maher Pasha, Ali, 162–63, 164, 166, 170–71, 172, 173–74, 175

Maliki, Nuri al-, 47, 82

mandate system and mandatory powers: Arab Nationalist confrontation against, xxiii; conference for instituting, 5; creation of and concept of, xxiii, 205–6n8; independence of mandated states, 25, 41, 205–6n8

Marshall, George C., 14, 181–82, 216n90, 233–34n53

Maysalun, Battle of, 41–42

McMahon, Henry, 6

Mein Kampf (Hitler), xiv, 16

Middle East: anti-American sentiments in, 13–14; anti-British sentiments in, 189; anticolonial sentiments and Axis interventions, xiii–xiv, 2; Arab leadership quarrels, 70–72; British interests in, defense and security of, 2–3, 78–79, 80–82, 84, 166–68, 187–88, 231n17, 232n19; British policy toward, 187, 196; food aid for, 227n25; German opinion of Arabs, 2, 4, 74–75, 206n1 (chap 2); German policy toward, 33–34, 67, 76–82, 218n128; importance of understanding, xiv–xvi, 1–3, 181–82, 190–91; important role of, 181–82; political history of, xi, xiii–xv, xvi, xxi–xxiii, 1–3; US attitudes toward colonialism, xvi; US relationship with countries in, 1; Western intervention in affairs of, xv–xvi; WWI and German-Ottoman instigation of uprisings, xxi–xxii, 185

Mohammad Reza Pahlavi, Shah of Iran, 108, 112, 115, 177

Montgomery, Bernard Law, 3, 169
Morocco, 12–13, 29–30, 74, 75, 95,
    156, 189, 199–200, 226n2
mufti and grand mufti, 205n4. *See also*
    Husseini, Amin Al-
Muslim Brotherhood, 21, 30, 36, 171,
    174, 176
Muslims. *See* Islam and Muslims
Mussolini, Benito: Brenner Pass meet-
    ing, 61; British interests, threat to and
    attack on, 80–81; colonial expansion
    activities, xxiii; North African oper-
    ations, 8; Tripartite Pact, 8; troops
    positioned in Libya, xvi; Zionist
    movement, support for, 15

Nahas Pasha, Mustafa, 32, 164, 165,
    172, 174, 175–76, 193, 194
Nasser, Gamal Abdel, xv, 30, 32, 174
National Defense University, xv, 3, 161,
    189
National Intelligence University, 3, 161
nationalism and strong nation concept,
    36. *See also* Arab Nationalism
Nationalsozialistische Deutsche
    Arbeiterpartei (NSDAP): Arab inter-
    ests in, 9–11, 32–33; militant Islamist
    ideology and worldview of, 72;
    Palestinian cells, 32–33; party mem-
    bership abroad, 11; spread of idea of,
    7, 10
Near East: Allies political initiatives in,
    187; anti-British propaganda cam-
    paign in, 15–16; anti-Italian senti-
    ments in, 53; challenge to British
    interests, 2, 14, 81–82; overthrow
    of governments in, xiii; pro-German
    and Axis sentiments, 10
Near East Radio, 16, 37, 208n32
Nicosia, Francis, 9, 10–11, 17, 19–20,
    32, 56
Nile Delta, xvi
North Africa: Allied landings in, 89;
    anticolonial sentiments and Axis
    interventions, xiii–xiv, 29–30; Arab
    soldiers serving with Axis forces, 73;

Italian troops in, 8. *See also* Afrika
    Korps
Nuri As-Sa'id, 32, 36, 41, 45–46, 47,
    48, 50, 54, 69, 197, 204

Office of Strategic Services (OSS), 189–
    90, 234n11
oil and oil fields: Bahrain resources,
    143, 145–46; British interests and
    security of, 2, 50, 64, 66–67, 81, 176,
    216n90, 232–33n27; German attacks
    on, 59, 89; Iranian oil reserves, 100–
    101, 103, 104, 105, 115; Iraqi con-
    trol of, 64, 66; Italian oil needs, 81;
    Japanese oil needs, 134–35; Kuwait
    resources, 135, 136; postwar oil pol-
    icy, 147; sabotage activities, 110;
    Saudi Arabia oil resources and US
    interests, 132–33; short war and need
    for, 80
Oman, 146–47
Ottoman Empire: army reforms, 40;
    army security role, 40; collapse of,
    41, 183; German relationship with,
    xxi; Iraq regions, administration of,
    39–42; Middle Eastern borders and
    collapse of, xxiii, 5; WWI and instiga-
    tion of Arab uprisings, xxi–xxii, 185

Palestine: anti-Allied sentiments in,
    4, 132, 184; anti-British propa-
    ganda campaigns in, 1, 8–9, 11–14,
    15–16; Arab Nationalism movement
    in, 9–12, 184; Arab Revolt (1936),
    17–21; armaments for, 131, 132;
    British appeasement of Arab griev-
    ances, 54; British interests in, defense
    and security of, 2, 8, 14–15, 84,
    187; British mandate status, 6, 9, 14,
    205–6n8; British pledges to support
    autonomy of, 5–7; distrust narra-
    tives in, 190; Fascist and Nazi inter-
    ests in, 9–12, 22–33, 38; German
    policy toward, 33–34; German pro-
    paganda operations in, 7, 10, 11, 13,
    16; German support for insurgents

in, 19; German-Arab collaboration, xxi–xxii, 23–33, 193; independence for, 38, 198; insurgency potential in, 3; Italian interests in, 14–17, 20, 38; Italian propaganda operations in, 15–16; Jewish homeland in, 5–6, 8, 15, 20–21, 26–27, 33, 184, 186; Jewish immigration into, xiv, 22–25, 97, 184; NSDAP activities, 32–33; oil reserves in, 144–45; Palestinian-Israeli dispute, diplomatic double-speak and, 5–6; partitioning of, 20–21, 33; political history of, 4–5; pro-German and Axis sentiments, 7–14; Soviet interests in, 20; victim-ization narratives, 9; weapons for, 20
Palestine Broadcasting Service, 16, 37
Palestine Liberation Organization (PLO), 30
Palmach units, 96–97
pan-Arabism: decline of, 188–89; German National Socialism and, xiv; Greater Syria plan, 22–23
pan-Turanism (pan-Turkism), 121–22
Paris Peace Conference, xxii, 6, 14
Paris Protocols, 58–59
Peel Commission and plan, 5, 7, 17, 20–21, 33
Persian Corridor supply line, 100–101, 112–15
Phalanges, 34–35
Poland, xiv, 13, 60, 146, 198, 234–35n1
propaganda: Allied operations, xiv, 1; anti-American sentiments, pro-paganda to counter, 16; anti-Brit-ish Axis propaganda, xiv, 1, 84; anti-British campaign in Egypt, 1, 166, 171, 175; anti-British campaign in Iraq, 48, 214n51; Arab enemy aliens participation in, 73; German operations in Palestine, 7, 10, 11, 13, 16; German WWI operations, xxi; Italian operations, 14, 15–16, 136; leaflet campaigns, 16, 66, 93; Nazi propaganda in Iran, 102, 104, 222n13; NSDAP activities, 32

Qaida, al-, 189
Qassam, Izz Ad-Din Al-, 17–18
Qatar, 137

Rabin, Yitzhak, 97
radio: British broadcasting activities, 16, 37, 207–8nn31–32, 208n34; Egyptian broadcasting activities, 16, 37, 207–8nn31–32; Fascism introduction through, 189; French broadcasting activities, 207–8n31; German propaganda operations in Palestine, 7, 10, 13, 16, 37; impact of, 3; Iranian broadcasting activities, 16, 37; Iraqi broadcasting activities, 16, 37, 214n51; Italian anti-British propaganda campaign in Palestine, 15–16, 37; Italian broadcasting activi-ties, 119, 136, 207–8n31; propa-ganda value of broadcasts, xvi, 189
Radio Algiers, 207–8n31
Radio Baghdad, 16
Radio Bari, 7, 15–16, 37, 119, 136, 207–8n31
Radio Berlin, 7, 16, 37
Radio Berlin-Zeesen, 7, 16, 37
Radio Cairo, 207–8n31
Radio Tehran, 16
Raeder, Erich, 78, 79, 167, 177, 181, 218n134
railroads: Berlin-Baghdad Railway, xxi, xxii; Berlin-Istanbul railroad, exten-sion of, 135; German study of Iraqi lines, 77; in Iran, 104, 112
Red Sea, 2, 141–42
Reza Pahlavi, Shah of Iran: British-Soviet invasion of Iran, 111–12; death and burial of, 108, 112, 224n57; governing model of, 47; regime change in Iran, 69, 107–8, 112, 164, 223n34; relationship with Germany and German influence over, 102, 104, 107–8, 177
Ribbentrop, Joachim von: Afghanistan operations, 151, 153–54; Arab enemy aliens, use of, 73; Arab Legion, formation of, 29; Egyptian

operations, 107; German propaganda operations, 10; Husseini, meeting with, 26; Iranian operations,
108; Iraqi operations, 49, 59, 76–77,
80–81; Saudi Arabia operations, 131;
Syrian operations, 90, 94; Turkish
operations, 94, 121, 123, 124
Rodinson, Maxime, xiv
Rommel, Erwin: defeat of, 73; desert
combat operations, xiii, 3, 187; intelligence operations in Egypt, 168–69;
lessons learned from fighting, xvi;
supplies and troops for, 9, 177, 180;
threat to British interests, 78, 84
Roosevelt, Franklin D., 12–13, 111–12,
113, 124, 146, 147, 177, 181–82,
233–34n53
Royal Air Force (RAF): Anglo-Iraqi
War, 67–68; intelligence operations
in Egypt, 165; Iraqi air bases, 48,
49–50, 63, 64, 65, 66–67, 68–69, 70,
196, 198, 201–3; Near East Radio,
16, 37, 208n32
Russia. *See* Soviet Union/Russia

Sadat, Anwar, 2, 32, 174, 178, 179
Salafi and Salafism, 21–22, 209n57
San Remo Conference, 5, 6
Saudi Arabia: armaments for, 127, 128,
130, 131–32; British interests in, 126,
127, 129, 130; food aid for, 227n25;
German and Axis interests in, 32,
126–33; Italian interests in, 128, 129–
30; Italian support for pilgrimages to,
14; Japanese interests in, 133, 134–
35; US and oil resources in, 132–33
Secret Intelligence Service (SIS, MI-6),
190, 234n11
Shah of Iran. *See* Mohammad Reza
Pahlavi, Shah of Iran; Reza Pahlavi,
Shah of Iran
sherief, 206n2 (chap 2)
Shinseki, Eric, 98
Sidqui, Bakr, 47, 197
Soviet Union/Russia: alliance between
British, Iran, and, 103, 106–7, 114,
118, 119; Arab forces to fight in,

71–72; counteroffensive against
Germans, 98; German invasion of,
8–9, 59, 78, 79, 81, 100–101, 106,
176–77, 181; intervention in affairs
of Middle East, xv–xvi; Palestinian
interest of, 20; POWs spying for
Germany, 11; protocols for aid to
Russia, 113–14; Turkey, relationship
with, 119–20, 194
Special Operations Executive (SOE),
16, 37, 208n32, 208n34
Stalinism and Joseph Stalin, 9, 11, 100,
119–20, 121, 125, 151, 157, 167,
175, 184
Suez Canal: Axis attacks on, 59, 61, 78,
79, 80, 81, 85, 89, 142, 177; Axis
control of, 167, 231n17, 233–34n53;
British defense of, xvi, 67, 167,
216n93; British interests and security
of, 2, 67, 84, 187, 216n90; British
troops in canal zone, 160; challenge
to British interests, xxii; Egyptian
defense of, 164; fight over control of,
xv; Italian share of control to, 14
Sunni insurgency, 43
Sykes-Picot Agreement, xxii, 4, 6, 9, 22,
43, 90, 183
Syria: air bases in, 58–59, 87, 88,
90–91; anti-British propaganda in,
1; Arab soldiers serving with Axis
forces, 73; bomb and weapons stock-
pile in, 111; British appeasement of
Arab grievances, 54; British attack
on, concerns about, 59; conflicting
interests of British and Free French
in, 89–90; distrust narratives in, 190;
economic embargo against, 88–89;
Exporter operation, 69, 85, 92–97;
foreign intervention, feelings about,
42; French forces and Maysalun battle, 41–42; French mandate status,
5, 85–86, 96, 205–6n8; German and
Axis interests in, 85, 87–96, 97–98,
110–11; German invasion of, 81;
German Nationalist model to unite
Arabs, 92, 98; Greater Syria plan,
22–23; independence for, 86–87,

91, 92, 96, 97, 198, 199; insurgency potential in, 3; Iraq revolt, support for, 91; majority and minority populations and sectarian conflict, 42, 86, 220n2; Paris Protocols, 58–59; strategic importance of, 86; Vichy French control of, 85, 87–93, 96
Syrian Socialist Nationalist Party, 34

Taliban, 188–89
Torch, Operation, 1, 8
Tripartite Alliance, 118, 119, 125
Tripartite Pact, 8
Tripartite Treaty of Alliance, 103, 106–7, 114, 118, 119
Tunisia, 15, 29–30, 58–59, 73–74, 75, 187, 189–90
Turkey: alliance between Great Britain, France , and, 118, 119, 125; alliance with Allies, 117, 224n64; armaments for, 124; declaration of war against Germany, 125, 225n3; declaration of war against Japan, 125; Gaylani transit to Germany through, 122–23; German invasion of, 81; Germany and Axis, relationship with, 117–18, 119–25, 225n3; Husseini transit to Germany through, 122, 123; Italy, relationship with, 119; mediation offers by, 124; neutrality of, 91–92, 111, 117–18, 119–20, 124–25, 194, 225n3; pan-Turanism (pan-Turkism), 121–22; Soviets, relationship with, 119–20, 194; strategic importance of, 117–18; Syrian-Axis operations, 91–92, 93; trade agreement between Germany and, 120–21; Vichy France, relationship with, 123–24

United States (US): American Exceptionalism, rise of, 12; British imperialism, attitude toward, 13–14; colonialism, attitudes toward, xvi; food aid for Middle East, 227n25; intervention in affairs of Middle East, xv–xvi; intervention in Egypt, 78; Middle East countries relationship

with, 1; neutrality of, 113; Saudi Arabia oil resources and interests, 132–33

Versailles Treaty, 9, 22, 23, 117
Vichy France: Arab soldiers serving with Axis forces, 73; Catapult operation, 88; control of Syria by, 85, 87–93, 96; Exporter operation, 69, 85, 92–97; Iraq, relationship with, 69; Paris Protocols, 58–59; regime change in, 189–90; subversive actions against, 190

Wavell, Archibald: Churchill, relationship with, 231n15; dismissal and replacement of, 231n15; Egyptian operations, 163, 166–67, 180, 231n15; Iranian operations, 105, 109; Iraqi operations, 59, 61–63, 65–67, 70, 216n90; Syrian operations, 59, 87–88, 90, 92–93, 94, 96; Turkish operations, 124
Wilson, Woodrow, 6, 205–6n8
World War I (WWI): anticolonialism and Arab Nationalism, xxii–xxiii, 6, 183–88; Central Powers and instigation of Arab uprisings, xxi–xxii, 185; ending of, 14
World War II (WWII): Arabic viewpoint on, xv; Middle East theater, importance of understanding, xiv–xvi, 1–3, 190–91

Yemen, 129, 130, 137–41, 165, 226n12
Young Egypt Party, 34, 35

Zionist movement: British pledges to, 5–6, 183; homeland in Palestine, 5–6, 8, 15, 20–21, 26–27, 33, 184, 186; immigration into Palestine, xiv, 22–25, 97, 184; Mussolini support for, 15; origins of, 1; US support for, 13

ABOUT THE AUTHORS

Youssef H. Aboul-Enein is a U.S. Navy Medical Service Corps commander, Middle East foreign area officer, and author of *Militant Islamist Ideology: Understanding the Global Threat*, and *Iraq in Turmoil: Historical Perspective of Dr. Ali al-Wardi from the Ottomans to King Feisal*, both published by the Naval Institute Press. The first book was named among the top 150 most influential books on terrorism by the peer-reviewed on-line journal, *Perspectives on Terrorism*. He currently is adjunct military professor and Islamic studies chair at the National Defense University Dwight D. Eisenhower School for National Security and Resource Strategy (formerly the Industrial College of the Armed Forces), and adjunct faculty for Middle East Counter-Terrorism Analysis at the National Intelligence University. From 2006 to 2009 he served as a senior counterterrorism adviser, warning officer, and instructor on militant Islamist ideology at the Joint Intelligence Task Force for Combating Terrorism (JITF-CT) in Washington, DC. In 2010 Commander Aboul-Enein returned to JITF-CT as senior adviser and subject matter expert on violent Islamist ideology. Commander Aboul-Enein was country director for North Africa and Egypt, assistant country director for the Arabian Gulf, and special adviser on Islamist militancy at the Office of the Secretary of Defense for International Security Affairs from 2002 to 2006. At the Office of the Secretary of Defense, he helped prepare Defense Department officials to engage in ministerial-level talks with their counterparts in countries from Morocco to the Persian Gulf. He has attended many working-level interagency meetings on counterterrorism, disarmament, and Middle East regional security issues. Among the interagency working groups he has participated in are Libyan WMD disarmament, coordinating the first Defense Ministry–level bilateral talks with Algeria, arranging the freedom of 407 Moroccan POWs held by the POLISARIO Front, and Saudi energy infrastructure security in the wake of the 2006 Abqaiq refinery attack.

Commander Aboul-Enein has published many articles on Islamist militancy, Arab affairs, and Middle East military tactics for *Military Review*, the *Infantry Journal*, the *Marine Corps Gazette*, Small Wars Journal.com, and the *Foreign Area Officer Journal*. Commander Aboul-Enein is author of *Ayman Al-Zawahiri: The Ideologue of Modern Islamic Militancy*, published by the

U.S. Air Force Counter Proliferation Center in March 2004. He is coauthor with Dr. Sherifa Zuhur of *Islamic Rulings on Warfare,* published by the Army War College in October 2004. Commander Aboul-Enein is engaged in a long-term project to highlight Arabic works of military interest in the pages of the U.S. Army's *Armor* and *Infantry* journals. He is currently working on a multipart series highlighting the memoirs of War Minister Mohamed Fawzi of Egypt for the U.S. Army *Infantry Journal.* He has highlighted in U.S. military journals excerpts of memoirs by Egyptian, Syrian, and Algerian generals. Commander Aboul-Enein is cited in two Project Air Force/RAND studies on Islamist radicalism and has served as a distinguished judge for the 2012 and 2013 Secretary of Defense/Chairman of the Joint Chiefs of Staff National Security Essay Contest. Aboul-Enein was also a distinguished judge for the 2012 Galileo Intelligence Community Essay Contest, sponsored by the director for National Intelligence. His education consists of a B.B.A. from the University of Mississippi (Ole Miss), an M.B.A. and master's in health services administration from the University of Arkansas at Little Rock, an M.S. in strategic intelligence from the National Intelligence University, as well as an M.S. in national resource strategy from the Industrial College of the Armed Forces. Commander Aboul-Enein's operational tours include Liberia, Bosnia, and the Persian Gulf. His personal awards include the Army Commendation Medal presented by Gen. Tommy Franks, the Joint Service Achievement Medal presented by the commandant of the Joint Forces Staff College, and the Defense Meritorious Service Medal (two awards) awarded by the Secretary of Defense and the Defense Intelligence Agency's deputy director for analysis. Commander Aboul-Enein is rated proficient in the Egyptian, Peninsular, Levantine, Modern Standard, and Iraqi dialects of Arabic by the Defense Language Institute.

Basil H. Aboul-Enein is a former captain in the U.S. Air Force, serving from 2007 to 2012. He attended the University of Central Arkansas, receiving his bachelor of science in family and consumer sciences. He received his dual master's degrees in clinical nutrition and public health from Texas Woman's University and the University of Texas Health Science Center in Houston, respectively. He also holds a master's degree in military history from Norwich University. Prior to entering the U.S. Air Force, where he held the position as chief public health commander and medical intelligence officer of the 14th Medical Squadron at Columbus AFB, Mississippi, he worked in several academic institutions and medical facilities, including Baylor College of Medicine and the USDA WIC nutrition program for the city of Houston. Basil has taught undergraduate nutrition courses at Houston Community College and San Jacinto College, and is currently teaching at East Mississippi Community College while pursuing his doctorate using his GI Bill education benefits. He has published articles on Islamist militancy, Arab political history, and Near East military campaigns of World War II for the *Infantry*

Journal, Foreign Area Officer Journal, and *Air & Space Power Journal,* as well as several health-care-related manuscripts in peer-reviewed public health journals. While on active duty, he tested proficient in the Egyptian, Iraqi, and Levantine dialects of Arabic by the Defense Language Institute.